The Essential Senghor

The Essential Senghor

African Philosophy and Black Aesthetics

from *Liberté 1, 3 & 5*

Léopold Sédar Senghor

Edited and translated by

DOYLE D. CALHOUN, ALIOUNE B. FALL, AND CHEIKH THIAM

Duke University Press *Durham and London* 2026

Project Editor: Ihsan Taylor
Designed by Courtney Leigh Richardson
Typeset in Garamond Premier Pro by Westchester Publishing Services

Library of Congress Cataloging-in-Publication Data
Names: Senghor, Léopold Sédar, 1906–2001 author | Calhoun, Doyle D., [date] editor | Fall, Alioune, [date] editor | Thiam, Cheikh editor
Title: The essential Senghor : African philosophy and Black aesthetics / Doyle D. Calhoun, Alioune Fall, Cheikh Thiam, Léopold Sédar Senghor.
Other titles: African philosophy and Black aesthetics
Description: Durham : Duke University Press, 2026. | Includes index. | Contents: "Léopold Sédar Senghor (1906–2001): A Reintroduction"—Negritude: A Humanism for the Twentieth (and Twenty-First) Century—Constitutive Elements of a Civilization of Negro-African Inspiration—Negritude Is a Humanism of the Twentieth Century—Negritude and Modernity; or, Negritude Is a Humanism of the Twentieth Century—Concerning Negritude—Negritude, as the Culture of Black Peoples, Shall Not Be Eclipsed—For a Modern and Negro-African Philosophy—As Manatees Go to Drink from the Source—Negritude, Aesthetics, and Philosophy—What the Black Man Offers—The Contributions of Negro Poetry to the Half Century—Negro-African Aesthetics—The Function and Meaning of the First World Festival of Negro Arts—For a Negro Criticism—From French Poetry to Francophone Poetry; or, The Contributions of Negroes to Francophone Poetry—Oral Tradition and Modernity—Negritude, Métissage, and the Dialogue of Cultures—The Problem of Culture in French West Africa—Perspectives on Black Africa; or, To Assimilate, Not Be Assimilated—Why an Indo-African Department at the University of Dakar?—Negritude and Mediterranean Civilization—French and African Languages—The Dialogue of Cultures
Identifiers: LCCN 2025033841
ISBN 9781478038603 paperback
ISBN 9781478033677 hardcover
Subjects: LCSH: Black people—Race identity | Politics and culture | Negritude (Literary movement) | Civilization, Western | Intercultural communication | Cultural relations | Black people | Africa, Sub-Saharan—Civilization | Africa—Civilization | French-speaking countries
Classification: LCC DT549.76.S46 A2 2026 | DDC 305.896—dc23/eng/20251117
LC record available at https://lccn.loc.gov/2025033841

Cover art: Léopold Sédar Senghor, 1978. Courtesy UNESCO / Dominique Roger and Wikimedia Commons.

Contents

Translators' Note

The texts assembled here are translations of the final, definitive editions of Senghor's prose, as published in the volumes *Liberté 1* (1964), *Liberté 3* (1977), and *Liberté 5* (1993). However, these texts all had a life of their own—as lectures, conference papers, prefaces or postfaces, forewords or afterwords, academic articles, essays, or speeches—before they were edited and printed (or reprinted) in the *Liberté* volumes. This heterogeneity on the level of genre and genesis helps explain some of the rhetorical features of certain texts as well as the diversity of bibliographic apparatuses deployed. For instance, texts that began their lives as speeches typically provided minimal citations, even in their edited form in the *Liberté* volumes, whereas texts conceived initially as academic articles or essays generally have more robust bibliographic information in the original. We provide details of original publication (which Senghor often includes at the end of his texts) in the first, unnumbered note for each text. While we have chosen to group essays thematically, and not in strict chronological order, it is imperative to keep this publication information in mind as one reads and engages with Senghor's texts, since their contexts of publication differ widely, in terms of both setting and historical moment. The earliest text here was published in 1937, under colonization and still decades before independence (1960); the latest was published in 1983, in the wake of Senghor's resignation from the presidency (1980).

More than a translation, we have sought to offer a critical edition for readers in English. Thus, we have provided complete bibliographic references for Senghor's citations (which, in the original texts, are often incomplete or missing), corrected and noted obvious errors, and introduced bibliographic references in the notes where they are absent, including many implicit or unattributed citations. In the case of multiple versions or editions of a given text cited or mentioned by Senghor, we have tried to reference the edition used by Senghor wherever possible; when necessary, we have cross-checked inventories of books held in Senghor's own collections. In some cases, we have had to rely on modern editions. We have also noted instances where Senghor's citations or translations appear to be incorrect or modified. Inevitably, we could not be truly exhaustive in this bibliographic labor, though in the process we have consulted editions in libraries and archives in the United States, France, and Senegal. Our hope is that the present volume at least gives a more complete sense of the sheer range of Senghor's citational practice.

In addition, we introduce discursive notes to clarify or explain relevant historical, cultural, literary-historical, and linguistic (including etymological) details that might otherwise escape the attention of contemporary readers. In particular, we have done so with an eye to matters related to Wolof and Sereer languages and cultures. For Wolof citations, we typically provide modern transcriptions in the notes but retain Senghor's original orthography in the body of the text; we follow this practice because Senghor often makes precise points regarding the transcription of African languages, whether implicitly or explicitly (famously, Senghor did not believe Wolof had geminate consonants, and his spelling reflected this assumption). However, we have preferred modern orthography for common Wolof words that occur frequently in the body of the texts (i.e., *Kocc Barma* instead of *Kotche Barma*, *boroom* instead of *borom*, *tagg*, not *taga*). Along these lines, we use contemporary terminology and spelling for African languages (e.g., "Sereer" for *sérère*, "Pulaar" for *poular*).

In the case of the French *peul* and *Peul*, used throughout Senghor's texts, we have drawn the following distinctions in English: We use the words "Pulo" (singular) and "Fulɓe" (plural) to refer to the people, based on the Pulaar roots *pul-/ful-* (*peul* is a French spelling of the Wolof word *pël*, used to designate speakers of Pulaar). For the language, we use the term "Pulaar." Senghor very occasionally uses the word *poular* to refer to what he calls "a Senegalese dialect of *peul*," in which case we translate *poular* as "Pulaar" and *peul* as the macro-language "Fulah" but include Senghor's French *poular* in square brackets. The Tukolor (from the French colonial designation *toutcouleur*) are Pulaar speakers who were traditionally sedentary, as opposed to the Fulɓe, who were itinerant; we use the terms "Haalpulaar" (singular) and "Haalpulaaren" (plural), which literally means "speakers of Pulaar," to translate *toutcouleur*.

We have sought to retain Senghor's original use of italics, which might strike the modern reader as excessive, and capitalization, which can be inconsistent, for emphasis wherever possible out of faithfulness to Senghor's often academic, sometimes pedantic style. We have also retained his use of hyphens to draw attention to the etymology (usually Latin or Greek) of certain words (e.g., *é-mouvoir*). We have left the French term *métissage*, which designates both cultural and biological mixture and hybridity, untranslated because, more than a word, it is a key concept in Senghor's theoretical arsenal, one that draws on and resignifies the colonial-era *métis*, which was used throughout West Africa and much of the French empire to refer to the children of European and African unions.[1] We have tried as much as possible to preserve Senghor's original syntax in English, though some smoothing over has been necessary to ensure readability.

We discuss in detail the challenges of translating the constellation of terms in French related to Blackness and Black or Black African identity in our introduction. As we explain there, the French term *nègre* is especially fraught and complicated. Charged with the histories of enslavement and anti-Blackness—in fact, synonymous with "slave" in many eighteenth- and nineteenth-century texts—the term was rehabilitated by African and Afro-Caribbean writers working in French from the 1920s onward, most famously in the 1930s by the Negritude thinkers, among them Senghor, whose project was founded on reclaiming and "rehabilitating" this term. As Senghor writes in "Negritude, as the Culture of Black Peoples, Shall Not Be Eclipsed": "We have used the word *Nègre* to designate the Black man, despite the pejorative nuance people have wished to attach to it [. . .] precisely to rehabilitate this man with the word."[2] The translation of *nègre* into English has given rise to different approaches, including "Negro," "Black," leaving *nègre* untranslated, and even the N-word. Across the body of his work, Senghor deploys the terms *Nègre/nègre*, *Noir·e/noir·e*, and *Négroïde/négroïde*, as well as the prefixes *Négro-/négro-* (as in *négro-africain·e*, *négro-américain·e*, and *négro-espagnol·e*) and *Afro-/afro-* (*afro-américain·e*, *afro-latin·e*, *afro-français·e*) extensively, consistently, and with precision. He uses such terms both as substantives and adjectives (to modify words for peoples, languages, cultures, ways of being, art forms, and cultural artifacts). Most often, Senghor capitalizes terms such as *Négro-africain* when he is referring to a person or peoples (i.e., *le Négro-africain* or *les Négro-africains*), especially when these are definite nouns, and uses lowercase letters when the words are deployed as adjectives (e.g., *l'art négro-africain*), though there are some exceptions to this pattern (e.g., rarely, *un négro-african*). His capitalization of *nègre* and *noir* is somewhat less consistent. While Senghor often seems to use capitalization, like italics, for emphasis or to designate types or concepts (e.g., *l'Homme noir* and *le Noir* versus *des noirs païens*), this is not always uniform across his essays. In general, when used as adjectives, *nègre* and *noir* appear in lowercase (e.g., *les poètes nègres*, *le rhythme nègre*, *les peuples noirs*), and when used as nouns they are frequently capitalized, especially when definite. Following English convention, we capitalize "Black" in our translation, unless the word refers exclusively to the color, and capitalize "Negro" when used as a noun. However, when it is used as an adjective, we capitalize "Negro" only when the noun it modifies is capitalized in the original or when *nègre* (adj.) itself is capitalized in Senghor (we thus translate *Art nègre* and *Art Nègre* both as "Negro Art" but *art nègre* as "negro art"). We do this out of respect for Senghor's original text.

Senghor sometimes also combines terms related to Blackness in ways that might strike readers as redundant or paradoxical (e.g., *Nègres noirs*, "Black Negroes"). Put simply, Negritude, Blackness (*noirceur*), and Africanness (*Africanité*) in Senghor's work cannot, in English, be collapsed into a single signifier: "Black." For these reasons, we have decided to follow Senghor's usage, which he maintained until the 1990s, translating *nègre* as "Negro" and *noir* as "Black," except where these words are referred to *as words*, in which case, we leave them untranslated. The translation of *nègre* as "Negro" underscores the affinities between Negritude and the Harlem Renaissance and the New Negro movement, which Senghor discusses at length in these essays, but it also, in later texts, helps to telegraph the ways in which Senghor's language may have begun to appear dated in the last decades of the twentieth century. In our introduction, we discuss possible advantages and disadvantages of this approach.

This translation, from its inception to its completion, was a fundamentally collective undertaking. While we often arrived at preliminary drafts of individual essays separately, we worked over each text together, as a unit. One person would read the French original aloud; another, the proposed English translation; the third would listen to both. We would then revise, puzzling over a paragraph, a sentence, or—often—a single word. Occasionally, we would call on our colleagues and friends for their expertise in Wolof, Sereer, and Pulaar. Our process for rendering Senghor's prose in English was ultimately an exercise in collaborative translation, "co-translation," or even "multiple translatorship."[3] *Liggééyu tekki bi ñoo ko bokk* (The work of translation is shared). This axiom was even more meaningful given our shared fluency in English, French, and Wolof despite our distinct linguistic backgrounds: One of us is a native English speaker, while the other two are native speakers of Wolof and French, and one with working knowledge of Sereer. Beyond these linguistic particularities, our disciplinary orientations further enriched the collaboration. Although we each identify as scholars of Negritude and have studied and published in the field, our areas of specialization differ: One works on the philosophy of Negritude, another on African and Caribbean literature and cinema, and the third on African literature and decolonial theory from an Afro-diasporic perspective. The diversity of our linguistic and intellectual points of reference made this collaboration especially rich, stimulating, and enjoyable.

Our collaborative process also extended from our constant reflection on style and approach in translation, to our framing of Senghor and his reception in the critical introduction. One of the most significant challenges we faced while translating, rereading, and reintroducing Senghor to an Anglophone audience was striking a balance between acknowledging Senghor's contested and controversial political legacy and doing justice to the intellectual complexity of his work. Drawing on our own disciplinary orientations and training, we sought to show that while fields such as Francophone studies, Black studies, philosophy, and literary studies might have been institutionalized in the West within nationalist perspectives, when placed under the broader rubric of African studies, these areas of inquiry are mutually enriching, or mutually fecundating, to borrow a term frequently used by Senghor. This mutual enrichment or cross-pollination underscores not only the vital importance of translation to our disciplines but also the value of cross-disciplinary, collaborative translation work. It seems especially fitting that a translation of Senghor's works be the result of a collective effort and the fruit of cross-disciplinary exchange. Such a process exemplifies the spirit of Senghor's commitment to "conciliatory harmony" between different intellectual and linguistic traditions.

NOTES

1. On the history of the term *métis* under French colonialism, see Emmanuelle Saada, *Les Enfants de la colonie: Les métis de l'Empire français entre sujétion et citoyenneté* (La Découverte, 2007).

2. [See chapter 5, page 131, in the present volume.—Eds.]

3. Hanne Jansen and Anna Wegener, "Multiple Translatorship," in *Authorial and Editorial Voices in Translation 1: Collaborative Relations Between Authors, Translators, and Performers*, ed. Hanne Jansen and Anna Wegener (Éditions québécoises de l'œuvre, 2013), 1–39. On collaborative translation, see Anthony Cordingley and Céline Frigau Manning, eds., *Collaborative Translation: From the Renaissance to the Digital Age* (Bloomsbury, 2017).

Acknowledgments

This volume has been an enormous collective undertaking, spanning several years. The bulk of the work was completed during our summers spent together in Senegal: in Dakar, Nianing, and Palmarin. Above all, we are grateful to our friends and families who have given us the time and space to pursue this project and who have supported us in myriad ways.

We also wish to thank the two anonymous readers for Duke University Press who provided thoughtful feedback on our manuscript and suggestions for revision, all of which greatly sharpened how we framed this project. We are deeply indebted to the editorial and design teams at Duke, in particular Elizabeth Ault and Benjamin Kossak, for their support of this project at every stage.

Carrie Heusinkveld, Duarte Bénard da Costa, and Ian Boyd at the University of Cambridge were superhuman in their attention to detail with respect to various bibliographic and editorial dimensions of this project, in particular assisting us in completing the notes and references. Their work as research assistants was generously supported by Doyle Calhoun's Professorial Appointment Support Fund from the University of Cambridge. Ali Touilila helped us locate the correct edition of Henri Gaden's *Le Poular* (1912–14) containing the specific Pulaar text referenced by Senghor.

Friends and colleagues generously provided invaluable feedback on early drafts of our translations. These include: Hady Ba, Baba Badji, Walid Bouchakour, Ruth Bush, Omar Dieng, Souleymane Bachir Diagne, Charles Forsdick, Cajetan Iheka, Jill Jarvis, Marius Kothor, Khalid Lyamlahy, Christopher L. Miller, Bamba Ndiaye, Fatima-Ezzahrae Touilila, Tobias Warner, Lynn Palermo, Yankhoba Seydi, Vieux Toure, and Sura Qadiri.

Introduction

LÉOPOLD SÉDAR SENGHOR (1906–2001): A REINTRODUCTION

Doyle D. Calhoun, Alioune B. Fall, and Cheikh Thiam

Negritude therefore [...] will not disappear; it will play, once more, its role, an essential one, in the edification of a new humanism, more human because it finally will have brought together in their totality the contributions of all continents, all races, all nations.
—LÉOPOLD SÉDAR SENGHOR, "La Négritude, comme culture des peuples noirs, ne saurait être dépassé," 1993

A Poet-Politician at the Crossroads

Black, French, and African; poet, philosopher, politician; universalist, essentialist, theoretician of Negritude and *métissage*; colonial subject, anticolonial scholar, African head of state; student of the Latin trivium, specialist of African languages, Sereer traditionalist—Senghor can be described by many epithets, each seemingly contradicting the other. His vast and varied oeuvre, encompassing lyric poetry as well as writings on philosophy, aesthetics, linguistics, and politics, spans over half a century and both the colonial and postcolonial periods. Senghor's major prose works—collected and edited into a five-volume series titled *Liberté* (Freedom) and published by Le Seuil in Paris over the course of several decades—testify to a highly syncretic thought. Dense with intertextual references ranging from classical antiquity to contemporary continental philosophy and steeped in diverse philosophical and linguistic traditions, Senghor's writings nonetheless remain resolutely African: They return us always to the "source," insisting on the value and vitality of African languages, literatures, and worldviews. Senghor's work is that of a poet, linguist, philosopher, and politician who lived and theorized at the crossroads of multiple languages, cultures, and intellectual and spiritual traditions.

Senghor's biography reflects the pluralism, hybridity, and irreducible complexity that characterize his thought. Born in a small Sereer village on the Petite Côte of Senegal only a few hours south of Dakar,[1] Senghor spent his childhood in Djiloor before moving to Joal for his formal education and later to Ngazobil, where he attended a local seminary. Senghor's early years in Djiloor and Joal were clearly formative. It was here, in his father Diogoye Senghor's home, and under the tutelage of his uncle Waly, that he received the initial formation of a young Sereer and attended several poetic and historical performances. Later, these would play an important role in his political and intellectual career. In 1928, Senghor left the seminary to continue his studies in Paris at Lycée Louis-le-Grand and then at the Sorbonne. It was in Paris that Senghor met several other colonial students who would all become central figures in the Negritude movement and Black Internationalism more generally: namely, Aimé Césaire and Jeanne and Paulette Nardal, from Martinique, and Léon-Gontran Damas, from Guyana. In 1935, he would become the first African student to receive the French *agrégation*. Senghor subsequently taught French and African languages and civilization for several years in France before being drafted at the beginning of the Second World War. It was during this period, including his time as a prisoner of war in a Nazi internment camp along with other *tirailleurs* (African riflemen), that he wrote some of his most important poems, which would be published shortly after the war ended. Throughout the 1940s and 1950s, Senghor served in various roles in the French government, notably as secretary of state, minister counselor (*ministre conseiller*), and member of the Assemblée nationale, advocating successfully for the extension of French citizenship to all French territories. When he became the first president of the newly independent Republic of Senegal in 1960, Senghor embarked on a twenty-year tenure marked by significant challenges. His presidency witnessed intense dissent, at least one assassination attempt, and censorship of the local press. However, it was also characterized by the establishment of a multiparty democratic system—an approach that contrasted sharply with the many other African leaders of the time who declared themselves de facto lifetime presidents. Today, while Senghor's poetry remains widely celebrated and his contributions to the Negritude movement generally acknowledged, his political legacy in Senegal is complex, and his prose works are largely overlooked.

Although widely recognized as central to the history of African thought, Senghor remains a polarizing figure. He is viewed variously as a colonial apologist, an antiracist racist, a repressive head of state, a Pan-African visionary, and a thinker who prioritized art, language, and culture in ways that—some argue—failed to address the social, economic, and political challenges of national independence and those that emerged in its wake. The reality is that Senghor does not fit neatly into the expectations of what an anti-, post-, or decolonial writer and thinker should be. He does not readily align with the categories of the militant, the revolutionary, or the radical. In many ways, Senghor refused to embody any single identity, choosing throughout his lifetime to fully embrace his multifaceted and multihyphenate self. This was a lonely and challenging path to tread in a (post)colonial world that Frantz Fanon presented as thoroughly Manichaean[2]—a Manichaeism that has led to radical positions on both sides of the (post)colonial divide, often resulting in absolutist positions for all parties.

It is perhaps unsurprising, then, that Senghor is frequently decried for his ambiguous position vis-à-vis France's neocolonial policies in West Africa, for envisioning models of decolonization and national independence that were not predicated exclusively on state sovereignty, or for insisting on the compatibility of his philosophical understanding of Negritude, and its corollary the theory of *métissage*, with European modernity. As Paul Gilroy aptly observes in the first pages of *The Black Atlantic*, there remains little place within current discursive formations for such strategic, theoretical, or existential "in-betweenness," little room for "striving to be both European and black": "Where racist, nationalist, or ethnically absolutist discourses orchestrate political relationships so that these identities appear to be mutually exclusive, occupying the space between them or trying to demonstrate their continuity has been viewed as a provocative and even oppositional act of political insubordination."[3] For this reason, Senghor's thought, and by extension Negritude more generally, has been mired in debate, controversy, and, perhaps above all, misinterpretations, especially among Anglophone intellectuals, since its emergence in the 1930s, despite the consensus that Negritude is one of the foundations of African studies.[4]

A Double Marginalization

Today, Negritude appears to have lost the debate. On the one hand, the new millennium and, in particular, the year 2006 or L'Année Senghor (The Year of Senghor), as it was dubbed by the Organisation Internationale de la Francophonie, marking the centenary of his birth, brought about a reappraisal and celebration of Senghor's legacy, a brief period of what David Murphy has called "Senghormania."[5] An even more recent resurgence of interest in Senghor and Negritude has seen more than a dozen new book-length studies on the topics published in the past decade alone[6]—including much needed work on Senghor's own practice as an occasional translator, especially of American and British poets (such as Sterling Brown, Langston Hughes, Claude McKay, Gerard Manley Hopkins, T. S. Eliot, W. B. Yeats, Dylan Thomas).[7] On the other hand, in 2026—the 120th anniversary of his birth and the commemoration of twenty-five years after his death—Senghor's vast body of prose works remains largely inaccessible and greatly underread. His *Liberté* volumes, foundational texts in African studies and cognate disciplines, are out of print in French and difficult to access. Except for Mercer Cook's translation of a few of Senghor's speeches, collected in *On African Socialism* (1964),[8] Yohann C. Ripert's very recent *Senghor: Writings on Politics* (2025),[9] and a handful of well-known essays on Negritude, his prose has never been translated into English. Until now, Senghor's writings on African art, aesthetics, philosophy, and literature have not been collected into a single volume in either English or French.

The marginalization of Senghor's prose is particularly troubling given his role not only as one of the principal theoreticians of Negritude but also as one of the African scholars who wrote most extensively and published most widely on African languages, literature, art, philosophy, and history throughout the twentieth century. This negligence prompts a vital question: How has one of the key architects of a cultural movement and philosophical discourse so central to African studies become so overlooked today? Consider the following case in point. During a public lecture at the University of Cheikh Anta Diop in Dakar, one of the editors of this volume highlighted this issue by asking more than a hundred faculty members and students if they had read all five volumes of the *Liberté* series. Only a handful had done so, while most acknowledged being familiar only with Senghor's poetry. This unevenness in terms of access and engagement (familiarity with Senghor's poetry but only passing knowledge of his prose works) extends beyond students to established African and Africanist scholars who, despite critiquing Senghor, often base their assessments on limited readings of his work. Senghor is thus frequently reduced to widely circulated but decontextualized soundbites—"La colonisation est un mal nécessaire" (Colonization is a necessary evil) and "L'émotion est nègre, comme la raison héllène" (Emotion is negro, as reason Hellenic), for instance—that confirm oft-repeated characterizations about Senghor's Francophilia and colonialist apologism, but that ultimately obscure the depth, nuance, and sheer scope of his intellectual contributions.

One explanation for Senghor's marginalization stems from his dual identity as both a towering intellectual and a dominant political figure in Senegalese politics from the 1940s to the 1980s. His writings were frequently dismissed on an ad hominem basis, overshadowed by his role as a statesman. Compounding this treatment is the fact that the first generation of Senegalese university professors emerged from the cohort of students who experienced violent repression under Senghor's administration during the 1968 protests.[10] As a result, his intellectual contributions were often interpreted through the lens of his political actions.

A second reason for Senghor's marginalization lies in the fact that, as opposed to unequivocally radical figures such as Cheikh Anta Diop, Kwame Nkrumah, Marcus Garvey, Frantz Fanon, and Amilcar Cabral, who are particularly well received by the contemporary Pan-Africanist tradition, Senghor's intellectual and political legacies are characterized by nuance and an orientation toward conciliation and *métissage*. Above all, his philosophy of Negritude foregrounds a strong, Africa-centered search for meaning, an acknowledgment of the importance of experiences—including colonial ones that have undoubtedly transformed Africa in irreversible ways—and a firm belief that the very nature of life is movement, with every movement leading to exchanges. As he declares in his essay "Negritude and Mediterranean Civilization," "Since the upper Paleolithic period, and this is one of the characteristics of *Homo sapiens*, when two people meet, they often fight, but *they always mix*."[11] Far from rejecting the foundations of Euro-modernity, Senghor's vision sought to integrate African cultural and philosophical systems into a broader shared human framework where they would exist and contribute on the same footing as others.

Although Senghor's understanding of Negritude has often been presented as an essentialism veering toward an antiracist racism, his desire for syncretism, his refusal of binaries, and his attention to difference are precisely why he never ceases affirming the values of universalism and the promise of (future) mutual intelligibility. This seemingly paradoxical stance is in line with his conception of the universal as fundamentally plural. There is a deep irony in the general disregard for Senghor's work in contemporary scholarship on postcolonialism and decoloniality, given that the very forms of cultural hybridity and difference explored by Senghor have since become major features in postcolonial theory, even though these discourses rarely invoke, and even disavow, his work. As Robert Young puts it, "It is curious that while (crudely speaking) endorsing Fanon and dismissing Léopold Senghor, postcolonial theory itself in many ways comes closer to the latter's exploration of interrelated forms of cultural difference than the Manichaean world of Fanon."[12] For a generation of scholars and activists committed to radical opposition to Europe and to the pervasive structures of coloniality, Senghor's intermediary position—seeking a balance between African traditions and the ideals of Euro-modernity—has often been construed as obsequiousness to France. The new Pan-African and decolonial tradition, which calls for a radical rupture and complete epistemic "de-linking," has often dismissed Senghor's work, presented it as fundamentally paradoxical, or simply ignored it. This is symptomatic of a generation of "decolonising" scholarship which, as Olúfẹ́mi Táíwò suggests, tends to "neglect a significant class of African thinkers" in the name of a vaguely defined "Africa" that leaves little room for "any nuance or differentiation in the discussion of specific authors, works or even regions."[13] Senghor, for Táíwò, is one such unduly neglected thinker. As he puts it, "Our decolonisers are always talking about Senghor's terrible Francophilia. But when one reads deep studies of Senghor, *the complexity of his thinking* comes out clearly."[14]

Today, the opportunity has emerged to assess Senghor's work without the weight of historical animosity, now that many of the seasoned Africanists were either not yet born or were particularly young when Senghor stepped down almost half a century ago. This makes a renewed and more sustained engagement with Senghor's oeuvre not only possible but essential.

(Re)Reading Senghor

A now robust body of scholarship by French-speaking scholars illustrates the transformative potential that a deep engagement with the primary literature on Senghor's work can offer. We mention only a few notable recent examples here. Souleymane Bachir Diagne's *African Art as Philosophy* (2011), Gary Wilder's *Freedom Time* (2015), and Cheikh Thiam's *Return to the Kingdom of Childhood: Re-Envisioning the Philosophical Relevance of Negritude* (2014) and *Negritude, Modernity, and the Idea of Africa* (2023) all demonstrate the rich insights that access to Senghor's entire oeuvre can provide.[15] These studies offer close readings of Senghor's body of prose works as collected in the *Liberté* volumes—texts that remain largely inaccessible to non-French speakers. Such engagement allows for nuanced perspectives on Senghor's thinking on Black aesthetics and African philosophy, and especially Negritude, which emerges as a complex philosophical, political, and aesthetic theoretical framework that remains deeply embedded in and marked by the historical contexts out of which it developed even while it is able to engage contemporary theoretical discourses and speak directly to present social and political issues.

In *African Art as Philosophy*, for example, Diagne presents Negritude as a philosophy of African art developed in conversation with towering figures such as Henri Bergson, Teilhard de Chardin, Lucien Lévy-Bruhl, Karl Marx and Friedrich Engels, Leo Frobenius, and Pablo Picasso. By reading Senghor's scholarship as a serious philosophy that can stand on its own, Diagne challenges simplistic interpretations of Senghor's texts and demonstrates the value of engaging deeply and carefully with them. Focusing on the political writings of Aimé Césaire and Senghor, Wilder's *Freedom Time* foregrounds how these two thinkers and so-called colonial *évolués* responded to historical contingencies to chart paths forward for Martinique, Senegal, and the world out of the wreckage of colonization. In so doing, Wilder suggests, Negritude offers a means to rethink or "unthink" both France and the notion of the Republic. Finally, in *Return to the Kingdom of Childhood* and *Negritude, Modernity, and the Idea of Africa*, Thiam draws on the intellectual traditions of both African studies and Black studies to offer Africa-centered readings of Negritude, presenting Senghor as a fundamentally transdisciplinary thinker whose prose traverses the boundaries of philosophy, literature, political science, and anthropology, while drawing substantially on Sereer and Dogon world systems and ontologies.

Nuanced readings of Senghor depend on access to his work in the original French and a willingness to work across languages and all too often siloed disciplines. And yet, over six decades after decolonization in Africa, linguistic divisions across the continent and within the academy remain deeply entrenched. They are particularly evident in the sphere of knowledge production, where former colonial languages continue to dominate the processes of creating, acquiring, and disseminating knowledge in African and Euro-American academies. African studies, a discipline now dominated by Anglophone scholars primarily based in the United States and the United Kingdom, has perpetuated this divide. As a result, scholarship produced in French, Spanish, Portuguese, and even African languages is often marginalized or overlooked. A few Francophone scholars—almost invariably male—such as Cheikh Anta Diop, Aimé Césaire, Frantz Fanon, and more recently, V. Y. Mudimbe and Achille Mbembe, stand out as exceptions to this trend, gaining significant traction in African studies and in English translation. By comparison, the case of Senghor is particularly striking. While Senghor's work is frequently acknowledged as central, if not foundational, to the discipline, his contributions remain misunderstood because of the limited accessibility of his writings to Anglophone scholars. This issue diminishes the ability of the discipline to fully examine and appreciate the theoretical and historical-cultural underpinnings of Negritude as articulated by its most important thinker.

It is in this context that we are reminded of a poignant assertion made by Abiola Irele, the Nigerian scholar largely responsible for introducing and popularizing Negritude writings in English, half a century ago regarding the then quite recent English translation of Jean-Paul Sartre's canonical essay "Orphée noir" (Black Orpheus), which first appeared as a preface to Senghor's *Anthologie de la nouvelle poésie nègre et malgache de langue française* (Anthology of new negro and malagasy poetry in French) (1948). Irele wrote:

> While the concept of negritude has met with considerable success in French intellectual circles, though not without inspiring some controversy among certain French African elements, it has met with either suspicion or open hostility (and even ridicule) among English-speaking Africans. Much of this attitude arises, I believe, from grave misconceptions about the *real* aims of the movement in general, and in some cases, from prejudice and complete lack of knowledge. It is in this respect that the recent separate publication of Sartre's preface in an English translation comes as a welcome move.[16]

Just like Irele, we hope that this English translation of Senghor comes as "a welcome move" and that it will also save Senghor's scholarship from "grave misconceptions" about its real meanings and orientations and from "prejudice and complete lack of knowledge." Yet the goal of the present volume is not to defend Senghor but rather to make room, in English, for the complexity of his thought. It is indeed legitimate to ask if Senghor's universalist framework is sound. It is necessary to question whether Senghor's work takes seriously the realities of power. There is also no denying that he too frequently repeated some of the most despicable racist claims of the nineteenth century. Oyèrónkẹ́ Oyěwùmí had a point when she suggested:

> Senghorian negritude [. . .] is actually a result of Senghor's acceptance of European categories of essence, race, and reason and the linkages among the three. Senghor asserts that since Africans are a race like Europeans, they must have their own brand of essence. [. . .] Stanislaus [*sic*] Adotevi is correct when he writes that "negritude is the last-born child of an ideology of domination."[17]

However, to critique Senghor, we must do more than simply dismiss a large and complex body of work as that of a Francophile entrenched in coloniality: We must try to read him, closely, on his own terms and in his own time. We are reminded here of the words of Henry Louis Gates Jr. on what it means to historicize and critically reengage with a writer (Fanon) whose legacy has been overdetermined by the contexts of his reception:

> It means *reading* him, with an acknowledgment of his own historical particularity, as an actor whose own search for self-transcendence scarcely excepts him from the heterogenous and conflictual structures that we have taken to be characteristic of colonial discourse. It means not to elevate him above his localities of discourse [...] nor simply to cast him into battle, but to recognize him as a battlefield in himself."[18]

What Gates wrote in reference to Frantz Fanon might equally apply to Senghor. Even beyond the contentious debates around Negritude, a new translation of Senghor's work in English may reveal Senghor's intellectual production to be a generative yet largely untested battleground for ongoing conversations in African studies and related fields.

Translating Senghor's work into English is particularly urgent, as English is now the predominant language of African studies, though we might hope for a future translation of Senghor in Wolof or Sereer. Ensuring broad access to his texts is the necessary foundation for reinscribing Senghor and reestablishing his rightful place in contemporary discourses on African philosophy, Black aesthetics, political theory, and intellectual history. The very fact of translating Senghor opens up the possibility of revisiting other moments in African intellectual history. Moreover, making Senghor's works available in English provides a timely opportunity to build lateral conversations between traditionally siloed disciplines—such as literature, linguistics, anthropology, art history, history, and philosophy—all of which may contribute to the intellectual repositioning of Senghor's oeuvre within the larger discipline of African studies. This translation arrives at a decisive moment, marked both by a rehabilitation of Negritude and a call for "decolonizing" the field of African studies. In this volume, we aim to offer a space that makes it possible to engage with the complexity and nuances that a close reading of Senghor's prose works can bring—a close reading possible only if Senghor's work is available in English.

Translating Senghor in English also shows the extent to which his prose, in the original French, is itself an exercise of translation. Senghor transcribes and translates Wolof, Sereer, Pulaar, and other African languages into French but also constantly mimics syntactic and rhetorical features of these languages in his prose. In this sense, our translation also entailed a constant reflection on and experience of linguistic pluralism and how it is brought to bear on knowledge production in Africa. The careful and critical engagement with Senghor's plurilingualism that this volume offers, both in the text and in the notes, allows us to rethink the horizon of African studies outside the language divides inherited from colonization. It is perhaps not simply in rereading Senghor but in *translating* him that we find "the real answer to the questions of identitarian and exclusive nationalisms, grafted on the *génie des langues*."[19]

Put another way, the texts in the *Liberté* volumes all perform translation or (in Wolof) *tekki* as a process of cultural "unraveling."[20] By underscoring Senghor's irrigation of his texts with African languages such as Wolof, Sereer, and Pulaar, we highlight the potential of an Afrophone philosophical base, inclusive of autochthonous African languages and former colonial ones. In this vein, translating Senghor is arguably an exercise in revealing his prose to be an intercultural and intralingual contact zone predicated on a "special kinship" between languages, in Walter Benjamin's sense. "This special kinship," Benjamin wrote, "holds because languages are not strangers to one another, but are, a priori and apart from all historical relationships, interrelated in what they want to express."[21]

Although we acknowledge the hegemonic place that English occupies in African studies today, our translation illustrates the limits of a monolingual engagement with African experiences. By revealing the complex nature of Senghor's multilingual understanding of culture, our volume gestures also toward a conception of the practice of translation as an alternative to the broadscale rejection of "Western" languages from African cultural production. As Táíwò suggests, "While people are happy to line up behind Ngũgĩ [wa Thiong'o]'s declamations, hardly anyone bothers to consider alternative takes on the question of language from other African thinkers."[22] By no means do we diminish calls to write and publish in autochthonous African languages, such as those issued by Ngũgĩ wa Thiong'o. Rather, we invite African scholars to take seriously the diglossic nature of imperial languages and rethink plurilingualism as an antidote to both Western hegemony and extremist nativism in African studies. We posit translation as a possible way forward. As Ngũgĩ himself has suggested, "the fear of exacerbating divisions along language lines is obviously genuine—but the solution is not to continue burying languages and the means of African memory under a Europhonic paradise. On the contrary [. . .] *the solution lies in translation*."[23]

In what follows, we reflect on the process of translating Senghor into English. First, we provide some background on the *Liberté* series from which the essays collected in this volume are drawn. We then explore the notion of freedom (*liberté*) in Senghor's thought before discussing some of the challenges in translating his texts, including the key word *nègre*. Finally, we explain the rationale for the selection and organization of essays.

On the *Liberté* Volumes and "Freedom"

Shortly after national independence (1960) and in the wake of his first reelection (1963), Senghor began editing and compiling his prose works—some previously published, others unpublished—into a series of five volumes under the title *Liberté* (Freedom), published by Le Seuil. Along with *Nation et voie africaine du socialisme*, published in 1961 by Présence Africaine, the *Liberté* volumes are the only collections dedicated exclusively to Senghor's vast and varied philosophical, aesthetic, and political writings. They represent a concerted effort (and remarkable foresight) on the part of Senghor to conceive of his extensive nonliterary production as a cohesive oeuvre.

Already, in 1964, when the first *Liberté* volume was published, Senghor had amassed almost three decades' worth of essays, articles, and speeches. At this juncture, he was prepared not only to look back on his intellectual output, curate it, and define its throughlines, but also to look forward to a series of volumes to come, each of which would treat the "ideas" or "obsessions" around which the entirety of his production revolves and which would lend the *Liberté* volumes their respective individual titles: Negritude, humanism, nation, socialism, the "dialogue of cultures," and the "civilization of the universal."[24] In the preface to the first *Liberté* volume, *Negritude and Humanism*, Senghor characterizes the texts grouped together in the *Liberté* series as constituting his "principle prose works" across various genres: "essays, prefaces, articles, conference papers, speeches, allocutions." He notes that compared to the manuscripts, the texts collected in *Liberté* present variants, corrections, and changes, but most often deletions and the removal of unnecessary citations (though what we have found, in translating and editing Senghor, is that he frequently seems to have removed the *sources* cited).[25] Senghor's reflection on the series title (*Liberté*) is revealing:

> The writings collected here have as a general theme the *conquest* of Freedom, as the recovery and affirmation, defense and illustration, of the collective personality of Black peoples: of *Negritude*. National *Independence* can have no other meaning. As if by accident, new neighborhoods in Dakar bear the same name: "Liberté I," "Liberté II," "Liberté III." . . . But this is no accident in the year 1963.[26]

The choice of *freedom* not merely for title but as theme and rubric for the collected prose works is significant. On the one hand, it reflects and reasserts the role of Negritude itself as a *philosophy of freedom* in the wake of formal decolonization, positioning Senghor and the other Negritude thinkers as major theorists and architects of Black/African freedom and cultural liberation, as well as national independence—even if their preindependence political action sought, at times, forms of self-determination *without* or beyond state sovereignty.[27] The allusion to the Liberté neighborhoods in the Grand Dakar area, which he suggests had sprung up after independence but which really had been built up by SICAP (Société Immobilière du Cap Vert) beginning in the 1950s, seems a further attempt by Senghor to align his philosophical and political writings with a vision for a new, modern Senegal. On the other hand, there are evident paradoxes involved in Senghor's self-styling as an architect of freedom. Indeed, in 1964, the very year that the first *Liberté* volume was published, nearly thirty undercover Senegalese members of the Marxist-Leninist African Independence Party assembled in Cuba so as to prepare a "guerrilla war" against Senghor's regime, which they saw as neocolonial and oppressive.[28] Before and after independence, Senghor deployed questionable, often brutal tactics (including intimidation, imprisonment, torture, and assassination) to maintain power, forcefully quelling the anti-imperialist and anticapitalist student and union protests at the Université Cheikh Anta Diop in 1968, imprisoning political rivals such as Mamadou Dia, banning media deemed critical to his regime (including, famously, Ousmane Sembène's 1977 film, *Ceddo*), and even torturing and killing political dissidents and activists, the case of Omar Blondin Diop (1946–73) being especially well known.

This political legacy would seem impossible to square with any narrow understanding of the term "freedom." And yet it is undeniable that Negritude has played a central role in articulations and understandings of Black liberation. While Senghor the statesman made oppressive and at times abhorrent decisions that actively contributed to the *unfreedom* of Senegalese citizens, Senghor the philosopher-poet never stopped theorizing Negritude as a privileged site of what Nathalie Etoké calls "Black existential freedom." In this light, Blackness itself "must be theorized as a never-ending commitment to individual and collective freedom" and, further, "the meanings of Blackness expand our understanding of freedom and what it means to be human in a dehumanizing white supremacist world."[29] Senghor's writings reflect and confirm this conception of Blackness. Across the *Liberté* volumes, Blackness is the privileged site for Senghor's reflections not only on freedom but also on rhythm, poetry, beauty, language, art, and philosophy. Senghor theorizes Negritude as a set of fundamental values that enables all people of African descent to subvert the colonial dialectic by accepting and affirming their experiences of Blackness and Africanness. Despite the broad scope and incredible variety of Senghor's intellectual and literary production, all his work nonetheless shares a primary concern: to plumb the depths and elucidate the nature of the Black soul (*l'âme nègre*) while articulating a theory of Black liberation and a global—indeed planetary—vision of a symbiosis of human cultures. The latter prepares what he calls the "civilization of the universal," a concept that, across his oeuvre, remains a political horizon for Africa and for the world.

Translating Blackness: *Nègre*, *Noir*, Black, Negro(-)

"Blackness" in Senghor is, to borrow one definition of the "untranslatable," not a word that *cannot* be translated but "a word that one never stops (not) translating."[30] On the level of the word, the single most significant challenge in rendering Senghor's works in English today is the term *nègre*.[31] Readers familiar with the Francophone context and the histories of French slavery and colonialism will readily recognize the difficulties posed by translating into English the constellation of terms in French related to Blackness and Black or African identity, especially the notoriously fraught word *nègre*. From Jean-Paul Sartre's assertion, in "Black Orpheus," that the French language was "unsuitable" (*impropre*) for the articulation of Black subjectivities, to Franco-Cameroonian writer Léonora Miano's more recent suggestion, in *Afropea* (2020), that "Blackness" remains unthinkable and, ultimately, unsayable in French,[32] Blackness persists in French not only as an obstacle in and to translation but also as a generative site for thinking through questions of postcolonial untranslatability. The challenges of translating "Blackness" have given rise to a now robust body of scholarship and reflection.[33] However, we find it noteworthy that, with few exceptions (e.g., Lamine Senghor, Léopold Sédar Senghor, Achille Mbembe), such reflections are marked by a striking absence of Black African scholars' perspectives on these words. Critical engagement with the term *nègre* has overwhelmingly focused on its circulation in the Caribbean, the "Atlantic world," and the African diaspora, while its particular usages by writers in West Africa and on the rest of the continent remain underexamined.

For Anglophone readers unfamiliar with such debates, the stakes of translating terms such as *nègre, noir*, and the prefix *négro-*, all of which occur frequently in Senghor's texts, may be less clear.[34] Above all, these terms testify to the overdetermined lexical history of writing Blackness in French, a history whose contours have been shaped by the enduring legacies of colonialism and neocolonialism as well as Black resistance, internationalism, and activism. Both *nègre* and *noir* have been translated variously into English as "Black" and "Negro," or simply left untranslated; *nègre* has also, occasionally, been translated using the N-word in English (though the latter is closer to *sale nègre*).

English translations of *nègre* have had to grapple with the term's history of use not only as a racial epithet but also as a synonym for "slave" in colonial discourse, especially in French Caribbean texts.[35] Indeed, Doyle Calhoun notes, "by the nineteenth century—and perhaps even earlier—the idea of Blackness was thoroughly conflated with that of slavery; in French, the word *nègre* was the lexical sign of this conflation."[36] As Brent Hayes Edwards writes, the association, in fact, synonymity, between the words *nègre* and *esclave* ("slave") was "cemented in early dictionaries [. . .] in a phrasing copied in almost all the dictionaries of the next two hundred years."[37]

Importantly, Edwards points out the "heterological slippage" between *nègre* and *noir*, noting that these words circulated differently in different contexts structured by American racism and European colonialism—the Americas, Africa, and Europe.[38] These terms, moreover, were gradually rehabilitated by Black Caribbean, African, and French writers and activists, even before the Negritude writers, beginning in the 1920s. An early example of this rehabilitation is Lamine Senghor's 1927 essay "Le 'Mot' Nègre." In this essay, published in the radical periodical *La voix des Nègres*, Lamine Senghor draws a clear distinction between *nègre* and *noir*, identifying the latter, not the former, as a colonial imposition and part of a "divisive maneuver" intended to drive a wedge between Black subjects:

> They are extracting two new words out of the word *nègre*, in order to divide the race into three different categories, namely: "*hommes de couleur*," "*noirs*"—simply—and *Nègres*. The former are made to believe that they are "*hommes de couleur*" and neither *noirs* nor *nègres* (first category); the others are made to believe that they are "*noirs*" simply and not *nègres* (second category). As for the "leftovers" [Quant aux "restes"], they are *nègres* (third category).[39]

Maintaining a distinction between *noir* and *nègre*, Lamine Senghor went on to reclaim *nègre* as both honorific and rallying cry, in a move Christopher L. Miller characterizes as a "radical" and "space-clearing" rerouting (or uprooting) of etymology.[40] Senghor explained:

> We do not think that the word "*noir*" can serve to designate all the *nègres* in the world, given that all African *nègres* recognize with us that there exist, in various points of the continent, *nègres* as white as some European whites, *nègres* who have nothing *nègre* aside from their features and hair. We refuse to admit that only those who live in the depths of the Senegalese jungle, those who are exploited in the cotton fields of the

Niger valley, the sugarcane cutters in the plantation fields of Martinique and Guadeloupe, are *nègres*. [. . .] We do ourselves honor and glory by calling ourselves *Nègres*, with a capital *N*.[41]

There is much that could be said about these passages. In many ways, Lamine Senghor's radical expansion of the term *nègre* anticipates Léopold Senghor's own. But we focus on the fact that translating the words *nègre* and *noir* both as "Black" would not only produce a tautology in this text but also flatten a distinction central to Lamine Senghor's efforts to push the term *nègre* beyond chromatism, beyond "Black" as colonial phenotype.

This radical expansion of *nègre* is a major feature of Senghor's thought and of the Negritude movement more broadly. For Senghor, *nègre* designated less a racial or phenotypical concept based on geographical origins and biological essences than a definition of the human conceptualized through historical experience and psychology. Negritude was not a skin color but "a culture."[42] It is perhaps better translated as "Negrohood" than "Blackness." This becomes clear in Senghor's essay "Concerning Negritude" ("Problématique de la Négritude"). For Senghor, Negritude was expansive, capacious, and spiritual, whereas Blackness (*noirceur*) was concrete. Had this not been the case, Senghor writes, the Negritude writers would have chosen another word, such as *nigrité* or *nigritude*:

> It is true, people have not failed to reproach Césaire for choosing the word *negritude* over *negroness* [*négrité*]. Once again, the two words have the same meaning, formed as they are with suffixes having the same meaning; it is only that the suffix *-itude* is more learned. But, according to the Strasbourg grammarians, it serves to form less abstract words, designating a state more often than a quality. Which has allowed me, elsewhere, to use the word *Arabness* [*arabité*] in some cases, and *Berberitude* [*berbéritude*] in others. We also find the word *nigritudo* in Latin, in Pliny. It has a concrete meaning and signifies: "the fact of being black, the color black, blackness [*la noirceur*]." And the word *nigritude* exists in English with the same meaning—if we are to believe the *Harrap's* French-English dictionary. As we will see, however, in various places, the meaning has remained quite concrete. The originality of the French word is to have moved from the concrete to the abstract: from the material to the spiritual.[43]

In this vein, at the beginning of his essay "What the Black Man Offers" ("Ce que l'homme noir apporte"), Senghor extends his reflection on the use of *nègre* versus *noir*. Regarding the notoriously fraught term *nègre*, he writes, "I adopt the word following others: It is convenient. Are there Negroes [*Nègres*], pure Negroes [*des Nègres purs*], Black Negroes [*Nègres noirs*]?"[44]

Once again, we are confronted with the nonsynonymity of the terms *noir* and *nègre* and the risk of producing a tautology in English translation if we translate both as "Black" or both as "Negro," given that, the use of the term *noir* in French during the first decades of the twentieth century was in many ways closer to the English "Negro" than to contemporary uses of the word "Black." In the 1990s, the English word "black" effectively replaced the term *noir·e* in France, though, as Matthew B. Smith points out in the preface to his translation of Aimé Césaire's *Nègre je suis, nègre je resterai* (translated as *Resolutely Black*), "*Noir* has since reemerged as the term most frequently used to speak of black experience in France."[45]

If *nègre* and *noir* already pose problems in the original French, the terms used to translate these words into English—"Black," "Negro"—are also far from neutral. This is especially the case in our current historical moment, in the wake of intense anti-Black violence in the United States and the Francosphere and the rise of global Black Lives Matter movements in all corners of the globe. Such words (as well as their translation or resignification) are ultimately more than words: They are "*framing* gestures" that demarcate a particular semantic, and thus ideological, field related to Blackness. They are sites where "racial meanings are negotiated."[46] For these reasons, as Edwards puts it, "the best 'translation' of *nègre* . . . might not be a literal translation at all, but a linguistic nuance, an effect achieved in *a particular nongeneralizable discursive instance*."[47]

The question remains, then, how to translate *noir* and *nègre* as they appear in Senghor's texts. Edwards's caution against generalization is well taken. Senghor's *nègre* is not Césaire's, is not Fanon's, and so on; nor, in any given "discursive instance," should it be assumed that the best or only way of rendering *nègre* in English is "Negro" and *noir* as "Black," or vice versa. However, we have opted here for what some might consider a more or less "literal" translation: We translate *nègre* as "Negro" and *noir* as "Black." We have done this for two main reasons. First, as we write in our translators' note, across the *Liberté* volumes, Senghor deploys the terms *Nègre* or *nègre* and *Noir·e* or *noir·e* as well as the prefixes *Négro-* or *négro-* (e.g., *négro-africain·e, négro-américain·e, négro-espagnol·e*) and *Afro-* or *afro-* (e.g., *afro-américain·e, afro-latin·e*) consistently and with precision (even if his use of capitalization occasionally varies). Given this distribution, we have, in the process of reading and translating Senghor, reached the consensus that translating *nègre* and *noir* by the same word in

English ("Black") would flatten important nuances legible in the original French, both within and across texts, in ways that would distort or attenuate Senghor's arguments—namely, his theorization of Blackness. At the same time, the sheer frequency with which the term *nègre* is used, both as an adjective and as a noun, made leaving the word untranslated or consistently glossing it in square brackets somewhat unwieldly; "to be *nègre*" seems viable in English, but "*nègre* art" or "*nègre* rhythm" less so. Second, we take seriously Sartre's suggestion, in "Black Orpheus," that one of the foundations of Negritude is the very possibility of using the term *nègre*.[48]

For Senghor, to live the values of Negritude was also to use its key term, fraught and difficult as it may have been. This is perhaps why, like Aimé Césaire, who used the term *nègre* instead of *noir* well into the 2000s, Senghor retained the word *nègre* even when other, less embattled options became available (e.g., *noir·e, personne de couleur, black*). The adherence to the term *nègre*, in other words, is not just a political stand for these thinkers but a way of living out the values of Negritude. Césaire expressed this adherence to the term *as a philosophical way of being* in a late interview with Françoise Vergès, where he stated the original commitments of the Négritude writers: "Nègre je suis, nègre je resterai" (Negro I am, negro I shall remain).[49] It is understandable that the theoreticians of Negritude would want to retain this key term—the rehabilitation of which was so hard won and truly marked an "event" in the French language—even when the tides of culture and common usage seemed to have irreversibly shifted. In this, we should also honor Senghor's (and Césaire's) long-standing commitment to the term as telegraphing their commitment to being not simply "resolutely Black" but resolutely *nègre*.

Organization and Structure

As with any selection of texts, it could be said of the present volume that this or that important text has been left out. Our choice to focus on three of the five *Liberté* volumes for the present collection of essays is due to their thematic coherence. As Jane Hiddleston points out, "Volumes one, three and five successively track the evolution of negritude from the 1930s to the 1970s, whilst volumes two and four delineate [Senghor's] more practical reflections on African socialism."[50] In our choice of texts, we have attempted to strike a balance between a thematic focus on Negritude, aesthetics, and philosophy, on the one hand, and, on the other hand, a certain representativeness, that is, a sense of Senghor's prose oeuvre across the three volumes, given that the writings collected therein span almost five decades. There is also a pedagogical aspect to this selection: Put simply, these are works that we have taught in French and hope to be able to teach in English. In addition to making Senghor's work available to the greater Anglophone community, we have attempted to provide in a single volume a representative selection of his most significant philosophical and aesthetic writings. By doing so, we hope to facilitate the synthetic work necessary for a deeper understanding of this complex thinker, even for French-speaking scholars who may already have access to his extensive body of work. Senghor's oeuvre is vast, encompassing some 2,300 pages of prose across the five volumes. Presenting a curated selection of these texts can significantly ease the burden on scholars, who would otherwise expend considerable resources to engage more fully with his ideas.

We have sought to feature a set of texts in which Senghor articulates his understanding of Negritude, with a notable focus on his polemical defense of Negritude against critics who dismissed it as obsolete and passé. With these texts, we aim to enable scholars and students to revisit the core ideas of Negritude by situating it within a broader Africa-centered intellectual tradition, rather than confining it to the narrow framework of anticolonial resistance and the interwar period. It is important to note that Negritude has been predominantly understood and taught through the lens of Jean-Paul Sartre's and Abiola Irele's writings. Sartre's influential "Black Orpheus," often cited as the text that introduced Negritude to the world, and Irele's pivotal role in bringing Negritude to Anglophone audiences, framed the movement as a revolutionary response by Black students in 1930s Paris grappling with pervasive racism and France's colonial assimilationist policies. Within this framework, Negritude is interpreted as either a revolutionary cultural movement or the dual-natured counterpart to Pan-Africanism. As Irele put it, "Negritude is a version, a distinctive current, of the same cultural nationalism expressed in different ways among black people and at various times in their reaction against white domination."[51] Its historic, geographic, and conceptual scope has thus been somewhat limited to what one editor calls the "the narrow historical circumstances that enframed its emergence":[52] to the metropole, during the interwar period, as a response to colonial conditions and, specifically, France's assimilationist policies. However, this way of framing Negritude, while influential, has constrained the movement to a reaction disconnected from its deeper philosophical and cultural dimensions. Moreover, it does not reflect the timeline of Senghorian Negritude, which extends well into the last decades of the twentieth century and becomes a distinctly *African* humanism. Senghor himself explicitly rejected this reductionist view of Negritude, which he consistently framed as more than an anticolonial movement, grounding it instead in a longer intellectual and cultural history of Africa.

By including several texts that highlight Senghor's rejection of the traditional framing of Negritude, we highlight the complexity of Senghor's scholarship and move the critique of Negritude beyond the dichotomies through which it is often characterized. Our hope is that these texts encourage scholars and students alike to reexamine Negritude not as a simple reactionary schema but as a complex philosophical, aesthetic, and political framework centering Black/African humanity and in conversation with modern Europe and the rest of the world. We highlight Senghor's multifaceted vision of Negritude as a movement, rooted in African and Afro-diasporic cultures, that transcends simplistic binaries and continues to hold enduring relevance for African studies and beyond. This perspective offers a deeper and more nuanced understanding of its philosophical foundations.

The texts published in the *Liberté* volumes were originally arranged chronologically, which has certain advantages. This organization "reveal[s] both the significance of their timing, and the overlapping and evolving formation of [Senghor's] thought."[53] It also has the potential to situate Senghor's work in the context of its political and intellectual production, allowing us to better understand Negritude as a pragmatic philosophical engagement with clear political objectives that must be read in connection with the political atmosphere of the moment and the intellectual conversations of the time. The risk, however, is that a chronological structure presents Senghor's thought in terms of a linear evolution that might be divided into "early" and "late" works. The reality is that Senghor's thought is, in many ways, cyclical and recursive. Although he revisited and reformulated earlier concepts—and occasionally corrected or revised himself—he never fully abandoned them; his commitments and preoccupations remained consistent even as they took different guises and adapted to different discursive and political contexts. Moreover, Senghor frequently (and, by his own account, quasi-obsessively) revisited, reworked, and reprised earlier ideas and even entire passages from one text to another. This practice reflected in part the nature of certain texts (similar speeches were given on different occasions and in different venues and may have been developed later as articles or essays) and in part the fact that he was a busy head of state who drafted quickly, leading him to recycle parts of texts and, occasionally, to contradict himself. Senghor was also a strong polemist who saw himself as the defender of Negritude against the attacks of a young generation of African scholars who in 1969, at the conference of Algiers, declared it dead and buried.[54] We hope that these aspects of his writing, too, emerge in the present volume. For as Senghor himself was wont to say, *reprisal is neither redundancy nor repetition.*

The texts that follow have been grouped thematically, rather than chronologically, into three sections. The first, "Negritude: A Humanism for the Twentieth (and Twenty-First) Century," presents Senghor's major texts on Negritude as a Black/African humanism and philosophy, thus offering an overview of his formulation and successive reformulations of the term and its stakes, from its emergence in the 1930s, to the period of vehement critique in the sixties and seventies, to Senghor's reflections on its enduring relevance at the close of twentieth century as he began to envision Negritude in connection to the "civilization of the universal." Part 2, "Negritude, Aesthetics, and Philosophy," brings together a series of texts that reflect on Black aesthetics in the visual and verbal arts in Africa, the Americas, and Europe—namely, poetry, painting, sculpture, and music. Across these texts, Senghor's understanding of Negritude as an aesthetic philosophy emerges clearly and is articulated alongside and through insightful reflections on African oral traditions as well as the artistic, literary, and musical contributions of Black Americans and the Harlem Renaissance, in addition to French poets such as Arthur Rimbaud. The final section, "Negritude, *Métissage*, and the Dialogue of Cultures," introduces Senghor's philosophical and political vision for the new century, in which Negritude was to play a major role: a "civilization of the universal" characterized by *métissage*, a form of cultural hybridity and mixing without dilution. From his earliest texts—for example, "The Problem of Culture in West Africa"—to his last, "The Dialogue of Cultures," Senghor's vision for a syncretic African polis enriched by contributions from different languages and cultures emerges as Negritude's as yet unfulfilled political horizon.

NOTES

Epigraph: Léopold Sédar Senghor, "La Négritude, comme culture des peuples noirs, ne saurait être dépassé," in *Liberté 5: Le dialogue des cultures* (Seuil, 1993), 108.

1. There is no consensus on the exact birthplace of Léopold Sédar Senghor. While his official birth certificate lists Joal, oral historians often argue that he was born in Djiloor, a small community approximately fifteen minutes by car from Joal, where his mother lived.

2. Frantz Fanon, *Les Damnés de la terre* (La Découverte, 2002), esp. 44–45, 52–53.

3. Paul Gilroy, *The Black Atlantic: Modernity and Double Consciousness* (Harvard University Press, 1993), 1.

4. See Abiola Irele, "A Defence of Negritude," *Transition* 13 (1964): 9–11. Irele notes the particular "suspicion or open hostility (or even ridicule) among English-speaking Africans" regarding Negritude that results from "grave misconceptions about the *real*

aims of the movement in general, and in some cases, from prejudice and complete lack of knowledge" (3).

5. David Murphy, "Léopold Sédar Senghor: Race, Language, Empire," in *Postcolonial Thought in the French-Speaking World*, edited by Charles Forsdick and David Murphy (Liverpool University Press, 2009), 157.

6. These include F. Bart Miller, *Rethinking Négritude Through Léon-Gontran Damas* (Rodopi, 2014); Cheikh Thiam, *Return to the Kingdom of Childhood: Re-Invisioning the Legacy and Philosophical Relevance of Negritude* (Ohio State University Press, 2014); the special issue titled "Negritude Reloaded," *African Philosophy*, no. 11 (2015); Reiland Rabaka, *The Negritude Movement: W. E. B. Du Bois, Léon Damas, Aimé Césaire, Léopold Senghor, Frantz Fanon, and the Evolution of an Insurgent Idea* (Lexington Books, 2015); Gary Wilder, *Freedom Time: Negritude, Decolonization, and the Future of the World* (Duke University Press, 2015); Carrie Noland, *Voices of Negritude in Modernist Print: Aesthetic Subjectivity, Diaspora, and the Lyric Regime* (Columbia University Press, 2015); Jean-Pierre Langellier, *Léopold Sédar Senghor* (Perrin, 2022); Sébastien Heiniger, *Décolonisation, fédéralisme et poésie chez Léopold Sédar Senghor* (Classiques Garnier, 2022); Mohamed Aziza et al., *L'Héritage de Senghor* (L'Harmattan, 2022); Cheikh Thiam, *Epistemologies from the Global South: Negritude, Modernity, and the Idea of Africa* (University of KwaZuu-Natal Press, 2023; Routledge, 2024); Mamadou Diouf, Sarah Frioux-Salgas, and Sarah Linger, eds., *Senghor et les arts: Réinventer l'universel* (Musée Quai Branly, 2023); Ela Bertho, *Léopold Sédar Senghor* (Puf, 2023); Souleymane Bachir Diagne, *African Art as Philosophy: Senghor, Bergson, and the Idea of Negritude*, trans. Chike Jeffers (Other Press, 2023); Yohann C. Ripert, *Senghor: Writings on Politics* (Duke University Press, 2025).

7. See *La Rose de la paix et autres poèmes*, trans. Léopold Sédar Senghor with John Amery, ed. John Furness (L'Harmattan, 2001). See also Patrick Hersant, "'Une traduction du dedans': Hopkins dans le fonds Senghor," *Continents manuscrits* 21 (2023), http://journals.openedition.org/coma/10524.

8. Léopold Sédar Senghor, *On African Socialism*, trans. Mercer Cook (Frederick A. Praeger, 1964). John Reed and Clive Wake published an English translation of some of Senghor's prose and poetry as early as 1965. Reed and Wake, trans., *Senghor: Prose and Poetry* (Heinemann, 1965).

9. Ripert, *Senghor*.

10. For an overview, see Abdoulaye Bathily, *Mai 1968 à Dakar ou la révolte universitaire et la démocratie: Le Sénégal cinquante ans après* (L'Harmattan, 2018).

11. Léopold Sédar Senghor, "Négritude et civilisation méditerranéennes [*sic*]," in *Liberté 5: Le dialogue des cultures* (Seuil, 1993), 86 (our emphasis).

12. Robert J. C. Young, *Postcolonialism: An Historical Introduction* (Blackwell, 2002), 255.

13. Olúfẹ́mi O. Táíwò, *Against Decolonisation: Taking African Agency Seriously* (Hurst, 2022), 63.

14. Táíwò, *Against Decolonisation*, 63 (our emphasis).

15. Diagne, *African Art as Philosophy*; Wilder, *Freedom Time*; Thiam, *Return to the Kingdom of Childhood*; Thiam, *Epistemologies from the Global South*.

16. Abiola Irele, "A Defence of Negritude: A Propos of *Black Orpheus* by Jean Paul Sartre," *Transition* 13, no. 50 (1975): 39.

17. Oyèrónkẹ́ Oyěwùmí, *The Invention of Woman: Making an African Sense of Western Gender Discourses* (University of Minnesota Press, 1997), 20.

18. Henry Louis Gates Jr., "Critical Fanonism," *Critical Inquiry* 17, no. 3 (1991): 470.

19. Barbara Cassin, "The Energy of Untranslatables: Translation as a Paradigm for the Human Sciences," *Paragraph* 38, no. 2 (2015): 154.

20. In *The Tongue-Tied Imagination*, Tobias Warner uses the Wolof verb *tekki* to describe translation as a process of unraveling or untying semiotic knots. In Senghor's world, these semiotic knots call for multilingual engagement with his text that frames translation as an act of "pulling a thread that may unsettle others." Warner, *The Tongue-Tied Imagination: Decolonizing Literary Modernity in Senegal* (Fordham University Press, 2019), 7.

21. Walter Benjamin, "The Task of the Translator," in *Walter Benjamin: Selected Writings*, Vol. 1, ed. Marcus Bullock and Micheal Jennings (Harvard University Press, 1996), 255.

22. Táíwò, *Against Decolonisation*, 79.

23. Ngũgĩ wa Thiong'o, *Something Torn and New: An African Renaissance* (Basic Books, 2009), 95 (our emphasis).

24. Léopold Sédar Senghor, *Liberté 1: Négritude et humanisme* (Seuil, 1964), 7.

25. Senghor, *Liberté 1*, 7–8.

26. Senghor, *Liberté 1*, 7.

27. See Wilder, *Freedom Time*.

28. On this moment, see Fatoumata Seck, "The Cultural Underground of Decolonization," *Journal of Postcolonial Literary Inquiry* 10, no. 3 (2023): 287–309.

29. Nathalie Etoké, *Black Existential Freedom* (Rowman and Littlefield, 2023), 3.

30. Barbara Cassin, "Traduire les intraduisibles, un état de lieu," *Cliniques méditerranéennes* 2, no. 90 (2014): 26.

31. On philosophical untranslatablity, see Barbara Cassin, Emily Apter, Jacques Lezra, and Michael Wood, eds., *Dictionary of Untranslatables: A Philosophical Lexicon* (Princeton University Press, 2014). See also Michael Syrotinski, "Postcolonial Untranslatability: Reading Achille Mbembe with Barbara Cassin," *Journal of Postcolonial Writing* 55, no. 6 (2019): 850–62.

32. Jean-Paul Sartre, "Orphée noir," in *Anthologie de la nouvelle poésie nègre et malgache de langue française*, ed. Léopold Sédar Senghor (Presses universitaires de France, 1948), xviii. Miano leaves the English word untranslated in the French original: "This *blackness* that the French language has not allowed itself to think" ("Cette blackness que la langue française ne s'est pas autorisée à penser"). Léonora Miano, *Afropea* (Grasset, 2020), 94.

33. For discussions of the term *nègre* and other terms related to Blackness in French, see Laurent Dubois's introduction to his translation of Achille Membe, *Critique de la raison nègre* (La Découverte, 2013); Laurent Dubois, translator's introduction to Achille Mbembe, *Critique of Black Reason* (Duke University Press, 2017), ix–xv. See also Brent Hayes Edwards, *The Practice of Diaspora: Literature, Translation, and the Rise of Black Internationalism* (Harvard University Press, 2003), 26–68; Nigel C. Gibson, "Relative Opacity: A New Translation of Fanon's Wretched of the Earth—Mission Betrayed or Fulfilled?," *Social Identities* 13, no. 1 (2007): 69–95, esp. 73; Grégory Pierrot, "Nègre (Noir, Black, Renoi, Négro)," *Small Axe* 26, no. 2 (2022): 100–107; and Doyle Calhoun,

"Fanon's Lexical Intervention: Writing Blackness in *Black Skin, White Masks*," *Paragraph* 43, no. 2 (2020): 159–78. See also Corine Tachtiris, "Introduction: The Unbearable Whiteness of Translation," in *Translation and Race*, ed. Corine Tachtiris (Routledge, 2024), 1–30.

34. See N. Gregson Davis's translation of Aimé Césaire's *Journal of a Homecoming / Cahier d'un retour au pays natal* (Duke University Press, 2017), esp. 97.

35. Richard Philcox characterizes *nègre* as "that word dreaded by all translators of French Caribbean texts." Philcox, "Retranslating Fanon, Retrieving a Lost Voice," in Frantz Fanon, *The Wretched of the Earth*, trans. Richard Philcox (Grove, 2004), 247.

36. Calhoun, "Fanon's Lexical Intervention," 172.

37. Edwards, *Practice of Diaspora*, 26.

38. Edwards, *Practice of Diaspora*, 20,

39. Lamine Senghor, "Le Mot 'Nègre,'" *La voix des Nègres* 1 (January 1927), cited in Edwards, *Practice of Diaspora*, 31–32.

40. Christopher L. Miller, *Nationalists and Nomads: Essays on Francophone African Literature and Culture* (University of Chicago Press, 1998), 36.

41. Lamine Senghor quoted in Edwards, *Practice of Diaspora*, 32–33 (Edwards's translation).

42. Léopold Sédar Senghor, "Problématique de la Négritude," in *Liberté 3: Négritude et civilisation de l'universel* (Seuil, 1977), 270.

43. See chapter 4, page 107, in the present volume.

44. See chapter 8, page 190, in the present volume.

45. Aimé Césaire, *Resolutely Black: Conversations with Françoise Vergès*, trans. Matthew B. Smith (Polity Press, 2020), vii. For the original, see Aimé Césaire, *Nègre je suis, nègre je resterai: Entretiens avec Françoise Vergès* (Albin Michel, 2005).

46. Edwards, *Practice of Diaspora*, 38 ("*framing* gestures"); Tachtiris, "Introduction," 22 ("negotiated").

47. Edwards, *Practice of Diaspora*, 35 (our emphasis).

48. Sartre wrote: "Le Nègre [. . .] se redresse, il ramasse le mot de 'nègre' qu'on lui a jeté comme une pierre, dans la fierté" (The Negro [. . .] rises, takes up the word *Negro* which they had thrown at him like a stone, with pride). Sartre, "Orphée noir," xiv.

49. Césaire, *Resolutely Black*, 9 (translation modified).

50. Jane Hiddleston, *Decolonising the Intellectual: Politics, Culture, and Humanism at the End of the French Empire* (Liverpool University Press, 2014), 42.

51. Abiola Irele, *The African Experience in Literature and Ideology* (Indiana University Press, 1981), 91.

52. Doyle D. Calhoun, "Negritude and the Promise of African Literature," in *Intellectual Traditions of African Literature, 1960–2015*, ed. Cajetan Iheka and Jeanne-Marie Jackson (Cambridge University Press, 2026), 67.

53. Hiddleston, *Decolonising the Intellectual*, 42.

54. Lindfors Bernth, "Anti-Negritude in Algiers," *Africa Today* 17 (1970): 5–7.

PART I

Negritude

A HUMANISM FOR THE TWENTIETH (AND TWENTY-FIRST) CENTURY

I

Constitutive Elements of a Civilization of Negro-African Inspiration

You can imagine how embarrassed I was when I began reflecting on this report. *The Constitutive Elements of a Civilization of Negro-African Inspiration*? But, I wondered, had I not already dealt with the topic at the Paris Congress, in my report entitled *The Spirit of Civilization or the Laws of Negro-African Culture*?[1] I was all the more embarrassed when I reread the "Call" of the SAC (Société Africaine de Culture) [The African Society of Culture] defining the spirit of the Second Congress: "the lines of force or the magnetic field inspiring all creation, all cultural exchange in Negro-African society."[2] That is precisely what my first report strived to show. In other words: "all those original contributions (. . . totems, obvious facts and value judgments, vocabularies and style) which must, simultaneously, distinguish us from others, expose us to others, and link and connect us to the human family."[3]

But, upon further consideration, the question does not present itself in quite the same way. In my first report, the emphasis was less on Negro-African

Civilization (the sum of its technical and cultural works) than on *Culture*, that is, the spirit of this civilization (the sum of its values). On the other hand, I had disregarded social values that were not strictly cultural.

My point today is quite different. I intend to begin by defining the *conditions* of Negro-African civilization, by which I mean the physical environment and economic infrastructure, which largely determine the social and cultural superstructures. Some will cry out: "But that's the Marxist method." To this, I would reply that this method, which informs contemporary thought, cannot be ignored today. The Jesuit Fathers themselves, who have contributed so much to the progress of Marxology in France, do not deny the socialist philosopher's positive contributions. Moreover, Marx's thought is not without nuance, and the truth it expresses cannot be disputed. I will simply recall the following passage from Marx, quoted by Aimé Césaire in his report at the Paris Congress: "It is always in the direct relationship between the masters of the conditions of production and the direct producer—it is always in these relations that we discover the intimate secret, the hidden foundation of the entire social structure. Given the numerous and distinct empirical conditions (*natural and racial factors, historical influences acting from the outside* . . .), this does not prevent the same economic base (the same, at least, as far as the main conditions are concerned) from showing, in its manifestation, infinite variations and gradations which can be ascertained only through the analysis of the empirically given circumstances."[4] So, even for Marx, the economic factor is not the only *determinant* in the formation of society. Society is, in turn, determined by the natural environment. There is more, for the economic factor determines society only through certain mediations—races, families, groups of all kinds. Finally, superstructures react upon infrastructures and vice versa. This is the very meaning of the *dialectical* movement of history, at the end of which human *freedom* emerges.

This shows that our use of the socialist method is *humanist*. This method is only a framework. In particular, it is up to us to uncover the mediations and to define their roles. Ultimately, it is a matter of *explaining Man by man*.

For the originality of this presentation, if it has any, will be less to define the "laws of Negro-African Culture" than the "facts of civilization": social institutions such as cultural organizations and features, not to mention cultural "artifacts"—the "totems" and themes, to which the "Call" refers and which are found in all negro cultures, even in those of America, precisely because they include *human values of universality*, though they are specifically negro. Referring to our colleague Richard Wright, Jean-Paul Sartre writes: "Thus, if an American Black man [*un Noir des États-Unis*] finds that he has a vocation as a writer, he discovers this subject, at the same time. He is the man who sees the Whites from the outside, who assimilates the White culture for himself, and each of whose books will show the alienation of the black race within American society. *Not objectively like the realists, but passionately and in a way that will compromise his reader*."[5] "Passionately," then, and in a negro style. These "totems" and themes, though drawn from the source—how could it be otherwise?—are nonetheless oriented toward the *Future*. They are included here because of their permanent value. It would be easy for me—though it would be tedious—to show that most, if not all, these issues remain important in contemporary thought, or at least in art.

I. The Tropical and Agricultural Milieu

The term "race" can be discussed at length. That does not change the fact that the word corresponds to a reality, just like the word "civilization," which Marcel Mauss defines as "a set of sufficiently numerous and sufficiently important phenomena extending over a sufficiently considerable number of territories."[6] Regarding race, we can adopt the definition, following H[enri]. V[ictor]. Vallois, given by Dr. Jean Price-Mars in his report. It is a "natural grouping of man with a set of common hereditary physical characteristics."[7] What strikes me about the Negroes of America is the permanence not of Negro-African physical characteristics, but that of Negro-African psychic characteristics, despite their *métissage*, despite the new milieu. Do not speak to us of segregation. Of course, segregation partially explains the permanence of psychic features, particularly the gift of emotion; it does not explain everything, especially not among Latin American Negroes, where segregation is less of an issue.

I said, "despite the milieu." Because, over time, the milieu will have an effect. It is the milieu that first informs the economy, then society, and eventually brings about physical and psychological mutations that become hereditary. Here, then, we need to study the *Negro-African milieu*—and its effects.

The domain of Negroes in Africa is essentially the lands situated between the Tropics: the Sudanese [*soudanien*], Guinean, and Congolese countries, to which we need to add the region of the Great Lakes—countries covered with grassy savannahs or forests. These are hot countries—and humid the deeper you go into the forest; cattle-raising countries in the Sudanese [*soudanien*] savannahs, along the Guinean lagoons, and on the plateaus around the Great Lakes; farming countries here and there.

This shows that tropical Africa has been populated since early antiquity, since the apparition of Man. Let me remind you of the relevant pages in which

Dr. Jean Price-Mars sums up anthropologists' views on the issue. *Black Africa would be the cradle of Humanity*. All the conditions are there, were there, for that to be so; in any case, the heat and humidity, which are the source of life. And even the "mildness of the climate," if it is true that *Homo sapiens* first appeared on the high plateaus of the Great Lakes. I personally experienced the "sweetness of life" like nowhere else before in Entebbe, on the shores of Lake Victoria, in August.

This climate, hot and humid in the Guinean and Congolese forests—"unhealthy," European geographers add—certainly has much to do with the "negro temperament." It is a fact that this climate visibly acts on the nerves of Europeans, particularly on women. How could it not have done the same, for thousands of years, on Negroes? This would explain, at least partly, their extreme sensitivity [*sensibilité*].

But perhaps more than the climate, more than the cosmic forces, more than the sun and the moon, the plant and animal environments have acted on them. Hence, the importance of *trees* and *animals* in Negro-African mythology, and in the elaboration of totems and themes. Very early on, Negro-Africans devoted themselves to agriculture, and it is the agricultural milieu that best explains their society. I repeat, the Negro-African is a peasant who lives off the land and with the land. *Paysans d'Afrique occidentale* [Peasants of West Africa]: such is the title of one of the most famous works by the ethnologist Henri Labouret.[8]

I know that some geographers have developed the thesis that tropical soils are poor, which would explain the backwardness of exotic civilizations. This is the argument put forward by P[ierre]. Gourou in *Les pays tropicaux* [Tropical countries].[9] But others did not fail to counter these geographers with facts and to prove that Negro-Africans, in particular, were able to adapt their farming techniques to the nature of their soils. "These indications illustrate," Labouret concludes, "just how the natives of these different regions have shown their resolve to cultivate their fields, to make them produce maximum yields with the means at their disposal."[10]

However, J[acques]. Richard-Molard, who is sometimes inclined toward Gourou's thesis, cites P[ierre]. Viguier on this topic: "The information provided by the analysis inadequately reflects the agricultural quality of tropical soils. It is common and well-known that, in many cases, soils that appear to contain only a small amount of fertilizing elements after analysis can produce abundant harvests, while soils that are richer in nutrients according to chemical tests may yield poor results."[11] Agronomists realized this after having too hastily introduced European farming methods. Their science had failed, initially, where the practice of the Negro-Africans had succeeded—without "-ism," "-ology," or plough.

But Negro-Africans were familiar with nature; as we will see, they cultivated, in all senses of the term, both trees and animals.

In fact, several countries in Black Africa produce enough, on ostensibly poor soils and with modest tools, to feed populations with a density of up to three hundred inhabitants per square kilometer. That is the case of the coasts of the "Southern Rivers" and the countries of Benin. Between the dense forest and the sea, under a mild, open sky, "polders" provide oil and wine, grains and root crops in abundance. Even in the savannahs, as in my country of the Sine (Senegal), the density can reach fifty inhabitants per square kilometer.[12] If Black Africa is depopulated today, it is due neither to the poverty of its soils nor to the inexperience—let alone the laziness—of its peasants; it is due to the *Slave Trade*, which cost it some two hundred million human lives, at the very time when Europe was stretching its tentacles over the four other continents. As we know, it was precisely the peasant virtues of the Negro-Africans that were at the root of the slave trade. We can pose the question to Gourou: What was Europe like in the fourth millennium BC, when Egyptian civilization flourished—not to mention the Dravidian civilization that spread across India? According to ancient historians, most of its peoples were, then, nothing more than nomadic hordes.

One can therefore deny neither the agricultural and pastoral character of Negro-African civilization nor the fact that it dates back to the most ancient times. The exhibition *Peintures préhistoriques du Sahara* [Prehistoric Paintings from the Sahara][13] provides the latest evidence of this, for it reveals the ancientness and the extent of Negroes' settlement in Africa. Once again, as anthropologists and prehistorians had already pointed out, the climate was favorable. Unlike the European, who lived in cold weather for three to eight months of the year, the Negro-African thrived in the warmth of the savannahs and tropical forests, hunting, fishing, raising numerous herds, and harvesting up to several crops a year. We will consider the social consequences of this later.

First, we need to examine the *Negro-African man*, to define what has been called the "Black soul" ['*l'âme noire*'], by which I mean the Negro-African psychology. It was formed under the influence of the tropical climate and the agricultural and pastoral milieu.

II. The Psychology of the Negro-African or Consciousness and Knowledge

I had originally intended to call this chapter "Psychology of the Negro-African." But I have abandoned that idea. Upon reflection, it seems to me that, however important biological determination may be, along with the previously mentioned factors, it remains too little known. Moreover, what matters most is the consciousness that apprehends the real and constitutes an act of *knowledge* [*connaissance*].

Having said that, however, we must begin with the body: from physiological processes, neurosensory impressions, through sensations and behaviors, to arrive at consciousness, which Trần Đức Thảo defines as "outlined and repressed behavior."[14] From neurosensory impressions to consciousness, there is a whole series of relays, which, on the foundations of duration and *praxis*, transform matter-energy into ever clearer consciousness. I refer the reader to the first chapter of the second section of Thảo's work, entitled "The dialectic of animal behavior as the becoming of sense certainty." Drawing on [Jean] Piaget's work, the Vietnamese philosopher masterfully analyzes this dialectic of reality and intention, through which consciousness rises to the level of knowledge.

We are superior animals, but animals, nonetheless. It is thanks to the structures of our bodies, our nervous system, and according to certain laws, that we perceive things. Our psychology is the expression of our physiology, although, the former conditions and, in turn, surpasses the latter. This is why phenomenological psychology begins by analyzing and discussing the contributions of physiology, just as Sartre and Merleau-Ponty do.[15]

Let us return to the Negro-African. How surprised were Army psychologists when they realized that the Senegalese Tirailleurs were more sensitive to the caprices of the climate than Europeans; that they reacted to the slightest variations in the weather, the slightest events, even the slightest inflections of the voice! These warriors, whom we imagined to be brutes, these heroes, had a woman's sensitivity! And yet we had often said that *the Negro is a man of nature*. He is a man of the open air, a man who lives off the land. And let us take the word in its *cosmic* sense. He is a being with open senses, permeable to all solicitations, to the very waves of nature, without any filtering intermediaries—I do not mean without relays—between subject and object. A thinking man, of course, but first, shapes and colors, above all smells, sounds, and rhythms. And Aimé Césaire, the poet of Negritude, sings:

Hurray for the majestic Cedrate!
Hurray for those who have never invented anything
for those who have never explored anything
for those who have never vanquished anything
but they surrender, possessed, to the essence of every thing
ignorant of surfaces but possessed by the movement

of every thing
unconcerned to vanquish, but playing the game of the world

truly the elder sons of the world
permeable to all the breaths of the world
fraternal compass points for all the breaths of the world
deep lake bed for all the waters of the world
spark of the sacred fire of the world
flesh of the very flesh of the world, palpitating with the very
movement of the world![16]

In these often-cited verses, Césaire contrasts the Negro with the White man, the African with the European. And I know very well that this opposition simplifies the problem, but it is meaningful. As evidence, Sartre uses it again in "Orphée noir" (Black Orpheus),[17] when he opposes the negro peasant to the White engineer.

Let us consider the White European before the object: before the outside world, nature, the *Other*. Man of will, warrior, bird of prey, pure gaze, the European White man distinguishes himself from the object.[18] He holds it at a distance, immobilizes it, fixes it. Equipped with precise instruments, he dissects it in a merciless analysis. Driven by a will to power, he kills the Other and, in a centripetal movement, turns the Other into a means to a practical end. He *assimilates* the Other. Such is the European White man, as he was before the scientific revolution of the twentieth century.

The Negro is entirely different. American psychotechnicians have already noted that his reflexes are more natural and better adapted. Hence, his use in industry and in the Army's technical services, despite the fact that he represents a relatively lower proportion of the population of the United States of America. But let us return to our central theme. The Negro-African exists, first and foremost, in his color as in the primordial night. He does not see the object, he *feels* it. This is one of those verses from the Third Day—a pure sensory field.[19] It is in his subjectivity, at the tip of his sensory organs, that he discovers the Other. He is *moved* [*é-mu*], moving centrifugally from subject to object on the waves of the Other. And this is not a mere metaphor, since contemporary physics has discovered *energy* beneath matter: waves and radiation. Here is, thus, the Negro-African who sympathizes and identifies, who dies to himself in order to be reborn in the Other. He does not assimilate, he *becomes assimilated* [*s'assimile*]. He lives with the Other in symbiosis, he *is born-with [con-naît] the Other*, to use Paul Claudel's phrase.[20] Subject and object are dialectically confronted in the very act of knowledge, which is an act of love. "I think, therefore I am," wrote Descartes. The point has already been made: We are always thinking of *something*. The Negro-African might say: "I feel the Other, I dance the Other, therefore I am." But to dance is to create, especially when the dance is a dance of love. In any case, it is the best way of knowing.

Paradoxical as it may seem, the negro impulse, the Negro-African's active surrender to the object, is driven by *reason*. As Marx wrote to Arnold Ruge, "Reason has always existed, but not in a rational form."[21] Even more explicitly, Engels notes in his preparatory work for *Anti-Dühring*: "Two kinds of experience—one external, material, the other internal—: laws of thinking and forms of thinking. Forms of thinking partially transmitted through inheritance. A mathematical axiom, for example, is self-evident to a European. But certainly not to the Boshiman or the Negroes of Australia."[22] Negro reason, as it appears here, is not, as we can guess, the discursive reason of Europe, the *reason-eye* [*raison-œil*], but the *reason-touch*, sympathetic reason, which has more to do with *logos* than with *ratio*. This is the logos before Aristotelian hardening and sclerosis, the logos that is not pure diamond, but the word of life. This is what today's European science and philosophy are all about.[23] For this speech does not, without touching it, mold the object into rigid, logical categories; it stimulates things, piercing them with its rays to reach their surreality, or more exactly, their *subreality*, in its original humidity. *European reason is analytic by use, negro reason is intuitive by participation*, as I have already emphasized elsewhere.

I have often written that *emotion is negro*. I have been criticized for it. Unjustly. I do not see how else to account for our specificity, for this *Negritude*, which is the "sum total of the cultural values of the Black world," including the Americas, and which Sartre defines as "a certain affective attitude toward the world."[24] This would be the moment to mention a number of well-known testimonies. I prefer to rely on my childhood memories, on the vigils of the past. So many tears shed by implacable heroes! And the audience saw in them the sign of a noble soul. As my refined and sensitive mother used to say, "It is not human to not cry." But here is a common scene. Two relatives—or two friends—meet. They have not seen each other for a long time. The litany of greetings begins—according to a familiar rhythm:

–Do you have peace?
–Nothing but peace.
–Does your father have peace?
–Nothing but peace.
–Does your mother have peace?

–Nothing but peace.
–Do the people in your house have peace?
–Nothing but peace.

And they go on asking about one another: relatives, allies, friends, fields, and cattle. Then memories of bygone days come to mind. When certain facts are recalled, when loved ones are remembered, emotion fills their faces. They throw themselves into each other's arms, holding hands for a long time. And the greetings begin again, but this time to a rhythm with more pronounced contours, to the very rhythm of the poem, which tightens the chest, squeezes the throat, and expresses emotion. It is then that we burst into tears, and large tears flow.

What, then, is *emotion*? At first glance, it appears as a certain attitude of the body. Classical theories—those of [William] James and [Pierre] Janet—with a few variations, present it as a "physiological disorder," "a behavior that is less adapted to the given situation," "a behavior of failure," or, at best, as "an awareness of physiological manifestations."[25] It is true that emotion is accompanied by physiological manifestations that are perceived, from the outside, as disturbances. But let us take a closer look. The object produces, generally through the sensory organs, an excitation, which is translated into an impression and provokes a muscular reaction. That is the immediate, animal reaction. Thảo, who integrates phenomenology into dialectical materialism—I do not mean mechanistic materialism—soon discovers the complexity of the issue. "While excitation is going on," he writes, "and while muscular reaction is taking place, nervous pulsations accumulate: These are repressed and interiorized in the form of a series of impressions that are maintained with their *still present* meaning of attraction or repulsion. In this retention, the attractive or repulsive *sensation* is constituted as a lived experience that endures, is self-identical, and progressively penetrates into the immanent past."[26]

The *displacement* builds on this retention in order to go beyond it. Allow me to digress for a moment. Experience has taught us—my own experience has taught me—and tests have confirmed it: At this level, the reflexes of the Negro-African are, more than any others, spontaneous, *lived*. Not to say: *retained*. For retention, contrary to what one might think, is not inhibition: The impression is retained "in the living present" in order to be transformed into *sensation*, on which, once again, a *displacement* is based. And so the Negro-African reacts more readily to excitations; he naturally espouses the rhythm of the object. This carnal sense of *rhythm* is one of his specific characteristics. I will get back to this later. In this dialectic of behavior, displacement becomes *locomotion*, then "intentional movement," experienced by consciousness, thanks to the experience of the milieu. "In such a way are defined," Thảo continues, "the behaviors of joy, fear, and anger, where the meaning of sensation is no longer simply lived in the interiority of the internal sense, but appears in the phantom that is presented as an attractive, repulsive, or irritating object. The emotion is not the simple, purely subjective, movement of need; it implies the sense of the object as a *moving object* [*émouvant*]."[27]

But, then again, what is *emotion*? Sartre defines it as "a sudden fall of consciousness into the magical world."[28] But what, in turn, is the magical world? It is the world beyond the rational world, beyond the visible world of appearances, which is rational only because it is visible and measurable. This magical world is more real than the visible world. It is *surreal*. It is animated by the invisible forces that govern the universe and whose specific character is that they are harmoniously linked by sympathy with each other, on the one hand, and with visible things or appearances, on the other. As Eliphas Lévi writes, "There is only one dogma in magic, and it is this: The visible is the manifestation of the invisible, or in other words, in appreciable and visible things, the perfect verb corresponds perfectly to things that are inappreciable to our senses, invisible to our eyes."[29]

Let us take the example from earlier. Let us imagine that we are speaking of a mother who, after many years, welcomes home her son, a student in France. What moves her is that she is suddenly thrown backward, out of the real world before the "French presence." She is no longer the mother of the "civil registry." She is the mother of Negro-African tradition, who, beyond social obligations, is connected to her son by the umbilical cord of feeling, of the clan's *Vital Force*. She touches her son's hands and face as if she were blind, as if she wanted to feed off him. Her body, "the immediate experience of consciousness," reacts.[30] There she is, weeping and dancing, the dance of return, the dance of possession of her son with whom she has been reunited. She is no longer of this world; she is of the magical world of yesteryear, which partakes in the world of the dream. And she believes in this world, which she now lives, and which *possesses* her. As Sartre writes again, "In emotion, consciousness deteriorates and suddenly transforms the determined world in which we live into a world of magic."[31]

If we push the analysis further, we discover that the fabric of society itself, the relationships between men, and even the relationships between men and nature, that is, things, are made of magical bonds. "It is," as Alain put it, "the spirit wandering among things."[32] Beneath the rational, technical, structures of society, what shines through, upon analysis, are human, and therefore psychological, relationships: *relationships of consciousness*, in which imagination, the daughter of Desire, plays an essential role. The most rationalized society, the Soviet one, is no exception to the rule. Remo Cantoni, an Italian Communist, wrote the following regarding Russian Communism in the journal *Esprit* (May–June 1948): "Marxism, by converting itself into a popular, millenarian and apocalyptic faith, reinforces itself politically, since it draws into itself all the immense energies of religious faith."[33] There, then, is "faith," which we know to be linked to magic,[34] underpinning a society founded on reason and technology, imbuing it with a creative dynamism, creating the myths that are the true nourishment of the people.

This is even truer of Negro-African society. As we shall see, there, technical activities are always connected to properly social activities, and first and foremost to art, which is magic. And social activities occupy a primordial place over technical ones, especially over work. It is a society based essentially on human relations, and perhaps even more so on the relations between men and "gods," an *animistic* society, I mean, a society less interested in "earthly nourishment" than in spiritual nourishment. Here, material facts, especially "*Social Facts, are not Things*."[35] Hidden behind them are the forces governing them, animating these appearances, giving them color and rhythm, life and meaning. It is precisely this *meaning* that imposes itself on consciousness and provokes emotion. Even more precisely, emotion is the prehension [*saisie*] of the whole being—consciousness and body—by the irrational world, the irruption of the magical world into the world of determination. What moves the Negro-African is not so much the appearance of the object as its profound reality, its *surreality*, not so much its *sign* as its *meaning*. What, in a dance mask, moves him is, through the "image" and its rhythm, the unusual vision of "god." The sensible aspect of things, perceived in its singular particularities, is, to the very extent that it is so, merely the sign of the object's meaning.

In other words, emotion, in its initial form as a fall of consciousness, is, on the contrary, *the attainment of a higher state of knowledge*. It is "consciousness of the world,"[36] "a certain way of apprehending the world."[37] It is total knowledge, for "the moved subject and the moved object are united in an inseparable synthesis,"[38] I repeat: in a dance of love. A superior form of knowledge, then, as evidenced by the famous words of one of the twentieth century's greatest scientific minds, Albert Einstein, for whom "mystical emotion" is the source of knowledge and art.[39] It is exactly the source of negro knowledge and negro art, in which *e-motion* is *com-motion*.

III. Ontology and Religion

In my report at the first Congress, I attempted to outline, in broad terms, Negro-African metaphysics. I specified that it was an *ontology*, a science of *being*. "The Negro identifies *being* with life: more precisely with the *Vital Force*."[40] In other words, life is the expression of Vital Force. What is important, in this chapter, is that this ontology is still valid in the twentieth century, as is the Negro-African way of *knowing*.

Thus, for the Negro-African, "a vital force similar to his own animates each object endowed with *sensible* characteristics, all the way from God down to the grain of sand."[41] In other words, is this not what Father Pierre Teilhard de Chardin confirms when he writes: "This is to say that life can be legitimately considered as being pressurized, forever and everywhere in the universe,—erupting as soon as it can, wherever it can—and, where it emerges, intensifying as much as it can in the immensities of time and space?"[42] But what is *Life*? For Negro-Africans, it is a force, a living matter, that is, capable of increasing or losing its energy, of *re-enforcing* or *de-forcing* itself. The *Vital-Force-Being* is, thus, in vital connection with other forces, if it wishes to grow and not *perish* at least. This is what the physicist Erwin Schrödinger expresses, in scientific terms, in his book *What Is Life?* "What is the characteristic feature of life? When is a piece of matter said to be alive? When it goes on 'doing something,' moving, *exchanging material with its environment*, and so forth, and that for a much longer period than we would expect for an inanimate piece of matter to 'keep going' under similar circumstances."[43]

But we will be reminded that, in the current state of scientific knowledge, it is impossible to give life a definition that is satisfactory to everyone, even by having recourse to a *quantum* explanation; this is also the conclusion that the *Nouvelles littéraires* survey reaches.[44] I acknowledge this, and that is precisely why the concept of Vital-Force-Being, which pertains more to spirit than to matter, is a metaphysical concept. I merely wanted to show that it does not contradict the current data of science, that it is an extension of Physics, a *Metaphysics* in the etymological sense of the word, insofar as it relies on Physics in order to go beyond it. Is it not significant that this Negro-African concept reminds us of Father Teilhard de Chardin's thesis on the subject? For Teilhard de Chardin argues: "In virtue of the 'law of complexity/consciousness,' which has guided us so far, one may say that there exists in every corpuscle *two levels of operation*: one (let us call it tangential) binding physico-chemically, that is by way of complexity, the corpuscle in question to all the other corpuscles in the universe: the other (let us call it radial or axial) leading directly from consciousness to consciousness, and manifesting itself, on the level of humanity, in the different psychological phenomena, already mentioned, of unanimity and co-reflexion.

"Granted this, we have adopted the habit of reserving for 'tangential' effects (the proper domain of statics and entropy) *both* the name of energy and the privilege of constituting the primal matter of things; the 'radial' being then regarded as only a subsidiary effect or a fragile super-structure of the determinism of matter. But, turning the perspective upside down, why not decide on the contrary that, of the couple under examination, it is the radial that is primitive and consistent, the tangential being only a minor product statistically engendered by the interactions of the elementary 'centres' of consciousness, imperceptible in the 'pre-living,' but clearly discernible to our experience once matter has reached a sufficiently advanced degree of arrangement? From this point of view, if one accepts it, the edifice of physical laws would remain absolutely intact and valid in the domain of pre-life, where the radial does not yet exist for our eyes. But on the other hand, it would be possible for us to conceive that, where the interiorisation of corpuscles is sufficiently developed, the axial consciousness, at last capable of directly coiling on itself, *centre to centre*, escapes the peripheral servitudes of physico-chemical complexity. In this case, very far back (that is to say in the inanimate) all would continue to happen as if entropy were in command. But in front (that is at the critical point of super-reflexion), it would be entropy's turn to disappear, thus revealing and releasing the ultrareflected and irreversible portion."[45] Forgive me for the lengthy citation; these lines are crucial.

What is striking is the *human* value of Negro-African ontology, its cultural value. For what is *Culture* if not Man's effort to adapt to his milieu through social mediations, and to adapt this milieu to his generic activities? This is the moment to note the two fundamental features of Negro-African ontology. The first is that the *hierarchy of vital forces* expresses only the integration of the universe into the family or, perhaps more accurately, the expansion of the family to the size of the universe. God, who presides over the unity of the universe—the Negro-African is a monotheist—, is the Ancestor of clanic ancestors, and the clanic ancestors partake *in* and *of* his vital force. Just like cosmic forces such as the stars and lower forces embodied by animals, plants, and minerals. The second feature of this ontology is the prominent place that the living man, the Existent [*l'Existant*], occupies in the hierarchy of forces.[46] Man is the center of the universe. He has no other purpose than to reinforce his force, to make it more alive and more existent, to *realize* it into a person. When I say *person*, I mean a free being, the freest being there is. That is to say, *freedom*, which transcends contingent determinations, is at the heart of the problem; it is the umbilical cord of the world. Here we are, once again, brought back to the heart of the questions that the contemporary world explores.

And brought back to *Religion*—for what is religion? This is the question Man asks himself amid the anxiety of uncertainties and fears. The uncertainties of experience, then those of science, the determinations of which do not explain everything, especially not the essential. "Fear of no longer being able to move. Fear of not being able to get out. . . ."[47] Religion is an attempt to provide answers and solutions; the metaphysical leap to fill the gap: the link that unites Man to God, that is to the invisible, the indeterminate.

Here, as well as previously, the Negro-Africans' response emanates from their deeper selves, from their psychophysiology, from their relentless need for *communion*. And their solution is *humanist*.

First of all, Negro-African religion is an *agrarian religion*.[48] The Negro-African pantheon is one of the richest to exist. It is likely that, beginning with Pharaonic Egypt, the pantheons of Mediterranean religions, and particularly that of Greece, are of Negroid origin. But I want to focus on the agrarian character of the Negro-African pantheon. We will note that the gods, more precisely the *jinns*, are merely the manifestation of the stars, of natural phenomena—lightning, rain, wind, epidemics, rivers, mountains, seas—, of animals and plants: manifestations of the peasant environment. At the top of the hierarchy, one finds, everywhere and always, as the elders of God, the Sun or the Sky and the Earth. It is from this primordial couple that the jinn are born. The rain from the Sky fecundates Mother-Earth, from whom life emerges. It is the deep meaning of all agrarian rites that gives rhythm to the seasons and the days, the Black peasants' labor, from sowing to harvesting. From there, proceeds *totemism* and the cult of the Tree.

Negro-African religion is also a *family religion*. Of course, one finds, especially among the peoples of the Gulf of Benin, numerous communities of priests, each of which is in the service of a "god." But the priesthood is most often hereditary, and it is one's Ancestor whom one honors.[49] If this ontology is the *dogma* of Negro-African religion, *worship* is essentially expressed by way of sacrifice, in which appears the familial character of this religion. As I said in my report at the first Congress, "It is the head of the clan family who makes the sacrifices, for he is a priest by virtue of his character as the oldest descendant of the common Ancestor. He is the natural mediator between the living and the dead."[50] I would add that he cannot *intercede* for himself alone, but must do so for the entire community that he represents.

This leads me to compare and differentiate, simultaneously, religion and magic. Understood in its narrowest sense, *magic* can be defined, with Claude

Lévi-Strauss as an example, as "a system of operations and beliefs which attribute to certain human acts the same value as to natural causes."[51] In its broadest sense, magic is a dogma according to which "the visible is the manifestation of the invisible."[52] One can identify the definition of mysticism here. This is the meaning that I will retain. Thus, it appears that magic and religion delve into the same sources of *mysticism*. In traditional civilizations—as is the case in Black Africa—, religion is only an elaborate magic; it remains magic. Sacrifice is its most typical illustration. In sacrifice, as in magic, and according to *the law of the interaction of forces*, a superior vital force acts, in its *being*, upon an inferior force. But we shall see that magic does not subtend only religious activities; taking its roots from *animism*, it animates all Negro-African social activities.

IV. Society

More than anyone else, the ethnologists Leo Frobenius and Marcel Griaule have often emphasized the *unity* of the Negro-African universe. From God to the grain of sand, by way of Man, this unity is seamless. Man, as I said, in his quality as a *person*, is the center of this universe. More precisely, the center of the *family*. Family is the microcosm, the primary cell that, through expansion, is reproduced by all the concentric circles forming the various levels of society: village, tribe, kingdom, empire. We shall see shortly that these are not the only organs of society. The Negro-African is contained within a tightly knit network of vertical and horizontal solidarities, which are simultaneously linked to him and which sustain him. This is the most complete illustration of this truth touted today by socialism, according to which *Man lives and realizes himself only through and within society*.

In Black Africa, the *Family* is the *clan*, and not just, as in Europe, "father, mother, and child." It is not the household, but "all the people, living or dead, who identify with one another through a common ancestor." And we know that the lineage of Ancestors extends all the way to God. It is worth noting that an animal, or even a tree, is often integrated into the clan from the "indigenous" flora or fauna. This is the famous *totemism*, which is monstrous only in appearance. What is inhuman is to isolate man from his environment, to *domesticate* the Animal and the Tree. In Europe, this domestication goes so far as destruction, which breaks the equilibrium of nature and results in catastrophes denounced by scientists. To return to the family, its head, the firstborn among the living, is the link between the living and the dead, truly the umbilical cord that gives life to the world.

Here, then, is the family, as center and source—I say hearth [*foyer*]—where the flame of life, the Vital Force, is nurtured, growing and intensifying insofar as it manifests itself in living bodies, in more and more numerous and prosperous existents. We come to the major roles of the Child and the Woman in the family.

And first of all, the *Child*. The child is not that shapeless, bawling little larva who disturbs the nights of his parents. Negro-African parents raise him in an atmosphere of tenderness and freedom. It is a *self-education* that is not an abandonment of duties, but rather vigilant love. This is until the age of reason, when the boy and girl must bend to the harsh disciplines of *initiation* whence an accomplished young man—or a young girl—will emerge, ready to face life. The Negro-African family is not only looking toward the past, from where it draws fecundating traditions; it also looks toward the future: more precisely, the past prepares the future.

In Black Africa, *Woman* holds pride of place; or used to hold pride of place, for Arabo-Berber influence, followed by European influence, as well as the influence of nomadic civilizations have continued to diminish her role. This role is understandable given the agrarian nature of the Black world. Such an explanation is accurate, but there is more to it. As always, here, consciousness has translated the economico-social fact into *myth*. The woman, because she is the "permanent" member of the family and a giver of life, has been raised to the level of a source of vital force and guardian of the home, that is, custodian of the past and protector of the clan's future. In a relatively recent past, which has not entirely vanished everywhere, one belonged to the family of one's mother; the familial regime was that of *matriarchy*. Still today, among the Sereer of the Sine (Senegal), a child's first name is followed by that of his mother. For the people of my native village, I am still Sédar Nyilane: "Sédar (son of) Nyilane." In the past, this appellation must have been generalized: The patronym would be of a posterior usage. Regardless, among most Negro-African peoples, one belongs to one's mother's clan; and nobility is passed on through the mother, as is inheritance. If the maternal uncle passes on the inheritance, if the eldest male acts as head of the family, it is merely by delegation. Thus, we can understand the position occupied by the woman, the mother, in the family, the eminent role she plays in it, the respect with which she is surrounded, the freedom she enjoys. Contrary to popular opinion, the Negro-African woman is not in need of being liberated: She has been *free* for thousands of years.

Marriage is not the establishment of a new family, nor is it the integration of the wife into her husband's family; it is the alliance of two clans for the purpose of procreation, an alliance in which each clan, beginning with the two spouses, retains their personality and their freedom in cooperation. The wife, who continues to belong to her clan, brings her Ancestors into the common home; there, she sometimes sets up an altar. She has her own possessions as well as her own activity. It is she who takes care of the household and manages the domestic workers. An exemplary proof of her freedom is that, if she becomes widowed or merely offended by her husband, she returns to her clan, with her children and her belongings.

Another essential characteristic of the family is that it is a *democratic community*. Certainly, the *Head of the family* is, as his name indicates, the one who exercises authority. He administers the family's possessions by distributing tasks and harvests among the households. He is a priest—as we have seen—and a judge. But he acts only by delegation of the Family Council which, made up of the heads of households, gives its opinion on all important matters and supervises the actions of the Head of the family. Naturally, the deceased Ancestors are members of the Family Council by right. We do not forget to call on them with sacrifices and consultations, in which the magician and the "teller of hidden things" intervene. But the women intervene as well, either with their husbands in the privacy of the hut or, grouped together, directly with the Family Council when the issue is of interest to them. In a word, what characterizes the family on a social level is that it is a democratic community, in every sense, that it is at once a church, an administrative community, and a production and consumer cooperative, in which the head of the family combines, in his own person, the functions of priest, judge, and director of the cooperative.

If I may use another image, Negro-African society is a pyramid; better: a multistory tower, a ziggurat, but one that is inverted, its head at the base. As I have said, there is, above the family, constituting each of the levels, the village, the tribe, the kingdom, the empire. I will not go through them all: I will simply touch on the *village*.

Like the family, the Village has its singular character. This is already apparent in the name of the village. It is usually a descriptive word, borrowed from flora or fauna, from legend or myth, from the place or the character of the inhabitants. It is a "community of inhabitants";[53] primitively, it was a *community of kinship*. Most often, it is made up of one or several clans, each living in its own enclosure—the "compound"—or neighborhood.

As a community of kinship, the village, like the family, has its holdings, its land with fields and pastures, its logging and hunting grounds, its fishing waters, and sometimes its mines. It has its administration, its ancestral "gods," and its cooperatives, grouped into associations.

It is more than a community: It is a *commune*, but a commune-parish, the foundations of which plunge into the tombs of the Ancestor-Jinn. It is, first of all, a commune with its Municipal Council, made up of the heads of the compounds, presided over by the Head of the village. In ancient times, the Head of the village, appointed by the heads of the compounds, was "the eldest." Today, he is the wisest; for, today, under the White regime, the oldest is not necessarily the wisest. The "Council of Elders" administers the village, and the associations as well. In the old days, still following the example of the family, the Head of the village combined his administrative functions with those of the president of the Customary Court and of the parish "priest." As time went by, he abandoned these latter functions. This is consistent with a general phenomenon of *desacralization* under the influence of Arabo-Berber and European civilizations, which are Muslim and Christian. However, the ancient flame is not yet extinguished; the ashes of the hearth still burn, and the authority of the Head of the village retains something of the fervor of yesteryear.

I will speak of the structures of the tribe, the kingdom, and the empire, for the record. If I had the time, I would not overlook the organization of the model cities that flourished on the coast of Benin within the area that Élie Faure called "Black Greece."[54] Everywhere, we find the same structures, above all the same spirit of religious fervor and social communion. Sometimes, it is a constitutional monarch, who can take no major decision without the approval of a Senate. At other times, in the final analysis, we are dealing with a *democratic theocracy* in monarchical guise.

However, these organs—we will call them *vertical*—are not the only ones that simultaneously connect and sustain persons, existents. *Horizontally* organized, there are age fraternities, brotherhoods with secret rites, castes, and trade guilds. I will not insist on castes. They are in the process of extinction.

Age fraternities are public associations. Their originality lies not only in the fact that they are open to all but also in the fact that they necessarily include all individuals between two ages. For despite the name, they do not recruit annually. An age group comprises all individuals born within a given time frame, which extends over several years—five in general. In reality, it is not so much the ages as the *initiation* ceremonies that determine a group. We are therefore dealing with closed associations, which are based on initiation, hierarchy, and a strictly regulated discipline.

The age fraternity is essentially a *school*. But it is first and foremost a *religious order*, like all social groups in Black Africa. One enters as a novice, first undergoing initiation ceremonies. The purpose of these ceremonies, with their suggestive symbolism, is to make a knowing man out of an ignorant one; organized freedom out of childish anarchy; the birth to life out of the death of childhood. The age fraternity, I have said, is a school: the citizen's school.

Under the guidance of experienced masters, it teaches, in some cases for years, all that an honest man must know: mythology and magic, legends and customs, politeness and art—storytelling, poetry, song and dance. Ethics—we will see later what this consists of—is not neglected, however, and the body and will are subjected to the harshest of tests. It is this education, this discipline that constitutes the cohesion of Negro-African society. All the more so given that the age fraternity organizes, at regular intervals, advanced training courses [*stages de perfectionnement*]—right up to old age.

This is for boys, as girls have their own separate associations, which are less robust; maternity and housework will soon preoccupy them.

The age fraternity is also more than a cooperative; it is a mutual aid *society*. It assists in, or rather contributes to, the domestic celebrations of its members: births, weddings, funerals, and, above all, work in the fields. Finally, in the vein of other fraternities, it is an instrument of village administration. It has its own role in the community and its own place in the village Square, where village representatives deliberate.

Brotherhoods with secret rites could be compared to the religious, political, and cultural associations of Western civilization. The difference is that their organization, doctrine, and aims are secret. Each is a kind of *Free-Masonry*. They were numerous before European conquest; they have not yet disappeared. I will mention the Goli society of the Baoulé, the Goré of the Gouro, the Simo of the Baga, the Dou of the Bobo, the Do and Flankrou of the Sénoufo, and the Komo, Koné, Koré and Nama societies of the Malinké. Each society has its own ritual and one or more types of mask. Initiates wear them to the society's festivals, to its mysteries.

Unlike age fraternities, brotherhoods with secret rites are not open to all. Entry is by way of selection. Like the age-old fraternity, it [the brotherhood] has its own initiation, hierarchy, and discipline. In truth, the brotherhood with secret rites is a far more complex association than the age fraternity, both in terms of its organization—which still partially eludes us—and in terms of its aims. Although it is almost always a religious, and at the same time political and cultural, association, it most often focuses on one of these aspects or another. One brotherhood is concerned with the material prosperity of the group; another, with the health of its members; a third, with the observance of certain customs; a fourth, with the development of an art. Sometimes, the brotherhood has a clearly political aim. In a word, the essential role of brotherhoods with secret rites, which, depending on the case, serve as brakes, counterweights, or motors of official institutions, is that of animation and equilibrium. It is a matter of keeping society in line and unified, of avoiding setbacks, stagnation, and, above all, deviations.

Such associations, moreover, are to be found in any civilized society. They are one of the ways in which Negro-African society protects the *person* against the abstract tyranny of the official powers and the State. Nowhere else in the world is the State so reduced to its role of administration and arbitration. Monarchy, and chieftaincy in general, is strictly "constitutional." The problem of the "deterioration of the State" does not, did not arise in Black Africa: the deconcentration and decentralization of institutions—on both vertical and horizontal levels—had resolved it, to the great benefit of the people.

As for craft guilds, I will speak of these in the following chapter.

V. Property and Labor

It is due to the importance of the related problems of *property* and *labor* in contemporary society that we have deemed it appropriate to devote a distinct chapter to them. As we know, before being *Homo sapiens*, thinker and artist, Man was first *Homo faber*, that is, a producer, a laborer. If labor constitutes one of the major issues of contemporary society, it is due to the *desacralization* of ancient society. This desacralization broke the *unity* of civilization by dissociating thought and art from manual labor, of which they were the extension and fulfillment. It emphasized material values to the detriment of spiritual ones. This *desacralization* took concrete form in the creation of *private property*. This has, in effect, doubly alienated Man. On the one hand, by depriving him of the products of his labor, forcing him to ascribe to manual labor a disproportionate role. On the other hand, by denaturing labor itself, which has become a waste of life.

In Black Africa—and I am referring to traditional Africa—there is almost never any *property* in the European sense of the word, that is, an object that can be "used and abused," destroyed or sold. More precisely, the general means of production, in other words, the land and its resources—the resources of the soil and subsoil—cannot be owned. First of all, Negro-African animism considers the *Earth*, the main means of production for peasant peoples, to be a person, a jinn. The Ancestor of the clan, the first to clear the land and occupy it, made a pact with this jinn, sanctioned by a ritual sacrifice. The Ancestor made this pact not in his own name and for himself, but in the name of the collectivity and for the collectivity he embodied. Not only is the Earth a person, but so are the resources it contains: mines, waters, animals, trees.

Thus, in Black Africa, there is no "right of property" over the soil and its resources, not even a "right of possession," to use the expression of certain ethnologists. It is a matter of "right of use," of "usufructuary property," if we really want to use the word. Expressions such as "Master of the Land"—*lamane*[55] among the Sereer—or "the Leopard"—totem of the prince—"who owns the country" should not mislead us. The maxim of the King of Ashanti is significant in this respect: "I am the grandson of the Earth, who owns the world." The "eminent domain" of the soil belongs to the Earth-Jinn; the King or "Master of the Land," the most ancient descendant of the Ancestor, has only "useful domain"—and on behalf of the collective. As "master of the land," the clan chief's role is to ensure the integrity and proper use of collective lands. It is he who reserves certain parts for collective use: mines, water, pastures, forests. It is he who distributes fields between households, instituting a rotational system so that the same households do not always have the good or bad land. It is he who ensures that the rotation of crops and the fallowing of land are carried out correctly.

As "usufructuary property," collective lands are *inalienable*, for the reason that one can only alienate what belongs to oneself. Even the conquest of a country cannot lead to land ownership: "Labor [*le travail*]," writes Maurice Delafosse, "or more precisely, perhaps, the productive action of man, is considered the only source of property, but it can confer the right of property only on the object it has produced."[56] One is therefore the owner not of the soil but of the harvest, not of the river but of the fish caught, not of the trees grown in one's field but of the fruit picked, not of the animals of the forest but, under certain conditions, of the game killed. The nature of the labor determines the nature of the property. Depending on whether the labor is collective or individual, the property is collective or individual. Thus, the products of the family fields and herds are collective, family property, while the products of individual fields are individual property. Depending on whether clothing or work tools come from the family or private budget, they are collective or individual property, even if they are to be divided among individuals.

The advantages of this regime are easy to recognize. Since labor, like the general means of production, is usually collective, the products of labor are collective property. Hence the first major advantage: Every human being is assured of the "vital minimum" and can thus satisfy the basic needs of food, clothing, and shelter, the sine qua non of spiritual fulfillment. And there is another benefit, scarcely less important: the acquisition of the superfluous, a luxury necessary for the realization of the person, is made possible by individual labor.

Although they never placed emphasis on the *individual*, Negro-Africans did not neglect the *person*, as is too often said. The realization of the person lies less in the quest for singularity than in the deepening and intensification of spiritual life. "For a collective form of property to be an effective aid to the individual," writes Jacques Maritain, "it must not have as its endpoint a depersonalized possession."[57] In Black Africa, Man is connected to the object of property, as we have seen, by the legal bond of custom, but also and above all, by a mystical bond. Man feels himself to be a person—granted, a clan person—before the object of property, which is, in turn, felt to be a person. Thus, ownership of the means of production is no longer something abstract and illusory. The laborer feels that he is not a mere component of his land or his tool. He feels, he knows, that his intelligence and his arms are laboring freely on something living and very much his own.

And labor itself is not alienated. It is not a burden, but a source of joy. Because it is *free*, it allows for the intensification, the realization of *being*. In Negro-African society, we will point out here, working the land is the noblest form of labor. This kind of labor enables the accord of Man and the universe: it is carried out to the rhythm of the cosmic forces. And the Negro-African, feeling in unison with the universe, lends rhythm to his labor, accompanied by musical instruments. Work songs by the thousands—songs of the peasant, the shepherd, the fisherman, the craftsman—songs that *accomplish* the work. negro work, negro rhythm, negro joy, which is liberated by labor and thus liberated from labor.

However, there are not only peasants in Black Africa. There are also shepherds in the savannah, fishermen, craftsmen, and traders everywhere. Although simpler in structure than European society, Negro-African society is, and was, no less structured and balanced.

We will touch here on those who specialize in certain technologies and are grouped into *trade guilds* [*corporations de métiers*]. While agriculture, livestock breeding, house building, hunting, and fishing are practiced by everyone, subject to the division of labor according to age and gender, craft work is carried out by the trade guilds.

The *Trade Guild* is both a class and a caste. In both respects, it is characterized by religious and technical initiation, specialization and hierarchy, and finally, endogamy. Entry into the guild is hereditary or by apprenticeship.

Trade guilds are generally divided into several categories, each of which in turn has its own subdivisions. For example, among the Haalpulaaren of Senegal: (1) musicians, weavers, shoemakers, blacksmiths, and precious metalworkers; (2) manufacturers of wooden utensils and pirogues; (3) griots and singers.[58]

Members of trade guilds are the lowest castes in Negro-African society, at least in societies that have been subjected to Arabo-Berber influence. Admittedly, the contempt in which they are held is *one of the defects of Negro-African society*. However, we would be wrong to exaggerate this. This contempt stems from the dependence that craftsmen once enjoyed in the shadow of princely courts. But, even then, many of them were esteemed and even honored by the Prince. Above all, they were feared for the magical power they wielded. The fact remains that the trade guilds were among the essential workings of Negro-African society, which could not do without their services in the area of both the arts and the crafts, properly speaking.

The works of craftsmen present the same general characteristics as those of farmers and shepherds. They are steeped in religion and magic; they are rhythmic, accomplished in and through song; and they are divided into collective and individual labor. Even *industry and commerce* are not always immune to the demands of the Negro-African soul. As Maurice Delafosse writes, "Industry and large-scale trade are, most often, also carried out by collectivities that are no longer family-based, but corporative, or by associations."[59]

VI. Negro-African Ethics

We can now make out what constitutes Negro-African *Ethics*. It is founded on its ontology and realizes itself in its social activities.

As we have seen, living man, the Existent, is at the center of the universe. The activity of all creation, of all other vital forces, has no other purpose than the *personal realization* of the Existent and the reinforcement of his vital force. However, as this is merely the immediate and contingent expression of the clan reality, itself an emanation of God, it cannot be considered to be an end in itself. The *being* [*être*] of the Existent is only one integral part of the clan force, which, in turn, must be in accord with all the vital forces of the universe.

Ethics, in Black Africa, is *active wisdom*. For the living man, it consists of recognizing the unity of the world and of working in service of its ordination. His duty is therefore to reinforce his personal life, of course, but also to realize *being* in other men. This explains the place in society occupied by religion, which is, truly, the link between the living and the dead, and which, through them, unites God to the grain of sand; which explains the organization of this same society within a network of vertical and horizontal communities; which explains the cultivation of certain virtues, such as work, honor, filial piety, charity, hospitality. Hence the astonishment of the first European explorers when, disembarking, armed, along the "inhospitable" coasts of Black Africa, they were welcomed as messengers of the gods. All the authors of antiquity have praised, along with their warrior virtues, the peace-loving character of Black peoples. It is Queen Candace who proclaims her will to wage war only to defend the borders of her kingdom; these are "the Ethiopians whose sacrifices," according to Homer, "are pleasing to God"—because of their great gentleness.[60]

Some authors have denied the existence of a Negro-African ethics. Their error stems from the fact that they have poorly analyzed the "primacy of sensitivity and honor" which reigns in Negro-African society. *Honor* is, precisely, among the peoples of the savanna, the most meaningful expression of our ethics.

What, then, is *Honor*? It is the intellectualization of the feeling of the divine. As he emerged from the magico-religious world, and the ashes of the divine cooled in him, the Negro-African became aware of his *person* as an autonomous reality, and he reacted to preserve the integrity of this person. It is in this reaction that honor resides, which is, at the same time, feeling, consciousness, and vital deed. Honor is, in this way, an ideal of humanity and an act of life.

First, it is an ideal, which postulates excellence, if not perfection in all areas. Among the Wolof of Senegal, "the honest man," the *dyambour*[61] must possess the most varied qualities: physical beauty and strength, refinement and urbanity, material and moral wealth. Above all, the *dyambour* must "honor" other men by treating them as he would like to be treated: as a man.

To honor someone is, of course, to express outward signs of respect to him. Above all, it is to do him justice by granting him what is rightfully his by his sole quality as a *man*—materially and morally. *Justice* is, thus, placed at the very center of Negro-African ethics. It is what establishes—or reestablishes—*Peace*, this balanced ordination which constitutes the unity of the person, the community, and society, and is so dear to the heart of the Negro-African. To aid one's neighbor, to provide him with food and shelter as well as moral assistance, is to perform a work of justice. Although there were unemployed people in Black Africa, mentally or physically ill people, there were no beggars, much less hungry people during times of abundance.

As important as the duties toward one's neighbor and society are the duties toward oneself. In this case, it is a matter not only of requiring and receiving signs of respect but of protecting and affirming one's personality, one's *being*. Being is affirmed, essentially, by the cultivation of virtues, and, first of all, by loyalty, courage, and *generosity*, this final quality being the negro expression of justice. However, the person may be *o-ffended* [*of-fensé*], and, sometimes, circumstances deprive us of any effective response. We then have only one solution: to abandon our vital breath in order to save our personal life, our soul. *Suicide is the ultimate demand of honor.*

As we can see, Negro-African ethics is not European morality. It is not a catechism one recites; it is an ontology one *realizes* in and through society, and first of all within oneself and by oneself. Once again, unlike the European world, the Negro-African world is that of *unity*.

VII. Art

The study of Negro-African art provides us with a further illustration of this truth. I insisted on this in my report at the Paris Congress.[62] Art, in Black Africa, is linked to the deep life of agrarian and pastoral communities, to religion and to technologies. Art is a technology of approach or, better, of identification. It is a matter of acting upon the higher forces, of appropriating them by identifying with them—through gesture and speech, poem and music, dance and song, sculpture and painting.

I will recall the general characteristics of art, of Negro-African arts. First of all—one follows from the other—:

1 Art is, along with *production*, that is to say *work*, the generic activity of Man. The artist is the *Homo faber* who realizes himself as *Homo sapiens*. More precisely, perhaps, art is an aspect of production. It is art that gives its form, its style, its seal of humanity to production.
2 Art is *functional*. It is not entertainment, nor an ornament that is added to the object. It gives the object its *efficacy*, it *fulfills* it: it is art that gives the object its character as an object.
3 The arts are linked to each other because we are dealing with a civilization that is not divided against itself, a society where *unity* is the principal characteristic.
4 For the same reason, the work of art is made *by all and for all*, even though there are professionals in art and literature, literature being only one domain, among others, of art.
5 Because it is functional and collective, as well as *social*, art is *engaged*. I developed all these characteristics in my report at the first Congress. I need only recall them here.

Beyond these general characteristics, Negro-African art is expressed essentially by *image* and *rhythm*: by the *rhythmic image*. I gave many examples of this in my first report, drawing them, in turn, from the various arts: poetry, narrative, sculpture, painting, music, dance. My intention today is to attempt to analyze in depth the two features of the Negro-African *style*.

The Negro-African image is the *surrealist* image or, perhaps better, the *subrealist* image, in the sense that it expresses the reality that *sub-tends* appearances. It is not a rational equation but an *analogical* link, the participation of "two objects of thought," of the signifier and the signified, in the same subreality. As such, it is an expression of the mystico-magical world. Paraphrasing André Breton—in "Signe ascendant" [Rising sign]—I would say that it presupposes, "through the weave of the visible world, an invisible universe that tends to manifest itself."[63] If I were to stop there, I would seem to adopt the classic, Cartesian conception of imagination, a conception taken up by [Hippolyte] Taine and [Henri] Bergson, for whom there was an "an identity of nature between the sensation and the image, a power of actualization inherent to the image."[64] I would merely have colored it with a romantic interpretation, stemming from a cosmological naturalism.

The Negro-African image is richer, more complex. We explained, above, the negro emotion by the action of going beyond neurosensory impressions. In such a way that emotion is not a simple translation of these impressions but a *reaction of the subject* to them. There is indeed a fall from the world of determination into that of indeterminacy. But it is indeed emotion, I mean the *imaging consciousness*, which creates this magical world. It is imagination, daughter of Desire, that creates this *imagined nature* which bursts into our consciousness. In other words, the Negro-African image is born from the symbiosis of reality and Desire. More precisely still, *Desire* plunges, beyond appearances, into this deeper reality underlying appearances, whence it raises the images of the dream. Thus, the Negro-African imagination restores to *Man* his generic activity, "the freedom and meaningful activity of an imaging consciousness."[65] It is not the bull that the Baoulé sculptor brings forth, before us, but the vital force, the Spirit of the bull: the jinn of the brotherhood with secret rites. The image is not only a *symbol*—like any object, any form, any color—but an expression of Desire at the conjunction of reality: truly, a *creation*. Of the Negro-African's gift of *fabulation*, which is a gift of imagination, of this imagination that creates the *myth*. Myth, as you know, is a fabric of images, organized into a narrative, of the mystico-magical world. It is the natural expression of Negro-African thought. As Marcel Griaule writes, it is "a living thing, integrated into the social rhythm, felt and moved differently according to the seasons, circumstances, places, people," and which "does not allow itself to be apprehended like an object that one could hold in one."[66]

But the image does not express the *essential* reality, the subreality; it does not speak to our imagination and to our heart, it does not inspire emotion, the *shock* [*ébranlement*] of our being if it is not *rhythmed*. Rhythm is consubstantial with the image. It is, at bottom, the substance, the subreality of the image. Poetic truth identifies, here, with scientific truth, for which the *being* of being is *energy*, that is to say, rhythm. As I have said, *rhythm* "is the architecture of being, the internal dynamism that gives it form, the system of waves that it emits to others, the pure expression of the force which, by way of the senses, seizes you at the root of *being*."[67]

Two years ago, we saw that, in Black Africa, rhythm not only animated the image by giving it its form but also marked all Negro-African arts, up to the fables and proverbs, with its seal. This rhythm is complex. In dance, for example, it animates the mask and costume of the dancer as well as his movements, the shapes of the mask and of the costume as well as their colors: It subjects time and space to its influence. In poetry, rhythm is based on the accents—of pitch and intensity—of the syllables, but also on the words, even on the *phonemes* or sounds, whose recurrence, at more or less regular intervals, accomplishes the rhythm.

What characterizes Negro-African rhythm is precisely its *vital* character: regularity in irregularity, unity in diversity, in short, its variety beneath its appearance of monotony. Thanks to *syncopations* and *offbeats*, the equivalents of which are found in the plastic arts, this rhythm expresses, more than any other, life. It is the famous Negro-American *swing*, which comes straight from Africa and which is emphasized, here, by the *polyrhythm* of Negro-African works.

This shows that in Black Africa, art is not only *social* but *vital*. It accompanies and accomplishes activities of *production*. By this word, we must understand not only material production but also spiritual production; not only labor in the European sense but also the social activities of different groups, including activities of leisure. Art is vital since *production*, in the material sense, is the first expression—in time—of Man: his *generic* activity. But, beyond this material production, art expresses *Homo sapiens*, the inner life, by which he is essentially distinguished from the animal. The materialist Karl Marx asserted this truth forcefully in a posthumous work, which is, surprisingly, so poorly known.[68] Only Man can dream and express his dream in works that go beyond it. And, in this domain, the Negro is king. Hence the exemplary value of Negro-African civilization and the need to decrypt it so as to establish a new humanism on its basis.

Conclusion: For a New Humanism of Negro-African Expression

New autonomous or independent States are being born in Black Africa. For the past ten years, each year has seen new stars rise in the sky. In America, the reveille was sounded more than a quarter century ago, by artists and writers who had made the *pilgrimage to the sources*. But what are Black peoples doing, what will they do with their newfound freedom? It is obvious that freedom without consciousness is worse than slavery. The slave, at least, is aware of his slavery. *Cultural imperialism*, we too often forget, *is the most dangerous form of Colonialism: It obscures consciousness.*

What is striking about the Black peoples who have recently gained autonomy or independence is the *un-consciousness* of the majority of their leaders: their contempt for Negro-African cultural values. They are proud of the political freedom of their people; they do not realize that true freedom is that not of bodies but of minds. And here they are, importing Europe's political, social, and even cultural institutions as is.

Of course, parliamentary democracy and socialism have their virtues, as do unions, cooperatives, the police, and compulsory secular education. The issue is not blocking them as they pass through customs. It is, rather, above all, a matter of seeing what can be retained from them, and how we can root what is retained in Negro-African realities. As R. P. Lebret, the eminent founder of *Économie et Humanisme* [Economy and humanism], said to me, "Of course, cooperatives are excellent institutions. But before sticking them in the African bush, we should begin by studying whether or not they existed in Black Africa and, if they did, how to revive them in this light."[69] It is a fact that parliamentary democracy has existed and functioned, in Black Africa, in an original form, for millennia; it is a fact that a form of communitarian collectivism—which is the true form of socialism—has animated society and its groups. It is therefore surprising, and rightly so, that the young African States have made the police and the single-party system the main instruments of their action. Where, then, is the famous "socialist" thesis of the "deterioration of the State" in all this? I am well aware that an underdeveloped people gaining autonomy or independence requires a party with a large majority and the establishment of a rigorous disciplinary system, but all this must be done in the spirit of the Negro-African genius. It is not by importing European institutions, whether from the East or the West, simply as they are, that we will reach the desired goal: namely, real independence—not only for peoples but also for individuals.

Let us summarize the "themes" and "totems" of Negro-African civilization. First, there is the environment, the agricultural and pastoral milieu, which has shaped the body and, above all, the temperament and spirit of the Negro-African. The Negro-African is essentially characterized by his capacity to be moved, emotion being defined as projection into the mystico-magical world. In this world of *participation*, the main elements of the environment—the tree, the animal, the natural phenomenon, and the material fact—are experienced as analogical images [*images-analogies*], as *symbols*. This explains the original characteristics of Negro-African religion, society, and art. Here, religion is the doctrine and technique—dogma and rites—that connect living man to God through the Ancestors; society is the fabric of institutions that binds groups and individuals together. As for art, it is the most effective instrument of *communion*, the thread that conducts the vital impulse from one to the other. It is, on another level, the imagination that, at the confluence of desire and reality, creates *myths*, that is to say the living forms of the mystico-magical world.

The problem now facing us, the Negroes of 1959, is how to integrate Negro-African values—themes and totems—into the world of 1959. It is not a question of resurrecting the past, of living in the Negro-African Museum; it is a question of animating this world, *hic et nunc*, with the values of our past. This is, in fact, what Negro-Americans have begun to do.

First of all, there is no denying the industrial world. It is evident that, in order to raise (or simply maintain) the standard of living of their populations—which is the sine qua non of all human progress—underdeveloped countries must create an economic infrastructure and industries, even if these are only for the processing of raw materials. But, in this transformation of the milieu, they will be mindful of adapting their methods to the realities of the soil, climate, and race. The other year, an industrialist in Dakar complained to me that he was not obtaining the same yield from his workers as in France. I advised him to feed them well, provide them with good technical training, and allow them to sing while they worked. He followed my advice to the letter, and the results were not long in coming. The industrialist in question had only forgotten one thing: that he was dealing with Negro-African peasants.

Many Black intellectuals still regard *religion as "the opium of the people."*[70] If they are to be believed, it is a feudal relic, which we should eliminate if we wish to keep up with the contemporary world. The risk is of replacing one religion with another. The risk is of provoking the deviations we see in America and in African medinas, which are heterogeneous monsters in which European contributions are not fecundating virtues. Religion, whatever it may be, and more generally *faith*, is as necessary to the soul as bread, rice, or millet is to the body. In Black Africa, millet is being replaced by rice, which is less nourishing. The issue is not doing away with religion, or even replacing it; it is assigning religion its rightful place and purifying it by making it one of the elements of today's humanism.

What I have said about religion could be said about political and social institutions. The majority of the people of Black Africa, as well as of the Antilles and Latin America, have opted for a *socialist*, not to say *communist*, State. Throughout this presentation, I have tried to show that Negro-African civilization is a *collectivist and communitarian* civilization: a socialist civilization.

The mistake here is beginning from European socialism without first analyzing it. The mistake is not having understood its historical necessity—that, in its different forms, European socialism is the natural result of a specific situation.

The mistake is attempting to transplant, as is, the institutions that it advocates. The most important thing to retain from European socialism is its *method*. And this requires us to begin by analyzing Negro-African realities: geographical, historical, ethnic, economic, social, and cultural realities. Once this analysis has been carried out, it is a matter of determining the *current* value of the institutions and lifestyles born of these realities, and how to adapt them to the demands of the contemporary world. We will realize, then, that "parliamentary democracy," mutualist cooperation, and the division of labor, as they manifest themselves in Black Africa, are still valid, provided we are willing to renew them in light of European and Asian experiences. I say "Asian," speaking as an African, because our situation as underdeveloped countries brings us much closer to Asia than to Europe.

With respect to art, Europe has no lessons to offer us. We are in our own domain. The lessons of Negro-African art must be retained. As evidenced by the fact that contemporary European art has retained them all. For the past several years, Black students have been speaking a great deal about "socialist realism," forgetting that thousands of Soviet writers—Mayakovsky, Yesenin, Gorki—always rejected a narrow and blind realism, which only reached the surface of reality. Moreover, why seek elsewhere what we already find here, in Black Africa?

It is true, Mister [Maurice] Houis,[71] after reading the proceedings of our first Congress, feels obliged to offer us some lessons in the journal *Esprit*. And to assert the necessity of prior study of Negro-African languages, and to insist on the oral character of these languages. As if we had not been repeating these self-evident truths for some fifteen years. What Mister Houis fails to say—and should have said—is that *orality* is not only a feature of languages, but of all Negro-African cultural manifestations: Orality is one of their shared characteristics. It is the result of their spontaneity, of their appropriateness to their object. The problem is not as simple as Mister Houis believes. He sees only codification; but fixing languages by writing, if it offers certain advantages, does not make those advantages certain. Writing is synonymous with abstraction, and therefore with *impoverishment*. And how can we fix music, or simply Negro-African dance? In reality, it is less a question of fixation and codification than of analysis and conservation. For my part, in this area, I prefer the copy, the photograph, or better still, the sound film. This is the opinion of Mister Herbert Pepper, the well-known musicologist, who intends to create, at the ORSTOM (Overseas Scientific and Technical Research Office), an audiovisual museum of Negro-African arts.[72]

It is time to conclude this lengthy report. Paradoxical as it may seem, writers and artists must play, and do play, a leading role in the struggle for *decolonization*. It is up to them to remind politicians that politics, the administration of the city, is only one aspect of culture and that, consequently, cultural colonialism, in the form of assimilation, is the worst of all. It is up to them to analyze the *total situation* of their respective peoples and, on the basis of that analysis, to say what should be retained from their traditional civilization—values and institutions—and, above all, how to revive them, thanks to the leaven of external contributions.

However, in this confrontation, in this symbiosis, *Man* must be at the center of our concerns. We cannot build a modern State simply for the sake of building. Action is not an end in itself. We therefore must guard ourselves against a will to power that deifies the State, that crushes *Man* beneath the State. Ultimately, it is a matter of producing the Black man within a humanity that is on the path toward its *total realization* in time and in space.

NOTES

Léopold Sédar Senghor, "Éléments constitutifs d'une civilisation d'inspiration négro-africaine," in *Liberté 1: Négritude et humanisme* (Seuil, 1964): 252–86. The text was originally given as a talk at the Second Congress of Black Writers and Artists (1959), though with a slightly different title: *constructifs*, "constructive," instead of *constitutifs*, "constitutive." The text later was published in the double special issue of *Présence Africaine* dedicated to the proceedings of the Congress. Léopold Sédar Senghor, "Éléments constructifs d'une civilisation d'inspiration négro-africaine," "Deuxième congrès des écrivains et artistes noirs (Rome: 26 mars–1er avril 1959), vol. 1: L'unité des cultures négro-africaines, responsabilités des hommes de culture," special issue, *Présence Africaine*, no. 24/25 (1959): 249–79.

1. [Senghor is referring to his contribution to the First Congress of Black Writers and Artists held in Paris in 1956. See Léopold Sédar Senghor, "L'esprit de la civilisation ou les lois de la culture négro-africaine," *Présence Africaine*, Nouvelle série, no. 8/10, Premier congrès international des écrivains et artistes noirs (Paris-Sorbonne: 19–22 Septembre 1956) (1956): 51–56. As a "report" (*rapport*), Senghor's contribution was part of the second half of the congress program, which consisted of "three large reports" by specialists or a group of specialists. See "Appel: Unité et responsabilités de la culture négro-africaine," *Présence Africaine*, no. 24/25 (1959): 12.—Eds.]

2. [For the text of the "Call" ("Appel"), see "Appel," 11.—Eds.]

3. ["Appel," 12.—Eds.]

4. [Marx quoted in Aimé Césaire, "Culture et colonisation," *Présence Africaine*, no. 8/10 (1956): 192; the citation from Marx comes from Karl Marx, *Das Kapital* (Dietz, 1951), vol. 3, 841.—Eds.]

5. Jean-Paul Sartre, "Qu'est-ce que la littérature?," in *Situations II* (Gallimard, 1948), 126. [Jean-Paul Sartre, *What Is Literature?*, trans. Bernard Fretchman (Philosophical Library, 1949), 77.—Eds.]

6. [This citation of Mauss is the one cited by Césaire, without further attribution, in "Culture et colonisation" (191). The citation given by Senghor and Césaire appears to be a version of the definition Mauss gives in "Les civilisations: éléments et formes," in Lucien

Lefebvre, Émile Tonnelat, Marcel Mauss, Adfredo Niceforo, and Louis Weber, *Civilisation: Le mot et l'idée* (La Renaissance du livre, 1930). The citation reads: "On peut donc proposer la définition suivante d'une civilisation: c'est un ensemble suffisamment grand de phénomènes de civilisation, suffisamment nombreux, eux-mêmes suffisamment importants tant par leur masse que par leur qualité, c'est aussi un ensemble assez vaste par le nombre, de sociétés qui les présentent; autrement dit: un ensemble suffisamment grand et suffisamment caractéristique pour qu'il puisse signifier, évoquer à l'esprit une famille de sociétés" (88–89). However, Mauss reformulated his definition of "civilization" numerous times in his writings. For an overview, see Jean-François Bert, "Marcel Mauss et la notion de 'civilisation,'" *Cahiers de recherche sociologique* 47 (2009): 123–42.—Eds.]

7. [Jean Price-Mars, "La paléontologie, la préhistoire de l'archéologie: Au point de vue des origines de la race humaine et du rôle joué par l'Afrique dans la genèse de l'humanité," *Présence Africaine*, no. 24/25 (1959): 51. Price-Mars is citing Henri Victor Vallois, *Les races humaines* (Presses universitaires de France, 1944), 6.—Eds.]

8. Henri Labouret, *Paysans d'Afrique occidentale* (Gallimard, 1941).

9. Pierre Gourou, *Les pays tropicaux: Principes d'une géographie humaine et économique* (Presses universitaires de France, 1947).

10. Labouret, *Paysans d'Afrique occidentale*, 169.

11. [Pierre Viguier, *Le soudan français: Ressources et possibilités agricoles* (Imprimerie du Gouvernement, 1945), cited in Jacques Richard-Molard, *Afrique occidentale française* (1949; reprint, Berger-Levrault, 1956), 31.—Eds.]

12. For a study of Sereer agriculture in the Sine, cf. [Mission] Roland Portères, *Aménagement de l'économie agricole et rurale du Sénégal* (Gouvernement général de l'A.O.F., 1952). [Senghor gives the place of publication as Dakar, but it is Bambey.—Eds.]

13. Henri Lhote, *Peintures préhistoriques du Sahara: Mission H. Lhote au Tassili: [exposition au] Musée des arts décoratifs [Pavillon de Marsan, Palais du Louvre], Novembre 1957–Janvier 1958* (Les Presses artistiques, 1958).

14. Trần Đức Thảo, *Phénoménologie et matérialisme dialectique* (Éditions Minh Tân, 1951), 252.

15. Cf. Jean-Paul Sartre, *Esquisse d'une théorie des émotions* (Hermann et Cie., 1948); Maurice Merleau-Ponty, *Phénoménologie de la perception* (Gallimard, 1945). [Sartre's text was originally published in 1939, but Senghor had the 1948 edition in his collections.—Eds.]

16. [In his note here, as well as in "Éléments constructifs," in *Présence Africaine* (1959), Senghor gives only the reference "*Cahier d'un retour au pays natal* (Gallimard)." Gallimard never published an edition of the *Cahier*. The first version of the *Cahier* appeared in 1939, in *Volontés*, no. 2, then in Spanish translation in Cuba in 1943. The first publication in book form in French was the Bordas edition of 1947, followed by the "definitive" edition by *Présence Africaine* in 1956. Senghor is most likely citing the latter, or the fragment of the *Cahier* published in the *Anthologie de la nouvelle poésie nègre et malgache de langue française*, ed. Léopold Sédar Senghor (Presses universitaires de France, 1948). Aimé Césaire, "Cahier d'un retour au pays natal (Fragment)," in Senghor, *Anthologie*, 59. Here we have used the English translation by N. Gregson Davis: Aimé Césaire, *Journal of a Homecoming / Cahier d'un retour au pays natal* (Duke University Press, 2017), 127.—Eds.]

17. Jean-Paul Sartre, "Orphée noir," in Senghor, *Anthologie de la nouvelle poésie nègre et malgache de langue française*, xxxi.

18. Cf. Gaëtan Picon, *Panorama des idées contemporaines* (Gallimard, 1957). On a style of a contemporary spirit: "Although it was a very learned and subtle organization, the ancient system of knowledge had no other object than that world which is naturally discovered by the eyes of the body as well as the soul—and which emerges like the landscape when the sun rises: a universe on a human scale where thought and imagination seemed to be governed by a kind of visual realism" (25). And again: "Western philosophical tradition has always demanded this distance of observation" (26).

19. [This appears to be a reference to the Book of Genesis, to the third day, when God separates the land and sea and furnishes the earth with plants and trees.—Eds.]

20. [Paul Claudel, *Art poétique* (Mercure de France, 1907), 182.—Eds.]

21. [Karl Marx to Arnold Ruge, Kreuznach, September 1843. For the full letter, see Karl Marx, *Œuvres*, vol. 3, trans. Louis Evrard (Gallimard, 1982), 344.—Eds.]

22. [The citation comes from Karl Marx and Friedrich Engels, *Werke*, vol. 20 (Dietz Verlag, 1956), 529; it is possible that Senghor has translated directly from the German. The French term *Bochiman*, which Senghor uses, is from the colonial era; the people are the San of Southern Australia.—Eds.]

23. "We are witnessing a general decline in the idea of objectivity. Everywhere we find the researcher involved in his own research, and revealing it only by veiling it. The light of knowledge is no longer that unalterable clarity which rests on the object without touching it and without being touched by it: it is a troubled fulguration born of their embrace, the flash of a contact, a participation, a communion." Picon, *Panorama*, 2.

24. Sartre, "Orphée noir," xxix.

25. Sartre, *Esquisse d'une théorie des émotions*, 16–17.

26. Thảo, *Phénoménologie*, 254–55. [We have used the following English translation: Trần Đuc Thảo, *Phenomenology and Dialectical Materialism*, trans. Daniel J. Herman and Donald V. Morano (D. Reidel, 1986), 147.—Eds.]

27. Thảo, *Phénoménologie*, 259–260. [Thao, *Phenomenology and Dialectical Materialism*, 148 (translation modified).—Eds.]

28. Sartre, *Esquisse d'une théorie des émotions*, 49.

29. Lévi, cited by André Breton, *L'art magique* (Club français du livre, 1957), 14.

30. Sartre, *Esquisse d'une théorie des émotions*, 41.

31. Sartre, *Esquisse d'une théorie des émotions*, 45.

32. [Alain (Émile Chartier) quoted in Sartre, *Esquisse d'une théorie des émotions*, 58.—Eds.]

33. [Remo Cantoni and Claude Beigbeder, "Mythe et critique dans la culture marxiste," *Esprit* 145 (May–June 1948): 769.—Eds.]

34. Cf. André Breton: "In the eyes of many authors, magic and religion originally appear inextricably mixed." Breton, *L'art magique*, 19.

35. Jules Monnerot, *Les faits sociaux ne sont pas des choses* (Gallimard, 1946).

36. Sartre, *Esquisse d'une théorie des émotions*, 29.

37. Sartre, *Esquisse d'une théorie des émotions*, 30.

38. Sartre, *Esquisse d'une théorie des émotions*, 30.

39. [Einstein wrote: "The most beautiful thing we can experience is the mysterious. It is the source of all true art and science. He to whom this emotion is a stranger [...] is as good as dead." Albert Einstein, *Living Philosophies* (Simon and Schuster, 1931), 6.—Eds.]

40. [Senghor, "L'esprit de la civilisation," 53.—Eds.]

41. [Senghor, "L'esprit de la civilisation," 53.—Eds.]

42. Cited in Picon, *Panorama*, 632. The text was published in *Les nouvelles littéraires* (6 April 1950), on the occasion of a survey conducted by A. George, entitled "Qu'est-ce que la Vie?" [See André George, "Qu'est-ce que la vie?," *Les nouvelles littéraires, artistiques et scientifiques*, April 6, 1950, 6. See also Pierre Teilhard de Chardin, "Les singularités de l'espèce humaine" (1954), in *Œuvres: L'apparition de l'homme*, vol. 2 (Seuil, 1956), 293–369. Senghor later cites the text as "*Les singularités de l'espèce humaine* (Masson et Cie)," which seems to refer to the version of the text published in *Annales de paléontologie* 41 (1955); see note 45 in this chapter. The citation in Senghor and Picon seems to be a paraphrase of a longer passage in Teilhard de Chardin, "Les singularités de l'espèce humaine": "Si localisée et dispersée que puisse être la Vie dans l'Univers, elle deviendrait immédiatement incompréhensible scientifiquement si nous ne la considérions pas comme, depuis toujours, en pression partout. Qu'en un point quelconque des espaces sidéraux, dès lors, un astre apparaisse par chance où température, pression, gravité, etc., permettant la formation graduelle de très grosses molécules, et c'en est assez pour qu'aussitôt—en un tel point de coïncidence optimal entre 'corpusculisation d'agrégation' et 'corpusculisation d'arrangement'—la Vie s'accroche: et pour que, une fois accrochée, elle se concentre et s'intensifie jusqu'à se réfléchir sur elle-même,—si tout va bien."—Eds.]

43. Erwin Schrödinger, cited in Picon, *Panorama*, 628 (emphasis added). [Erwin Schrödinger, *What Is Life? The Physical Aspect of the Living Cell* (Cambridge University Press, 1944). We have used the following edition: Erwin Schrödinger, *What Is Life? With Mind and Matter and Autobiographical Sketches* (Cambridge University Press, 2013), 69.—Eds.]

44. [George, "Qu'est-ce que la vie?"—Eds.]

45. Pierre Teilhard de Chardin, "Les singularités de l'espèce humaine," *Annales de paléontologie* 41 (Masson et Cie., 1955), 48–49. [We have used the following English translation: Pierre Teilhard de Chardin, "The Singularities of the Human Species," in *The Appearance of Man*, trans. J. M. Cohen (Harper and Row, 1965), 365–66.—Eds.]

46. [Senghor is drawing a philosophical distinction, also present in Heidegger and Lévinas, among different forms of being, essence, and existence. He distinguishes between *l'existant*, "an existing thing or being, that which exists, existent," and *l'étant*, "being." The latter is distinct from (and a contingent element of) *l'être*, variously translated as "Being," "to be," or "being," as in *l'être humain* "the human being." When using the terms as nouns, we always translate *existant* as "existent," following translators of Lévinas, and *étant* as "being," but we include the original French in brackets in the case of the latter, where confusion might arise with *être*. See chapter 3, note 7, of this volume, where Senghor clarifies his terminology.—Eds.]

47. Teilhard de Chardin, "Les singularités de l'espèce humaine," 4. [Teilhard de Chardin, *The Appearance of Man*, 209.—Eds.]

48. Cf. Labouret, *Paysans d'Afrique occidentale*, 155 and onward.

49. Cf. Léo Frobenius, *Mythologie de l'Atlantide* (Payot, 1949), 170–76.

50. [Senghor, "L'esprit de la civilisation," 54.—Eds.]

51. Cited in Breton, *L'art magique*, 56.

52. Elias [*sic*; Eliphas] Lévi, cited in Breton, *L'art magique*, 14.

53. Labouret, *Paysans d'Afrique occidentale*, 109.

54. Cf. Frobenius, *Mythologie de l'Atlantide*, 98–112; R[obert] S[utherland] Rattray, *Ashanti* (The Clarendon Press, 1923); R. S. Rattray, *Ashanti Law and Constitution* (Clarendon Press, 1927). [Élie Faure, *Histoire de l'art*, vol. 2: *L'Art antique* (G. Crès et Cie., 1926).—Eds.]

55. [*Laamaan* in modern transcription.—Eds.]

56. Cf. Labouret, *Paysans d'Afrique occidentale*, 129. [Maurice Delafosse, *Les Nègres* (Éditions Rieder, 1927), 44.—Eds.]

57. Jacques Maritain, *Humanisme intégral: Problèmes temporels et spirituels d'une nouvelle chrétienté* (Fernand Aubier, 1936), 202. [The correct page is 193.—Eds.]

58. Cf. Labouret, *Paysans d'Afrique occidentale*, 46. [See also Senghor's essay "Perspectives on Black Africa," chapter 16 in the present volume, where he extensively discusses the caste system.—Eds.]

59. Maurice Delafosse, cited in Labouret, *Paysans d'Afrique occidentale*, 46. [Delafosse, *Les Nègres*, 46.—Eds.]

60. [*Candace* is the name Pliny gives to the Queen of the Ethiopians, a fact also mentioned in the New Testament (Acts 8: 26–27). It is the Latinized form of the Meroite term *Kandake*, the name given to queen mothers in ancient Nubia. Senghor's reference to Homer's characterization of the Ethiopians as a people favored by the gods stems from Book One of the *Iliad*, where the Ethiopians are characterized as a "blameless" people, whom the gods visit for feasts.—Eds.]

61. [*jàmbur* in modern transcription.—Eds.]

62. [Senghor, "L'esprit de la civilisation."—Eds.]

63. [André Breton, "Signe ascendant," in *Essais et témoignages* (La Baconnière, 1950), 44.—Eds.]

64. Cf. Ferdinand Alquié, *Philosophie du Surréalisme* (Flammarion, 1955), 171. For this analysis of the Negro-African image, cf. the same author; Alquié, *Philosophie du Surréalisme*, 166–82.

65. Alquié, *Philosophie du Surréalisme*, 180.

66. Marcel Griaule, "L'Inconnue noire," *Présence Africaine* 1, no. 1(1947): 21–27. [Senghor miscites this as "L'inconnu noir."—Eds.]

67. [Léopold Sédar Senghor, "L'esthétique négro-africaine," in *Liberté 1: Négritude et humanisme* (Seuil, 1964), 211–12.—Eds.]

68. [Senghor appears to be referring to Marx's *Le travail aliéné* (Alienated labor).—Eds.]

69. [Économie et Humanisme was a French Catholic association founded in 1941 by the economist and Dominican priest Louis-Josesph Lebret (1897–1966). It was also the name of the review, *Économie et humanisme*, founded by the association and referenced by Senghor here.—Eds.]

70. [This is an oft-cited statement of Marx (*das Opium des Volks*), from his "A Contribution to the Critique of Hegel's Philosophy of Right: Introduction," in Karl Marx and Friedrich Engels, *Collected Work*, vol. 3 (Lawrence and Wishart, 1975), 175.—Eds.]

71. Of the Institut francais d'Afrique noire (French Institute of Black Africa).

72. [Herbert Pepper (1912–2000) was a French musicologist, songwriter, and employee of ORSTOM; he composed the music for the national anthems of Senegal and the Central African Republic.—Eds.]

2

Negritude Is a Humanism of the Twentieth Century

For the past thirty years that we have been proclaiming *Negritude*, some people have fallen into the habit of accusing us of *racism*. The same people sometimes contend that "Negritude is an inferiority complex." Yet the same word cannot mean, without any contradiction, both "racism" and "inferiority complex."

No, Negritude is none of that. It is neither racism nor self-negation. It is rootedness in the self and confirmation of the self; of one's own *being*. Negritude is nothing other than the *African personality* of the English-speaking Negro-Africans. Nothing other than this "Black personality" discovered and proclaimed by the American *New Negro* movement. As Langston Hughes wrote, in a proclamation in the aftermath of the First World War: "We, creators of the new Negro generation, we want to express our *Black personality* without shame or fear.... We know that we are beautiful. And ugly too. The tam-tam cries and the tam-tam laughs."[1] Perhaps our only originality in the matter is to have tried to define the concept with rigor: to have intended to develop it as a weapon of combat, an instrument of liberation, and a contribution to the *Humanism of the Twentieth Century*.

But what is *Negritude*? Today, ethnologists and sociologists speak of "different civilizations." It is obvious that peoples differ in their ideas and languages, their philosophies and religions, their customs and institutions, their literatures and arts. Who will deny that Negro-African peoples, too, have a certain way of conceiving and living life? A certain way of speaking, of singing and dancing, of painting and sculpting, and even of laughing and crying? No one, of course, because, otherwise, we would not have been discussing "negro art" for the past sixty years and Black Africa would, today, be the only continent with neither ethnologists nor sociologists. But what, finally, is *Negritude*? It is *the sum total of the civilizational values of the Black world*, that is, a certain active presence in the world, in the universe. It is, as John Reed and Clive Wake say, a certain "*way of relating oneself to the world and to others*."[2] Yes, it is essentially relation with and movement toward the world, contact and participation with others. As such, Negritude, today, is necessary to the world: It is a humanism of the twentieth century.

The Revolution of 1889

But let us go back in time, to 1885, in the wake of the *Berlin Conference*. European nations had, with the partition of Africa, just finished carving up the planet. There were five or six of them, including the United States of America, all at their apogee, dominating the world. Without any complex, they were proud of their material power, even more of their science, and, paradoxically, of their *race*. It is true that it was not, at that time, a paradox. Arthur de Gobineau had left his mark and, by osmosis, influenced thinkers up to Marx. Marx, who gave his daughter's hand in marriage to a *métis*, was, of course, not racist, but he thought that the stage of colonization constituted progress for India. And [Benjamin] Disraeli could present himself as the grand theoretician of "that proud, tenacious, self-confident *Anglo-Saxon race* that no climate, no change could bastardize."[3] My emphasis. As the German Leo Frobenius writes, in *Le destin des civilisations* [The destiny of civilizations], "Each one of the great nations that deems itself personally responsible for the 'world's destiny' believes that they alone possess the key to understanding the Whole and other nations. That is an attitude from the past."[4]

More precisely, this attitude, "from the past," began to be shaken by the end of the nineteenth century with books such as [Henri] Bergson's *Essai sur les données immédiates de la conscience* [Essay on the immediate data of consciousness], published in 1889.[5] From the Renaissance, the values of European civilization were essentially based on *discursive reason* and *facts*, on *logic* and *matter*. Bergson, with a particularly dialectical subtlety, would meet the expectations of a public weary of scientism and naturalism. He showed that facts and matter, as objects of discursive reason, were nothing other than the superficial surface that we needed to transcend, with *intuition*, in order to have an in-depth vision of the *real*.

But the *Revolution of 1889*—that is how we will refer to it from now on—did not only affect arts and letters: It overturned the sciences. Still in 1880, a year before the invention of the word "electron," a distinction was made between *matter* and *energy*. The first was considered inert and immutable; the second was not. But what characterized both was their conservation and their continuity. They were both subject to a rigorous and mechanical determinism. Matter and energy were, so to speak, wholly eternal: They could change form, not substance. We were lacking only precise enough instruments of investigation and of measure to know them objectively in space and time.

Well, in less than fifty years, all these principles were to be surpassed, if not rejected. Thirty years ago, the new discoveries of science—quanta, relativity, wave mechanics, relational uncertainty, electron *spin*—had, with the concepts of matter and energy, unsettled classical determinism. [Louis de] Broglie revealed to us, beneath the surface of things, matter-energy or *wave-particle* duality; Heisenberg taught us that objectivity was an illusion and that we could not observe facts without modifying them; others taught us that particles acted on one another at the scales of the infinitely small as well as the immense. Thus, physicochemical laws could not, any more than things, appear immutable to us. They were only quite rough approximations, if not *probabilities*, even in the sole field and at the sole scale where they were valid. Scratching the surface of things, of facts, sufficed to open up horizons of instability that challenge our instruments of measurement, probably because these instruments are merely mechanical: material.

Beginning with these aforementioned discoveries, while combining dialectical coherence and dazzling intuition, scientific experimentation and inner experience, Pierre Teilhard de Chardin would transcend classical dichotomies by using a *new dialectic* in order to show us the living, pulsating, unity of the universe. Beginning, thus, with new scientific discoveries, he goes beyond the old dualism of philosophers and scholars, which Marx and Engels had not resolved by giving primacy to matter over spirit. He claims that the fabric of the universe is not composed of two realities but a single reality in the form of two phenomena, that there is no matter and energy, not even matter and spirit but *spirit-matter*, in the same way that there is *space-time*. Matter and spirit are both reduced to a "fabric of relations," that is, in [Gaston] Bachelard's terms, to *energy*, defined as a network of forces. Thus, there is only, in matter-spirit, a single energy that presents itself in two aspects. One, *tangential energy*, the one from the "outside," is material and quantitative. It links together, massively, all corpuscles that form matter. The other, *radial energy*, that of the "inside," is psychic and qualitative. It is a centripetal force. It organizes, while complexifying, the association, center to center, of particles within a corpuscle. Energy being force, it turns out that what is creative is radial energy, the "primary fabric of things," with tangential energy being only a residual product, "engendered by the interactions of the elementary 'centers' of consciousness, imperceptible in the pre-living [*pré-vivant*], but clearly discernible to our experience once matter has reached a sufficiently advanced degree of arrangement. [...]"[6] It follows that, in the pre-living, the physicochemical laws remain valid with the restrictions that we have defined above, whereas, in the living [*le vivant*], as we progress from plant to animal and from the animal to man, the *psychè* increases in consciousness to make itself and express itself in *freedom*. "To make itself," that is, to realize itself by, but also beyond, all material *well-being*, in the spiritual *more-being* [*plus-être*]. *To realize* itself, I mean to develop harmoniously, the two complementary elements of the soul: the heart and the head, intuitive reason and discursive reason.

What Is Negritude?

I will appear only to be developing a paradox in trying to show that, in its ontology, its morality, and its aesthetics, Negritude responds to contemporary humanism, as European philosophers and scholars have framed it since the end of the nineteenth century, and as Pierre Teilhard de Chardin, along with writers and artists of the middle of the twentieth century, present it.

First, Negro-African *ontology*. As far back as we can go into the past, from the Sudanese North to the Bantu South, the Negro-African has, always and everywhere, presented to us a conception of the world that is opposite to that of classical philosophy. The conception of the world in classical philosophy is essentially static, *ob-jective*, *dicho-tomous*, and, therefore, Manichean. It is based on separation and opposition: on analysis and combat. On the contrary, the Negro-African thinks the world, beyond the diversity of its forms, as a fundamentally moving, synthetic, but unique reality. This merits explanation.

It is significant that in *Wolof*,[7] there are at least three words to translate *spirit*,[8] while images must be used for the word *matter*.[9] Of course, the Negro-African is sensitive to the exterior: to the matter of beings and of things. Precisely, because he is more sensitive than the Albo-European, he *feels* things through all their sensible qualities—shapes, colors, smells, and weight, etc.—, which the Negro-African considers to be mere signs that one must interpret in order to surpass and reach the reality of beings. In the same vein as others—more than others—he distinguishes pebble from plant, plant from animal, and the animal from man, but, once again, the accidents, the appearances that distinguish these different forms of life only express diverse modes of the same reality. This reality is *Being* in the ontological sense of the word, that is, force. Thus, for the Negro-African, European *matter* is nothing but a system of signs that translates the only reality of the universe: *Being*, which is *spirit*, which is *force*. In this way, the entire universe appears to us as an infinitely small and, at the same time, infinitely great network of forces emanating from God and leading to God, who is considered the Force of all forces. It is he who *reinforces* or *deforces* [*déforce*] all other beings: all other forces.

We are not as far here as one would think from contemporary ontology. European ethnologists, Africanists, and artists use the same words, the same expressions to designate the ultimate reality of the universe they seek to know and express: "spider's web," "network of forces," "connecting vessels," "system of channels," etc. We are not even that far from scientists: physicists and chemists. There is no dead matter in African ontology, either: every being, every thing, be it a grain of sand, irradiates force—a sort of corpuscle-wave that, precisely, wisemen, priests, kings, doctors, and artists will use to aid in the fulfillment of the universe.

Because, contrary to general opinion, the Negro-African is not passive before the order—or disorder—of the world. His attitude is, fundamentally, ethical. If we have long been unaware of Negro-African *ethics* [*morale*], it is because it arises, naturally, from his conception of the world, that is, his ontology. So, naturally, that both were overlooked, and even denied, because they were not questioned during each generation.

Yet God was bored by all the potentialities that were within him, locked up, unexpressed, dormant and seemingly dead. And God opened his mouth. And he spoke in long, harmonious, and rhythmic words. And all the potentialities, all the possibilities that were there, expressed from the mouth of God, *existed* and had the vocation to *live*: to express God in turn, by playing the ordination of forces that came from God, toward God.

To better explain Negritude's ethics in action, I must back up a little. Each identified force of the universe—from the grain of sand to the Ancestor—is itself a network of forces, as contemporary physicochemistry confirms: a network of apparently contradictory but, in reality, complementary elements. It is in this vein that, for the Negro-African, the *man-person* is, of course, made up of matter and spirit, of body and soul, but, at the same time, of a virile element and a feminine element, and even of several "souls." Therefore, the man-person is an unstable fabric of intermingling forces: a world of affinities that seek to bond. As an existent, he is at once end and beginning: the end of the mineral, plant, and animal kingdoms but the beginning of the human kingdom. Let us leave aside, for a moment, the first three kingdoms and focus on the human kingdom. Above the man-person, and founded on him, this fourth world is built up in wider and wider, taller and taller, concentric circles that reach all the way to God and the entire universe. Each circle—family, village, province, nation, humanity—is, by vocation and in the image of the man-person, a *solidary society*.

So, for the Negro-African, *to live ethically is to live according to one's nature, a nature composed of contradictory elements but complementary forces*. It is to embellish the fabric of the universe, to tighten the threads of the cloth of the world. It is to go beyond the contradictions of elements in order to work toward the complementarity of forces, first within oneself, within the man-person, but also within every human society. Thus, it is in realizing these forces in light of their reciprocal complementarities, that man reinforces them in their movement toward God and, by reinforcing them, he reinforces himself; that is, he passes from *existent* to *being* [*étant*]. I do not exactly mean that he becomes "Being" [*être*].[10] For, in truth, only God is *Being*, and he is so with so much plenitude that creation, existents, fulfill themselves by expressing themselves in him.

Negritude's Contributions

Ethnologists have often praised the unity, balance, and harmony of Negro-African civilization: of Black society, which was *communalist* but also personalist, and in which, because it was founded on dialogue and the reciprocity of services, the group prevailed over the individual without crushing him, making him blossom into *personhood*. I would like to emphasize how these features of Negritude enable its incorporation into contemporary humanism, thereby allowing Black Africa to contribute to the Civilization of the Universal, which is so necessary in the torn yet *interdependent* world of this second half of the twentieth century. To contribute, first, to international cooperation, which must be and which will be the cornerstone of that civilization. It is thanks to these virtues of Negritude that decolonization was accomplished without too much bloodshed or hatred south of the Sahara and that a positive form of cooperation between former colonizers and former colonized, founded on "dialogue and reciprocity of services," was established; that a new spirit reached the UN, where crying *no* and pounding one's fist on the table are no longer signs of strength. Thanks to these virtues, peace through cooperation might be extended to South Africa, South Rhodesia, and to the Portuguese colonies if the Manichean spirit of the Albo-Europeans would open itself to dialogue.

In reality, the contribution of Negritude to the Civilization of the Universal did not begin today. In the field of literature and art, it dates to the revolution of 1889. Arthur Rimbaud had already made a claim to Negritude. But here I will evoke only the "Negro Revolution"—the expression comes from Emmanuel Berl—who helped shake the foundations of European fine arts at the turn of the century.[11]

Art, like literature, is always the expression of a certain conception of the world and of life: of a certain philosophy and, above all, of a certain ontology. The philosophical and scientific revolution of 1889 coincided with not only a literary revolution—symbolism, then surrealism—but also with a revolution, artistic revolutions, which were known, limiting ourselves to the plastic arts, as *nabism, expressionism, fauvism*, and *cubism*. A closed world of permanent and continuous substances, which must be reproduced, is being replaced by a world of live and unstable forces that must be tamed.

As far back as the Greek *kouroi*, Western European art has always been based on realism; the work of art has always been an imitation of the object.[12] It is, in the words of Aristotle, a *physéôs mimésis*. A corrected imitation, "embellished," "idealized," for the sake of rationality, yet an imitation, nonetheless. The interlude of the Christian Middle Ages is significant for the very reason that Christianity is of Asian origin, an origin profoundly influenced by Saint Augustine the African. For European artists of the twentieth century, for [Wassily] Kandinsky for example, "art begins where nature ends."[13] What, then, will the artist express? No longer *matter-object*, but *spirit-subject*, that is, his own interiority, his spirituality and, beyond that, the spirituality of his era. No longer through the techniques of perspective, modeling, or clair-obscure but, as [Jean René] Bazaine writes, "through the most obscure work of instinct and sensibility."[14] And [André] Masson specifies, "through a simple play of forms and colors legibly ordered."[15] This play of forms and colors is the play that we have already seen, that of vital "forces," that painters like [Pierre] Soulages describe explicitly.

"A play of vital forces." Here we come back to Negritude. As Soulages, specifically, used to tell me, the Negro-African aesthetic is that of "contemporary art." I find indirect proof of this in the fact that, if it is true that the consecration and spread of the new aesthetic revolution occurred in France, most of its promotors were Slavs and Germans, who, like Negro-Africans, belong to mystical civilizations of *meaning*. Of course, the revolution would have happened even without the discovery of Negro Art, but certainly not with such vigor, such assurance, such a deepening of man. The fact that an art of the subject and of the spirit—which had not even been rehabilitated yet by ethnologists—was born elsewhere, and, on top of it, among Negro-Africans, was proof of the values of humanity of the new message.

Beyond the aesthetic lesson—to which we shall return—what the earliest explorers of Negro Art were searching for was this: its "values of humanity," singularly its *unitary vision of the world* and of life, which had, for millennia, led to monotheism. For in Black Africa art is not a separate activity in itself and for itself. It is a social activity, a technique of life, and, in short, a *craft*. But, like prayer in the Christian Middle Ages, it is a major activity that fulfills all others: birth and education, marriage and death, sport, and even war. It is a matter of integrating all human activities—up to the smallest daily act—in the subtle play of vital forces: of familial, tribal, national, global, and universal forces. It is a matter of aiding in the creation of that harmonious play, subordinating inferior forces—mineral, vegetal, animal—to the play of the *human existent*, and the forces of human society to the play of the divine Being [*Être divin*] through the mediation of Ancestral Beings [*Étants ancestraux*].

A year or so ago, on the cliffs of Bandiagara in the Republic of Mali, I attended a celebration that was the microcosm of *Dogon* art. Although it was a pale imitation of the splendors of yesteryear, this concert-spectacle was the most significant expression of the Dogon vision of the universe. The celebration was sung and declaimed, choreographed [*dé-marché*] and danced; costumed, painted, and sculpted. The whole of the Dogon universe was featured in the symbiosis of art, as is the custom in Black Africa. The universe—heaven and earth—were therefore represented through the mediation of man, whose ideogram is undiscernible from that of the universe. Then came the world with masks, each of which featured, at the same time, a totemic animal, an Ancestor and a jinn, and others, which featured allogenous peoples: Fulɓe nomads and Albo-Europeans. The goal of the celebration was to re-create the universe and the contemporary world through the symbiosis of art—poem, song, dance, sculpture, and painting, used as techniques of integration—but in a more harmonious way, by making use of negro *humor*: a humor that redresses distortions at the expense of the Fulɓe immigrants and White conquerors. But this ontological vision was a *celebration*, that is, an artistic event as well: *a joy for the soul because a joy for the eyes and ears*, and re-creation because it is recreation.

It is perhaps—indeed, it is most certainly—this dimension of the aesthetic lesson that first seduced Picasso and [Georges] Braque when, around 1905, they discovered Negro Art in a *fang* mask and were inspired by it. I myself was also struck, at the very beginning of the Dogon concert-spectacle, even before I had tried to understand its meaning, by the harmony of forms and movements, the colors and rhythms that characterized it. This harmony, which, as a spectator, *moved* [*ému*] me, is that which, in the re-creation of reality, acts on invisible forces whose *appearances* are its signs to subordinate them to one another, complementarily, and to ordinate them to God through the mediation of man. By *appearances*, I mean the attributes of matter that strike our senses: forms and colors, timbres and tones, movements and rhythms. I said that these appearances were signs. They are more than that: They are signifying signs, "lines of force" of vital forces, in that they are used in their pure state with their sole virtue of form, of color, of sound, of movement, of rhythm. The other month, Monsieur [Pierre] Lods, a professor at the National School of Arts in Senegal, showed me the paintings that his students planned to exhibit at the First World Festival of Negro Arts. From the start, I was struck by the play of forms and colors, a play so noble and elegant. When I discovered that these paintings were not completely abstract, that they featured some women, princes, noble animals, I was almost disappointed. It was useless; the very play of colored forms rendered, perfectly, this elegant nobility that characterizes North Soudanese art.

Here, thus, is the aesthetic lesson. Art does not consist in photographing nature, but in taming it. In the same vein as the hunter who mimics the pursued animal's call, so do the two separate beings, reciprocally, the couple, the two lovers—in order to find one another and unite. The call is not the simple reproduction of the cry of the *Other*, it is a call of complementarity, a song: *a call-harmony to the harmony of union, which enriches by making more-being* [*plus-être*]. Once again, the negro lesson is that art is not photography, that, if there are images, they are rhythmed. I can suggest, create anything—a man, a moon, a fruit, a smile, a tear—by a simple assemblage of forms and colors (painting-sculpture), of forms and movements (dance), of timbres and tones (music), provided that this assemblage not be an *ag-gregation* [*a-grégation*] but that it be ordered and, in short, rhythmed. For it is *rhythm*, precisely the major virtue of Negritude, which gives the work of art its beauty. *Rhythm is nothing more than this movement of attraction and repulsion that expresses the life of cosmic forces*: nothing more than symmetry and asymmetry, repetition and opposition, in a word, the lines of force according to which the signifying signs—which are the forms and colors, the timbres and tones—are ordered.

Before concluding, I would like to insist on the apparent contradiction that we will not have failed to notice between contemporary European art, which focuses on the subject, and negro art, which focuses on the object. It is that the Revolution of 1889 began by reacting, necessarily, against the fetishism of the *object* and that the existentialist ontology of the Negro-African, if it is based on the *existing subject* [*sujet existant*], has God, the plenitude of Being, as *pole-object*. We will therefore have only noted nuances. It remains that for the contemporary European and for the Negro-African, the work of art, like the act of knowing [*connaître*], expresses the confrontation, the seizing [*étreinte*] of the subject and the object: "this penetration," Bazaine writes, "this great communal structure, this deep resemblance of man and of the world, without which there is no living form."[16]

Conclusion

The global reception of the First World Festival of Negro Arts, which occurred in Dakar, from April 1 to 24, 1966, is a final proof that Negritude is a humanism of the twentieth century. The great European and American nations participated either by sending works from their collections or even, in the case of the United States of America and of Brazil, their Black artists. It is significant that the "Arab" states of Africa were present in Dakar.

This is to say that the Civilization of the Universal feels implicated; from the beginning of the century, it is being built, in slow stages, on the ruins of racial hatred and intercontinental wars. It does not feel implicated without reason, for many of its features, which are presently becoming apparent, would not be the way they are if not for the fecundating contribution of Negritude.

In any case, the Negro of the twentieth century, the *Neo-Negro* [*Néo-Nègre*], in the words of my friend [Janheinz] Jahn,[17] means to contribute doubly to the Civilization of the Universal—the civilization of the twentieth century. On the one hand by bringing the wealth of his philosophy, his literature, and his traditional art; on the other hand, by showing the borrowings he has made, since the Renaissance, from other civilizations, singularly from European and Arabo-Berber civilizations. This was, precisely, the object of the First World Festival of Negro Arts: the manifestation of a humanism of the twentieth century.

NOTES

Léopold Sédar Senghor, "La Négritude est un humanisme du XXe siècle," in *Liberté 3: Négritude et civilisation de l'universel* (Seuil, 1977), 69–79. The text was originally given as a lecture at the University of Bayreuth (Bayreuth, Germany, May 19, 1966). An English version appeared as early as 1966, in *Optima*, a South African "quarterly review published in the interest of mining, industrial, scientific and economic progress"; Léopold Sédar Senghor, "Négritude: A Humanism of the 20th Century," *Optima* 16 (1966), 1–8. See also "Negritude: A Humanism of the Twentieth Century," in *The African Reader*, vol. 2: *Independent Africa*, ed. Wilfred Cartey and Martin Kilson (Random House, 1970), 179–92.

1. [The emphasis is Senghor's. The original reads: "We younger Negro artists who create now intend to express our individual dark-skinned selves without fear or shame. . . . We know that we are beautiful. And ugly too. The tom-tom cries and the tom-tom laughs." Langston Hughes, "The Negro Artist and the Racial Mountain," *The Nation*, June 23, 1926, 694, reprinted in *Within the Circle: An Anthology of African American Literary Criticism from the Harlem Renaissance to the Present*, ed. Angelyn Mitchell (Duke University Press, 1994), 59.—Eds.]

2. [Léopold Sédar Senghor, *Prose and Poetry*, selected and trans. John Reed and Clive Wake (Oxford University Press, 1965), 5.—Eds.]

3. [We have been unable to find a similar quotation attributable to Disraeli. It is possible that Senghor has misattributed a citation from Joseph Chamberlain (the secretary of state for the colonies from 1895 to 1903), who, in a speech made on the December 30, 1887, refers to the "greatness and importance of the destiny reserved for the Anglo-Saxon race, for that proud, persistent, self-asserting and resolute stock that no change of climate and condition can alter." The quotation can be found in Joseph Chamberlain, *Foreign and Colonial Speeches* (London: George Routledge and Sons, 1897), 6.—Eds.]

4. Leo Frobenius, *Le destin des civilisations*, trans. Norbert Guterman (Gallimard, 1940), 15.

5. [Henri Bergson, *Essai sur les données immédiates de la conscience* (Paris: Félix Alcan, 1889).—Eds.]

6. Pierre Teilhard de Chardin, *L'Apparence de l'homme* (Seuil, 1956), 363. [For an English translation, see *The Appearance of Man*, trans. J. M. Cohen (Harper and Row, 1965), 265.—Eds.]

7. A major language in Senegal.

8. *Xèl*, *sago*, or *dégai*. [*Xel* might be translated as "mind" or "intellect"; *sago* might be translated as "consciousness"; *dégai* is not a common Wolof word, but a nominalization of *dégg*, "to know, understand," and might be translated as "deep understanding," or *dégg-dégg*.—Eds.]

9. *Lef* (thing) or *yaram* (body).

10. [See chapter 1, note 46, as well as chapter 3, note 7, of this volume for a discussion of these terms and their translations.—Eds.]

11. [Emmanuel Berl, "La révolution nègre," *La Table Ronde* 8 (August 1948): 1280–1306.—Eds.]

12. [*Kouroi* is the term used for statues of nude young men in classical Greek sculpture.—Eds.]

13. [Various versions of this statement are often attributed either to Kandinsky or Chagall, though the original iteration of the saying seems to be traceable to Aristotle's *Physics*, in which he writes that "art in some cases completes what nature cannot bring to a finish."

See *The Complete Works of Aristotle: The Revised Oxford Translation*, trans. R. P. Hardie and R. K. Gaye (Princeton University Press, 1984), 340.—Eds.]

14. Cited in Jean Bouret, *L'Art abstrait: Ses origines, ses luttes, sa présence* (Le Club français du Livre, 1957), 65. [Jean Bazaine, *Notes sur la peinture d'aujourd'hui* (Floury, 1948), 35.—Eds.]

15. Cited in Bouret, *L'Art abstrait*, 45.

16. Bouret, *L'Art abstrait*, 1. [Bazaine, *Notes sur la peinture d'aujourd'hui*, 11.—Eds.]

17. [Jahn uses the term *neoafricanische*, "neo-African." Janheinz Jahn, *A History of Neo-African Literature*, trans. Oliver Coburn and Ursula Lehrburger (Faber and Faber, 1968). For the French translation, see Janheinz Jahn, *Manuel de littérature néo-africaine: Du XVIe siècle à nos jours; De l'Afrique à l'Amérique*, trans. Gaston Bailly (Resma/SEDIM, 1969). For the German, see *Die neoafrikanische Literatur: Gesamtbibliographie von den Anfängen bis zur Gegenwart* (Eugen Diederichs, 1965). See also *Geschichte der neoafrikanischen Literatur* (Eugen Diederichs Verlag, 1966).—Eds.]

3

Negritude and Modernity; or, Negritude Is a Humanism of the Twentieth Century

Nit moo di garab u nit
(Man is the remedy of man)
—Wolof proverb

I have chosen to speak to you today about *Negritude* in relation to modernity—in other words, I intend to present Negritude to you as a contemporary humanism—because the matter is topical. Numerous observers, even historians and philosophers, have noted the fact that, within the greatest world power, the United States of Africa, an ethnic minority—namely, Negroes—plays a role greater than the size of its population. And they do so in such essential areas as the arts and entertainment. And these observers tie this phenomenon to the growing influence of minorities worldwide—an influence that is growing because it is in the throes of rebellion. And they remind us of the influence of jazz on contemporary music and, before that, of *Negro Art* on the School of Paris, that is, on twentieth-century art. To focus purely on the relations between Europeans and Africans: The French called us "racists" when the word "Negritude" exploded like a stinking bomb, in Paris during the 1930s, in the heart of the Latin Quarter; while today, Her British Majesty's subjects deem the fusion realized by the Negritude and *African personality* movements to be *shocking*.

What Is Negritude?

But, since we are indeed concerned with Negritude: *What is Negritude*? In a recent interview, published by the newspaper *Dakar-Matin*, Professor Abiola Irele, of the University of Ifé, in Nigeria, responded to the question as follows: "I am a defender and a partisan of Negritude insofar as I see, in this movement, a desire to return to oneself. I even accept it as an absolutely necessary positive narcissism. I think that we should even exaggerate it, lending it dimensions proportionate to the degree of alienation. At the latest Edinburgh conference, I argued that Negritude is a philosophy that postulates a cultural action adapted to the spiritual and sociological conditions of the Black man. *It is a humanism of universal scope*."[1] I underscore the last sentence: it is the very topic of this conference. I have cited Irele at such length because he is an Anglophone and because the imperialism of the Great Whites wished to use Anglophone Negroes from Africa to fight the Negritude movement, just as it wishes to use "Marxist-Leninists" today.

But again, what is *Negritude*? If we are to really think about it, the word has two meanings: subjective and objective, particular and universal, actual and eternal—insofar as spirit is eternal. It is this first meaning of the word that Irele defines. In this sense, Negritude is, essentially, a rejection and an engagement, a negation and a going beyond of negation through synthesis: through symbiosis.

I refer here to my own experience, for it was in seventh or eighth grade, during the third or fourth year of secondary school, that I discovered the question and began to militate. It was at the *collège* Liebermann, in Dakar, which used to be run by the fathers of the Holy Spirit. We were already a handful of *protesters*, who, even though we were relatively privileged, demanded other privileges, among which was to have white bedsheets. The director would always remind us of our parents' low beds and pagnes, thereby denying us even the honor of having a *civilization*, because we were "savages" in the etymological sense of the term: "men of the bush." I used to protest all the more vigorously because, my father being a landowner, I had experienced, in the countryside, our *Negro-African civilization*, which was a certain non-European way of thinking the world and of being in the world, of conceiving and living life—a certain way of eating and working, of laughing and crying, of dancing and singing, of painting and sculpting, and also, above all, of praying. But the militant that I was becoming felt, despite all this, the weakness of this civilization, and that this weakness was of a technical nature. And I swore to steal from Europe the instruments of its superiority: its machines, of course, but mostly the spirit of those machines, I mean its *discursive reason*.

Objectively, as a civilization, Negritude is the sum total of values not only of the peoples of Black Africa but also of Black minorities from America, and even from Asia and Oceania. It is, thus, as Jean-Paul Sartre writes in "Orphée noir" [Black Orpheus], "a certain quality common to the thoughts and behaviors of Negroes."[2] *Subjectively*, Negritude is a will to assume the civilizational values of the Black world, to live them for oneself, after having fecundated and actualized them, but also to make them be lived in and by others. In this sense, it is, to use Irele's expression, "a humanism of universal scope."[3] To help you better grasp this, I invite you to read the doctoral thesis of Mrs. Erica Simon, a professor at the University of Lyon, but of Scandinavian origin through her mother, entitled *Réveil national et culture populaire en Scandinavie* [National awakening and popular culture in Scandinavia].[4] Here, she shows us how during the nineteenth century, the Scandinavian peoples, humiliated by the great European powers, sought the values of this *Northern spirit* beyond their respective national identities. This alone could help them form a solid cultural and political unit in Europe (the economic was not yet on the agenda). In an article published in the *Revue de la Société des études germaniques* [Journal of the society of Germanic studies] and entitled "The University of Grundtvig," Mrs. Simon went so far as to compare the notion of Negritude to that of *Folkelighed*.[5] I would compare it, more appropriately, to that of *Nordicity*—we could just as well have said *Negroness* [*Négrité*], since the Latin suffixes *-itudos* and *-itas*, have the same abstract value.

This is to say that Negritude, as a cultural movement, is not a racism, not even an "anti-racist racism," to use Sartre's formula. As we know, under the influence of characterology, one of whose inventors was the Franco-Senegalese philosopher Gaston-Berger, ethnology has ended up destroying the idea of a unique civilization and even more the idea—still embodied by the "European Society of Culture"—of a European civilization superior to all others. As Marcel Mauss and Paul Rivet, my professors at the Institut d'ethnologie de Paris [Institute of Ethnology of Paris] taught me, each ethnicity, each people, has its own civilization, which is the succulent fruit of geography but also of history, of race, even more so of language: of life in society.

After defining Negritude in this way, I would like to articulate, concretely, its two aspects, one after the other. But, by describing the second as a living movement, I will say, at the same time, the extent to which it is a *humanism of the twentieth century*.

Negritude, as an objective civilization, is an idea, I mean, a philosophy and a life, a theory and a practice, an ethics and an art. But, first of all, it is an *idea*. Africanists have often noted that those who are called "primitives" not only have a coherent philosophy but also live their ideas and live off of their ideas. I will not go this far, because only *initiates* who have reached the final stage of initiation have deciphered all the signs of the world and penetrated all its meanings. Yet even the average Negro-African—the peasant, the shepherd, or the fisher—is generally concerned with mastering, through his speech, the cosmic forces, that is, mastering his life as a man.

Negro-African philosophy, as we live it and as Africanists confirm, is an *ontology*, a science of *being*. From one Black people to another, there are a number of differences, even if we limit our reflection to Africa, as I will do throughout this presentation, but its meaning remains the same if we know how to interpret myths. For, in Nigritie, every science, every form of instruction, appears in the form of myth: the analogical image. That is why I will start, here, with the myth of creation, which is, at the same time and in a meaningful way, the myth of the *Word* [*Parole*]. I borrow it from the *Dogon* people of Mali, whom Marcel Griaule and his disciples have made famous.[6]

Thus, according to the Dogon myth, it is Amma, the uncreated and all-powerful God, who created all beings and all things. In the past, beings and things took the form of roughly sketched ideograms, contained within the egg of the world, composed of a double placenta. It is from this mother-egg, fecundated by Amma's speech, that the two first humans emerged. One, having rebelled against the paternal authority, introduced disorder along with defilement into the world and was transformed into a fox. The other, Nommo, put to death and resuscitated, descended from the sky to the earth with an arch that contained, besides the eight first ancestors of humans, all animals, plants, minerals, and elements that inhabit the universe.

However, all these beings [*êtres*] were, in fact, shapeless and mute—among others, men appeared as silent fish. It is to Nommo that God would give the mastery of speech, and he would take on the responsibility of teaching it, at the same time as technology, to shapeless *existents*,[7] and first to men. It is in this way that the learning of language [*langage*] coincided not only with that of technology but, before that, with the development of the human body and the improvement of his appendages: with our emergence from animality. Marx and Engels, [Jean] Jaurès and [Pierre] Teilhard de Chardin have said exactly this.

Meanwhile, behind the myth, we must provide a knowledge [*une connaissance*] for phenomena *confabulated* in this way—a knowledge that is also a rational and coherent but not necessarily logical explanation. There we have the definition of philosophy. As Alfred and Maurice Croiset write, "Greek philosophy was born the day a thinker tried to find a rational and systematic explanation for all things."[8]

It is precisely that, in a number of Negro-African languages—as seems to have been the case for all Negro-African languages—all men, all animals, all plants, all minerals, all identifiable things, up to abstract beings, that is, all existents, are classified into grammatical categories or "noun classes." There are twenty-one in *Pulaar* [*poular*], a Fulah [*peul*] dialect of Senegal. Beyond phonetic, morphological, and syntactical considerations, this classification follows, primarily, semantic, that is, rational reasons. Drawing thus on grammar—ultimately on language [*langage*]—and following the Abbé Alexis Kagamé,[9] Janheinz Jahn[10] uncovers, in Negro-African ontology, *force* as the very essence of *beings* [*étants*], as it is expressed in the root *-nt-* in Bantu. Thus, in the context of noun classes, *muntu* designates "force endowed with intelligence"; *kintu*, "forces that . . . are set into action only after the intervention of a Muntu"; *hantu*, "force that situates every event in time and in space"; *kuntu*, "finally . . . 'the modal force,' the laugh or beauty, for instance, constituting, 'for the Bantu, authentic forces.'"[11] It is thus the fact not precisely of *having* force as attribute but of *being* force as substance that constitutes the shared quality and, in reality, the shared identity of *beings* [*étants*]. This has been true since Father Placide Tempels, translating "Bantu" thought, posited that "being [*l'être*] IS force."[12] All major Africanists and, first, African informants and researchers, have confirmed this fundamental principle of African ontology, which could, as well, be articulated in this way: "The fabric of matter is energy."

Before going further, let us analyze this principle, which perhaps more than any other distinguishes Negro-African philosophy from classical European philosophy. Up to the nineteenth century, for more than two thousand years, European thought, neglecting the brilliant intuitions of an entire line of Greek philosophers, has more or less depended on Aristotle's thought, in which the humid and vibratory *logos* crystalized in rigid categories that no longer correspond to or translate moving, living reality. For classical philosophy, thus, beings are discrete substances, created by God, of course, but existing independently: *in se* and *per se*. It is a *static* ontology. For the Negro-African, on the contrary and once again, being is not a substance that has force as an attribute; it is force itself that is the substance of being. *Being-force* [*l'être-force*] is *energy*, that is, a spirit, an always moving life, capable of increasing and decreasing, of enrichment and alteration. It is a *vital force*, which subtends men and animals, plants and minerals, and even natural phenomena: everything that is identifiable.

Thus, rather than being one next to the other, separated and seemingly unable to communicate with each other—in any case, with no action on each other—every being-force, every *ntu*, can, by means of its natural nature and its own movement, influence an other all the more easily if the other is *subordinated* to it. The world of forces is, thus, a system of connected vessels: a communion of *existents* between each other and in Being. For this influence is exercised, from the perspective of primogeniture, from God, *a force in himself and by himself*, which gives, increases, or diminishes force. According to the principles of this hierarchy, there are, first, the first men and ancestors, then among living things, old and young peoples, honest people, that is prosperous people, and others. After human forces, there are animal, vegetal, and mineral forces, hierarchized according to the same ranks of primogeniture, which is nothing but the sign of *pre-eminence* [*pré-cellence*] and which the law of *precedence* [*pré-séance*] translates. This is why I said earlier "by means of its natural nature and its own movement." Because primogeniture, in itself, is not enough. We must add to it good actions, that reinforce force, and bad actions, that deforce it. That is to say, this ontology, first and foremost, refers to the *Human*.

We have often noted that, within the system—better, within the solidary community of the universe—Man is at the same time subject and object of the universal movement, means and end, form and center. By the authority of God, as we have seen, Man-Nommo teaches the Word and, thus, completes creation as the master of the play of forces, the substance of which he enriches or empties—up to death. This explains the labels *anthropocentrism* and *anthropomorphism* given to the Negro-African vision of the universe.

But what, exactly, is this *Man*? In all versions of Negro-African philosophy, Man is presented to us as a complex being [*être*]—the most complex after God—and as having several "souls," that is, several spiritual principles. Geneviève Calame-Griaule has discovered eight "souls" or *kikinu*—to which naturally, we must add the *vital force* as substance[13]—that make up "personality." What is noteworthy, at first glance, is the equilibrium created by all these souls. They are divided into two groups of four, which each contain two twins. The first group, located in the head, is made up of a male principle, expressing intelligence and will, and a female principle, conveying intuition and emotion, to which correspond two negative opposing principles. The second group, located in the genitals, is made up of analogous principles, yet related to sexuality in its dual physical or practical aspects (procreation) and spiritual or sentimental (love) aspects. We understood the importance of sexuality in Negro-African civilization, but in this context, far from being an obsession that produces disequilibrium, it is a set of elements that work together toward the formation of the personality. Consulting the synoptic table of *kikinu* provided by Geneviève Calame-Griaule, one notes that "reason and will are introduced into sexual life,"[14] while intuition and emotion, which pertain to sex, are introduced into intellectual life. Especially given that every human contains within themselves the same male and female principles, with, depending on sex, a nonexclusive predominance of masculinity or of femininity. Thus, Man appears to us, at the center of the Negro-African Weltanschauung, as the equilibrium of a *binary rhythm*: an ambivalence, better, a *symbiosis*. This anthropocentrism, which becomes anthropomorphism, goes as far as to divide all existents, all elements of the universe, into male and female.

But how does *Man* activate, direct, and order the universal system of solidary forces? It is that he understands the cosmogony, the structures and the hierarchy of the system: the series—ascending and descending—of *beings* [*étants*] and, therefore, of powers. It is also that, understanding these things, he knows how to set them in motion. But it is not useless to revisit these binary structures, which are more complex than they appear. There is, for men, the vertical plane of primogeniture, illustrated by *age classes*, but also the horizontal plane of structures, illustrated on the one hand by sociocultural groups or *brotherhoods* and on the other hand by socio-professional groups or *corporations*. We will not reexamine the top of the hierarchy: God. Nor will we reexamine animals, plants, minerals. Nor natural phenomena such as clouds, wind, and rain.

As we consider this horizontal or structural order, it is time to go further in our analysis, to show more explicitly what this system of connected vessels, in which one goes from man to stone and vice versa as if they were of the same nature, consists of. Our evening tales hum with these stories in which a woman transforms into a hyena as easily as a stick transforms into a warrior.

Following the cosmogony of the *Fali*[15] of Cameroon, [Jean-Paul] Lebeuf recounts: "The Papaya Tree planted itself at the center of the earth destined for men and engendered a first couple of human beings of opposing sexes who twice birthed two twins. In turn, the Turtle and the Toad mated, the Turtle to a crocodile . . . the Toad to a lizard . . . , and they gave birth to two couples of male twins. These couples, along with the four wives born from the children of the Papaya

Tree constituted four couples that are at the origin of the *Fali*."[16] Since all *ntu* can only become *beings* [*étants*] of the *Being* [*l'Être*], it follows that the procreations and changes, as well as all avatars, are nothing but enrichments and impoverishments of the same vital force, of the same *being* [*être*]. On the basis of this ontological truth, each being [*étant*] and above all each existent, as we have seen in the case of Man, is ambivalent, more precisely multivalent, for each is composed of several elements, several parcels of vital force—which, among others, it received from its ascendents—, all of which can undergo physical or moral, material or spiritual variations. These variations occur according to the laws of *participation*.

There you have it, the word is out, and beyond the word, the concept that explains, in addition to the structures, the organization and the functioning of the world. Thus, since the same force animates the universe, one of its elements can, by transformation and under the influence of certain psychophysiological laws, take on another density, another form. More precisely, a certain quantity of vital force can pass from an *existent* to another. But for this to occur, the two *beings* [*étants*] must be united by at least one element or any other link. This link can be an *affiliation* (from father to son, for example), a *correspondence* (from a color to a sound), an *analogy* (between the situations of two existents), and finally an *identity*, which facilitates everything. That is all for the nature of the link. However, the link can connect one existent to another (for example a man to a tree), an element or, more concretely, a modality to another (a sound to a color), still yet a physical element to a moral modality. The list of reincarnations [*avatars*] is not exhaustive, far from it. We could say, in a word, that the universe is a dictionary, a fabric of metaphors, a vast network—obverse and reverse—of signifiers and signifieds but in which the participating, communing correspondences operate in both directions from the sign to the sign, but also from the sign to meaning, and vice versa. Even if he does not understand all its meanings—not just each existent, I say, each form and each color, each sound and each smell, if not each movement, and even rest and silence—everything, for the Negro-African, is a sign, and every sign has a meaning.

One might wonder, and you will wonder, why. It is, essentially, for ethnic reasons. In fact, the ethno-characterologists have classified the Negro-African among the *Fluctuants*. Yet the Fluctuants are characterized by the depth and vigor of their affectivity, the rapidity and violence of its reaction. Their intelligence, "concreto-sensory," is expressed more readily with images than with concepts. The richness of their interior life, fully oriented toward the realities of the soul, is underscored. In the past, Negro-African *intuitive reason*—in particular, their power of emotion and fabulation—was explained by the contrasts and violence of the African climate. *Portentosa*, "maker of marvels," that is how the Latins called Africa. But not the Greeks, for whom Africa was the continent beloved by the gods, where men, *Ethiopians*, that is Negroes—who had invented religion and law, writing and art—were the most ancient, the most beautiful, the most religious, and the wisest. I refer you to the doctoral dissertation, entitled *Sources grecques de l'histoire négro-africaine* [The Greek sources of Negro-African history], that a Cameroonian Jesuit, Father Engelberg Mveng, has just written.[17]

Prehistory confirms the opinion of the Greeks. Since the end of the Second World War, the discoveries of prehistorians confirm this opinion, namely the thesis of [Henri] Breuil and Teilhard de Chardin according to which it is in Africa that, for the first time, man emerged from animality.[18] For, Teilhard explains, far from being an inhospitable land, Africa had, on the contrary, the climate most favorable to the evolution, by abrupt mutation, of the large anthropoidal primates, first toward *hominins*, then toward the men that we are. Today still, from Ethiopia to South Africa, the highlands of eastern Africa offer us the grace of earthly Paradise: the sweetness of life. Among anthropoid primates, *hominins* emerged in this earthly Paradise as bipeds with an upright stature. Thanks to the coordinate action of the hand and the foot, of the hand and the brain, they would become, after some tens of millions of years, *Homines abiles*: not only omnivorous primates but also primates capable of building and using tools. Capable too, without a doubt, of articulating the first words of a coherent thought. This was a little less than four million years ago in the highlands of Oriental Africa.[19] Yves Coppens, a member of the French expedition that discovered, three years ago, in the Omo valley in Ethiopia, the oldest human skeleton, dating back 3,700,000 years, writes, "Thanks to these Hominins of the lower Pleistocene era, Africa, currently and without a doubt, has an advantage of at least 1,000,000, perhaps 2,000,000 years over toolmaking humans."[20] Thus, hominins lived for forty million years, and men for nearly four million years,[21] in Africa, on lands where nature is generous and the climate clement. Here, amid the familiarity of animals and plants, of terrestrial and celestial phenomena, men learned to know all existents in their forms and their movements, their activities and their respite, their screams and their silences, their struggles and their accords. In short, in the prodigious tangle of their links and correspondences, their participations and unions, they learned to identify the meaning beneath the sign. Hence, these symbolic images, these *archetype-images* that lie dormant in the depths of our memories and from which negro art conjures them with an essential force.

Negro-African Civilization

Given these explanations of ethnic psychology, which I unfortunately do not have the time to develop, it is now a matter of saying how and in what circumstances Man sets in motion, directs, and orders the universal system of solidary forces. We will, thus, address the major matters of *religion*, *ethics*, and *art*. But, in reality, in this Negro-African civilization, one of the most distinctive features of which is *unity in coherence*, art is essentially a technology, more precisely, a set of technologies, in the service of ethics, which is in itself merely the practice of religion, of which ontology, which we have just discussed, is the dogma.

One of the most profound questions that human anxiety asks of religion is that of death. In the Negro-African case, what does the network of vital forces strive for, and to what end? We will answer this question by borrowing a more modern language—in the same vein as "Negritude as subject." We will respond to it by underscoring two features of our ontology: the idea of Fecundity and the idea of Man.

First of all, and once again, the idea of *Man*. It has often been said that, in Negro-African philosophy, God was remote, indifferent, ineffective. This is not correct. It is truer to note the role of demiurge that God has given to Man. It is Man who, authorized by the All-Powerful Being, completes creation. It is also Man whom God has tasked to restore the order of the system when it is troubled and to maintain it by reinforcing it. For creation is always incomplete. Better, God has, so to speak, united all creation, all *beings* [*étants*] in the service of the *Existent* par excellence, that is the living man. Not only animals and plants, minerals and other elements, but also the Dead, his Ancestors, have placed themselves in his service.

This brings us to the idea of *Fecundity* or procreation, which, along with the idea of force, haunts, even obsesses, the Negro-African consciousness. The first artworks of humanity, in the form of soapstone fertility statutes enlivened, already, by negro rhythm, expressed this. It is to this idea that creation corresponds. It is, thus, as if all things were locked in God's breast, immobile and mute, shapeless and barely sketched out. If God named them with his speech to give them life, it is in order to dilate and reinforce his vital force: to make his BEING *more-being* [*plus-être*], in more and more numerous and varied forms. In living bodies. As the Jola of Senegal say, "God holds in reserve the infinity of souls to be born, which, united to the reincarnated souls, will come to renew, indefinitely, the surface of the earth."[22]

In Man's main function, ethics blends with mysticism, of which it is, ultimately, only the practice. Since all vital forces are emanations of God, and since God's will lies in the multiplication and augmentation of these forces, *morality* [*morale*] will, for Man, consist of acting in a way that is in conformity with this will, that is to say: it will consist of inciting the birth of new forces and reinforcing existing forces. And Man will act through the action of a series of material and spiritual technologies.

It is, first of all, a matter of inciting the birth of new vital forces, which often are, after all, nothing but the reincarnations of the dead Ancestors. Hence all the ceremonies, all the rites surrounding events and actions such as marriage, birth, naming, sowing, and harvesting. It is also a matter of increasing the existing forces, as is the case in different professional activities: that of the blacksmith as well as the weaver, that of the fisher as well as the hunter. It is not only a matter of increasing existing forces and creating new ones; these forces must also be restored when they are altered or diminished. And they are always so, when the network, the order of solidary forces, is troubled by a mistake, whether voluntary or not. This mistake, like a defilement, corrupts, spoils the forces connected to the guilty party by the participating correspondences we have analyzed above.

To play its major role as pilot, conductor, ruler—better, as permanent creator of the world—Man uses at the same time, or alternately, technologies that emanate simultaneously from religion, craft, and art. I will begin by taking two examples borrowed from religion and craft: from sacrifice and the forge.

Sacrifice is, in Black Africa, the essential act of worship. Even in a country like Senegal where *animists*—the followers of traditional religion—do not make up more than 10 percent of the population, sacrifice is the most common way of invoking the divine. It is the only form of worship that unites all Senegalese people. In Black Africa, sacrifice appears much more as the gift of an object, an offering, than as the slaughter of a victim. It is one of the features of Negritude, where the tree prevails over the animal. Be it an animal, a drink, or any other food, it is a matter of offering to the dead Ancestors an earthly food they will transmit to God. There is, of course, in the offering, vital substances like water or blood. But the proper virtue of the sacrifice is to *revitalize* these substances in the sense more of reinforcing than of renewing. This revitalization is incited by the intention of the sacrificer, the will of the Ancestors, and, above all, God. But also by the words of the sacrificer. On the primordial importance of the *Word*: As a sonorous projection of human personality, it possesses, like the human body, "the four elements"—water, air, earth, and fire—to which we add oil. Like the human *being* [*l'étant humain*], it possesses, along with the vital force, the "eight souls" of which I have already spoken. To summarize, as an expression of the essence of Man, containing, in addition to all the elements, the oil of fertility, the Word is a nourishment, but a vivifying nourishment. The Word is sperm.[23] During the sacrifice, Ancestors receive revitalized nourishment, which makes them relive the sweetness of life. And, in return, by the grace and will of God, they increase, through the sacrificer, the vital forces of the *orants*. In the case of defilement, of a disturbance to the order, there is not only revitalization but also purification. For purification is nothing other than revitalization by means of the elimination of corrupted elements: dead elements.

Second example: that of the work of the *blacksmith*. I invite you to read Laye Camara's novel.[24] The son of a blacksmith, he has described for us, in his autobiographical novel *L'enfant noir* [The Black child], his father's work on a piece of gold jewelry. We will not dwell on the general technique of the blacksmith but on that of the goldsmith. But then, while he works on the jewelry, the goldsmith—in the ancient sense of the word—prays: chants incantations. And at the same time, his *griot*, his troubadour, sings his praises. And at the end, the griot starts to sing the song of the completed jewelry—the work of art. And, in turn, the blacksmith dances "the glorious dance."[25]

These pages from Laye Camara that I summarize here are interesting in many regards. They show the role, in Nigritie, of religion—which is a philosophy—, of craft—which is a technology—, and of art. Religion is, in effect, at the beginnings of the technology, and in the past, the blacksmith received during his apprenticeship a religious initiation before a technical one. Traces of the former are still present in the blacksmith's incantation that is a prayer to *accomplish* the technical labor of the worker, in order to give him the oil and something like the grace of beauty. It is because, south of the Sahara, the two visible and invisible, material and spiritual, profane and religious, technical and artistic worlds are nothing but the obverse and reverse of the same fabric: of the same reality. The weaver sings when he weaves. And his words are feet and hands at work, replicating the tensioner and the shuttle.

I am forgetting neither the griot's song nor his final dance, which appear to us, first, as the expressions of a profane art. Art is never profane in Nigritie; it is never mere entertainment. The griot's song and dance are, on the one hand, in order to increase the blacksmith's vital force—in reward—and, on the other, to accomplish the beauty of the jewelry by insufflating it with a final grace. However, the blacksmith dances in turn: to *express* his joy. Because, in Black Africa, one dances first *by oneself*, if it is not *for oneself*. This brings us to negro art.

Since the beginning of the century and the radiance of the School of Paris; since the beginning of cubism and surrealism, we have spoken a great deal about *Negro Art* in Europe and in America. In order to assert, at times, that it disregarded the notion of beauty, thereby reducing this art to an ethnological document and, at other times, in order to assert that it was a form of religion or magic, thereby confusing it with a talisman. None of these definitions are exactly true. Negro art is all that at once, and something else, and it has a profound sense of beauty. This is where I will begin.

I have in my papers a peculiar text that I collected while in captivity at *Frontstalag 230*.[26] My informant, a Senegalese townsman, described to me the ideal form of beauty for a young woman. She is the color neither of ebony nor of golden red but of a dark bronze. Her lips are well drawn without drooping. Her waist is slim and curved but with no excess. *Beauty* is, thus, for the Negro-African the norm but also the measure, the accord: in one word, the *harmony* that unites complementary, if not contrary, elements. In our *gymnic* songs, the young girl praises her fiancé for being "black" and "tall"—that is the norm in my *Sereer* ethnic group—but also for being "slender and strong." She sings, "Kiin o baal, jag fo nut, jag fo ngel." That is, "The man with black skin, handsome at rest, handsome in the arena." In reality, the ordinary word that means "handsome" is *mos*, while *jag* means "in tune [*accordé*]." The athlete is handsome because he is as in tune with the repose of the home as with the wrestling games of the arena. And the beautiful poem is the one that "is pleasing to the heart and the ear." That is to say that negro art goes beyond the pleasure of the senses—without denying it.

Its first characteristic is to be a *total art* because it integrates all arts and makes them collaborate, as is the case in dance and lyrical theater. Every ceremony, every public manifestation is, at the same time, an artistic activity. Today still, the complete athlete is one who knows how to both wrestle and dance, how to sing and compose poems. The effective political rally is one that begins and ends with song, with dance.

The second characteristic of negro art is to be a *technology*. Contrary to what Europeans believe, each art—dance and music, song and poem, sculpture and pottery, painting and weaving—is a precise technology that includes a theory with its own vocabulary but also a practice which aims at efficacy. A technology, then, albeit one that plays on the double register of the useful and the beautiful, the profane and the religious. The weaver's pulley is, at the same time, a sculpture, just like the scepter. The calabash, a household utensil, is an engraving, and the pagne, the garment par excellence, a tapestry. And all these objects are magical, like jewels, for they protect more than they adorn. The artwork is a receptacle of forces that reinforce the vital force of the user and the efficacy of the instrument, which also is a bearer of force. *Negro art is a technology of essentialization toward more-being* [*plus-être*].

I would like to illustrate these characteristics of negro art with two examples drawn from dance and poetry.

I have always considered *Dance* to be the first art invented by man, even before the emergence of *Homo sapiens*. Animals dance. It is the most natural, the most spontaneous way, of expressing oneself. That is why, in Nigritie, everyone dances, and the elders who are the wisest dance more than the youth. As soon as dance rises to the level of ceremony—in the village, the brotherhood, the corporation—it unites all arts, where every element has its meaning. Dancers wear, on their bodies, clothing whose forms, material, and colors each have a meaning. Their faces are hidden with masks. An orchestra, which brings together instruments of percussion and melody, accompanies the dancers' steps. Not to mention spectators who often join in the dance and, most often, accompany it with their songs and their clapping of hands. Because in Nigritie, in every ceremony, in every spectacle, one is a spectator and an actor at the same time.

As for the dance itself, it is a sculpture-painting in motion: thanks to the clothing, masks, and painting, but especially thanks to the steps and figures of the dance, which, expressing participating correspondences, are *rhythmed images*. I watched, some years ago, in Côte-d'Ivoire, the dance of the Bull-Moon. The dancer wore a mask in which the curves, following the laws of the image-symbol's multivalence, are, at the same time, the crescent moon, the bull's horns, the cornucopia, the horns of abundance, that is to say, expressions of *Fecundity*. And the dancer danced furiously, expressing the generous force of the Bull with brisk movements of the feet, the arms, and the head.

I have said that the crowd was singing. They were singing a poem. Allow me to recall the definitions that the Fulɓe of my country give to the poem: "words that are pleasing to the heart and ear." That is to say that the poem is, at the same time, teaching and artwork. But also insemination [*ensemencement*], I mean, effective action because it acts on the heart. It is that the poem is an elaborate exercise of Speech. I will not repeat the virtues of Speech, its power of fecundation. It is enough for me to recall that Speech, as a fecundating power, is necessary for all art; better, for all technical and professional activity. The blacksmith as well as the weaver, the painter as well as the sculptor speaks, sings his artwork, while working. Without this, it would not be accomplished because it must carry a vital force. We have seen this in the case of the goldsmith. But since the poem's speech is beautiful and good speech par excellence, we must examine why, and in what way, it is such, when beauty and goodness are indistinguishable.[27] What essentially separates poetry from prose in Black Africa is its style, its manner of saying things; but before that, the things that are said—even though in Africa, less than in Europe, one should not separate substance from form. For it is form that will lead me to the substance.

In Senegal, as I have experienced it, but also among all the Negro-African peoples whose poetry I have read, poems appear, on first reading, as a fabric of metaphors and comparisons: a fabric of catachreses. And one must have it explained to them, because the correspondences they convey, if they express essential realities, are specific to the community in question, to the village, to the clan, though a knowledgeable African—or Africanist, for that matter—easily identifies with the myths the archetype-images. Poems, more than tales and fables, thus express what is essential: birth and death, the jinn and the Ancestors, work and war. They speak above all in a more concise and forceful way: a denser way.

What further distinguishes a poem from prose is *style*. It is a matter of saying things—more precisely, forces and their interactions—in an unusual and strong way, in a fecundating way. Hence, the often archaic style, which extends occasionally to using language that has become obsolete. These stylistic devices relate to vocabulary, figures of speech and of thought, and, finally, to rhythm.

Vocabulary is all the more important in Negro-African languages insofar as the roots of words are felt in their concrete value in such a way that the word almost always conveys an image. I shall add that poetic vocabulary, often sprinkled with rare words, employs many proper names—of Ancestors, places, families—that are, in themselves, charged with emotion and meanings.

But, once again, the Negro-African poem—like sculpture, painting, dance—is a fabric of signifying catachreses. There is not only an abundance of figures of thought—comparisons, antitheses—but also of figures of speech. Whether it is parallelisms or asymmetries, anaphoras or chiasms, alliterations or assonances, plays on words referring to timbres or meanings, sounds are always *pregnant* with images that establish correspondences between things, between forces, between *beings* [*étants*]. It is a taught, directed poetry in which the poet's intention is, moreover, as effective as his expression. The fact remains that the poet's intention is revealed more by his desire for efficacy than by the clarity of his expression. The ambivalence, the multivalence of negro art—in which, teeming, the signified and signifiers become undistinguishable—has often been noted. This adds to the force of beauty because it adds to the mystery.

But this—the expression—is effective, sets forces in motion, only if the poem itself is animated by *rhythm*, the imperious negro rhythm, which is monotone at first glance. In the past, all oral works, even the tale, were recited, declaimed in a monotone rhythm and a high tone. If I take the example of the gymnic poems of my ethnic group, the *Sereer*, these may be declaimed or sung. In both cases, the rhythm follows strict laws that one can express in mathematical formulae. Here, the verse is not determined by a fixed number of syllables but by accents of intensity as in ancient Germanic poetry. There is poetry whenever an accented syllable occurs at a regular interval. The discrepancy between the number of syllables and the number of accents allows us to transcend the apparent monotony in order to adapt the rhythm of the poem to that of the soul. It is this extreme freedom, beyond the tyranny of the basic rhythm marked by the tam-tam, that constitutes the originality of negro rhythm, all trembling with syncopations and offbeats that are accented in the singing of the poem.

For the poem reaches its own ontological efficacy only if it is sung. In most Negro-African languages, there is not a specific term to name the poem, which is frequently called by the same word as the song: *gim* in *Sereer* and *woi* in Wolof of Senegal, *nii* in Dogon of Mali. The song takes its pleasant and beneficial force—pleasant and beneficial because also purifying and fecundating—from the supplement of oil it contains. This oil gives the sung word its harmony, which comes from the pitch of the sounds and their melodic symbiosis. That is why the voices of women, above all those of young women, which are the highest and the most melodic, are also the most effective.

In this way, the poem admirably summarizes what I have tried to demonstrate to you concerning man's role of creation in the world. And, here, how could we not give poetry its etymological sense of *poiesis*, of "creation"? The poem, that is, the rhythmed and sung word, is the very example of the work of art, of the action of art, which recharges the energetic batteries of the world. The poem, so to speak, is the fecundating sperm of the world. And may no one refute "Negro sensuality," which exists firmly as a source of life and of dreams, precisely because it is not an obsessive eroticism. Consider, then, that there is biological fecundation, there is procreation, only if man, by the tenderness of his well-oiled words, sweetly makes his wife's heart melt. We have not, so far, spoken enough about Black tenderness.[28]

Negritude Is in Tune with the Twentieth Century

It is precisely the mission of the *New Negro* to make known all the values, all the virtues of Negritude: above all, those that align with the contemporary world and that, in symbiosis with those of other civilizations, must serve to build the Civilization of the Universal. From Negritude-object, we will move on to Negritude-subject. The new Negro, as Jean-Paul Sartre says, "wishes to be a lighthouse and a mirror at the same time; the first revolutionary will be the annunciator of the Black soul, the herald who will tear Negritude from himself in order to give it to the world, half-prophet, half-partisan, in short, a poet in the precise sense of the word 'vates.'"[29]

I have frequently noted that since the *Cultural Revolution of 1889*, since the scientistic blindness of the twentieth century was healed, the new discoveries of the Euramerican culture—even in the area of science—have corresponded, paradoxically, to the intuitions and experiences, the theories and practices of Negro-African civilizations. Meanwhile, in the realm of art, we consciously found our inspiration in the values of Negritude—though they were not always well interpreted. It is these convergences that I would like to note first before articulating how the militants of Negritude, conscious of such convergences, intend to draw all implications from them.

I perceived and noted these convergences, yet again, at the beginning of the year, while reading the French academician Jacques Rueff's book entitled *Les dieux et les rois* [Gods and kings] and subtitled *Regards sur le pouvoir créateur* [Perspectives on the power of creation].[30] Jacques Rueff's point is of a philosophical order. It is to fill in the "void" separating the human sciences from mathematics and the natural sciences. In short, it is—in the very spirit of philosophy, which is theory, a general vision of the universe—to show that all sciences, including the science of nature, are "social sciences." We see to what extent his point, initially, aligns with Negro-African philosophy. Naturally, I will not stop at this reference alone. I will add others, such as a remarkable text by Gaëtan Picon, published in 1957.[31]

As we know, the first and fundamental problem that philosophy faces is an epistemological one: What is the ultimate reality, the fabric of the universe? And, first, can we prehend it and with what means? For classical philosophy—we alluded to this—the real is an objective thing, given once and for all, situated in a defined space and time and, by that very fact, measurable. Of course, this "thing" can be endowed with force or spirit, but these are nothing but attributes, "accidents" of the substance. Naturally, "things" can be known because they are seen, touched [*atteintes*], and measured by the mind: by intelligence and experimentation in which the mind [*l'esprit*], remains at a distance. As Gaëton Picon puts it, the philosophy of discursive reason was a "visual realism."[32] That is why I have called it a *reason-eye*. For the brilliant essayist, this classical thought lasted until Hegel. I believe it lasted until the Cultural Revolution of 1889, until Bergson, until Rimbaud's "I am a Negro."

Thus, since the end of the nineteenth century, thanks to the new physics, the new art, that is, the new *poiesis*, the new philosophy, we are abandoning the spirit of objectivity: of *thingism*. We no longer believe ourselves to be capable of contemplating the thing *as such* [*in se*]. We can only hope to prehend it alive, warm and palpitating: in an *embrace* [*étreinte*], which blends the subject with the object, emotion with intelligence, and experience with experimentation, passion with vision, feeling with perceiving.[33]

The standing in the contemporary university system of the humanities, particularly ethnology, sociology, and linguistics, proves more than anything else that the *reason-embrace* [*raison-étreinte*] occupies a place that is more and more important in research and teaching, education and training. Even in the most abstract science, mathematics, intuition is again playing its role. And here it is that peoples belonging to the ethnotype of the *Fluctuant*, like the Japanese, show themselves to be capable of being good mathematicians. Already, at the University of Dakar, it is in the medical field, but also in mathematics, that the proportion of Negro-African teachers, in any case, of Senegalese teachers, is the highest. I do not need to insist, for it is evident, after everything that I have said in the second part of my intervention, that Negro-African thought, which is "intuition, feeling, and lived experience,"[34] converges readily with contemporary thought, which "stops being the thought of the world so as to become the lived experience of the world, the identity of speech [*parole*] and of the real."[35]

"The identity of speech and the real," Gaëtan Picon writes. I would like to dwell on this expression in order to try to define the role of *Speech*, in contemporary thought as it pertains to the Negro-African idea. For, in this twentieth century, a certain number of philosophers, among the greatest—Kierkegaard, Heidegger and Jaspers, Sartre and Merleau-Ponty—have considered linguistics as one of the major instruments of philosophy and speech as one of its keys. It is true that linguistics had, previously, been renewed, I mean created, by scholars some of whom were my professors, namely [Joseph] Meillet and [Antoine] Vendryès; true that ethnologists, sociologists, and writers have, since then, been insisting on the values of the sign and the image, of style and communication.[36]

"Identity of speech and the real." Martin Heidegger goes further—toward the Negro-African—in his philosophy of language, arriving at the following proposition: the poet's word is "the foundation of being." The philosopher has arrived at that conclusion through an insightful historical analysis of the Greek *logos*.[37] If he has chosen the Greek people—this people which all modern minds, from Marx to Lenin, have admired—it is because they are at the origin of European thought and because they have always been able to retain the primary fecundating humidity of reason in its double power of vision and embrace [*étreinte*]. To unveil the secret and, as it were, the nature of speech, Heidegger began with the verb *légein* and the noun *logos*, to examine the respective but converging evolution of their meanings and, first of all, of the meanings they had at the very origins of Greek thought: from Homer to the pre-Socratic philosophers of whom I spoke above and who wrote in verse or, at least, in poetic prose. *Légein*, thus, originally signified "to lay down or lay open" [*étendre*] or "to leave, extended, before, gathered together" [*laisser-étendu-devant-rassamblé*] before signifying "to pre-sent," "ex-pose," "to speak"; while *logos* meant "gathering gatheredness" [*pose receuillante*] or, more explicitly, "gathering which makes manifest" [*recueillement rendant manifeste*] or, better, "gathering and apprehension of the being of *being*" [*recueillement et apprehension de l'être de l'étant*].[38] We are not so far from the Negro-African philosophy of the word. For in Negro-African philosophy as well, as we have seen, to speak is to gather the vital force, the being of *being* [*l'être de l'étant*], in its preliminary form in order to extend it here by giving it a form, that is, an existence.

Let us return to Heidegger to note that his *logos*, like that of the Greeks, in its arranging, fabricating function, is a demiurge: it is *poiesis*, that is production, creation. And poetry as well, in the modern sense of the term: in the sense of the "speech that establishes" the Sacred. Like Nommo: the Negro-African Word [*Verbe*]. This is what the German philosopher explains to us regarding Homer, the founder of Greek poetry, but also regarding [Friedrich] Hölderlin, one of the founders of modern poetry, in which "it is more salutary for thought to wander among strange things than to settle in clear things."[39]

We have just seen how man apprehends the ultimate reality of the universe, and even how he creates it. For contemporary thought, it is now a matter of articulating what this reality is, in other words, what is the fabric of the universe. For this, I will refer to Jacques Rueff, who, beginning from a quantic vision of the universe, in the way that nuclear physicians conceive of it, arrives at the same vision as sociologists and economists, jurists and philosophers. In his conclusion, entitled "Ultimate Confession," he summarizes himself as follows:

"I believe:

> that the individual, which is foundation of the universe, is *wave and crepuscule, matter and spirit*;
>
> that he is a medium of *behavior*, the latter is a *spontaneous outburst* that responds to surrounding circumstances, not a passive presence indifferent to the external world;

> that all behavior is the expression of *psychism*, which is merely a manner of *existing* (*exister*)—that is, a way of reacting to stimuli coming from the rest of the world;
>
> . . .
>
> that the psychism is the internal aspect and *indeterminacy* the external aspect of one and the same reality, which is that of the quanta of existence, known in the living world as individuals."[40]

I have italicized the important words, which express contemporary ideas on the issue. I would like to show that we have already encountered these ideas in Negro-African ontology: "the binary foundation of existence," "energy as first matter of the universe," "structure" and "interaction" as characteristics of life, "behavior" . . . which "always presents a certain margin of indetermination" and which is the manifestation of the "individual psyche," and finally, "complementarity," which opens onto the Humanism of the twentieth century. These are the same words and expressions that Jacques Rueff has used to title his book's paragraphs.

Even though I spoke about it at the time, I did not insist on the *dualist* character of the Negro-African universe. Everything is either to the left or to the right, above or below, at the fore or behind. More significantly, everything is, in Nigritie, either male or female. And beings and their modalities (forms and colors, sounds and rhythms) are grouped in two or multiples of two and always with interruptions that inject life into the process: such as asymmetry to disrupt the monotonous parallelism, the ternary rhythm to launch the movement, and, in the binary rhythm itself, the offbeat and the syncopation, which give the movement its *force*.

This brings us to the notion of *energy*, understood as the ultimate reality, the fabric of the universe, that for contemporaries leads to the symbiosis of wave and corpuscle, matter and spirit. We recognize, here, one of the major ideas of Pierre Teilhard de Chardin, who, in an antimaterialist dialectical reversal, postulated the preexistence of spirit over matter. I discovered that the socialist orator Jean Jaurès had already claimed, at the end of the previous century, that matter is "infused with thought, or rather, that it is nothing but thought itself, obscure and confused, and looking for its way."[41] Yet still, as we have seen, Negro-African mythology is more nuanced, as it posits, before the God-Spirit, the primordial placenta: *matter*.

Nothing proves that energy is the fabric of the universe better than *behavior* [*comportement*], which is the *re-action* of the existent to its environment. Not even the behavior of living matter but that of matter which, a priori, seems to be inert, dead, like the ninety-two basic elements that physicists have inventoried. Physicists teach us that the quasi-totality of the universe is made up of "stellar matter," that is, of very small atomic cores composed of protons and electrons, "sexed" into negative and positive corpuscles, males and females, in the same vein as Negro-African cosmogony. At the superior level, the atom, according to Louis de Broglie, "would be comparable to a small solar system made up of electrons playing the roles of planets and gravitating . . . around a positively charged central sun."[42] Niels Bohr, we know, will later offer us a more complex system. In the final analysis, reality would appear as "grains of energy," each of which is, at the same time, wave and corpuscle and which, depending on its form [*avatars*], becomes inertia-matter or movement-spirit. But what is most remarkable is not the movement of the grains of energy but the fact that we cannot assuredly predict them at this microscopic level, even though we can calculate the probability; for, like living individuals, these corpuscles react to their environment: they have a behavior, which is the product of the *inter-actions* between and among the grains of energy and existents. As Jacques Rueff writes, "These interactions vary according to the nature of the order they generate. Our anthropomorphic interpretation of the universe always invests them with the character of *forces of attraction*, since these are the foundation of our theoretical explanations of the physical world. Depending on the level at which they operate, they may be given various labels: exchange forces within the nucleus; electric or electromagnetic forces within the atom or the molecule; tropisms, appetencies, or appetites in an animal being; the *will* in the thinking being. In every case, regardless of the level at which they operate and notwithstanding our ignorance of their real nature and basic cause, they may genuinely be considered the coalescing agents of existence."[43] My emphasis.

This citation is characteristic. Characteristic, first of all, of the contemporary mind's tendency to reintroduce *unity* in the universe and in life despite the multiplicity of sciences and disciplines of thought, despite the often contradictory explanations of scholars and thinkers. It is also that, from the atomic core of stellar matter to the human brain, we have discovered the spirit *beneath* the fabric and *as* the fabric of the universe: Everything becomes force because everything is progressive *consciousness* and will. As is the case in Negro-African philosophy and its panpsychism. Ultimately, the binding force, better, the driving force, which is at the same time, the reality of the universe, is the *structure*, that is, the network of interactions linking together the grains of existence in the individual, individuals in our planetary society, the suns and planets of the universe. This vast network appears to us at the end of Jacques Rueff's analysis, as a binary system, better, as a system of complementarities founded on union: on love that, as Teilhard de Chardin would have it, completes and enriches by making *more-being* [*plus-être*]. As we have seen, the Negro-African does not say anything other than this, especially when it comes to the role and action of Man in and on the world.

Thus, within the fundamental problem, which is that of epistemology, Negro-African thought provides more or less the same answers, though it does not always use the same modes of knowledge as contemporary thought. Both refer to Man.

I know that, since the interwar period, we have been speaking of a "new humanism," which the neo-Thomist Jacques Maritain helped to make fashionable with his suggestively titled work *L'Humanisme intégral* [Integral humanism].[44] In truth, modern humanism was not born yesterday. It was born, in Europe, on the ruins created by the Revolution of 1789. From Hegel to Teilhard de Chardin, a double line of thinkers, atheists and believers, founded it, some by challenging metaphysics, others more often by creating a new one. I will only cite, here, Nietzsche, Marx and Lenin, Bergson and Kierkegaard, Husserl and Heidegger, Sartre and my compatriot Berger.[45] Modern humanism, founded on the convergent thought of all these philosophers, can be summarized as follows: *Man making the world and making himself through the world.*

Paleontologists and ethnologists have shown us that it is by drawing *on* and making use *of* the surrounding nature, by *reacting* to it, that man emerged from animality. First Hegel, then Marx and Engels, were, however, the first to present man as a product of his generic activity. I refer to Engels's *Dialectics of Nature* and to a posthumous work by Marx entitled *Alienated Labor*.[46] Pierre Teilhard de Chardin, himself a paleontologist, will reiterate and reinforce this argument. But that is not all. "It is said that man is the being [*être*] through whom each existent reveals itself; he is the revealer of things."[47] I do not think that "the formula is ambiguous," as Gaëtan Picon writes.[48] Already in the *Alienated Labor*, Marx explains that it is our senses, trained by the hand and the brain, that enrich nature, which has become "part of human consciousness."[49] Marx's successors—I am thinking of Husserl and Heidegger, but also of Sartre and Teilhard de Chardin—had the merit of insisting on the virtues of *speech*—which Marx and Engels had mentioned in passing under the name of "language" [*langage*]—as founder or, perhaps more justly, as revealer of being, coinciding with being.

I will not insist on the convergence that exists between contemporary humanism and, in the form of myth, Negro-African humanism: It is the same conception of the role as well as of the genesis of man. It is Nommo, the Man-

Verb, who does not create but contributes to creation: It is he who does not create but reveals the being through religion, ethics, and art.

Nor do I need to insist on the *religious* question, which is a fact of the contemporary world. The trials of certain Soviet writers are the best proof that *Holy Russia* is not dead. All the way to the Second Vatican Council, during which the Third World, Black Africa in particular, played a nonnegligible role of humanization. This was, once again, the best way to defend the divine, transcendental character of religion against the interpretations of European theologians, which were all too logical, all too juridical, prone to transform religion into formulas: into pills.

Finally, there is no need to insist on the humanization of contemporary morality. In this context as well, the evolution of the Catholic Church is characteristic, as, in the Third World, for example, it gives priority to the spirit of productivity over the spirit of poverty, to charity over chastity. It is noteworthy that, last year, in eastern Africa, where the first humans emerged, Pope Paul VI praised Negritude.

But it is still in the realm of art, the expansion of which coincides with Euramerica's entry into the civilization of leisure, that the convergence between the two humanisms becomes a symbiosis. Today, we know enough about how, at the beginning of the century, the artists of the School of Paris—painters, then sculptors—encountered Negro Art and worked to assimilate its virtues, how European musicians, in turn, drew inspiration from negro music by way of America. And we would not be comprehensive if we did not signal the general influence exercised by the research of ethnologists specializing in the civilizations of Asia, the Americas, and Africa. Yet, among these, Negro-African civilization is undoubtedly the most distant from the European model.

After reading my article on "Negro-African aesthetics"[50] in the journal *Diogène*, the painter Pierre Soulages said to me, as a kind of commentary: "It is the aesthetics of the twentieth century." I could say, in turn, that the aesthetics of the School of Paris expresses, in modern terms, Negro-African aesthetics. I was a little more convinced of this fact when I read last month in the weekly gazette *L'Express* an article by Pierre Schneider, notably entitled "Matisse: The Painter of Emotion."[51] If the article has retained my attention, it is, first, because Matisse was, along with Picasso, the most important painter of the School of Paris; and Schneider organized the largest exhibit of Matisse's work—painting, sculpture, and drawing—ever, which is being held currently at the Grand Palais; but, above all, because the features retained as characteristics of Matissean art are the very characteristics of Negro Art.

Primarily, art's *utility*, as a technology of essentialization: of participation in the Vital Force. "I would like it to be useful," Matisse said of his oeuvre. And also: "The particularity of modern art is to participate in our life." "The essential" for Matisse, who insisted on color, "was," Schneider notes, that through color, he had found "the old emotional core of men."[52] I would like to dwell on this notion of *emotion*, which in the past I had presented as the cornerstone of Negritude, with the formula—for which some reproached me—that "emotion is negro, as reason Hellenic." Of course, I was being simplistic, but the truth of the idea still holds. I explained myself in my lecture at the Second Congress of Black Artists and Writers,[53] beginning with the definition that Sartre gives in his *Esquisse d'une théorie des émotions* [Outline for a theory of emotions]: "A sudden fall of consciousness into the magical world."[54] I know that there is a physical, animal reaction to emotion, but this is a good thing, ultimately, a disturbance of consciousness that descends from the world of visible and clear things to the one of invisible and vague things, from the world of static appearances to that of dynamic realities, the world of the reason-eye [*raison-œil*] to that of the reason-embrace [*raison-étreinte*]. Schneider appreciates this, writing: "An art founded on intelligence, identifies things; an art founded on emotion identifies with things. The work of art is not a discourse on a subject but a dialogue with it. Imitation gives way to participation."[55] *Participation*: the keyword of Negritude.

It is the power of emotion and the desire for participation that explains, in Matisse, the abandonment of the techniques of classical painting that emerged out of the Renaissance and his adoption of this so special style that I can only qualify as "negro." The modern painter abandons "gradations, the model, shadows, perspective, all that allows him to give the illusion of space, volumes, and weight"[56]: the illusion of objective truth. He thus renounces visual realism in order to create a subjective painting, born under the spell of emotion and provoking not the pleasure of the mind but rather the joy, an often serious, even anxious joy, of the soul. It is in this way that he simplifies the forms, that is to say, the outline of things, replacing it with colors, but flat colors. In the manner of Negro-African painting-sculpture, the essential character of which, once again, is that it is *rhythmed*.

As we have said, it is not a matter of representing this reality, that of the Renaissance, in which everything is a discrete object, where each element of the object is placed next to another, separated and distinct; rather, it is a matter of *re-creating* the world of inner reality, where everything is linked to everything else, everything participates in everything else in an identificatory similitude or in a complementary difference. It is a matter of articulating the ultimate reality of the universe, which is an *interaction* of vital forces: *rhythm*.

This is why Matisse simplifies outline and color to give them more force. The simultaneous repetition and opposition of lines (straight and curved) and colors (in flat tones) gives to the work of art its analogical images and its rhythms: the *rhythmic images* by which I define the poem. These are the anaphoras and chiasms, the alliterations and assonances of a word, the parallelisms and asymmetries that we have noted in the Negro-African poem. With the following difference: that the "figures of thought" of classical painting completely give way to "figures of language." Paradoxically, this painting that tends toward abstraction is, by this very fact, the most *emotive*. In the same way as negro art and Celtic art, whose affinity in abstraction can be explained only by the power of emotion. It is that by using rhythmic signs, which function like image-symbols instead of photographical images [*images-photographies*], a world of objects has been replaced by a world of idea-feelings, a world of intelligible evidence by a world of obscure but fecund forces: *creative* forces.

Conclusion

I have compared Negritude to a contemporary humanism, you might guess, to arrive at a positive conclusion. We militants of Negritude had already begun formulating this proposition in the Latin quarter in the years leading up to the Second World War. Negritude was not, it is not, a racism; it is rather a panhuman humanism that, as such, addresses all races, all continents, but, first, White Europeans and Negro-Africans, who, because they are the most distant from each other, are the most complementary as civilizations. We know that colonization is a universal phenomenon, one that, along with its negative aspects, has certain positive aspects. All the more so because, since the beginning of *Homo sapiens*, when peoples encounter one another, they fight, certainly, but no longer annihilate one another: they mix [*se métissent*]. And above all, they mix their civilizations. This is the most important, for there is no true culture besides that of the *Soul*.

Today, thanks to the improvement and multiplication of means of communication, the world is contracting; men are growing closer to one another. If the old process were to continue, the result would be a general exchange of blood, ideas, and technologies. Yet it very well seems that even if biological *métissage*—the least important kind—occurs naturally, even in the USA, even in South Africa, and despite all restrictions, cultural *métissage*, initiated at the beginning of the century, seems poised to be stopped by opposing imperialisms that each want to impose their particular civilization as a "universal civilization." We militants of Negritude have had the opportunity to clarify our position with the *European Society of Culture*. It was in Rome, before 1960, the year of African independences; this moment gave our thesis its true dimension, its cultural dimension. That thesis is: It is not for Europe to impose on the world its civilization as a universal civilization, even if we are the first to acknowledge the fecundating power of some its values, such as the spirit of method and organization, for which rationality means efficacy. It is for all of us, together—all continents, races, and nations—to build the *Civilization of the Universal*, to which every different civilization will contribute its most creative values—most creative because they are the most complementary.

The civilization of the twenty-first century—which is being prepared by today's civilization—will surely be *superindustrial*, that is, technological. It will be a *humanism* or a *barbarism* insofar as the peoples of the Third World, and among them Black peoples, will have brought their contributions to this civilization. Like Plato, Aristotle, the founder of European rationalism, gave primacy to intuitive reason over discursive reason, while bringing together the two reasons. This we all too often forget.

NOTES

Léopold Sédar Senghor, "Négritude et modernité ou la Négritude est un humanisme du XXe siècle," in *Liberté 3: Négritude et civilisation de l'universel* (Seuil, 1977), 215–42. The text was first given as a talk "to Scandinavian Universities" in May 1970; the talk was repeated at the Universities of Lund, Stockholm, Uppsala, and Helsinki.

[Epigraph: In modern transcription: *Nit moo di garabu nit*. The original proverb says, *Nit, nitéëy (mooy) garabam* (The remedy of the person is to act like a person).—Eds.]

1. Interview with Abiola Irele, in *Dakar-Matin*. [We have not been able to locate an interview with Irele in any issue of *Dakar-Matin*, published from September 1969 to May 1970, when Senghor left Senegal for his talks in Sweden and Finland.—Eds.]

2. Jean-Paul Sartre, "Orphée noir," preface to Léopold Sédar Senghor, *Anthologie de la nouvelle poésie nègre et malgache de langue française* (Presses universitaires de France, 1948), xv.

3. Abiola Irele develops this idea in "Negritude-Literature and Ideology," *Journal of Modern African Studies* 3, no 4 (1965): 520, 523.

4. Erica Simon, *Réveil national et culture populaire en Scandinavie: La genèse de la 'højskole' nordique, 1844–1878* (Presses universitaires de France, 1960).

5. [Erica Simon, "L'Université de Grundtvig," *Études Germaniques* 22, no. 3 (1967): 445–48.—Eds.]

6. Cf. Marcel Griaule, *Dieu d'Eau* (Du Chêne, 1948); Geneviève Calame-Griaule, *Ethnologie et langage: La parole chez les Dogon* (Gallimard, 1965), 93–103.

7. By "existent" [*existant*], I mean what is living, while "*being*" [*étant*] must be understood in a more general sense as a contingent element of Being [*l'Être*]. [See chapter 1, note 46, of this volume for a discussion of these terms and their translation.—Eds.]

8. Cf. Alfred Croiset and Maurice Croiset, *Manuel d'histoire de la littérature grecque à l'usage des lycées et collèges* (Fontemoing, 1990), 221.

9. Cf. Alexis Kagamé, *La philosophie bantu-rwandaise de l'Être* (Académie royale des sciences coloniale, 1956).

10. Cf. Janheinz Jahn, *Muntu, l'homme africain et la culture néo-africaine*, trans. Brian de Martinoir (Seuil, 1958). The original text, in German, appeared in 1952 with Diedrichs Verlag in Dusseldorf-Cologne. [Jahn Janheinz, *Muntu: Umrisse der neoafricanschen Kultur* (Eugen Diederichs Verlag, 1952).—Eds.]

11. Janheinz, *Muntu*, 111–14.

12. Placide Tempels, *La Philosophie bantoue*, trans. A. Rubbens (Présence Africaine, 1949), 35.

13. Calame-Griaule, *Ethnologie et langage*, 32–48. [Senghor writes *kikinu*, not *kikínu*, as it is spelled in Calame-Griaule.—Eds.]

14. [The citation comes from Calame-Griaule, *Ethnologie et langage*, 44; the "synoptic table" appears on the preceding page.—Eds.]

15. [The Fali are an ethnic group of northern Cameroon and northeastern Nigeria. The word *fali* comes from Pulaar and means "perched," referring to the way the Fali settlements are perched on the sides of mountains.—Eds.]

16. Cited by Louis-Vincent Thomas in "Pour un programme d'études théoriques des religions et d'un humanisme africains," *Présence Africaine* 37, no. 2 (1961): 68.

17. Engelbert Mveng, *Les sources grecques de l'histoire négro-africaine: Depuis Homère jusqu'à Strabon* (Présence Africaine, 1972). [Senghor gives the publication year as 1969, but he also owned the 1972 edition.—Eds.]

18. The last Congress of African Prehistorians, held in Addis Ababa, locates the emergence around 5,500,000 years BC. [Senghor is referring to the Seventh Pan-African Congress of Prehistory and Quaternary Studies (Addis Ababa, Ethiopia, 1917).—Eds.]

19. Cf. the preceding note.

20. Yves Coppens, "L'Afrique équatoriale: Une étape de l'histoire de l'humanité," in *Cahiers des explorateurs: Bulletin de la société et des voyageurs français* 19 (December 1967): 18–19.

21. "5,500,000 years," according to the Congress of Africanist Prehistorians.

22. Thomas, "Pour un programme," 61.

23. Cf. Calame-Griaule, *Ethnologie et langage*, 48–57.

24. [Camara Laye, *L'enfant noir* (1953; reprint, Plon, 1976).—Eds.]

25. [Laye, *L'enfant noir*, 35.—Eds.]

26. [Frontstalag 230, also known as Camp de la Chauvinerie, in Poitiers, was one of the camps where Senghor was held as a prisoner of war during World War II.—Eds.]

27. In Senegal, beautiful young women are called *baxai* by young men, which means "goodness" [*bonté*]. [*Baxai* or, in modern transcription, *baaxaay*, is less common compared to the substantive *mbaax gi*, "goodness"; both are based on the adjective *baax* "good."—Eds.]

28. Cf. Calame-Griaule, "Physiologie de la Fécondation par la Parole," in *Ethnologie et langage*, 74–80.

29. Sartre, "Orphée noir," xv.

30. Jacques Rueff, *Les dieux et les rois: Regards sur le pouvoir créateur* (Hachette, 1968).

31. Gaëtan Picon, "D'un style de l'esprit contemporain," in *Panorama des idées contemporaines*, ed. Gaëtan Picon (Gallimard, 1957), 5–36.

32. [Picon, "D'un style de l'esprit contemporain," 25.—Eds.]

33. [Senghor is inflecting Bergson's thinking of the *étreinte*. Bergson wrote that "if there is finality in the world of life, it embraces life in a single, indivisible embrace [*étreinte*]." Henri Bergson, *L'évolution créatrice* (Félix Alcan, 1908), 47. For an overview of Bergsonian thought in Senghor, see Souleymane Bachir Diagne, "Bergson et la pensée de L. S. Senghor," *La lettre du Collège de France* 29 (2010): 10–11.—Eds.]

34. Jahn, *Muntu*, 105.

35. Picon, "D'un style de l'esprit contemporain," 30.

36. Cf. Georges Gusdorf, *La parole* (Presses universitaires de France, 1953). [It is possible Senghor was referring to a later edition, from 1956 or 1960.—Eds.]

37. [In addition to texts such as *Being and Time*, *What Is Called Thinking?*, and *On the Way to Language*, Senghor likely also has in mind Heidegger's essay "The Origin of the Work of Art" (Der Ursprung des Kunstwerkes) (1935–36), which was published by Reclam in 1950 and again in 1960, but drafted much earlier, in the 1930s. For an English translation, see "The Origin of the Work of Art," trans. Julian Young and Kenneth Haynes, in *Martin Heidegger: Off the Beaten Track*, ed. Julian Young and Kenneth Haynes (Cambridge University Press, 2002), 1–10. For an overview of speech, language, and the *logos* in Heidegger, see Joseph J. Kockelmans, ed., *On Heidegger and Language* (Northwestern University Press, 1972); Françoise Dastur, *Heidegger: La question du Logos* (Vrin, 2007). On Heidegger and Senghor, see Roxanna Curto, "Senghor and Heidegger: Negritude's Appropriation of German Phenomenology," *French Literature Series* 37 (2010): 27–41; El Hadj Ibrahima Sall, *Le lieu des regards: Martin Heidegger lecteur de Léopold Sédar Senghor* (Les éditions Maguilen, 1990).—Eds.]

38. [Senghor is drawing these translations from Heidegger's understanding of thinking as *gathering*; for an overview of these meanings and translations, see Adam Knowles, "Gathering (*Sammeln, Sammlung*)," in *The Cambridge Heidegger Lexicon*, ed. Mark A. Wrathall (Cambridge University Press, 2021), 349–51.—Eds.]

39. Cited in Pierre Trotignon, *Heidegger: Sa vie, son œuvre avec un exposé de sa poésie* (Presses universitaires de France, 1965), 112, 113.

40. Rueff, *Les dieux et les rois*, 313. [We have used the English translation from Jacques Rueff, *The Gods and the Kings: A Glance at Creative Power* (Macmillan, 1973), 245–46.—Eds.]

41. Cited in Henri Guillemin, *L'arrière-pensée de Jaurès* (Gallimard, 1966), 22, after *La Dépêche de Toulouse* (June 25, 1891). [The citation from Jaurès comes from an open letter to Camille Pelletan published on the front page of *La Dépêche*. Jean Jaurès, "Dieu: À Monsieur Pelletan," *La Dépêche de Toulouse*, June 25, 1891, 1.—Eds.]

42. Louis de Broglie, *Matière et Lumière* ([1937; reprint, 1941; and] Albin Michel, 1961), 75, cited in Rueff, *Les dieux et les rois*, 16–17.

43. [Rueff, *Les dieux et les rois*, 31; Rueff, *The Gods and the Kings*, 19–20.—Eds.]

44. [Jacques Maritain, *L'Humanisme intégral: Problèmes temporels et spirituels d'une nouvelle chrétienté* (Fernand Aubier, 1936).—Eds.].

45. Inventor of the *futurology* [*la prospective*], the *métis* Franco-Senegalese Gaston Berger was born in Saint-Louis in Senegal at the end of the twentieth century.

46. Karl Marx, "Le travail aliéné," trans. Maximilien Rubel, *Revue socialiste* 3 (February 1947): 161. [Friedrich Engels, *Dialectique de la nature*, trans. Denise Naville (Librairie Marcel Rivière, 1948).—Eds.]

47. [We have been unable to locate the precise source of this citation; it is possibly a biblical reference or an allusion to Heidegger's *Dasein*.—Eds.]

48. Picon, "D'un style de l'esprit contemporain," 34.

49. [Marx, "Le travail aliéné," 161.—Eds.]

50. Léopold Sédar Senghor, "L'esthétique négro-africaine," *Diogène* 16 (1956): 43–61.

51. Pierre Schneider, "Matisse: Peintre de l'émotion," *L'Express*, April 20–26, 1970, 86–89. Cf. also *Liberté 1: Négritude et humanisme* (Seuil, 1964), 202–17. [Senghor is referring readers to his essay "L'ésthetique négro-africaine" (Negro-African aesthetics).—Eds.]

52. [Schneider, "Matisse," 88.—Eds.]

53. [The talk, which was entitled "Éléments constructifs d'une civilisation d'inspiration négro-africaine," was published by Présence Africaine; Léopold Sédar Senghor, "Éléments constructifs d'une civilisation d'inspiration négro-africaine," in Deuxième Congrès des écrivains et artistes noirs [Rome, 26 mars–1er avril 1959], vol. 1, "L'Unité des cultures négro-africaines," special issue, *Présence Africaine* (1959): 249–79. Cf. Léopold Sédar Senghor, "Éléments constitutifs d'une civilisation d'inspiration négro-africaine," in *Liberté 1: Négritude et humanisme* (Seuil 1964), 252–86.—Eds.]

54. [Jean-Paul Sartre, *Esquisse d'une théorie des émotions* (1938; reprint, Hermann, 1975), 62.—Eds.]

55. [Schneider, "Matisse," 88.—Eds.]

56. Schneider, "Matisse," 87.

4

Concerning Negritude

In my opinion, and regardless of what is being said, we are currently witnessing the triumph of negritude (as I myself understand it, in any case).
—LÉON-GONTRAN DAMAS, "La Négritude en question," 1971

If I have chosen to address the question of Negritude at the start of this colloquium, it is because our former colonizers have continually posed the matter from the outset, and throughout our respective emancipation movements, whether we were Negro-Americans or Negro-Africans.

They treated us as colonial subjects [*sujets*] or as second-class citizens [*citoyens de seconde zone*]. More profoundly, they denied, on the one hand, that we had a *civilization*—at least a civilization that was equal to, yet different from, their own. On the other hand, they denied us the right to recognize this *difference*, to cultivate it, and to demand, in its name, a form of equality that was not identical but complementary. Nothing is more illustrative in this respect than the document entitled "Radicalism and Sedition among the Negroes as Reflected in their Publications," published by the American Senate in 1919.[1] We find therein the remarkable sentence: "Underlying these more salient points is the increasingly emphasized feeling of a race consciousness, in many of these publications always antagonistic to the white race, and openly, defiantly assertive of its own equality and even superiority." I emphasize the term *race consciousness*.

What is worse, White people managed to raise the matter of Negritude among Negroes themselves. I am not targeting those who disagree with us with respect to the content of Negritude, its basic tenets. It is good for the concept to be examined, discussed, deepened, and enriched from generation to generation. I will come back to this. I am speaking about the growing number of those who go about spouting more or less the following language at us: "Why speak of Negritude and define ourselves by race or by the color of our skin?" And, in a reversal of roles, taking effect for cause and victim for executioner, they conclude, sententiously: "Racism calls for counterracism." We heard similar statements at the Pan-African Festival of Algiers [1969], which, as we all know, was inspired by the desire of certain so-called "revolutionaries" to undermine Negritude, and even Arabism.

The issues of Negritude can thus be expressed as follows.

1 Are there, for Negroes, specific problems arising from the sole fact that they have Black skin or that they belong to a different *ethnicity* than White people and East Asians [*Jaunes*]?
2 What are these problems and in what terms are they posed?

But we must define the word before going any further.

What Is Negritude?

The term "negritude" has often been contested as a word before being contested as a concept. And other words have been proposed as substitutes: *melaninness* [*mélanité*], *Africanness* [*africanité*]. One could go on. And why not *Ethiopianness* [*éthiopité*] or *Ethiopianity* [*éthiopianité*]? I am all the more at liberty to defend the term since I was not the one who coined it, as has often wrongly been claimed; it was Aimé Césaire.

First and foremost, there is the fact that Césaire formed the word according to the most orthodox rules of the French language. I refer you to Maurice Grévisse's grammar of French, *Le Bon Usage*,[2] and to two studies that the University of Strasbourg dedicated to the suffixes *-ité* (from the Latin *-itas*) and *-itude* (from the Latin *-itudo*), which my friend Professor Robert Schilling shared with me.[3] These two suffixes, used with the same meaning in Low Latin, serve today to form abstract nouns derived from adjectives. They express a condition or a state, a quality or a flaw, and the manner of expressing them. It is in this way that the *Petit Robert* defines the word "Latinness" [*latinité*]: "1. Way of writing or speaking Latin. Latin character; 2. (1835) the Latin world, Latin civilization. *The spirit of Latinness.*" Following this model, we could also define Negritude as "the Negro's manner of expression. Negro character. The negro world, negro civilization." Césaire, Damas, and I—the first defendants of Negritude in France, rather than its founders—never claimed otherwise.

It is true, people have not failed to reproach Césaire for choosing the word *negritude* instead of *Negroness* [*negrite*]. Once again, the two words have the same meaning, formed as they are with suffixes having the same meaning; it is only that the suffix-*itude* is more learned. But, according to the Strasbourg grammarians, it serves to form less abstract words, designating a state more often than a quality. This has allowed me, elsewhere, to use the word *Arabness* [*arabité*] in some cases, and *Berberitude* [*berbéritude*] in others. We also find the word *nigritudo* in Latin, in Pliny. It has a concrete meaning and signifies "the fact of being black, the color black, blackness [*la noirceur*]." And the word *nigritude* exists in English with the same meaning—if we are to believe *Harrap's* French-English dictionary.[4] As we will see, however, in various places the meaning has remained quite concrete. The originality of the French word is to have moved from the concrete to the abstract: from the material to the spiritual.

Therefore, to return to the matter of Negritude, Césaire defines it as follows: "Negritude is the simple acknowledgment of the fact of being Black, and the acceptance of this fact, of our destiny as Black people, of our history and our culture."[5] Indeed, as I had a chance to explain in a recent talk, "Negritude and Modernity," the word—and, consequently, the concept—has a double meaning: objective and subjective.[6]

Objectively, Negritude is a fact: a *culture*. It is the sum total of the values—economic and political, intellectual and moral, artistic and social—not only of the peoples of Black Africa but also of Black minorities of the Americas and even of Asia and Oceania. I am speaking of the peoples of Black Africa who built civilizations and developed the arts that historians, specialists of the human sciences, and art critics discovered and began glorifying at the turn of the century. To avoid focusing solely on Negro-Americans, whose ancestors came from Africa, anthropologists, ethnologists, and sociologists have frequently underscored the civilizational affinities between the Black peoples of Africa, Asia, and Oceania. Greek writers had already acknowledged these affinities, calling all Black peoples *Ethiopians*, only distinguishing between "Easterners" (Asian) and "Westerners" (African). Is it not significant that the writing system of the first Indian civilization—that of Mohenjo-Daro and Harappa—which flourished around 2500 BC, served to express a Dravidian language: a Black people's language?[7]

Subjectively, Negritude is "the acceptance of this fact" of civilization and, prospectively, its projection in history as it unfolds, in the negro civilization to be reborn and fulfilled. This is, in short, the task the militants of Negritude set for themselves: to accept the civilizational values of the Black world, to realize and fecundate them, with foreign contributions if necessary, in order to live them by oneself and for oneself, but also to make them be lived by and for Others, offering in this way the contribution of the new Negroes [*les Nègres nouveaux*] to the *Civilization of the Universal.*

It is therefore understood that in the current exposé, the word "negritude" refers to the concept in its most general sense, thus encompassing all of the cultural movements initiated by a luminary or by a group of Negroes: the Niagara and *Negro Renaissance* movements in the United States; the Haitian School movement in the Antilles; the Anglophone *African Personality* movement in Africa; and the Francophone movement of "Negritude" in both the Antilles and in Africa.

Beyond terminology, the *quarrel of Negritude* arose from several causes, which get to the heart of things—to the complexity of the concept. These are, besides the ambivalence of the term, the disagreements between Anglophones and Francophones, Negro-Americans and Negro-Africans, as well as the conflict between generations. But let us not forget that the dispute first arose because of White people and continues to be fueled by them on all sides.

Anglophonie and Francophonie

In the dispute between Anglophones and Francophones, I shall distinguish both the pretext and the cause.

First, the pretext, which arises from the persistence, between the English and the French, in the spirit of Fashoda,[8] of petty rivalries to maintain a predominant cultural influence over Black Africa. I am not taking sides; I am merely observing. People went so far as to reproach us for having used a "French word" to name the essence of Black civilization. As if we were not *Francophones*, as if, in elaborating the concept, we had not been inspired in part by Negro-Americans and, more specifically, by the movement Alain Locke had baptized under the name *Renaissance*, which is of French origin. Both languages and thus both civilizations have influenced one another greatly.

I do not wish to dwell on the pretext, as it was White people who raised it and, fortunately, as this colloquium proves, the spirit of Fashoda is dwindling in Black Africa. What I would like, however, is to put forward an argument here that to me seems important. Often, in Senegal, when we are faced with a problem, we turn to our Negro-African civilization to examine the matter: to see if this civilization does not offer us the most effective solution. And it is not uncommon that it has offered that to us, be it in the realm of politics or economics, culture or health, as several of the papers you will hear during this conference shall demonstrate. So then I wondered if our languages might provide a concept similar to negritude. And indeed, this concept exists. In Pulaar, for example. In this Negro-African language, which is spoken throughout the region spanning from Mauritania to Tchad, across four thousand kilometers, *pull-o* means "the Pulo, the Pulo man."[9] Numerous words have been formed from the radical *pul-*, two of which are of particular interest. There is, on the one hand, *pul-aa-gu*, which means, according to [Henri] Gaden,[10] "the sum total of qualities characteristic of the Fulɓe." On the other hand, *pul-aa-gal*, which means: "the manner in which these qualities are manifested by an individual Pulo." These are, in short, the two meanings that correspond respectively to *objective* negritude and *subjective* negritude. In fact, *pulaagu* belongs to the noun class for which the suffix *-gu* serves to form abstract words indicating a state or a quality, whereas *pulaagal* belongs to the noun class for which the suffix *-gal* serves to form words indicating "a manner of being or acting." There is even a verb *fu-laa-de* which means "to behave like a Pulo." The verb is interesting because, among other reasons, it is in the *middle voice*[11] and because the three aforementioned words (*ful-aa-de, pul-aa-gu*, and *pul-aa-gal*) indicate that the action performed or experienced, in the grammatical sense of the terms, falls back on the subject.

Significantly, English-speaking Negro-Africans asked us: "But why have you coined a term that makes reference to color in order to express this idea which is so dear to us?" We reply that we did so in order to respect the facts: linguistic rules and ethno-sociological realities. In nearly every language, the word used to name a people's civilization refers to the country, to the ethnicity, or perhaps to skin color. "Latinness," "Germanness," "Indianness," "Europeanness" refer to the ethnicity or to the country. But there are also some words designating people that invoke color: "Ethiopian" (from the Greek *aithiops*, "burnt, black"), "Sudanese" (from the Arabic *sudan*, "black"), "Beidane" for Moor (from the Arabic *beidan*, "white"). From which "Ethiopianness," "Sudaneseness," and "Beidanness" are formed. White people see us as *Black* people, and, in our Negro-African languages, we see ourselves and call ourselves as such, without shame and even with a bit of pride.

Even more significantly, I know that our Anglophone brothers have begun to use the term "African personality." This expression can only be translated into French by the word "Africanity" [*Africanité*]. It is the sum of African peoples' civilizational values. But African peoples, to simplify the question, belong to at least two civilizations: the Arabo-Berber civilization and the Negro-African civilization. Hence, it follows that "African civilization," unified in the way Leo Frobenius believed it to be (he dedicated a book to the topic that bears the same title) has two different cultural expressions of which it is the symbiosis. "African personality," therefore, could not legitimately designate Negritude. If we wish to "call a spade a spade," we must, just as Negro-Americans do, use the words "blackness" or "Negroness."[12] Especially since the English suffix *-ness* corresponds to the French *-ité* and *-itude*. It is true, as I mentioned earlier, that I have found the word "nigritude" in *Harrap's* English-French dictionary, but there it means, concretely, "blackness [*noirceur*]."

The most justified criticism that English-speaking Negro-Americans level at us is that, having been trained by the French, we too frequently lapse into abstraction. It is true that, as Francophones, we are often quick to draw conclusions and create concepts from insufficiently studied material, for which we hasten to invent new words. Under the influence of Anglo-Saxon pragmatism and that of the Black temperament, our Anglophone brothers opted to study the Negro-African Man, the *Homo aethiopicus*, concretely: in his physical environment, according to his anthropological and ethnological features, and ultimately his social life, with a particular focus on its cultural manifestations. And in their universities, they have created numerous *Institutes of African Studies*, in the same vein as American *African Studies Centers*.

All of this, of course, is true. And yet the truth is not that simple. Those of us who, during the 1930s and '40s, initiated the "Negritude Movement" in the French-speaking world had started off pursuing—or were pursuing concurrently—their studies in linguistics, ethnology, and even prehistory. And despite their ethos of abstraction, the French had founded, not only in North Africa but also in Black Africa, research institutes whose mission was to study, in addition to the people, the structures and the characteristic elements of Arabo-Berber and Negro-African civilizations. I acknowledge that, since Independence, we French-speaking Negro-Africans have had a tendency to put the political before the economic and the economic before the cultural—instead of inverting the order of the terms, that is to say, the order of priorities and investments. This was obvious at the Pan-African Festival of Algiers, where some people wanted to relegate Negritude and Arabism to the folklore museum.

And so the truth is not that simple: it is more nuanced. This is to say, together, Anglophone and Francophone Negroes, we must lead the charge on two fronts: one on the level of concrete field and laboratory studies, the other on the level of dialectics and, more precisely, conceptualization. Especially since, as I have already demonstrated for Pulaar, our languages, too, have a whole series of processes for the formation of abstract words, *concept-words*. In our ideological struggle—for that is the crux of the problem—we simultaneously require facts, which scientific research alone can provide, as well as concepts, which are the other instrument of dialectical reasoning. This is why, far from limiting ourselves to "Negritude" and "Negroness" [*négrité*], we have taken up or created terms such as *négrie* or *nègrerie* (the global Black community), *Négritie* or the older *Nigritie* (the country of Black people), and *Négrisme* (Black ideology in the sense of subjective negritude).

Negro-Americans and Negro-Africans

The dispute between Negro-Americans and Negro-Africans is less serious than it appears. In reality, it is a matter of a simple gap—in time and in space. First and foremost, this is due to the fact that the shared language between Negroes from the United States, on the one hand, and Anglophone Negroes from the Antilles and Africa, on the other, facilitated understanding and, consequently, unity of action. And then, among Francophone Negro-Americans and Francophone Negroes from Africa, the French-speaking Antilles served as a link. It is thanks to the Martinican Paulette Nardal, founder of the *Revue du Monde noir* in the 1930s, that I met Alain Locke and Mercer Cook; thanks to the Guyanese Léon Damas, that I met Langston Hughes and Countee Cullen. I met them but, more importantly, read them. It is in this way that the movement of Negritude, in the general sense of the term—the discovery of Black values and the realization by the Negro of his condition—started in the United States of America. The founders of "Negritude" in the French-speaking world never ceased to acknowledge this, as Léon Damas affirmed yet again last month in the March 16, 1971, issue of the weekly newspaper *Jeune Afrique*.[13] It is from the interview he gave in this paper that I have drawn the epigraph to my talk. Our movement, which started in Paris, was greatly favored by the Niagara Movement, the Negro Renaissance, and even by Garveyism.

Before going any further, I would like to examine these three movements. Which will allow us to better distinguish the essential elements of the problem—to better judge the convergences and divergences between Negro-Americans and Negro-Africans.

One must always start with W. E. B. Du Bois, who was, in fact, as Lilyan Kesteloot writes, the real "father of the Negritude movement,"[14] since he was the first to conceptualize it in its totality and its specificity, its particular aspects and its finality, its objectives and its methods. For Du Bois, there is first the condition of the Negro in the United States of America. Then, there is the *image* that the White man has of him, which is that of a second-class citizen: of a man-child, feckless and moronic, with intellectual and moral qualities that are not, and cannot be, developed. This image was also engrained in the Negro's mind. "It is a peculiar sensation, this double-consciousness, this sense of always looking at one's self through the eyes of others, of measuring one's soul by the tape of a world that looks on in amused contempt and pity."[15] It is these feelings, which I have emphasized, that led the White man to impose on the Negro, in American society, an objective condition that can be called, broadly, "racial discrimination": The Negro, treated as a subhuman, is denied some of his rights in all spheres, whether in economics or politics, culture or social welfare.

After having thus analyzed the condition—subjective and objective—of the Negro-American from a theoretical perspective, Du Bois spells out the goals that needed to be reached in order to deliver the Negro from this condition. First of all, it was a matter of erasing the image of the *senseless childlike Negro* from the minds of White people, and more importantly the minds of Black people, by replacing it with the authentic image of a classical Africa, perceived as a civilization: "a self-sufficient universe." Thus would arise, for the Negro-American, the desire—and a sustained effort—to "be himself, before anything else," akin to the new image of the African. On the other hand, it was a matter of ending "racial discrimination," that is, all the barriers—economic and political, cultural and social—that made Negroes second-class citizens. In short, it was a question of transforming the Negro-American internally and externally at the same time. Internally, through education and training; externally, through an increasingly intense pressure on the American government and public opinion.

It is these two goals that Du Bois's theoretical and practical engagements address. First, *The Souls of Black Folk*, his major work. One can now say that the source of Negritude springs from this work. But this thinker was also a man of action who played an important role in the life and organization of the movement: in the Americas, of course, but also in Europe and in Africa. Here, I will note only the decisive role he played in the creation of the National Association for the Advancement of Colored People (NAACP), whose journal, *The Crisis*, he edited; as well as his other role in organizing the first four "Pan-African Congresses," serving as general secretary for the first of these.

The ideas behind W. E. B. Du Bois's action would be discussed, deepened, and expanded not only in the United States but also in the Antilles and in Africa. They did not influence us directly, however. When I say "us," I am referring to Negro-Africans in general and the founders of the Francophone movement of Negritude in particular. These ideas influenced us through Marcus Garvey and the Negro Renaissance.

By putting an emphasis on Africa, its ancientness, its nobility, and its beauty, and by directly engaging the Black masses and not just the intellectuals, Garvey gave his movement global resonance, as his militantly titled weekly journal, *The Negro World*, would have it. And, in actual fact, it is the convergence of Garvey's movement with the Pan-African Congresses that influenced, primarily and most profoundly, Black African politicians: Blaise Diagne and Galandou Diouf, members of the French parliament from Senegal, but above all, future Anglophone leaders such as Nnamdi Azikiwe, Kwame Nkrumah, and Jomo Kenyatta. I will be sure not to forget the proletarian current that, despite its communistic tendencies, was not less influenced by Du Bois and Garvey. I recall *La Voix des Nègres* [The Negroes' voice], a Parisian newspaper, led by Tiemoko Garan Kouyate and Lamine Senghor in the wake of the First World War.

However, in the Latin Quarter in the 1930s, we were above all responsive to the ideas and action of the Negro Renaissance, some of the most dynamic representatives of which we met in Paris. Damas has mentioned this in his interview. As for me, I used to read *The Crisis* and *Opportunity*, the newspaper of the National Urban League, regularly; but also the *Journal of Negro History*, which had been founded by Carter G. Woodson and featured numerous articles about Africa. But my bedside reading was *The New Negro*—"the manifesto-anthology," as Jean Wagner puts it—, which Alain Locke had edited.[16] Nanci Cunard's *Negro Anthology*, published in 1934, was to join it in my library.[17] As we will soon see, it turns out to be less the theory than the practice of Negritude, I mean the novel and more importantly the poetry of the Negro Renaissance, that influenced us.

Having thus analyzed Negro-American influences, where does the gap originate? I do not mean the dispute. It arises from the historical, geographical, and cultural context. It is, fundamentally, because Negro-Americans and Antilleans, even the Francophones, have inherited, in their blood and soul, a painful past of enslavement. For one, two, three centuries, they were cut off physically and, more seriously, spiritually from the source, which had for more than five million years sustained, *informed*, their ancestors: cut off from Mother Africa. For, it is now proven that the rise of the humankind began in Africa some 5,500,000 years ago.

For us Negro-Africans, the situation was different. We were, practically, the first young people to pursue higher education in Europe. Most of us had first lived in rural areas, where White people were scarce, in a civilization that had not yet disintegrated and that preserved, along with its moral foundation, its human qualities [*sens humain*] and its harmony. As I read the first pages of Leo Frobenius's *History of African Civilization*, I relived my *Sereer* childhood in the Kingdom of the Sine—even though this "kingdom" had been reduced to a "protectorate."[18] I relived, among other scenes, the king Koumba Ndofène Diouf's visits to my father. During these visits, all feelings were noble, all demeanors polite, and all words beautiful. Later, in Dakar, at the Catholic middle school, when the headmaster wanted to shame us for our past, by denying that we had a "civilization," we did not fail to react strongly, even though we were seminarians. This is when the idea took hold in the deepest part of my being [*au plus profond de mon moi*]: the *idea*, rather than the word, of a *different, yet equal, Black civilization*. Since these middle-school years, my goal or, more precisely, my life's mission has been, I believe, to prove and to live out this idea. And my case is not exceptional; it is, on the contrary, typical. That is why I mention it.

Black students of my generation thus set off for Europe, minds and senses fully alert, eager not only to learn the arts and sciences of White peoples but also to discover evidence of the greatness of Africa and its African peoples. Hence, our interest in ethnology, among other sciences. It was then, during the interwar period, the great era of Europe's discovery of Africa. Historians and prehistorians, ethnologists and linguists, especially writers and artists, in England, in Germany, and above all in France, contended for the discovery of Africa in its remote antiquity, its most original originality: *Ur-Africa*, as the Germans used to say. This was the moment of the "Negro Revolution," as Emmanuel Berl puts it, in which the Negro-Americans participated. This revolutionized European music and visual arts and was not without consequence for European thought and its literature—despite what has been said about it.

European scholars, artists, and writers thus taught us to better understand African life, not in its living flavors but in its irreplaceable civilizational values. The role of Negro-Americans was different. They did not exactly teach us to rebel morally but rather to organize socially if not politically and, above all, *to create*. The poets of the Negro Renaissance who influenced us the most were Langston Hughes and Claude McKay, Jean Toomer and James Weldon Johnson,

Sterling Brown and Franck Marshall Davis. They showed us the value of the movement through action: the possibility, by first creating works of art, of reviving and redeeming Negro-African civilization.

I mean "the influence" of Negro-Americans on Negro-Africans. But, because the *conditions*, the respective experiences, of Negro-Americans were different from Negro-Africans, the negritude of each of the two groups, consequently, had to take on different colors. To better understand these differences within the unity of negritude, one need only to read carefully *The Militant Black Writer*, a book published by the University of Wisconsin.[19] In the first part, entitled "African Voices of Protest,"[20] Mercer Cook examines contemporary Negro-African literature, while Stephen E. Henderson examines Negro-American literature in the second part, entitled "Survival Motion: A Study of the Black Writer and the Black Revolution in America."[21] I noted, in Henderson, these meaningful lines, from Leroux [*sic*] Bennett: "The whole corpus of the tradition . . . is compressed into the folk myth of *Soul*, the American counterpart of the African *Negritude*, a distinct quality of *Negro-ness* growing out of the Negro's experience and not his genes. *Soul* is a metaphorical evocation of Negro being as expressed in the Negro tradition. It is the feeling with which an artist invests his creation, the style with which a man lives his life. It is, above all, the spirit more than the letter: a certain way of feeling, a certain way of expressing oneself, a certain way of being."[22]

Our entire conception of Negritude—as a state and as an expression—is confirmed in these lines. Better, even the choice of the word—and the idea—of *Soul* recalls a certain popular and African way. It was in 1941, in a "Senegalese" prisoner-of-war camp. As I discussed with my companions, peasants, the respective qualities of White Europeans and Negro-Africans, one of them, Mbaye Diop, told me in Wolof: *Ñoo nu ëpp xel, noo leen ëpp fit.*[23] Which means: "They have more spirit than us, we have more *soul* than them."[24] It remains the case that Negroes from the other side of the Atlantic, be they from the United States of America, the United States of Brazil, or the Antilles, insist on the specificity of their condition given their unique experience: on social heredity more than biological heredity. And some Antilleans who identify with Marxism, like the Haitian René Depestre, go so far as to reduce Negritude to this *historical* experience and speak of "mysticism," of "mystification" even, when it comes to those who, like me and numerous Negro-Africans, focus on ethnicity.

Without sharing their opinion, I, as a Francophone, understand them all the better. Of course, Francophone Negroes from Africa experienced neither deportation to the Americas nor slavery on the plantations. However, the French politics of *assimilation* has, in some ways, I mean morally, exiled and subjugated us: *depersonalized* us. Hence, a trauma that African Anglophones have not felt, do not feel. It remains the case that to accuse us of "mysticism" alone, as Depestre does, is to jump too quickly to conclusions. But we have now reached the last part of my talk, which will address the questions raised by *the conflict of generations.*

Conflict of Generations

It is natural, as a famous writer would have it, and it is good that young people begin life with "insults in their mouth."[25] When I detect echoes of Damas, Césaire, or Senghor in the poems that young French-speaking Black writers send me to read, I have a hard time fighting off the urge to yawn. And I think to myself: "This is not good." And, as I read, I hear a writer less than thirty years old exclaim: "Césaire, Damas, and Senghor's Negritude must be surpassed, it is already surpassed," I clap with ten hands as we say in Senegal.[26] Once again, every generation, every thinker, every writer, every artist, every politician, must, in his own way and for his part, deepen and enrich Negritude. Must go beyond the Negritude of his predecessors. *But to go beyond is not to renounce,* especially since going beyond does not imply superiority but difference in quality: a new way of seeing, living, and speaking, according to new circumstances. Naturally, Negritude should be transposed from the Francophone to the Anglophone world. The problem should therefore be, for young poets, for example, to surpass Countee Cullen, Claude McKay, and even Langston Hughes. *That is the question.*

I thus will begin by agreeing with Tchicaya U Tam'si, who, when asked, "What is Negritude?" responds: "Negritude is a matter of generation as well as of a school of thought. I am of a different generation and another school of thought, and I am a laugher who cannot resist the urge to burst out in laughter whenever someone tries to teach me a lesson."[27] Tchicaya does not, therefore, reject Negritude; he only wants to add his contribution to the movement, freely. And he does so magnificently, because his poetry is one of the newest from the continent while remaining Negro, and even Congolese.

Then there is Wole Soyinka, who tells us: "A tiger does not proclaim his tigritude, a tiger pounces." I refer you to the German Janheinz Jahn's *History of Neo-African Literature.*[28] On pages 242 and 243 of the French edition, he points out that White critics had already hurried to make the essential proposition, "the tiger pounces," vanish in order to sow discord between African partisans of Negritude and those of *African personality.* But let us give the floor to the Nigerian writer quoted by Jahn: "I was trying to distinguish between propaganda and true poetic creativity. I was saying in other words that what one expected from poetry was an intrinsic poetic quality, not a mere label."[29]

In reality, this is an old debate: It dates back to the dawn of the movement. Du Bois declared himself proud to be a "propagandist." However, Alain Locke, his spiritual son, preferred to "choose art and put propaganda aside."[30] We had the same conversations among Francophones in the 1930s and the 1940s. And I was inclined to the solution recommended by Soyinka. Thus, in 1948, I wrote the following about our friend David Diop, who was taken from us too soon: "We have no doubt that David Diop will continue to grow in humanity as he grows in age. He will understand that what constitutes the Negritude of a poem is less its theme than its style, the emotional warmth that gives life to words, that transmutes speech [*la parole*] into verb [*le verbe*]."[31] Moreover, Jahn agrees with us when he concludes after quoting Soyinka: "The theorists of Negritude did not have any other pretense. . . ."[32]

The disagreement is therefore not between "negritude" and "tigritude," and [Es'kia] Mphahlele does not particularly shock me when he promotes an "individual realism," because he is a Negro and, being himself, he cannot but express "his way of being negro." It is indeed true that the zebra cannot get rid of its stripes, nor the tiger its tigritude, and that one only can go beyond one's ethnic and historical determinations—which is the particularity of the artist—by accepting them.

This is not where the real disagreement lies. It is between men of culture and men of politics, between the ideology of Negritude and the ideologies that in Europe, Asia, and the Americas serve the interests of the imperialisms vying for world dominion. This was evident at the Pan-African Festival of Algiers. In fact, the major newspapers and academic journals of the White world delighted in seeing Negritude attacked by Negroes, and they blew the whole thing out of proportion. Not to mention the reactions of the Asian world, which, although more circumspect, was no less attentive to these events.

But, starting with the aforementioned interview with Léon Damas, let us consider the arguments presented against Negritude by the politicians. The main question of the interview is: "Not all critics of Negritude identify with melanism, on the contrary. Moreover, at the Festival of Algiers, the attacks against Negritude were apparently of two origins: on the one hand, (Black) Africans such as the Guineans and Congolese (Brazzaville), etc.; on the other hand, the Arabs, who saw in Negritude, it seems, a culprit of the division of the continent. Is it not, in fact, negative to insist on the reality of color while Africa attempts to unite beyond its differences?" This is the question, clearly articulated. Let us see in what way.

In the case of the Arabs, they would be ill-advised to reproach Negroes for cultivating their differences, since the Arabs had done the same before the Negroes: first in the Nada (Renaissance) movement, a movement of Lebanese origin, then in today's Arabism. On the other hand, to divide the African continent on the basis of language is hardly more positive than doing so on the basis of color. This is particularly true in that none of the founders of Negritude ever focused on color, but rather *ethnicity*. Yet, ethnicity, as we know, refers not only to race and its physical qualities but also to culture and its "civilizational values." Values that the militants of Negritude have always exalted. And if today the younger generation raises the battle cry *Black is beautiful*, it is because White people had started by insulting the color of our skin and that insult needed to be challenged. Moreover, every ethnicity, every people, has sung the praises of its physical characteristics, as positive qualities, as a beauty standard. In Senegal, the *Sereer* sing of the beauty of the "lean and black" athlete in their gymnic poems, and the Fulɓe, in their love poems, of the young girl, "with a red-copper complexion," as the Greeks in the past, of their goddesses "with white arms."

Coming back to the Arabs, far from vilifying Arabism, we were the first ones, I believe, to speak of *Africanity*, not in the subjective sense or in a self-conscious way to describe Black culture but in the objective sense of "African Civilization," which I have defined as "the symbiosis between Arabism—more precisely, *Arabness* [*Arabité*]—and Negritude."[33] What constitutes the true strength of this conception of Africanity is that this dialectical symbiosis can be traced back to prehistory or, in any case, to protohistory. And it was then understood as a superior achievement of Man. When I speak of Arabs, I have in mind White Mediterraneans from the South: I think of Berbers and Semites. Father Engelbert Mveng could provide us with meaningful insights on this issue.

Negritude and Marxism

Thus, the real problem lies not in the opposition between Negritude and Arabism. It lies in the opposition between these concepts—dare I say, between these ideologies—and the ideologies that currently prevail in the great nations of Europe, Asia, and the Americas: more specifically, the ideology referred to as *Marxism-Leninism*. It is significant that the delegations of Guinea and Congo-Brazzaville are the ones that most violently condemned Negritude. And, if the official Arab delegations, which were more consequential in the defense of their national cultures, have refrained from condemning Arabism, their young Turks did not hesitate to relegate Negritude and Arabism to the museum of antiquities, however. It is along these lines that Mister [Mahjoub] Faouzi writes, in the August 12, 1969, issue of the weekly *Jeune Afrique*: "Algiers has proven the incoherence and error of any racialization of thought. It has shown that the African artist and the African intellectual, far from confining themselves to a blissful admiration of history, or to its facile glorification, are taking up the techniques developed in the very culture of the colonizer so as to put them to use for the cause of the nation and that of Africa."[34]

In short, if we have understood Mister Faouzi, it is a matter of extracting the essence from the European culture of the former colonizer, that is, technical, discursive reason. And why do this? In order to support the "national cause" and the "African cause," understood as political independence—and, I shall add, economic growth. For in this case, it is neither a question of the independence of the mind, which is the prerequisite to all forms of independence, nor a question of cultural development, which should be the ultimate goal of all economic growth. Mister Faouzi makes two mistakes, which consist in believing in the superiority of discursive reason, which thus far has been privileged by Europeans, over intuitive reason, which has been privileged but not exclusively exercised by Negroes.

It is true that White Europeans have made classical logic their tool of choice—not for two thousand years but at least, let us say, since Descartes. But this reign of discursive reason will not have lasted more than three centuries out of the five and a half million years of humanity's existence, even though, from the middle of the nineteenth century onward, logic became dialectical: nonlinear. In any case, as you know, in the past hundred years or so, epistemology has undergone a veritable revolution, as shown by the development of human sciences—anthropology, ethnology, sociology, linguistics—which, though not very metaphysical to begin with, became structural, functional. Today, to know an object does not mean to isolate it by severing it from its environment in space and time. It is no longer to abstract it from its principal sentient [*sensible*] qualities, as if from its vital forces and vigor [*de ses sucs et de sa sève*], from its blood. Above all, it is not to keep it at arm's length from the subject, who, like an impassible God, contemplates a world created from all eternity and for all eternity. Contemporary knowledge is a confrontation between the subject and the object. It is a participation, a communion, in which subject and object simultaneously contemplate and are contemplated, act and are acted on. It is a coupling of the reason-eye [*raison-œil*] and the reason-touch [*raison-toucher*]. But this is the way in which ethnologists, with the terms "participation" and "communion," have always defined the knowledge of Negroes.

I know that the so-called Marxist detractors of Negritude criticize me for having written, "Emotion is negro, as reason Hellenic." And they have concluded from this that I deny Negroes of any rational capacity, any reason. But how can one know what I meant by isolating a statement from its context? For it is obvious here that "emotion" means "intuitive reason," just as the word "soul" does for Negro-Americans, and "reason" refers to European "discursive" reason. I need only the triumph of the new epistemology as evidence that the latter is not superior to the former. Not to mention the opinion of the very founders of rationalism. Aristotle, who is certainly not the creator but the curator of Greek rationalism, would, like Plato, privilege intuitive reason over discursive reason, and Descartes, the founder of modern rationalism, positioned "feeling," alongside "thinking" and "will," as one of the expressions of *reason*. Thus, "Marxists" have misread their authors, including Marx himself.

I do not need any other proof besides the priority they give to the political and the economic over the cultural, to quantity over quality, confusing growth and development, as do the capitalists in opposition to the lessons of Marx and Lenin. In his *Differentialist Manifesto*, one of the foremost Marxists in France, Henry Lefebvre, writes: "This double aspect, namely the real priority of the economic over the fictive yet active primacy of the political, constitutes a social structure doomed to failure. Insofar as socialism, renouncing difference, adopted this structure (this model), it too sees itself as being doomed to failure. What does this failure consist of? The dissolution of essential social relations."[35] However, Marx, before Lenin, distinguished between growth and development. In a posthumous manuscript published by the *Revue socialiste* and entitled "Alienated Labor,"[36] the founder of "scientific socialism" elaborated on this idea, showing that even if economic growth met "animal needs"—eating and drinking, clothing and shelter—, it was merely a means of achieving the ultimate ends of Man, whose "generic activity" and its fulfillment involve the creation of works of art in view of making these into sustenance for himself and for other men, his brothers. And, for Marx, what characterizes them while giving them a human quality is their *beauty*: the conjunction, in these works of art, of Man and the World, of the individual and the universal. In the sense that the entire universe is reflected *in* and measured *by* the individual work, whereas Man, in his individual consciousness, is expanded to the dimensions of the universe; also in the sense that this conjunction is of a spiritual order because it is a qualitative rather than quantitative equilibrium. The passages from Marx that I am referring to explain the failure during the twentieth century of the primacy of the economic as well as the political. And this failure can also be observed in communist as well as in fascist or simply bourgeois countries. Why do young people from all regimes revolt in the name of culture: in the name of *the right to be different*? As Henri Lefebvre writes, "Development, restored to its fullness, implies an enrichment, an *unreduced* complexification of social relations. It is (and can only be considered) *qualitative*. It assumes the *creation* of forms of social life, of 'values,' of ideas, of ways of living, of styles. In short, the creation of differences."[37]

Among the people, young and old, who identify with Marxism-Leninism in order to excoriate Negritude, there is a more serious issue than the primacy given to the political or even to the economic. It is their contempt for their national culture, although they may deny it. As if the birth of cultural movements often likened to Negritude were not at the root of all European national renaissances. I will mention only three examples: Germany, Scandinavia, and Russia.

In Germany, the liberation movement began to take shape from the mid-eighteenth century onward with Klopstock and Wieland, and especially the authors of Sturm und Drang. Germans are no longer expected to attend French schools, or even English ones; students are presented with popular poetry and German myths, and *discursive reason* is discredited. "Reason," writes [Johann Georg] Hamann, "reveals nothing more to us than what Job had already seen, namely, the misfortune of birth, the supremacy of death, the inutility and insufficiency of human life, for we know nothing, and we feel within ourselves passions and instincts for which we do not understand the causes."[38] If Goethe is among the greatest minds of world literature, it is, undoubtedly, because he possessed genius; it is also because, as a direct heir of the Sturm und Drang movement, he started off by being *German*. Indeed, he is the founder of modern German poetry.

As for Scandinavia, I refer you to Mrs. Erica Simon's text *Réveil national et culture populaire en Scandinavie* [National awakening and popular culture in Scandinavia].[39] In this text, Simon explains how, at the beginning of the nineteenth century, during and after the Napoleonic wars, the Scandinavian peoples, occasionally occupied—humiliated, in any case—by the great European powers, began to search for the "spirit of the North" in their shared culture: the values that would enable them, by awakening their sister civilizations, to form a solid cultural and political ensemble on which they henceforth would rely. One will notice that here, as in most cases, cultural awakening is born of occupation, humiliation, if not conquest. As another French journalist wrote just last month, "It is not poverty that drives people to revolt, but humiliation." Equally interesting and noteworthy is the parallel that Mrs. Simon draws between Negritude and *Nordicity* [*Nordicité*] in her article, "Grundtvig University," published in the *Revue de la Société des études germaniques*.[40]

Let us now discuss Russia, which, as you might guess, is the most interesting case. Here, as in Scandinavia, the country's invasion by foreign armies and the occupation of a part of the national territory triggered a cultural revival. First, the occupation gave rise to a resistance movement against the French, which led to liberation and eventually engendered a more deliberate cultural movement: the *Slavophile* movement. Alexis Stepanovich Khomiakov was one of its leaders. He never forgot his family's hasty flight on the arrival of Napoleon's troops and the burning of their family home in Moscow. Although only a young man—he was born in 1804—he declared, "I will urge the Slavs to rebellion" against all Europeans of the West. As in Scandinavia, the movement was primarily philosophical and literary. It was at the source of the cultural renaissance that in Russia would produce masterpieces in all areas of thought and art: philosophy and literature, visual arts and music.

I would like to make two observations regarding the Slavophile movement. The first is that it, too, has been compared to Negritude.[41] On the other hand, there is the fact that if present-day Russians, the Soviets, have "surpassed" the "Slavophile movement," they have not disowned the cultural renaissance that it engendered, and they have remained, in action if not also in theory, Slavophiles or, better, *Slavs*. Today, certain articles from the *Molodaya Guardia*, or the "Young Guard," the official newspaper of the Communist Youth, attest to this.

In doing so, the Soviets managed to reconcile fidelity to their ethnicity, to their national culture, with their fidelity to the spirit, as well as to the letter, of Marx's writings. Indeed, with respect to ethnic determinations, Marx writes: "It is in each case the direct relationship of the owners of the conditions of production to the immediate producers—a relationship whose particular form naturally corresponds always to a certain level of development of the type and manner of labor and hence to its social productive power—in which we find the innermost secret, the hidden basis of the entire social edifice, and hence also the political form of the relationship of sovereignty and dependence, in short, the specific form of state in each case. This does not prevent the same economic basis—the same in its major conditions—from displaying endless variations and gradations in its appearance, as the result of innumerable different empirical circumstances, *natural conditions, racial relations, historical influences acting from outside*, etc., and these can only be understood by analyzing these empirically given conditions."[42] This, then, explains the influences—and, consequently, the role—of ethnicity, which can be defined, in line with the terms I have underscored here, as the result among human beings of the symbiosis of racial, geographical, and historical factors.

To those who deny the reality of ethnicity and race, and therefore their influences on civilization, I offer as a counterexample this text from Marx, the value of which has been confirmed by the emergence of new human sciences, such as ethnology and characterology. As we know, *ethnology* is the science whose object is the study of ethnic groups, focusing less on their physical traits than on their customs and institutions. *Characterology* is a twentieth-century science whose object is the study of characteristics, that is, the ways of feeling, thinking, and living that distinguish one individual from another. Under the influence of ethnology, it quickly occurred to characterologists to expand their studies from the individual to ethnicity. It is along these lines, with researchers such as Paul Griéger, that a new science was born: *ethnic characterology*. A science that sought to determine, even more clearly than ethnologists had done, the irreducible originality of each civilization. As Griéger states, "Just like individuals, human groups, with their own psychobiological constitution, could neither feel, nor think, nor even act in the same way. Each has its particular ways of conceiving existence, and of adopting, with respect to values, a specific attitude. On the level of psychological reality, the *oneness of humanity* [*l'unité humaine*] is a fact; it does not eliminate another aspect of the truth, that of the *diversity* of collective as well as individual characters."[43]

It will be difficult for our detractors to object to the new human sciences. But perhaps, to come back to Marx—and to Lenin, from whom I could quote similar texts—, they will consider him outdated compared to Mao Tse-tung, their new idol. It so happens that the case of the Chinese leader, far from contradicting the thought of Marx and Lenin, of which he proclaims himself an orthodox disciple, in fact confirms this thought and in a rather decisive way.

For the originality of Mao's ideas lies in his rejection of the Soviet model. In fact, even if he does not expressly state it, he wanted to do to Lenin, the *Russian*, what Lenin had done to Marx, the *German Jew*. Challenging the Russian model, he wanted the Chinese to reflect on Marxism by themselves and for themselves—as free individuals, without any complexes. In doing so, Mao Tse-tung remains faithful to the spirit of Marx and even to his word. In fact, it is Engels, commenting on Marx, who draws our attention to the fact that Marxism is not a "dogma" but a "method": a "path" not a "model," as Henri Lefebvre writes. He specifies: "The Model, which is an obsession and a phantasm of specialized political apparatuses, came after Marx and Lenin. It is not a 'Marxist' concept. This is why Marxism is dismembered, and the dialectic suppressed. The Model prescribes a predefined growth, according to the demands of power and its strategy. The Model should be identical for all. It imposes identity or simulation. It manipulates people and enables their intimidation. The 'path' does not impose; it proposes. Paths differ; the path is that of difference."[44]

Thus, to our detractors, some leftist and others Maoist, I say that the only way to be truly faithful to Mao Tse-tung is to reject the "Chinese model" for Africa and to seek, in the path of the Chinese thinker, a sui generis model for Black Africa and the Antilles—not to mention the United States of America or the United States of Brazil. The debate is not a recent one; we began engaging it in the 1930s against our peers who prioritized Marxism over Negritude. Our argument was, and still is, that Culture is superior to Politics, of which it is the precondition and the ultimate goal. In other words, Man is at the beginning and at the end of development. Put a different way, *Marxism should not only be revised but also rethought by Black intellectuals and according to the values of Negritude.*

Conclusion

It is true that we did not, as our so-called "revolutionaries" did, wait for Marx, for Lenin, or for Mao Tse-tung to examine our situation and to work toward building for ourselves a model—cultural, political, economic, and social—in tune with the values of Negritude as well as those of modernity. We do not reject the civilizations of Europe, America, and Asia. Nor do we refuse to borrow from those ideologies—liberal capitalism or democratic socialism, Russian or Chinese Marxism-Leninism—that the imperial powers currently vying for dominion over the world, and particularly over Africa, make use of, and from which we, the militants of Negritude, might acquire and learn something. But, like American *management* after the old European capitalism, like Lenin after Marx, we should, after Mao Tse-tung and Nehru, *think and act by ourselves and for ourselves, as Negroes* [*en Nègres*].

One of our own, the philosopher Gaston Berger, a *métis* born in Saint-Louis, in Senegal, at the end of the previous century, founded *futurology* [*la prospective*], the science which allows us to study the future evolution of the world in order to predict it. This science, ultimately, teaches us that the civilization of the twenty-first century will be that of the universal, to which each ethnic group [*ethnie*] and each nation will contribute. I say "will be" because it is not inevitable that, as Césaire wrote, each "will be present at the gathering of giving and receiving [*au rendez-vous du donner et du recevoir*]." Only those ethnic groups and nations that believe they possess a singular message and who desire, consciously, to spread that message will play a part in building the *Civilization of the Universal.*

It is here that Negritude as subject converges with Negritude as object. Indeed, since the beginning of the century, the militants of Negritude began spreading our civilizational values, and acting according to their word—for every art is *Speech* [*Parole*]—, and helping to construct the most human civilization because it is made of necessary differences: the complementary differences of ethnic groups and of nations.

NOTES

Léopold Sédar Senghor, "Problématique de la Négritude," in *Liberté 3: Négritude et civilisation de l'universel* (Seuil, 1977), 268–89. The text was originally published as an essay in *Présence Africaine* 78, no. 2 (1971): 3–26; it was first given as a talk at the *Colloque sur la Négritude* (Dakar, April 12–18, 1971).

[Epigraph: Léon-Gontran Damas, "La Négritude en question," *Jeune Afrique*, March 16, 1971, 59.—Eds.]

1. U.S. Department of Justice, "Radicalism and Sedition among the Negroes as Reflected in their Publications," *New York Times* (November 23, 1919), 107. [https://nyti.ms/3DnzwBJ.—Eds.]

2. Maurice Grévisse, *Le Bon usage* (J. Duculot et Librairie A. Hatier, 1964), 13.

3. [Robert Schilling (1913–2004) was a French historian and Latinist.—Eds.]

4. [*Harrap's New Shorter French and English Dictionary* (G. G. Harrap, 1971).—Eds.]

5. [For the original citation, see Aimé Césaire, cited in Jacqueline Sorel, *Léopold Sédar Senghor: L'émotion et la raison* (Éditions Sépia, 1995), 53.—Eds.]

6. [The talk was given in 1970 and later published as Léopold Sédar Senghor, "Négritude et modernité ou la Négritude est un humanisme du XXe siècle," in *Liberté 3: Négritude et civilisation de l'universel* (Seuil, 1977), 215–42.—Eds.]

7. [Senghor discusses this issue in depth in chapter 17 of this volume, "Why an Indo-African Department at the University of Dakar?"—Eds.]

8. [The Fashoda Incident, or Fashoda Crisis, was the climax of territorial disputes between Britain and France in East Africa at the end of the nineteenth century.—Eds.]

9. [*Pulo* is the singular form of *Fulɓe*.—Eds.]

10. Henri Gaden, *Le poular: Dialecte peul du Fouta sénégalais* (Ernest Leroux, 1913–14).

11. [Middle voice (sometimes "middle marking") is a controversial typological notion. Typically, it is defined as a type of grammatical or verbal voice indicating that the "the 'action' or 'state' affects the subject of the verb or his interests." John Lyons, *Introduction to Theoretical Linguistics* (Cambridge University Press, 1968), 373. At the time Senghor was writing (ca. 1970s), definitions of middle voice were largely based on studies of ancient Indo-European languages.—Eds.]

12. Cf. Mercer Cook and Stephen E. Henderson, *The Militant Black Writer in Africa and the United States* (University of Wisconsin Press, 1969).

13. [In the interview, Damas recalls his friendship with Langston Hughes and affirms the "great inspiration" that the Negritude thinkers had taken from the Harlem Renaissance and the New Negro movements. "La Négritude en question," *Jeune Afrique* March 16, 1971, reprinted in *Critical Perspectives on Léon-Gontran Damas*, ed. Keith Q. Warner (Three Continents Press, 1988), 14.—Eds.]

14. Lilyan Kesteloot, *Anthologie négro-africaine: Histoire des textes de 1918 à nos jours* (Marabout University, 1967), 15.

15. Epigraph to the work of Jean Wagner (Doctoral Thesis), entitled "Les Poètes nègres des États-Unis: Le sentiment racial et religieux dans la poésie, de P. L. Dunbar à L. Hughes" (Librairie Istra, 1963). [The original citation is from W. E. B. Du Bois, *The Souls of Black Folk: Essays and Sketches* (A. C. McClurg, 1903), 3.—Eds.]

16. [Alain Locke, ed., *The New Negro: An Interpretation* (Atheneum, 1925).—Eds.]

17. [Nanci Cunard, *Negro Anthology: 1931–1933* (Wishart and Co., 1934).—Eds.]

18. Leo Frobenius, *Histoire de la civilisation africaine*, trans. H. Back and D. Ermont (Paris: Gallimard, 1936). [For the original, see *Kulturgeschichte Afrikas* (Phaidon, 1933).—Eds.]

19. [Cook and Henderson, *Militant Black Writer*.—Eds.]

20. [Mercer Cook, "African Voices of Protest," in Cook and Henderson, *Militant Black Writer*, 3–62.—Eds.]

21. [Stephen E. Henderson, "Survival Motion: A Study of the Black Writer and the Black Revolution in America," in Cook and Henderson, *Militant Black Writer*, 63–129.—Eds.]

22. [Senghor provides the original English citation in a footnote; we have reproduced it in the running text here. Lerone Bennett, *The Negro Mood and Other Essays* (Johnson, 1964), 89, cited in Cook and Henderson, *Militant Black Writer*, 115.—Eds.]

23. [We have modernized Senghor's transcription for clarity.—Eds.]

24. [*Fit* in Wolof means "courage, valor," not "soul" as Senghor translates it here.—Eds.]

25. [The expression "*l'injure à la bouche*" is perhaps a citation from Roger Martin du Gard's "La Sorellina." See *Les Thibault*, vol. 2 (Gallimard, 1955), 154.—Eds.]

26. [In Wolof: *Taccu ak samay fukki loxo*.—Eds.]

27. [Interview with Tchicaya U Tam'si in *Afrique* (July 1966): 57, cited in M. A. Anis Ben Amor, "Champ de tension entre littérature africaine et surréalisme d'Aimé Césaire: À Dambudzo Marechera" (PhD thesis, Humboldt University), 2010), 62.—Eds.]

28. [Janheinz Jahn, *A History of Neo-African Literature: Writing in Two Continents*, trans. Oliver Coburn and Ursula Lehrburger (Faber and Faber, 1968). For the French translation, see Janheinz Jahn, *Manuel de littérature néo-africaine: Du XVIe siècle à nos jours; De l'Afrique à l'Amérique*, trans. Gaston Bailly (Resma/SEDIM, 1969). For the German original, see *Geschichte der neoafrikanischen Literatur* (Eugen Diederichs Verlag, 1966). See also *Die neoafrikanische Literatur: Gesamtbibliographie von den Anfängen bis zur Gegenwart* (Eugen Diederichs, 1965).—Eds.]

29. [Jahn, *A History of Neo-African Literature*, 266.—Eds.]

30. Cited by Jean Wagner, who, in his monograph, discusses the debate on pages 172–84. [Wagner, "Les Poètes nègres," 172–84.—Eds.]

31. Léopold Sédar Senghor, ed., *Anthologie de la nouvelle poésie nègre et malgache de langue française*, with a preface, "Black Orpheus," by Jean-Paul Sartre (Puf, 1948), 137.

32. [Jahn, *A History of Neo-African Literature*, 266; the English reads, "This is just what the theorists of negritude claimed."—Eds.]

33. Cf. my presentation "The Foundations of Africanity" ["Les fondements de l'Africanité"] in *Négritude, Arabité, Francité* (Dar Al-Kitab Allubnani, 1969), 45–120.

34. [M[ahjoub] Faouzi "Dans Alger en fête," *Jeune Afrique*, August 12–18, 1969): 27.—Eds.]

35. Henri Lefebvre, *Le Manifeste différentialiste* (Gallimard, 1970), 37.

36. Karl Marx, "Le travail aliéné," trans. Maximilien Rubel, *Revue socialiste* 3 (February 1947).

37. Lefebvre, *Le Manifeste différentialiste*, 38.

38. Cited in Fernand Mossé, *Histoire de la littérature allemande* (Éditions Montaigne, 1959), 387.

39. Erica Simon, *Réveil national et culture populaire en Scandinavie: La genèse de la 'højskole' nordique (1844–1878)* (Puf, 1960).

40. [Erica Simon, "L'Université de Grundtvig," *Études Germaniques* 22, no. 3 (1967): 445–48.—Eds.]

41. Cf. "Encounter the West: The Ideological Responses of Alexis S. Khomiakhov and Léopold Senghor," a thesis presented by Janet G. Vaillant, Harvard University: "La lutte contre l'Ouest: Les réponses idéologiques de S. Khomiakhov et Léopold Senghor."

42. Karl Marx, *Le Capital: Critique de l'économie politique*, Livre 3: *Le procès d'ensemble de la production capitaliste*, trans. Julian Borchardt and Hippolyte Vanderrydt (V. Giard et E. Brière, 1901–2), 387–88 (emphasis in Senghor). [Senghor is possibly citing a later edition. For the English cited here, see Karl Marx, *Capital: A Critique of Political Economy*, Vol. 3, trans. David Fernbach (Penguin Books, 1981), 927–28. The same passage from Marx is cited in Aimé Césaire, "Culture et Colonisation," *Culture française* 5, no. 1 (January–February 1963): 18. For the original German, see "Das Kapital: Kritik der politischen Ökonomie, Dritter Band," in *Marx-Engels-Gesamtausgabe*, vol. 2 (1861–63; reprint, Dietz, 1989), 766–67.—Eds.]

43. Paul Griéger, *La Caractérologie ethnique—approche et compréhension des peuples* (Puf, 1967), xv.

44. Lefebvre, *Le Manifeste différentialiste*, 40.

5

Negritude, as the Culture of Black Peoples, Shall Not Be Eclipsed

To begin, I shall say quite simply that we Senegalese, as your guests today, are particularly delighted to be among you. First, during my years as a student in the Latin Quarter, in the 1930s, there were Antilleans among my closest friends. I also have many Antilleans as collaborators in Dakar: Martinicans, Guadeloupeans, and Haitians. Finally, if our friendship is such for the Antilleans—and I consider it mutual—it is due to a core that unites us. Of course, there is the color of our skin. For, in Senegal as in the Antilles, there is every shade: from light bronze to the blue-black praised by our popular poets. Above all, beyond our black or bronze skin, there is a common culture, a *Black culture*, which is precisely the crux of the matter I wish to discuss with you, as this talk's title suggests: "Negritude, as the culture of Black peoples, shall not be eclipsed."

I would like to assure you without further ado that I will not be speaking about politics except, in passing, about cultural politics. For several reasons. The first is that Martinique and Guadeloupe are *départements* and, as such, members of the French Republic. And one of the principles of Senegal's international policy is noninterference in the internal affairs of other States. This also explains why I will not speak about politics here in Haiti, at least not in this lecture. My second reason is that, since the 1930s, more than forty years ago, I have always put culture before politics. What distinguished us then—I mean that little group of students who launched the Negritude movement, including Aimé Césaire and Léon Damas—was that we thought, and I still think, that politics should be at the service of culture and not culture at the service of politics, as—alas!—too many politicians and too many writers from the Third World believe. This is why Senegal allocates around 33 percent of its operating budget to education and training: in a general sense, to culture.

I have given this talk its title quite consciously. You will find it, perhaps, a bit provocative. Indeed, today Negritude is contested by every ideology raised against Africa, whether from the right or the left, as well as by certain Africans themselves, including the youth, who tell us that Negritude is now a struggle, or even a concept, that is obsolete. I do not believe so for the reasons I shall develop later.

First, I will try, once again, to define *Negritude*.

Negritude is, first of all, objectively, "the sum total of the civilizational values of the Black world." It is, to speak like the Germans, a *Neger sein*, a "being-Negro." Not merely a "Negro being" but a "Negro thinking" [*un penser nègre*], an original vision of the world, a Weltanschauung, to speak, once again, like the Germans. Among other essential works, I refer you here to the great German ethnologist Leo Frobenius's *Histoire de la civilisation africaine* [History of African civilization], which was our bible in the Latin Quarter.[1] This first meaning is, generally, the one I give to the word "Negritude."

There is another meaning to the word. It is "the concrete way, for each Negro and for each Black people, to live as a Negro [*vivre en Nègre*]" by responding to their material and psychological, natural and social, environment. In fact, to be Negro is not simply a state, a set of objective situations, but it is also a concrete action of the individual as well as of the Black collectivity: of Black peoples. It is not a simple state, a "being-there," a *Da-sein*, a being-acted-upon [*être-agi*]; it is above all an acting [*un agir*]. This second meaning of the word is the meaning preferred by Aimé Césaire, who coined and launched the word "Negritude" in the 1930s.

Nine years ago, in an article entitled "Jewishness and Negritude,"[2] the sociologist Albert Memmi, a Jew of Tunisian origin, invited us, the founders of the Negritude movement, to deepen our analysis of the concept, to expand and enrich it. As I have written recently, in an introduction to Memmi's work, we were conscious of the plurality of meanings that the word "Negritude" covered.[3] If we did not respond immediately to Albert Memmi's invitation, it is because we were still in the midst of battle and we needed to bring all of the meanings together in a single discourse, like a sledgehammer used for striking our enemies. I believe the time has come not only to distinguish between the various meanings of the word, as we have done for some time now, but also to enrich our vocabulary by means of our conceptual arsenal.

I will therefore reserve the word "Negritude" to mean the "way of living as a Negro," and I will propose "Negroness" [*négrité*] to designate "the sum total of values of the Black world." Indeed, as I learned from a linguistic study from the University of Strasbourg on the French suffixes *-itude* and *-ité*, words ending in *-ité* serve to create more abstract words while words ending in *-itude* have a more concrete meaning.

That is not all. There is also the total sum of people, more precisely, of Black peoples. Albert Memmi did not retain the word "Jewry" [*juiverie*], because of its pejorative nuance, and substituted the word "Judaicity" [*judaïcité*] to designate the "Jewish community." I will not follow his approach here. If we have used the word "Negro" [*Nègre*] to designate the Black man, despite the pejorative nuance people have wished to attach to it, it was precisely to rehabilitate this man with the word. We will do the same by calling the "sum total of Black men and Black peoples" Negrery [*négrerie*]. Indeed, the suffix *-erie* expresses a concrete ensemble: a collection or a collectivity. As for "all the countries inhabited by Negroes," I propose to take up the old term *Nigritie* to designate this.

Once again, this is not our first attempt to enrich our vocabulary, namely, our conceptual arsenal. Some told us that this was artificial— as if Black peasants, whether Negro-African, Negro-American, or Antillean, were oafs even though they possessed keenness of both body and spirit. Go to Africa and you will see that the peoples who are spread out along the same latitudes as you, in the Sudano-Sahelian religion, are the tallest of Negroes, the slenderest, with lean muscles made for running, and at the same time the blackest, and often the bluish black. In a word, the "most beautiful," as my Three Graces, the three poetesses of my village, used to sing.

To confirm that the enrichment of our conceptual vocabulary is not a rhetorical exercise in vain, I will use the example of the Fulɓe. In Senegal, the Fulɓe represent 25 percent of the population. Beyond my country, they are spread across some four thousand kilometers in the Sudano-Sahelian zone, from Mauritania in the west to Chad in the east. The Fulɓe, thus, offer us an example by enriching their vocabulary to designate the different aspects of the Fulɓe world and, first, of Fulɓe culture. In this way, they coined the word *pulaa-gu* to designate "the set of qualities characteristic of the Fulɓe," with the suffix *-gu*, which serves to form abstract nouns. It is again in this way that they created the word *pulaa-gal* to designate the "way of being Fulɓe" with the suffix *-gal*, which serves to form concrete words. To name the Fulɓe ethnic group, they have the words *Pul-o*, "Pulo," in the singular, and *Ful-ɓe*, "Fulɓe," in the plural, the suffixes *-o* and *-ɓe* being reserved uniquely for humans. To recognize that not all "Pulaar speakers" belong to the Fulɓe race, as is the case in my country, one refers to the people of the Pulaar language with the term *Halpulaar-en*, the suffix *-en* serving to form words designating "a group of people." People will ask: "And the country of the Fulɓe?" It so happens, precisely, that the Fulɓe do not have a specific territory but that they live, once again, to the north, all along the Sudano-Sahelian zone. This is why the root *-pul/-ful* signifies "dispersed."

As evidenced from these definitions, Negritude, which in this talk I will continue to consider in a general sense, is first of all a culture, that is to say, a reaction by individuals in society to adapt to their milieu and to adapt their milieu to themselves. Albo-Europeans, from the dawn of Greek civilization in southern Europe, endeavored, by privileging discursive reason, the reason-eye [*raison-œil*], to "make themselves," as Descartes said, "masters and possessors of nature."[4] They began by analyzing all the elements of the universe, even their inner world, in order, thus armed, to master nature by making it an instrument of their will and power. By contrast, the attitude of Negro-Africans, but also of Negro-Asians, was to privilege intuitive reason. From the beginning of time, since the first founders of agrarian cultures in the valleys of the Nile and the Indus, they attempted to make contact with the Universe through their senses, through their *reason-touch* [*raison-toucher*] not in order to oppose nature but, in a reciprocal embrace [*étreinte*], in order to unite with it.

The acuity of their senses and of their reason-touch explains, along with the taste for life, the communitarian spirit, precisely the *communal* [*communial*] spirit, of Negro-Africans, but also the Black peoples of Asia, Oceania, and America. We find this meaning and this spirit in all activities, all manifestations of individuals as Black peoples of precolonial Africa. In political life, it was the principle of accountable participation that brought together all the socio-professional groups and all the age groups in the exercise of power, even in the case of monarchical regimes. In socioeconomic life, it was the craftsmen's corporations and the rural cooperatives that played such a significant role in production and exchange. In religious life, it was, alongside the priests of national religions, along with the members of the brotherhoods of more or less secret rites who acted as a counterbalance within this civilization founded on the equality of parts, on social harmony.

Nothing better expresses this sense of balance and, more generally, of beauty than *Negro Art*, where we find, in symbiosis, the communal spirit and the taste for life that I was speaking of earlier. The communal spirit, which perceives the secret connections unifying the visible and invisible worlds, matter and spirit, nature and man—secret, because they are not initially manifest. The Black artist translates all these connections through symbolic images—or "analogical" images, as mentioned by the surrealists. It remains the case that these images would not be poetic if they were not also rhythmed.

What foolish remarks have not been said and written about negro rhythm? Idle minds have assimilated it to monotony, to death, whereas it is passion or, better, an expression of life. It is Albo-European rhythm that is monotone, with its sempiternal symmetries, which we expect at fixed times and places, whereas negro rhythm, even in America and especially there, becomes, under the influence of emotion, an explosion of surprise: of asymmetrical parallelisms. You can recognize the Negro-American *swing*.

It is hardly surprising that Negro Art, in the aesthetic sense, has become, since Rimbaud's cry "I enter into the true kingdom of the children of Cham,"[5] since Picasso's amazement before a negro mask, since the trumpeter's heart-wrenching refrain in Harlem, the aesthetic of the twentieth century. This is why, a year or so ago, I titled one of my talks in Scandinavia "Negritude Is a Humanism of the Twentieth Century."[6] To allow you to grasp the modernity and the humanistic character of Negro Art at once, I could not do better than to refer you to the great art critic Élie Faure: on the one hand, to his "History of Art"; on the other hand, to his introductions to "Oriental Art" and "Greek Art,"[7] not to mention *L'Homme et la danse* [Man and dance],[8] a posthumous work that contains, among others, two articles entitled "Incarnations of Black rhythm" and "Black rhythm."[9]

In these "introductions," Élie Faure opposes, beyond Greek art, Albo-European art to the arts of all other peoples and continents. For this art, the offspring of discursive intelligence, "mystery [. . .], as well as the symbol, are found to be repugnant. It describes; it does not suggest."[10] With respect to Greek art, the critic had concluded: "It is, undoubtedly, anthropomorphic. [. . .] It is not anthropocentric."[11] Which I translate as: It is not humanist in the sense of the Universal. Which, by contrast, other arts are: those of the Middle East, India, Insulinde, China, Japan, the Maghreb, and pre-Columbian America. Not to mention Black Africa. Western, European "objectivism," which leads to realism or naturalism, is opposed to Asiatic but above all African "subjectivism," which is made of imaginative emotion and "which aims for expression more than description, character more than form, and, to speak like Baudelaire, infinitely more for spirituality than beauty."[12]

On hearing the last sentence, you will think that it is in contradiction with this, "this" being the negro sense of beauty. It only appears to be so. The originality of negro art—and the two articles I have mentioned from *L'Homme et la danse* prove it—is precisely that here the violence of emotion and the purity of form, flesh and spirit, in short symbol and rhythm, are unified, rather than opposed, and mutually reinforce one another. As I have often said, it is in sensuality that Black spirituality incarnates itself, alive. Beauty is not merely the art of Black men, it is also their entire person: their body, their clothes, their movements. It is in "Black rhythm" that Élie Faure speaks of the "sculptural beauty of the Negro, highlighted by the bronze sheen that seems to emanate from this beauty, alight on it, and to increase despite its density, to shape it with the insistence of a mold, to make of it a black sun that illuminates its surroundings. Singular among men, for they live more or less naked in the light, they have conserved the unity of formal grace and power that ancient statuary taught us. Through this unity, we entered into a still-living world, one contemporaneous with our vestimentary indiscretions in which a woman retains, from head to toe, the precise undulation of the volumes swelling her erect breasts, pure hips, arms flowing in a single stream, the mass of the skull, and the full cylinder of the neck, a sculpture of muscle and bone that necklaces and chignons accentuate—an elusive and irresistible splendor."[13]

This lengthy quotation serves to complete the demonstration that the aesthetic emanating from this negro art is that of the twentieth century, just as Negritude is an essential contribution to the humanism of our time. Of course, since the eighteenth century, the "exotic" arts have contributed much to Western art and, among them, the arts of Iran, China, and Japan, not to mention Arabo-Muslim art. It remains the case that negro art has contributed the most—it is true, by way of the school of jazz in America and the Paris School in France. Regarding India, as René Grousset acknowledges in his preface to *L'Inde* [India],[14] Indian art can be explained only by the essential values introduced by Black Dravidians. He specifies: "Our dear Jouveau-Dubreuil, proud of his Antillean origins, used to say to me with affection, 'Indian aesthetics? It is tropical, it is creole.'" It is in the same vein that Mister Alfred Foucher, on the eve of the Second World War, maintained, in disregard of the threatening racisms, that the aesthetics of eternal India remained, above all, "Dravidian," that is to say, *Black*.

One might be surprised that, despite such vigorous testimonials coming from such eminent writers, artists, and critics, Negritude has been, since its inception, the object of no less vigorous attacks. We will therefore examine these: their nature, their motivations, and their reasons.

Albo-European idealogues from Europe and America have all, in turn, launched attacks on Negritude, which they discerned, early on and with a remarkable security of judgment, to be an ideology. And, indeed, it is. The only difference is that it is founded not on race but on ethnicity. As you know, ethnicity is complex: a symbiosis of history and geography, race and culture.

The attacks from the English-speaking world were among the most representative, if not the most virulent. It is in this vein that Samuel W. Allen, in a talk given at the University of Indiana in October 1966, wrote: "The emphasis placed on the concept of 'negritude' in African writings in French has inspired an opposing force, of the same intensity, in the rejection of this concept by Nigerian practitioners of the morose art [*l'art morose*]. They have, along with their Ghanaian partners, resisted what they perceive to be a cultural imperialism, imposed by a foreign source, that is, French-speaking Africans. Their reaction has been summarized by Wole Soyinka in his oft-cited remark that the tiger does not strut about, here and there, declaring its 'tigerness' [*tigritude*], and thus there is no reason for the Negro to declare his 'negritude': '*The tiger does not stalk about crying his tigerness* [*tigritude*].'"[15] It is in the same vein that certain English-speaking Negroes from Black Africa, such as the South African [Es'kia] Mphahlele, reproached the Negritude poets for creating a popular and collective poetry. I will distinguish between the two accusations.

They reproach Black writers of French expression, first, for the fact that the word *negritude* is a French word. From there, it is only a small step to accusations of "cultural imperialism," a step they readily took. I will not dwell on refuting this accusation, which simply proves that a certain English-speaking world, ten years ago, was still in the midst of what I call the "Fachoda mentality": petty quarrels between the English and the French.

The accusation becomes more serious when they reproach us for creating a "new Black poetry," which claims to be rooted not only in the color of our skin but also in the values of Black culture, a poetry that takes up these values on the level of the people, or even on the level of ethnicity, more than on the level of the individual. For the attacks in question are directed above all at poetry, which is the main art. If we take a close look at these attacks, we will discover that what they are asking of us is to create a poetry in the manner of the English of the twentieth century: to *fabricate*—that is the right word here—an individualist, intimist poetry. As if we were a people from a civilization in decline and not a young, conquering people in its ascension.

I will not dwell on Soyinka's quip, because, fortunately, over the past decade significant progress between Francophone and Anglophone writers in Black Africa has been made in the common struggle for the renaissance of Black culture. It is Wole Soyinka himself who, just a few days ago, convened a seminar of Black writers from Africa and Asia that included Black Dravidians and Black Americans to reflect on the "specificity of Black culture." He chose Dakar for this purpose. And the symposium eventually gave birth to a *Union of Writers from the Black World*, open to the entire diaspora.

Bringing these two accusations together, I will note that it is the American writers of the *Negro Renaissance*—W. E. Burghardt Dubois, Langston Hughes, Countee Cullen, Claude McKay—who, along with Haitians like Dr. Price-Mars, gave the signal for the Black renaissance of the twentieth century. Let me underscore, in passing, that "renaissance" is a word of French origin. And they began by choosing Black skin as a rallying sign. It is Langston Hughes who proclaimed, on June 23, 1926, in the journal *The Nation*: "*We younger Negro artists who create now intend to express our individual dark-skinned selves without fear or shame.*"[16] Which I will translate as: "We, the young Black artists who are creating now, we have the will to express our individual, Black-skinned personalities without fear or shame." And it is true that, before them, and at all times, popular poets from Black Africa sang of Black beauty as well as Black poetry, for it is the same word that names both the song and the poem. This is the case of the gymnic poets of my native village, Joal, which has since become a city, who sing of the blue-black skin of their champions. Thus, one of my Three Graces sang, and I noted:

The indigo-colored flank
May I measure it with a silver meter.
Ndiaye Khamad, come sing with me
The Splendid One, from Ndoubabe [*le Splendide—là de Ndoubabe*][17]

You will have noticed the "*là*," which in Antillean Creole became the definite article.[18] And the second woman modulated, singing the "song":

My night will not be solitary
For I know[19] the feast songs
I, the Lion of Lat Dior,
The beloved of the people, (champion of) Koumba!

In doing so, my Three Graces and the popular poets of Africa, to take this example, are doing nothing other than what the Greek poets were doing when they sang of the characteristic features of their ethnicity and their civilization. Like Homer, who sang of the "blue-green eyes" of the Greek goddesses and of their "white arms." All features that characterized the first Indo-Europeans—Greeks, Latins, Gauls, Germans, Slavs—when they reached the luminous shores of the Mediterranean.

Regarding the public and collective nature of the "New Negro and Malagasy poetry in French," I refer you to the preface, entitled "Orphée noir" (Black Orpheus), that Jean-Paul Sartre wrote in 1948 for my anthology, which bears this title.[20] The philosopher demonstrates in his study what distinguishes the oppressed White person from the oppressed Black person and why "Black poetry in French, today, is the only great revolutionary poetry."[21] I will not summarize this poetry today but rather freely comment on it: to show how it does justice to the idea by which all poetry is not subjective or personal but individual.

Between the White worker and the White bourgeois, explains Sartre, there is class opposition and only that, whereas between the Black worker and the White bourgeois, there is a triple conflict: of class, certainly, but also of race and above all of culture. There is no popular poetry in Europe—nor in America—because in a society that has passed from feudalism to capitalism, the struggle is developed, objectively, on the terrain of material interests by scientific and technological means. The arguments here are those of discursive reason, and the words used are the least poetic, that is to say the most plain and precise, which designate the object without any mediation: without symbol or song.

Poetry, indeed, a colorful and rhythmic speech, is a creation of subjectivity: of emotion. This, precisely, is the greatest gift of Negroes. Sartre notes, moreover, that if they are oppressed, it is less as workers than as "Negroes," with all the disdain that is attached to that word. "Thus he is driven to authenticity," writes the philosopher, regarding the Black worker; "insulted and subjugated, he picks himself up again, picking up the word *nègre* which has been thrown at him like a stone, proclaiming himself a Black man, before the White man, with pride."[22] Those who say "authenticity" and "pride" are referring, beyond the plastic beauty of forms and colors, to the values of civilization, of ethnicity: to the public and collective values that must be praised, exalted in exultation. And it is only in this way that Black men, as Sartre suggests, will join White men—and the East Asians [*les Jaunes*], I will add—to create the "revolution," which must be objective and subjective at the same time: political and poetic, but above all, social. I will come back to this.

I shall add to Sartre's argument that poetry in precolonial Black Africa was also public and collective. And it has remained as such to this day, when the *xawaare*,[23] or poetry nights, at our Daniel Sorano National Theater draw a large audience. Going further, I shall say that one of the fundamental characteristics of negro art is, precisely, its public and collective character: its popular nature.

The argument raised most often against Negritude is that it is a "cultural movement" and that, as such, it is eclipsed by the demands of our Third World condition. Indeed, our opponents explain, the primary task of Black men, above all Negro-Africans, is, in the manner of the Arabs and Asians, to free themselves from imperialism, colonialism, and neocolonialism. This requires a political vision, but above all political action, which Negritude can only distract from. Étienne Léro and the members of his group, already over forty years ago, treated us with such language that we hear still all too often in meetings of Afro-Asiatic writers: "Politics first, for political liberation will naturally give rise to cultural liberation."[24]

Rest assured I will keep my promise: I will not lapse into "politicking." I am simply positioning myself so as to respond on the terrain of our second group of opponents. Once again, it is a question not of ideological politics but of cultural politics. To continue to reassure you, I will cite a definition of "revolution" given by Manuel Alegre, the representative of the Portuguese Socialist Party, at a recent meeting of the Socialist Parties of Southern Europe: "Revolution is, before all else, a project of transformation of the economic and social structures of a country, a project of social justice, a *project of civilization*."[25] My emphasis. The true revolution, "true" because modern, you see, is less a political project—that is not even mentioned here—than an economic and social project, even better, a cultural project.

In the 1930s, despite our respect for Léro and his school, we responded by arguing that their thesis led to a confusion of culture and politics or, more precisely, to subordinating culture to politics when it should be the other way around. We acknowledged, and still acknowledge today, the *priority* of political action, not its *primacy*, which should be reserved for cultural action. I will go even further by asserting that, concerning the cultural vision, it should indeed take precedence—not over action but over political vision. Here, I am not saying anything new for a Marxist familiar with Marx. Indeed, in a posthumous text titled "Alienated Labor" published in *La Revue socialiste*,[26] Marx himself wrote: "[The animal] produces under the domination of direct physical need while man produces even when he is free from physical need and produces truly, indeed, only in freedom from such need. The animal produces only itself, while man reproduces the whole of nature. The animal's product is directly part of its physical body, while man steps out freely to confront its product. The animal builds only according to the standard and the need of the species to which it belongs, while man knows how to produce according to the standard of every species and always knows how to apply the intrinsic standard to the object. Man, therefore, creates according to the laws of beauty."[27] All of this is to say that, in the order of priorities, of *primum vivere*,[28] if politics precedes culture, so does the economy, but it is culture—meaning the integral development of *Homo sapiens*—that is the ultimate goal. Therefore, I assert that man, in other words, his "generic activity" as creator, is at the beginning and end of development. The society envisioned by the founder of scientific socialism is one where, thanks to progress in the sciences, particularly in technology, production will reach such a level of abundance that people can, after only a few hours of work, dedicate the rest of the day to the generic activity of man: to creation "according to the laws of beauty."

Thus, far from being eclipsed by the revolutions, and ideologies, currently upending the world, Negritude inscribes itself in this vision, the goal of the human project. A militant of Berberitude attempted a similar project in an article published in the July 1973 issue of *Les Temps modernes*, of which the editor is none other than Jean-Paul Sartre. "Lenin," he affirms in support of his thesis, "who worked his entire life for the unity of the working class in Tsarist Russia, represented by more than one hundred and seventy nationalities, did not hesitate to take a clear position on cultural and linguistic issues before the proletariat seized power."[29] He cites, among others, these lines from Lenin: "A democratic state must unequivocally recognize the total freedom of different languages and repudiate any privileges of one of these languages."[30] You can sense how relevant this statement is today, for within la Francophonie, not only have former colonies, now independent, like Senegal, reclaimed their languages without repudiating French, but also within metropolitan France, the Basques, Bretons, and other Occitans can, most legally, recover their cultural heritage through their language. The editorialist of the left-wing newspaper *Le Monde* emphasized this modern phenomenon of the primacy of culture on November 15, 1974, in connection to Arafat's success at the UN: "The event shows to what extent disputes related to race, nationalities, and religions, in a way, transcend political quarrels."[31]

However, our critics, far from disarming, pull out their trump card: "Negritude is racism." When someone—an American, for example—is accused of racism, they might ask, "Would you give your sister in marriage to a Negro?" The founders of the movement—figures like Césaire, Damas, [Paul] Niger, and Price-Mars—would respond that they are Antillean and, by definition, *métis*. We Senegalese could reply that, being at the border of Negro-Africans and Arabo-Berbers, we are as well. If I count the members of my family in the African sense of the term, including nieces and nephews, and encompassing spouses and children, I observe, alongside the predominance of black blood, if I may express it that way, white blood and even yellow blood, with the three blood groups O, A, B, and, alongside the Muslims, Catholics, Protestants, and Jews. If, instead of accusing Negroes, our critics accused Arabs, or especially

Jews, the latter would respond: "How can you forget all the suffering we endured, all the pogroms we were victims of, not to mention the crematoriums?" It is not to you, Antilleans, that I will teach the long suffering of Negroes, which lasted for three and a half centuries, with twenty million deported to the Americas. And you know, despite everything, that we have remained without hate: that we have transformed our suffering into joy and the long wail into song: a work of beauty. This is *Negritude*.

Nonetheless, in the early years of the movement, in the Latin Quarter, Negritude was intentionally, I admit, a kind of moral ghetto, a ghetto tinged with racism to the extent that, in the enthusiasm of returning to the sources and discovering the Black Grail, as Sartre put it, we found the Albo-European values insipid: the discursive reason with its rigid logic and mathematical coldness, with its nature truer than nature and its symmetrical, monotonous parallelisms. And Césaire tossed the bomb that exploded: "*2 and 2 make 5*!" That, too, is Negritude, where you find symbiosis and rhythm.

However, we were not slow to leave this ghetto. I have mentioned elsewhere, more than once, my personal experience. How two years of reflection in the *Frontstalags*, as a prisoner of war, helped me break out: healed me of the Black ghetto. Thus, for two years, I had ample time to reflect on the "Greek miracle" and, both upstream and downstream of the Greeks, on the other miracles that had chosen it but first preceded it—to reflect, singularly, on Egyptian civilization, the mother of all civilizations.

I will not go as far as my compatriot Cheikh Anta Diop, whose well-known thesis states that the Egyptian civilization was entirely the work of Negroes. In the current state of scientific knowledge, what strikes me is that it was essentially the work of Negroes of the "Ethiopian" type, engaged in the cultural momentum that, according to Pierre Teilhard de Chardin, kept Africa at the forefront of human progress from the emergence of Man to the Upper Paleolithic period. The Greeks, moreover, who, from Homer to Strabo, never ceased to praise the "Ethiopians," meaning the Blacks, have taught us that, according to the Egyptians themselves, the essential elements of their civilization were brought to them by the "Ethiopians," inventors of Religion, Law, Art, and Writing. This Negroid substrate is found all around the Mediterranean and in the south of Asia, from the Middle East to the Far East. It remains the case that it is the contributions of new peoples, as shown by Alexandre Moret among other scholars—anthropologists, historians, prehistorians—that have allowed the Egyptian civilization to flourish and endure, following its course for some four thousand years.

It remains the case that the Greeks still offer us perhaps the most fruitful example of cultural *métissage*. In any case, it is they who were the privileged object of my reflections, within the barbed wire enclosure, during the Second World War. The Greeks who, according to Élie Faure, had arrived on the shores of the Mediterranean as hordes of savages: tall and with white skin, blue eyes and blond hair. There, Césaire tells us, they discovered a people, sweet and polite peoples, who knew how to sculpt and paint, but, firstly, how to sing and dance. And the Greeks united with these Pre-Hellenics who, according to Jean Vercoutter, had "skin of a reddish-brown color, often dark."[32] United in this way with these Pre-Hellenics, the Greeks founded the first European civilization worthy of the name, the seeds of which, in the sixteenth century of the Christian era, would blossom during the Renaissance. As we know, it is the Renaissance, with the Slave Trade, that marks the beginning of modern times, where Negroes, despite and because of the trade, played and continue to play the role that you know and of which Jean-Paul Sartre in the final pages of "Orphée noir" writes: "Thus," he concludes, "Negritude is dialectical; it is not only or above all the blossoming of atavistic instincts; it represents going beyond a situation defined by free consciences. Born of Evil and pregnant with future Good, Negritude is a sad myth full of hope, living like a woman who is born to die and who feels her own death even in the richest moments of her life; it is an unstable rest, an explosive fixity, a pride that renounces itself, an absolute that knows it is transitory: for whereas it is the herald of its birth as well as its death throes, it remains the existential attitude chosen by free men and lived absolutely, to the bitter end."[33]

I must conclude. Like Jean-Paul Sartre, I believe that "Negritude is a dialectic"; I do not believe that "it will give way to new values." More precisely, I believe that in the Civilization of the Universal, which we have entered with the last quarter of the century, Negritude will constitute—already constitutes, I have shown—a set of essential contributions. It therefore will not disappear; it will play, once more, its essential role in the edification of a new, more human humanism, for it will have united in their totality all the contributions of all continents, all races, all nations.

Joyous Antilleans! If I have come to you from my native Senegal, which is not as far away as you might think, since we occupy on the other side of the Atlantic the same latitudes, it is to help you to affirm yourselves in the pride of your situation. Like all the great civilizations that first flourished along the latitudes of the Mediterranean, yours is based on a Negroid substrate. Among the contributions fecundated by this substrate, there are, playing a major role, those of the Latins and singularly of the French, of which you should also be proud precisely for the role that they played in the elaboration and edification of the Civilization of the Universal.

I said this a year or so ago, while giving the inaugural lecture of the chair of Francophonie at the Sorbonne. This is nothing other than the most modern enterprise of civilization at the scale of the planet, of the *noosphere*, which unites the most contradictory and yet most fecund values: flesh and spirit, intuition and discursion, speech and rhythmic song. We can and do count Antilleans among some of the greatest workers of this *Revolution*, to return to Sartre's term: Saint-John Perse and Paul Niger, the Guadeloupeans; Aimé Césaire and Édouard Glissant, the Martinicans; Jean Price-Mars and Jacques Roumain, the Haitians, alongside a Pleiad of other Antilleans and in all domains.

All this is to say that the virtues of Negritude are neither exhausted nor eclipsed. They are, more than ever, necessary to the new world emerging on the cusp of the year 2000. And necessary, first and foremost, to Francophonie, of which you are an integral part. I would say, an essential part, for you are situated yet again at the crossroads of *métissages* or, to speak once more like Césaire, "at the gathering of giving and receiving."

NOTES

Léopold Sédar Senghor, "La Négritude, comme culture des peuples noirs, ne saurait être dépassée," in *Liberté 5: Le dialogue des cultures* (Seuil, 1976), 95–109. The text was first given as a talk in Haiti in February 1976. For a recording, see "Conférence du président Léopold Sédar Senghor" (February 1976), Repository Collections and Archives, Duke University Libraries, accessed July 9, 2025, https://idn.duke.edu/ark:/87924/r42z16p81.

1. [Leo Frobenius, *Histoire de la civilisation africaine* (Gallimard, 1936).—Eds.]

2. [Albert Memmi, "The Negro and the Jew / Negritude et Judéité," *African Arts* 1, no.4 (1968): 26–29; Albert Memmi, "Negritude and Judeity," *European Judaism: A Journal for the New Europe* 3, no. 2 (1968–69): 4–12.—Eds.]

3. [Senghor had praised Memmi's work in *Le Monde*, but here he seems to be referring to a short text written in 1962 and intended to be inserted in the American edition of Memmi's *Portrait du Colonisé, précédé du Portrait du Colonisateur* (Buchet-Chastel, Corrêa, 1957), published in English as *The Colonizer and the Colonized*, trans. Howard Greenfeld (Orion Press, 1965), which Memmi dedicated to "the American Negro, also colonized." See Guy Dugas, "Négritude, Négrité, Judéité, Lusitanité: Correspondances croisées de Senghor avec Albert Memmi et Armand Guibert," *Continents manuscrits* 23 (2024): n.p., n14, https://doi.org/10.4000/12jtx.—Eds.]

4. [Senghor is referencing a passage in part 6 of Descartes's *Discours de la méthode* (1637); for an English translation, see René Descartes, *A Discourse on the Method*, trans. Ian Maclean (Oxford University Press, 2006), 51.—Eds.]

5. [Arthur Rimbaud, *Une saison en enfer* (Brussels: Alliance Typographique, 1873), 10.—Eds.]

6. [Léopold Sédar Senghor, "Négritude et Modernité ou la Négritude est un humanisme du XXe siècle," in *Liberté 3: Négritude et civilisation de l'universel* (Seuil, 1977), 215–42. See also, in the same volume, Léopold Sédar Senghor, "La Négritude est un humanisme du XXe siècle," 69–78. The former was given as a talk to "Scandinavian countries," the latter as a lecture at the University of Bayreuth in Germany.—Eds.]

7. Élie Faure, *Histoire de l'art*, vol. 1: *L'Art antique* (Éditions G. Crès et Compagnie, 1926), "Introduction à l'art oriental (1923)," 27–33, and "Introduction à l'art grec (1923)," 103–16.

8. Élie Faure, *L'Homme et la danse* (Pierre Fanlac, 1975).

9. Élie Faure, "Incarnations du rythme noir," and "Le rythme noir" in *L'Homme et la danse*, 35–43, 45–56. Cf. "Incarnations du rythme noir," in Élie Faure, *Les trois gouttes de sang* (Malfère, 1929), 103–27; and "Le rythme noir," *Art et Médecine* 6 (March 1931): 19–24.

10. Faure, *L'Art antique*, 28.

11. Faure, *L'Art antique*, 114.

12. Faure, *L'Art antique*, 114.

13. Faure, *L'Homme et la danse*, 50–51.

14. René Grousset, *L'Inde* (Plon, 1949), 9–11.

15. [Samuel W. Allen (1917–2015), who often wrote under the penname Paul Vesey, was an American writer, literary scholar, and lawyer. We have been unable to find the text of this October 1966 talk at Indiana University.—Eds.]

16. [Senghor is citing Langston Hughes, "The Negro Artist and the Racial Mountain," *The Nation*, June 23, 1926, 692–93.—Eds.]

17. [The song was composed by a relative, Koumba Senghor, for Senghor's brother, Simon, and sung to Senghor by his great-grandmother Marône. *Ndoubâbe* refers to the European neighborhood.—Eds.]

18. [Senghor is referring to the fact that, in Antillean Creole, the definite articles *la*, *lan*, *a*, *an*, and *nan* are placed after the nouns they modify, in contrast to French, where they precede the noun.—Eds.]

19. One must understand: "I know *how to make* feast songs."

20. Jean-Paul Sartre, "Orphée noir," in Léopold Sédar Senghor, ed., *Anthologie de la nouvelle poésie nègre et malgache de langue française* (Presses universitaires de France, 1948), ix–xliv.

21. [Sartre, "Orphée noir," xii.—Eds.]

22. [Sartre, "Orphée noir," xiv.—Eds.]

23. [Senghor writes *khévarés*. *Xawaare* are evening social gatherings in which poetry plays a central role.—Eds.]

24. [Étienne Léro (1910–39) was a Martinican writer and cofounder of the Marxist and Surrealist journal *Légitime Défense*.—Eds.]

25. Manuel Alegre [de Melo Duarte], "Le Parti socialiste portugais a résisté au projet totalitaire," *L'Express*, February 2–8, 1976, 46–47.

26. Marx, "Le travail aliéné," trans. Marx Rubel, *La Revue socialiste* 8 (February 1947): 163.

27. [Senghor is citing Marx's "Alienated Labor"; we have used an English translation from *The Portable Karl Marx*, edited by Eugene Kamenka (Viking, 1983), 139–40.—Eds.]

28. [*Primum vivere* is the first half of a well-known Latin phrase, *primum vivere deinde philosphari*, meaning "Live first, then philosophize."—Eds.].

29. [Rejala M'barek, "Spécificité culturelle et unité politique: Arabophones et berbérophones en Algérie et au Maroc," *Les Temps modernes*, July 1, 1973, 2250; the citation from Lenin comes from *Lénine*: *Œuvres complètes*, vol. 20: *Décembre 1913–août 1914* (Éditions sociales, 1959–60), 233.—Eds.]

30. Lenin, *Lénine*: *Œuvres complètes*, 233.

31. [The article appeared on the front page of *Le Monde*, above the fold, with the subheading "L'impasse." Henri Pierre, "L'accueil triomphal réservé à M. Arafat à l'ONU suscite consternation et colère en Israël," *Le Monde*, November 15, 1974, 1.—Eds.]

32. Jean Vercoutter, *Essai sur les relations entre Égyptiens et Préhellènes* (Maisonneuve, 1954), 103.

33. [Sartre, "Orphée noir," xliii.—Eds.]

6

For a Modern and Negro-African Philosophy

La Pensée africaine [African thought] was originally a doctoral thesis defended at the Sorbonne. At the time, it had the originality of being the first thesis on Black culture, if not the first on Negritude, to receive "distinction" [*la mention 'très honorable'*] in France. I am writing this preface less for that reason than for the following: the work of Professor Alassane Ndaw is, both in terms of style and thought, a work of *honesty*. I use this term in the sense of the humanist Jean Guéhenno, who said of French that it was a "language of gentility [*gentillesse*] and honesty [*honnêteté*]," that is to say, a clear and precise language. Here, it is not a matter of summarizing Ndaw's work—this is accomplished in the "Introduction," followed by the "Overview"—but of focusing on certain issues, namely the "forms of knowledge [*savoir*]," discussed in the first chapter, and supporting Professor Ndaw's argumentation, even if this means strengthening it by means of additional arguments and examples.

In his "Introduction," the Senegalese philosopher not only specifies the subject of his dissertation but also raises—not without nuance or courage—the dual question that the professors of the Sorbonne, no doubt, did not fail to ask and which Negro-African readers will not fail to pose: (1) Is there a traditional Negro-African philosophy as, for example, there is an Indian or a Chinese philosophy? (2) If this is the case, can we, on that basis, establish a modern Negro-African philosophy?

In response, Alassane Ndaw has raised two additional questions: "What is philosophy in the technical sense of the word? What is human thought in general and, specifically, Negro-African thought?" This means that he has played the game, positioning himself within the field of contemporary Western *Euro-American* philosophy and, as one might say, "on the opponent's turf."

Before coming back to his answers, I would first like to attempt to give a brief historical definition of Greek philosophy, from Theogonic poetry to Aristotle.[1] For it was the Greeks who founded *Philosophy* in the sense that Euro-Americans understand it. Having provided this historical overview, I will then, first, return to Ndaw's questions. Then, I will focus on some major examples, showing that Negro-African thought is capable of giving us—it has already given us—a philosophical vision of the world. Third, I will outline this vision: this "discourse of the world," as Jean Granier would say.[2]

First, we will dwell on the meaning of the word "philosophy" among the Ancient Greeks.

Philosophia[3] or "philosophy," for the Greeks, was the love of—and, thence, the quest for—*sophia*. The latter is generally translated as "wisdom," but this meaning is the result of a long process of simultaneously generalizing and deepening the meaning of the word. *Sophia* originally meant skill in the manual trades, ability in the arts, specifically in the art of playing the flute or the lyre, then talent. It is only later that the word came to mean "technical knowledge," "science," and, finally, "wisdom," that is to say, understanding [*connaissance*] of the principles that, underpinning phenomena, explain and produce those phenomena: create them. It is in this final sense of "philosophy" that Aristotle occasionally uses the term, as in *Metaphysics* or *Nicomachean Ethics*. It is also in this sense that Descartes, the founder of modern thought, uses the word "philosophy."

The wise person, therefore, ought not only know [*connaître*] what proceeds from the [first] principles but also possess the truth about the principles themselves.[4] "Therefore wisdom would be both intuitive reason and science, a science equipped, so to speak, with a head and dealing with the highest truths."[5] These lines are of capital importance, especially since it is Aristotle who, completing and fulfilling Greek philosophy, thereby establishes Euro-American philosophy.

How did we arrive at this point? Let us say, first, that in the *philein* ("to love") of philosophy, the aspect of searching [*recherche*] is even more important than the aspect of *love*. Philosophy, for Socrates, is, even before the answer, the questioning of the questioner. It is a relentless search that mobilizes all the faculties of reason and the soul. A search that draws on technical, not merely scientific, knowledge [*connaissances*], forms of knowledge that support one another reciprocally, dialectically. It remains that these scientific and technical forms of knowledge are not acquired for their own sake. They are acquired in order to live better, body and soul, by being virtuous, so as to arrive at the possession of the supreme good, the nature of which we will examine shortly. It is in this way that, from knowledge to its lived application, philosophy is transformed into an ethics [*morale*]. More than a science, *Ethics* [*la Morale*] is a conduct—in one's personal and communitarian life—that is just, measured, and balanced. As Alain writes in his *Propos* [Remarks], "The ancient sages, of whom Socrates is the best example, lived more or less like saints."[6] I would say, like gods. We will return to this as well.

This explains why the first philosophical writings were Theogonic poems. But let us come to the first philosophers worthy of the name. From Thales to Anaxagoras, as well as Anaximenes, Anaximander, Heraclitus, Parmenides, Pythagoras, Empedocles, and Leucippus, it is significant that the first Greek philosophers most often titled their work *Péri Physéos*, "on nature" or, better, "on the origin of things." Behind appearances, they placed water, air, fire, or one or more elements, as the first cause, the substance underlying "phenomena," to use a contemporary term. Some present phenomena as being immutable, unchangeable, while others show them to be mobile and endowed with perpetual movement. Still others locate the ultimate reality in the harmony of numbers, up to Anaxagoras, who places the *noûs*, the mind [*esprit*], at the origin of things. We thus realize that before being an ethics, Greek philosophy was a going-beyond of physics: it was a *metaphysics*.

From Socrates to Aristotle, Greek philosophy would consolidate its conquests by augmenting, in the *noûs*, the activity of intuitive reason. It is not that Socrates did not advance metaphysics or ethics; his merit was to have tried to base them in science by creating the conditions of science: of the authentic *épistêmê*. And he was successful, once again, by systematizing questioning, by making a tool of it, that is to say, a critical method, that alone leads to truth, the essential criteria of which is the noncontradiction or coherence of ideas.

I will not dwell long on Plato, even though he is widely considered to have been Socrates's best disciple and to have founded the philosophy of the subject. Paradoxically, it is his style that I will focus on and that, as we will see, will serve my argument. This style, borrowed from Socrates and which, according to Alcibiades in *Phaedo*, "possessed" those who listened to him. And, to specify: "His words, yes, the words of that man bring tears to my eyes, and I see so many other people seized by the same emotions!"[7] It is this vivid speech of Socrates, assimilated by Plato, that, far from sophist rhetoric and in his supple, often familiar style, makes ample use of myths and analogical images to teach his disciples, his readers.

To this point, I will invoke a remark by the Croiset brothers, the great Hellenists: At the beginnings of Greek literature, the philosophers who wrote in verse were more convincing than their prose-writing emulators. It is essentially, I will specify, that philosopher-poets convinced their readers by *charming* them in the etymological sense of the term—by enchanting them with analogical images, melody, and rhythm.

It is time to move on to Aristotle. Although a disciple of Plato, he strikes me as the most authentic successor of Socrates. For Socrates was the first to conceive and to go about realizing philosophy, less as an encyclopedia than as a total form of knowledge that, grounded in a sure science, a *physis*, aimed to go beyond it in order to become *metaphysics*. Yet the latter must be lived within an ethics that, though of a happy medium, leads us, thanks to virtue, to the possession and enjoyment of the Supreme Good.

Beyond Socrates's dialectic method, Aristotle's decisive and essential contribution is to have defined the rules of *Logic*, which lead to truth, as with "a certain resemblance and affinity between subject and object."[8] He did so, initially, by distinguishing the different elements of the soul and, within the soul, the elements of reason. It was a matter of developing an encyclopedic science. "And yet," he writes in *Nicomachean Ethics*, "there are three main factors in the soul that control action and truth: sensation, reason, and desire."[9] Contrary to J[ules]. Tricot, I will translate *noûs* as "reason." Indeed, this term means both "intuitive reason" and "discursive reason," the latter corresponding to *dianoia*.[10]

Thus, the primary work of philosophy is, by means of *dianoia*, to establish a science, a solid *épistêmê*. Solid because it will have encompassed all aspects and all domains of nature, especially of *physis*, and because it will have, beforehand, relied on a method as well as precise, generative principles.

This is why Aristotle penned treatises on the principal aspects of nature and Man, of which the most important are *On Philosophy, Organon, Metaphysics, Physics, On the Soul, Nicomachean Ethics*, and *Politics*. After research and discoveries, it is a matter of defining and enumerating all aspects of nature, all "phenomena," as contemporary philosophers put it: all physical and material facts, of course, but also psychic and even spiritual facts.

However, in order to uncover and enumerate these facts and, above all, in order to explain them with clarity, precision, and coherence, it was first necessary to invent an appropriate method of analysis and exposition, but also to define the axioms or first principles on which to base a reasoning or relevant demonstration in which the arguments are connected to each other like the links of a chain.

It is in this way that, in reasoning, in order to locate the truth and explain it through demonstration, one makes use of three elements, according to Aristotle: (1) the object, whose properties and attributes are made apparent through analysis; (2) principles, that is, the first truths, indemonstrable but evident; and (3) the rules of formal logic, which apply reasoning or demonstration to reach a sure conclusion.

That is all for scientific truth, which is necessary for action and which results from a symbiosis of sensibility [*sensibilité*], reason, and desire. It remains that science is not an end but a means. From the first sentence of *Nicomachean Ethics*, Aristotle indicates the objective of science to us: "Every art[11] and every inquiry, and similarly every action and every choice, is oriented toward some good, it seems. It has also been rightly declared that this good is that toward which all things are oriented."[12] But what is this *Good*, with a capital *G*? It is the "Sovereign Good," which the philosopher likens to "happiness." But what, in turn, is happiness? Aristotle tells us that "happiness is a certain activity of the soul in accord with perfect virtue." And he specifies that "it is the nature of virtue that we must examine."[13]

We've now moved from Science to Ethics [*Morale*]. This fact is important enough, from a philosophical standpoint, to be underscored. I will come back to it. "The principle of moral action," Aristotle continues, later on, "is also free choice, and the principle of choice cannot exist without intellect and thought, nor without a moral disposition, for good conduct and its opposite in the realm of action do not exist without thought or without character."[14]

But what, then, is "virtue" for Aristotle and, thus, ethics? This has often been presented on a purely intellectual level. In reality, Aristotle's ethics is at the crossroads between that of Socrates and that of Plato. It participates both in understanding [*entendement*] and the soul. It proceeds from *synésis*, or intelligence, and *phronesis*, that is, prudence or practical knowledge. It is the ethics of good measure: *mèden agan*.[15]

All this has not yet gotten us to the supreme good, to happiness, for we have not yet reached the "perfect virtue" associated with the "theoretical wisdom" that Aristotle discusses in Book Ten of *Nicomachean Ethics*. In the case of theoretical wisdom, it is wisdom in the ultimate, fullest sense of the word. The Greek *théôria* or "theory" is, in fact, not exactly the act, but rather the action of seeing, observing, contemplating, and assimilating. And yet, Aristotle specifies, perfect virtue, true wisdom, the supreme good, and, whence, happiness, is to exert one's "activity" on "the highest of all objects."[16] But, beyond the sciences, namely mathematics and physics, these ultimate objects are those of *metaphysics*, of the eternal and pure form, that is to say: God. And it is for the philosopher to specify in this way the aim of his philosophy: "Therefore, one must not heed those who advise man, because he is human and mortal, to limit his thought to human and mortal things; rather, man must, insofar as possible, make himself immortal and do all that he can to live according to the noblest part of himself."[17]

If I have focused on Aristotle, it is, once again, because by fulfilling Greek philosophy, he founded, in the same movement, *Philosophy*, all while organizing the sciences but going beyond them: psychology, logic, ethics [*la morale*], and metaphysics—which, to this day, still constitute the teaching of Philosophy. All modern Euro-American philosophers, from Descartes and Hume to Heidegger and Teilhard de Chardin, owe something essential to Aristotle. Is it not Descartes who tells us that "reason" is "thought" [*le penser*], "desire" [*le vouloir*], and "feeling" [*le sentir*]? And does Teilhard de Chardin's "creative union" not recall Aristotle's "theoretical wisdom"? Because, for Aristotle, all that is living has a soul and all that lives in nature is swept up in a universal movement of love toward God, as living thought, as thought in action [*pensée en acte*].

It is time to come back to Alassane Ndaw. Let us return, then, to the Senegalese philosopher who, let us recall, raises, in the introduction to his dissertation, a twofold question that is the object of his research: "What is philosophy today? What is human thought and, specifically, Negro-African thought?"[18]

To the first question, he responds: "Philosophy is a rigid discipline because it constitutes the theoretical engagement of bringing to a successful conclusion the investigation of ultimate causes using demonstration or proof. It is the critique of its own method, just as the objective givens that are its foundation constitute the guarantee of its scientific purity and rigor."[19] Nothing essential is missing from this Ndawian definition of philosophy in the Euro-American sense of the word: the search for ultimate causes, demonstration by means of logical reasoning, or the production of facts. Nothing is lacking: neither critical questioning nor a certain assimilation of philosophy to science.

Later, Alassane Ndaw raises the second question: "What does it mean *to think*?"[20] To which he responds: "We will consider this word both in the current sense of the action and effect of thinking and in the ideal sense of what has been thought; but thought, in this acceptation, is not only logical and rational representation but also the result of imagination and poetic intuition."[21] And, to specify: "Thought, thus understood, does not necessarily require the demonstration of proposed ideas or a basis in real givens in order to retain the character of what is proper to it."[22]

This last clarification is of major importance. Just like this other notion, according to which thought and philosophy always suppose "a great capacity for abstraction." This is what allows one to best understand the "Ndawian" definition of "African thought," which some, such as myself, readily call "philosophy." "What is presently called African philosophy," Ndaw writes, "is nothing other than an attempt to give a conceptual basis to the vision of reality specific to the peoples of Africa."[23]

Alassane Ndaw having raised the problem of philosophy and, at the same time, that of thought, let us see, then, if there is a Negro-African philosophy or only a Negro-African thought.

That there exists a Negro-African thought can no longer be denied after the discovery, at the beginning of the century, of *Negro Art*—what André Malraux has defined as the power of the imagination and the fruit of poetic intuition.[24]

Regarding Negro-African philosophy, this has been a topic of debate, and numerous studies have been dedicated to it since Father Placide Tempels's *Bantu Philosophy*, which caused a scandal in 1949.[25] Alassane Ndaw's study, building on these earlier studies as well as others concerning Negro-African civilization, has the merit of considering the issue with rare precision and depth.

But let us return to Aristotle, who tells us, in *Metaphysics*, that "the science called philosophy is generally considered to have as its object the first causes and principles of beings."[26] We should not understand the word "science" in its twentieth-century sense, for the Greek word *épistêmê* simply designates authentic knowledge. Most Africanists, even before 1949, tell us that there is a Negro-African philosophy in the sense of the first Greek philosophers, including Aristotle, in the sense of a *metaphysics*. It is no coincidence that our traditional philosophers, such as the Senegalese Kocc Barma, were called "masters of knowledge," *boroom xam-xam*, to take the Wolof example. Nor is it a coincidence that this second term, *xam-xam*, has exactly the same signification as *épistêmê*.

And yet our sages, like the first Greek philosophers, based their science of wisdom, their philosophy, on what they considered to be the "primary elements": water, earth, fire, and air—to which the Macedonian philosopher will add ether. As if to echo this, Dominique Zahan, in his major work entitled

Religion, spiritualité et pensée africaines [African religion, spirituality, and thought]—thus there *is* an African thought!—writes: "Earth, sky, and water, these are, in effect, the notions that, in Africa, governed the constitution of a materialist [*de la matière*] philosophy and religion."[27] But Aristotle, still in *Metaphysics*, critiques both materiality and the multiplicity of principles identified by his predecessors, including Plato's "Ideas."[28] It is in this way, as we have seen, that beyond physics, Aristotle erected a *metaphysical* knowledge, not to say a science, that allowed him to find what he was seeking: an immaterial, spiritual substance that would be the first cause and ultimate end of all beings. It is, beyond Anaxagoras's *noûs*, God, thought that is conscious of itself, that thinks itself perfectly. As Aristotle specifies, "Intelligence thinks itself by capturing the intelligible."[29]

Later, we will see that the Negro-African sages, too, going beyond the primary elements of matter, beyond even the unique principle, the *Vital Force*, will locate God.

But Alassane Ndaw has not eluded one of the fundamental objections made to the idea of "Negro-African philosophy." Indeed, we are told that, in order to elaborate a *metaphysics* and, from there, a philosophy, one must first scientifically establish a physics. But how could this be done with a "prelogical mentality" that, lacking abstract words, thinks in images?

In the second part of this preface, it will be a matter of responding to this objection, a significant one, and to others.

As we know, Lucien Lévy-Bruhl, the inventor of the "prelogical mentality," ended up retracting, in his *Notebooks* of 1949, conceding that mythical, mystical thinking was more or less present in all humans.[30] Among those who criticized, with the utmost pertinence, Lévy-Bruhl's thesis, I will retain the name of Alexis Kagamé, a Rwandan from Central Africa.

After publishing a study entitled *La philosophie bantu-rwandaise de l'être* [Bantu-Rwandan philosophy of being], Mister Kagamé, wanting to produce a more general, and thus, more solid study, gave us his most important work: *La philosophie bantu comparée* [Comparative Bantu philosophy].[31] Most important indeed, for the Rwandan philosopher had, previously, drawn on some "405 titles or studies." Let us recall, in particular, chapters 2 and 3. In the chapter entitled "Les Bantu et leur civilisation" [Bantus and their civilization], Kagamé reminds us that "no human group can perpetuate itself without existing within a civilization, the condition of its survival."[32] I will retain, among the eleven criteria of an "objective civilization" that he lists, only what is sufficient for my argument: "a linguistic system," "an effective economic system," "a set of technical knowledge," "a set of scientific knowledge," and "a system of deep (or philosophical) thought, which will surely be true if it is implicitly lived."

We will return to this final detail of philosophical thought, lived as reality. In the meantime, I would like to say that there is a science, a Negro-African *épistêmê.*

As we have seen, in order for science to exist, one must establish in precise ways the phenomena or facts and, in addition, connect them in a coherent logic [*raisonnement*]. One must, moreover, apply them to reality, to nature, in order to put these to human use, thanks to technology [*la technique*]. As Descartes writes, it is a matter of making oneself "master and possessor of nature."[33]

To return to Aristotle, man understands facts through his experience, which is "a knowledge of the individual."[34] It is the senses, instruments of our experience, which, thanks to sensation, "provide us with the most authorized knowledge of individual things."[35] It is, precisely, the case that Negro-Africans have particularly developed senses, as if with a juvenile freshness. This gives a remarkable depth to their experience of nature, for, Zahan writes, "perhaps nowhere besides the black continent has the sensible world been so researched, observed, probed, thought."[36]

"Thought." This last word is not the least important, for it is in drawing on experience—what Aristotle considered one of the three modes of human understanding—that man begins to think. The Greek philosopher clarified, in fact: "Experience seems to be of the same nature as science and art, but, in reality, science and art come to men by the intermediary of experience."[37] Once again, we must understand, by the word "art," technology [*la technique*] in general, especially since the Greek word is *technê*, from which "technique" originates.

Yet the same philosopher specifies in *Topics* that "there are two types of dialectical reasoning: induction and syllogism."[38] He adds: "In the case of induction, it is the movement from particular cases to the universal. [. . .] Induction is a more convincing and clearer process, more easily known by means of sensation, and thus accessible to the layman. But reasoning has greater force and is more effective for responding to naysayers."[39] Once again, I prefer André Cresson's translation in *Aristotle*, at least for this last proposition: "Syllogism"—for that is what it is about—"is more pressing and more effective for controversy."[40]

Men of experience, full of good sense because strongly rooted in nature, Negro-Africans make use of induction above all "to think" and reason on the basis of "feeling." However, they are not averse to syllogism—far from it. Alexis Kagamé even dedicates a paragraph to the topic, titled "Syllogism, the sign of reasoning," in chapter 3 of *La philosophie bantu comparée.* He writes: "In Bantu culture, syllogism is always elliptical: one sometimes formulates one of the premises and moves on to the conclusion."[41] Even better, Alassane Ndaw speaks to us of Bambara "syllogism."

All this—and we could multiply the examples—shows that, in truth, although each people may favor a given form of reasoning, but above all a given expression, human thought remains identical to itself on all continents, among all races, ethnicities, and nations. This is one of the solid truths that Alassane Ndaw forcefully exposes by drawing on the works of the foremost specialists: ethnologists, sociologists, and philosophers, including the Lévy-Bruhl of the *Notebooks*. All men thus reason by means of induction and deduction, without forgetting the hypotheses, advanced on the basis of facts and experience. They will reply to me: "But above all on the basis of experimentation." To which I would respond: "Yes, but experimentation already existed on every continent before the invention of the steam engine."

Our devotee of the "prelogical mentality," hardly perturbed, will then put to us, the sledgehammer argument: "Moreover, as we know, Negroes think in images and not in concepts. The best evidence of this is that they do not have abstract words."

Alexis Kagamé has also responded to this argument. We know that Bantu languages are languages with nominal classes. In these, we organize not only all beings but also ideas. "To express the abstract," clarifies Kagamé, "the *Bantu* system introduced a special class, marked by the classifier *bu* in 'interlacustrine' Africa. This *bu* has the variants *bo, o, vu*, and *u*. In languages of the 'Senegalo-Guinean group'—*Sereer*, Pulaar, Wolof, Jola, etc.—we find, but multiplied, the ability to create abstract words. This is the case in Pulaar. In Pulaar [*poular*], the Senegalese dialect of Fulah [*peul*], we can form abstract words in nine of the eighteen noun classes of the singular."[42]

Our contrarian launches a final arrow, a poisoned one: "It remains that Negro-Africans prefer to speak in analogical images, in myths, above all when it comes to expressing ideas."

It is true, and the deepest, most solid part of Ndaw's study is in the first chapter, where he explains style or, better, *Black Speech*. We will come back to this. It remains that not only can the Negro-African think in terms of concepts, but moreover, as Paul Griéger shows in *La caractérologie ethnique* [Ethnic characterology],[43] thought characterized by a "predominance of images" is not only a feature among Black people; it is a feature of all the Fluctuants: Mediterranean peoples, Latin-Americans, Japanese, etc. Better: This predominance of the imaginary is also found among the Introverts, including the Scandinavians and the Germans, who are the best examples. In his *Psychological Types*, C[arl]. G.

Jung writes of the German ethnotype: "He creates theories for his own sake, apparently taking into consideration existing, or at least possible, facts, but with a very clear tendency to move from the ideal to the pure imaginary."[44] Who would dare assert that German thought is inept at philosophy?

More broadly, since what I call the Revolution of 1889, with the *Essai sur les données immédiates de la conscience* [Essay on the immediate data of consciousness],[45] a new philosophy has emerged, which is expressed as much, if not more, through the analogical image than through the concept. Besides Henri Bergson, I am thinking of Pierre Teilhard de Chardin and Martin Heidegger. Through the valorization of intuition and, consequently, the analogical image, it is the primacy of thought, of linear, discursive logic that is itself called into question. All of this, moreover, had been facilitated by the meteor Arthur Rimbaud streaking across the poetic skies.

This brings us back to the Negroes' imagination. Why do they express themselves through analogical images rather than concepts? First, it is because Negroes, as well as other races and ethnicities, in order to understand nature and act on it, have at their disposal, as Aristotle told us in chapter VI, 2, of *Nicomachean Ethics*, "sensation," "reason," and "desire," or, to use the modern terms of Descartes, who will take up the idea in his *Meditations*, "feeling," "thinking," and "willing" [*vouloir*]. It happens, moreover, that Negroes have a sensibility [*sensibilité*] that is, as Dominique Zahan has emphasized recently, deep and nuanced at the same time.

I myself have often emphasized the "psychophysiology" of Negroes: their "power of emotion." And ethnologists have gone so far as to speak of the "sensuality" of their sensibility, all while emphasizing its "purity." This is an important feature that my own experience confirms. I remember the UNESCO General Conference held in Florence—the fifth, I believe. I spent, then, I confess, a good part of the conference in the museums, with François Mauriac. At the sight of the paintings, statues, and even monuments, I was overcome—I "trembled," I would say in Senegalese terms—by a sensual emotion. And yet no feminine thought caressed me. It was like during my first communion. Therefore, I say that, for the Negro, spirituality is rooted, *in-carnated* in the flesh.

Still in his first chapter, at the end, Alassane Ndaw extensively discusses the Negro-African imaginary, which is expressed, in speech, through symbolic images and, in discourse, narrative, or poetry, through myths. He sees the reason for this in the fact that the Negro-African mind, without abandoning analysis, emphasizes synthesis, better, symbiosis, but above all this other fact that, if it draws a distinction in the universe between the visible and the invisible, man and the world, the profane and the sacred, this same mind [*esprit*] unites the two sides of being by means of the concrete signs that analogical images are.

As I have often said, in Negro-African languages, words are "pregnant with images," especially when they are modified with classifying suffixes or prefixes, as in the Bantu languages and the semi-Bantu languages, such as those of the "Senegalo-Guinean" group. Hence the insistence of our sages, our philosophers, on recalling the class or etymology of the word. This is, in short, what Martin Heidegger often does. I refer French-speaking readers to two works by the German philosopher, translated under the titles *Introduction to Metaphysics*[46] and *Essays and Lectures*.[47] They will see there how Heidegger, by returning to etymology, that is, to the source of essential, and today the most abstract, words, shows us that they are still pregnant with images as long as the writer restores their original, strong, full, total meaning. Such is the case, in Indo-European languages, with words like "being" [*être*] and "speech" [*parole*]. And Heidegger concludes: "In this setting out, language was poetry insofar as, in language, being becomes speech. *Language is the original poetry, in which a people articulates being* [*dit l'être*]. Conversely, the great poetry, through which a people enters into history, is what begins to give shape to the language of that people. The Greeks, with Homer, created and knew this poetry. The language was present in their being [*être*], as a departure into being, as a shaping of being [*étant*], which reveals being [*étant*]."[48] My emphasis.

This is a crucial text that helps us better understand Negro-African poetry and why, whenever it comes to expressing being, the Negro-African resorts to poetic expression. It is time to recall, first of all, that poetry, like philosophy, is a novel vision of the world in which man is inserted, *incarnated*. Subsequently, poetic expression is essentially made up of the analogical images, melody, and rhythm that are most apt to allow us to intuitively grasp the being in the world presented by the poet. I refer the reader to an essay by Jean Cohen entitled *Le Haut langage: Théorie de la poéticité* [High language: Theory of poeticity],[49] which confirms both Heidegger's theory and the value—the meaning—of Negro Speech. Cohen writes: "In poetic language, freed from all opposition, words regain their self-identity and, at the same time, their total semantic fullness."[50] And furthermore: "Poetry, on the contrary, intensifies language to the point of making it pathetic (which makes one feel). Its function resides in a qualitative transformation of meaning, which it conveys—through the intermediary of images, sounds, and rhythm—from the world of concepts to that of affectivity."[51]

If the Negro-African makes use of abstract words, it is mostly when he is confronted with material, concrete, technical problems: when it comes to being "master and possessor nature." And also in his explanations and comments on artistic, religious, and philosophical thought. I am thinking of the teachings provided in the schools of initiation. However, when it is a matter of expressing the Beautiful, the Good, Being in its truth, of making men grasp these essential realities, or more precisely, of prehending [*saisir*] men—Leo Frobenius's sense—through these realities, then the *Homo niger* employs poetic language in the manner of Heidegger's Greeks, with, among other things, symbolic images. A significant proof of this phenomenon is provided, once again, by the Croiset brothers, who noted that the early Greek philosophers, in order to be more convincing, had to express their thoughts in verse. And Plato, after them, used the language of myth, which is nothing but a long allegory made of metaphors.

Even better, the language of the sciences, including that of mathematics, is metaphorical. It is merely that, here, metaphor is reduced to its structure, to its quantity. Souleymane Niang, Dean of the Faculty of Sciences at the University of Dakar, provided relevant evidence of this truth in a lecture given on April 12, 1971, at the colloquium on Negritude entitled "Negritude and Mathematics."[52] In this lecture, Professor Niang began by showing how, in contemporary mathematics, intuition played a necessary role, one at least as important as that of logic. After which, he emphasized that, thanks to this role, the power of Negro-African emotion could contribute to the development of mathematical research and pedagogy.

I will stop at the first part of the mathematics professor's lecture. Having advanced that "mathematical language needs [. . .] a supporting lyrical language," which allows for the forging of "ideographic symbols," he asserts that "Mathematics is built from the sensible physical world, that is, from reality, and develops by means of intuition." Going further in his explanations, he specifies the relationship between intuitive reason and discursive reason or, more precisely, between intuition and logic by showing how they complement each other through collaboration: "Mathematical activity is exercised, first, on the concrete, and intuition, driven by emotion, then gives an initial schematization or idealization, from which, thanks to logic, the abstract construction of a theory is elaborated, the entire basis of which essentially relies on the emotive power that the real can have on the researcher." And to conclude: "Emotion plays a crucial role in Mathematics, especially in the field of research," which, I would add, is essential.

The reader will now better understand two things: on the one hand, how all languages, even the most abstract, such as Mathematics and Philosophy, are more or less metaphorical; on the other hand, how the Negro-African is capable of abstraction. It is not surprising, therefore, that in Senegal it is in Mathematics that we have the most highly qualified professors. Moreover, as is known, Mathematics originated in Egypt: in an Egypt, at that time, Blacker than it was White.

In the second part of this preface, it was indeed a matter of proving, as Alassane Ndaw had suggested, that there is not only a Negro-African thought, capable of abstraction and, consequently, coherent reasoning, but also of effective science in its applications to nature: *épistêmê* and *technê*, as the Greeks said. I will not return to the Neolithic Negroids, who were the "first settlers of the eastern valleys," according to Alexandre Moret,[53] and whose descendants, more or less mixed [*métissés*], invented the world's first three scripts: Egyptian, Sumerian, and Indo-Dravidian. Instead, I will focus on medicine or, more precisely, Negro-African pharmacopoeia. Indeed, even before European colonization, the magicians and other healers of Black Africa knew how to diagnose and treat diseases, as numerous studies have shown. Among others, I will cite: *Les plantes bienfaisantes du Ruanda-Urundi* [Beneficial plants of Rwanda-Burundi] by J[ean]-M[arie] Durand,[54] *La médecine indigène au Ruanda* [Indigenous medicine of Rwanda] by A[rthur] Lestrade,[55] and *La pharmacopée sénégalaise traditionnelle: Plantes médicinales et toxiques* [Traditional Senegalese pharmacopoeia: Medicinal and toxic plants] by Mister [Joseph] Kerharo.[56]

Thus, Negro-Africans have founded sciences, including Medicine, and numerous technologies in various domains: agriculture, livestock farming, writing, industry, etc. However, the question posed by Alassane Ndaw returns: "Do they have a thought, a philosophical one?" With Ndaw, we have partially answered it. It is therefore proven that, by being able to perceive, with depth and not without nuances, the various aspects of phenomena, and having, moreover, at their disposal a large number of abstract words, Negro-Africans have succeeded, through hypothesis, induction, and deduction, in creating sciences and technologies with effective applications.

In regard to Negro-African philosophy, we have seen that it exists, as evidenced by numerous studies that can be found in the bibliographies of both Alassane Ndaw and Alexis Kagamé. Focusing on the former, it is a matter of summarizing the main lines of his thesis, by emphasizing the essential ideas that confirm that there in fact exists a Negro-African philosophy. But before that, I would like to invoke here, against persistent prejudices, the testimony of a contemporary philosopher, Roger Garaudy, who specializes in the dialogue of civilizations. He directs, moreover, the *International Institute for the Dialogue of Civilizations*.[57]

Responding to my question, "What is philosophy?," Garaudy commented as follows:

> The consequence of this state of affairs (reducing Philosophy to that of the West) is a frightening narrowing of the very conception of philosophy. In this reductionist perspective:
>
> –philosophy is a matter solely of intelligence (and not of life, in its fullness and totality);
>
> –intelligence is defined solely by the concept and its logical handling.
>
> It is in this sense that Nietzsche accused Socrates of being "an abnormal man" because he reduced reality solely to the concept, whereas there are more things on earth and in heaven than can be contained in the concept: love, poetry, sacrifice, faith, etc.
>
> Only Marx, on the side of action and the transformation of the world, and Nietzsche, on the side of the affirmation of life, have surpassed this one-sided intellectualism.
>
> In my opinion, philosophy started to decline from the moment it substituted the knowledge of our concept of things for the knowledge of things. [. . .]
>
> Today, in the West, we are witnessing a double degeneration of philosophy.
>
> 1 Either it is eliminated in the name of the positivist and scientistic prejudice according to which "science" would be an end in itself, and where one pretends to define reality as if not only God but also man were absent from it, leading to the "theologies of the death of God," or to the philosophies of the "death of man" (Foucault).
> 2 Or knowledge is made the sole object of knowledge, as a decadent literature makes "the act of writing" the object of the novel or as a decadent painting makes "the act of painting" the object of the painter.
>
> If we distance ourselves from this Western conception of philosophy (which seems to me to be one of the aims of the dialogue of cultures), we access a broader view of philosophy, as it has flourished in the rest of the world:
>
> –it concerns life in all its dimensions (and not only intelligence);
>
> –it concerns all of man's relationships with the world and the divine.

In this universal perspective, we can define philosophy as "the way in which men conceive and live their relationships with nature, with society, and with the divine."

From this point of view, we can distinguish three fundamental types of philosophies:

1. *Mystical philosophies* of man and his self-knowledge, to become aware of his true nature and to achieve identification with the absolute (examples: Hinduism, Buddhism, Taoism, the African worldview, Zen);
2. *Prophetic philosophies*, beginning from God and his revelation to man to make him participate in the continuous creation of the universe (examples: Zarathustra, Judaism, Christianity, Islam);
3. *Critical philosophies*, retreating timorously to the act of knowing [*connaître*] and based on the dualism of subject and object. (Garaudy's emphasis)

I have quoted Garaudy at such length because he is not only a professor of philosophy but an authentic philosopher—his work attests to this—and a Marxist. From his letter, I gather that philosophy is reduced neither to the concept nor to logic, nor merely to the "critique of knowledge"; that it is essentially, as he emphasizes, "*the way in which men conceive and live their relationships with nature, with society, with the divine.*" In this sense, there is undeniably a Negro-African philosophy, and this is what Alassane Ndaw's thesis demonstrates, pertinently, in chapters II, III, IV, V, and VI. This is why—because philosophy is defined as the knowledge of being or, to use Aristotle's expression, of the "highest truths"—I would like to begin here by focusing on the two notions of truth and being.

For Aristotle, as we have seen, *truth* is always "a certain resemblance and affinity between the subject and the object." Since the Macedonian philosopher, not much has been added to this definition. Jean Granier, who, in a remarkable work, gives us a modern, contemporary definition of philosophy by presenting it as a relationship between "thought and its correlate," specifies: "Truth cannot be an immediate and total revelation; it is conquered on *appearances*, in a difficult struggle with the plurality of phenomena."[58] We should remember this clarification and note that it is Granier who emphasizes the word "appearances."

With respect to *being* [*être*], Aristotle, after recognizing that its meanings were numerous, concluded: "Therefore, Being, in the fundamental sense, not as a mode of Being, but Being in the absolute sense, must be Substance."[59] Since then, nothing has been added to this definition. The *Grand Robert* defines being as: "That which is." What is important resides not in this tautology but in the note, placed in parentheses: "Practically only used for what is living and animated, or what is imagined as such." As before, we will add Granier's commentary: "If truth always implies being, and thus being is coextensive with it, being, on the other hand, is more extensive than truth, since it supports negativities that lie beyond the true and the false. [. . .] Truth, therefore, is not the entirety of being; it is only a certain arrangement of meaning within being."[60] This leads the French philosopher to define philosophy as "the interpretation of the world."

This brings us back to Alassane Ndaw and to Negro-African philosophy as a "discourse of the world," to use Granier's expression. It is, indeed, a matter of the "interpretation" of *nation* in the sense understood by the Arabs, that is, as the set of African peoples living south of the Sahara among whom ethnologists have identified, since Abbé Henri Grégoire and his work *De la littérature des nègres* [On the literature of Negroes], a culture worthy of the name.[61]

But, before focusing on the main features of this philosophical knowledge [*savoir*], it is necessary to revisit its Negro-African modalities, emphasizing once again the value of *intuition* in the psychophysiology of Negro-Africans. It has been said—not only by Aristotle but also, and especially, by so many philosophers of the twentieth century, including [Henri] Bergson and Teilhard de Chardin, and even contemporary mathematicians, as we have seen—that intuition is at the beginning and the end of *knowing* [*connaître*]. For Bergson, intuition is "immediate consciousness, a vision that is barely distinguishable from the object seen, a knowledge which is contact and even coincidence."[62] Through intuition, man "settles into the movement and adopts the very life of things."[63] This is what Africanists mean when they speak of Negro-Africans' knowledge through "participation." This is why I speak of knowledge through amorous conjunction with the Other, of a death of the self so as to be reborn in the Other, or, to speak like [Paul] Claudel, a *cobirth* [*co-naissance*] *to the Other*. This sensual, rhythmic, carnal knowledge is expressed through symbolic images and myths.

Nothing is more foreign to Negro-African thought than the epistemological break between intuitive and discursive reason. It is the second feature I would like to emphasize here. As Professor Kutto [Essomé][64] notes, definitions of the soul, and even of thought, in sub-Saharan Africa, are always expressed through bodily images: "breath," "shadow," the "double," "clavicular grains," the "phantom," the "heart," the "brain."

This dual implication of spirit and body, of the idea and the thing, of thinking and feeling means that Negro-African thought can be bent toward neither materialism nor intellectualism—I do not say spiritualism. As we will see shortly, between the subject and the object, between man and being, there is nature, there is the cosmos, traversed by the senses. These senses gather a thousand aspects, a thousand images, which translate and signify being and which are interpreted by thought, by reason, alternately intuitive and discursive, intuition and logic. This means that Negro-African thought is dialectical: it plays on both keys, the two tableaux of the world and, therefore, of knowledge.

The third feature of Negro-African thought is that it is practical as well as theoretical, as shown by Alassane Ndaw in the sections of the first chapter entitled "Mythical Thought," "Divination," "African Thought and Mystic Life," "Initiation and Knowledge."[65] African thought becomes knowledge through the primary means of myth, which is a narrative woven with symbolic images. But, in order for this myth to become knowledge, it needs not only commentaries, in which the Master, the Initiator, makes use of concepts expressed through abstract words, but also lived realizations: practice.

It is this practice, in divination, initiation, and mystic life, that Alassane Ndaw describes in these sections. Thus, in divination by the *pomdo* or the *kala*, in initiation ceremonies, and more generally, in manifestations, particularly the ceremonies of mystic life. All the means of art are, then, employed: mask, song, poem, dance, theater. It is a matter of practicing, of living knowledge—and intensely—through the powerful means provided by art. It is a matter of living the analogical images, the symbols: the myth. As summarized by the Senegalese philosopher, "Mystic life appears as a *practice of symbolism*, a practice of purification in which enters not only the intellectual prehension of the meaning of symbols but also the intuitive prehension of meaning, that is to say, the total, immediate, and indivisible vision of the ontological relationship between man and cosmos."[66] My emphasis. An admirable sentence, because nothing is lacking to characterize Negro-African knowledge; and yet no word is superfluous.

The fourth feature of this specific thought: Knowledge coincides with *being*. "In the very act of this vision," writes Alassane Ndaw, "man makes a metaphysical leap that transforms him and makes him discover his true nature."[67] Truly, knowledge [*connaissance*] becomes cobirth [*co-naissance*].[68]

Fifth feature: Between man and the cosmos, the visible and the invisible, intuition and discursion, the signifier and the signified, there is a gap, a zone of silence, a secret, which is at once imperfection and perfection. Of the importance of the secret in Negro-African knowledge, of silence in Negro-African speech, in poetry, to take this major example.

Sixth feature, a paradoxical one: What ethnologists have alternately called the "dialectic," the "polyvalent logic," and the "superlogic" of Negro-African thought: this is what Alassane Ndaw alludes to in writing: "The initiatory process proposes to the disciple a systematic and global circuit. Systematic, because the knowledge communicated at each stage, far from being an anarchic sum, is logically articulated, providing a reasoned image of the universe, a logical and progressive framework, corresponding to what can, without hesitation, be described as methodological."[69] And the philosophy professor notes that "we find here a concern proper to modern thought, namely the concern for rigor, for order."[70] This is not the first time we have noted the encounter [*rencontre*] of Negro-African epistemology and modern epistemology.

It is on the basis of this epistemology, as a theory of Negro-African knowledge, that Alassane Ndaw has, once again, laid out the fundamental elements of what he calls *Negro-African philosophy*.

The Senegalese philosopher describes this ordered universe, this cosmos containing man, for us in chapter II, according to the modalities that we have just defined, and that are informed by the psychophysiology of the Negro-African.

The Euramerican conceives of the cosmos abstractly through the notions of space and time, with time assimilated to space. In contrast, the Negro-African perceives space-time also as a single category, which is placed in the same nominal class but, moreover, as a reality, felt and lived by man: as a quality—not as an abstract, geometric quantity. In a word, the Negro-African lives space and time, the mythical space-time, personally, but in society.

What best characterizes the Negro-African cosmos, besides the primacy accorded to the real, lived existentially, is its anthropocentrism and, consequently, its *humanism*.

To return to myth, it is in this way that man and the cosmos reciprocally reflect one another and maintain, between them, multiple links that are expressed in symbolic images, in correspondences. Man is the microcosm of the macrocosm that is the cosmos. But, even better, their correspondences are the signs of forces, of reciprocal actions. It is on the model of Man and the cosmos that society will be erected, will be organized: the household, the altar, the temple, the village, the kingdom.

We will better understand this truth by referring to the *mythology of origins*, as Alassane Ndaw explains it. Not only was the world created for *Man*, but it has also been realized by Man: by a hero or, often and better, by a couple that substitutes themselves for God, a couple in which God is incarnated. And *Woman*—this is not a detail—has often played an important role in this. And in the work of creation. Man supports benevolent jinn against the malevolent jinn. And his most essential, most human activities consist in nourishing, in fortifying the positive forces, among which are the Ancestors. He does so, preferably, in ritual ceremonies by resuscitating mythical time thanks to the techniques of art, which produce vital force: thanks, once again, to the mask, the song, the poem, the dance, and even drama, that is, theater.

The third characteristic of the Negro-African cosmos, we will have noticed, is the *symbolism* through which it is expressed. The household, the altar, the temple, the village, and the kingdom do not only represent Man and the cosmos by a logic of intuition, a logic of the imaginary: They respond, in parallel and complementarily, to a practical logic. The household, the village, and the kingdom are composed and organized effectively. They are operational. We have seen here, in the case of interpretation, the prehension of the world, a symbiosis of the imaginary and the concrete, of the rational and the real, of the spiritual and the material.

After having described, or more precisely defined, the Negro-African cosmos, in which man is inserted, like a microcosm, and with which he maintains dynamic connections, Alassane Ndaw will, in chapter III, focus on the notion of the *person* in order to define it in turn. While he still situates the person within the cosmos, he will emphasize the person's situation within its group, that is, their family and ethnicity, in short, in their society.

To the *persona*, a Latin concept enriched by Christianity, Ndaw opposes the Negro-African concept. The person in the Euramerican sense is an autonomous and responsible being, an individual who occupies a determinate social rank, with duties and honors. To this concept, which is taken to be entirely rational, Negro-African thought opposes a notion that is more complex because it is more social than individual.

I have said "more complex." Indeed, the Negro-African person is, vertically, rooted in their family, in the primordial Ancestor if not in God; horizontally, they are connected to their group, to society, and, as we have seen, to the cosmos. It is because the person is not oppositional that they are enriched and flourish through the bonds of reciprocity, which they actively maintain.

Thus, it is well before birth that the person, in the form of their "pre-existing soul," is taken in charge by an entire lineage of ancestors, down to the placenta, to the "Primordial Mother," who began to *inform* them.

As for the fabric of the person themself, Negro-African thought presents the person to us as complex, as I have said, formed, as it were, of several material and spiritual components. The Dogon and Bambara present us with four of these elements,[71] of which the most original, the most essential, is the *double*, the "point of fission" at the border of the conscious and the unconscious.

However, as we have hinted when speaking of the cosmos, as the product of a family-individual and society-individual dynamic, the whole being linked to the universe, the Negro-African person can develop and flourish only through the stages of familial and social life, from prebirth to the beyond, passing through birth, dentition, puberty, menopause, and death.

Alassane Ndaw dwells at length, and rightly so, on the *Formation of the Person and Initiation*, emphasizing the latter. It must be underscored that initiation is not limited to the stage of puberty, although this is the principal one; it begins at birth and can involve more than six stages, even lasting a lifetime. The teaching of doctrine—let us dare say: of *Philosophy*—and of ritual is conducted as much by peers of the same age group as by elders. The goal of this is to make the individual a complete *person*. Contrary to the prejudices prevalent in Euramerican opinion, it is a matter of making the individual a man of knowledge and duty, someone who is both intellectually free and morally strong. And if sexuality occupies a significant place in this teaching, it is to maintain not an erotic tension but a sensual sense of Beauty. As I like to say, in Black Africa, spirituality is embodied: incarnated in the flesh.

Therefore, alongside theoretical teaching, there is especially, once again, practical teaching through ritual ceremonies in which art is created, is realized, and, at the same time, realizes the person in their fullness: through the mask and dance, the mingling of music and song, through the symbolic image, melody and rhythm, which produce poetry in the etymological sense of the word, that is to say, *creation*.

This is the purpose of initiation as well as its meaning. At each stage, it involves the self dying in order to be reborn in the Other: in the child, the adolescent, the adult, the elder, the Ancestor, and God. We will come back to this. To be reborn more knowledgeable, stronger, more beautiful, happier because more of a *being* [*être*].

I will not dwell on chapter IV, which deals with "kinship," because the subject began to be addressed in the previous chapter and is not essential. I therefore come to chapter V, entitled, "Knowledge of God or the Conception of the Divine in Negro-African Thought."[72]

As Madeleine Barthélemy-Madaule observes in *Bergson et Teilhard de Chardin*,[73] Western thought, reacting against the Middle Ages and from Descartes all the way to Bergson, has gotten in the habit of separating religion from philosophy. If Father Teilhard victoriously broke away from this tendency, it is because he incorporated religion, as Barthélemy-Madaule writes, into a "total and harmonious vision of phenomena."[74] This is what Alassane Ndaw demonstrates with respect to Negro-African thought in chapter V.

The first question that arises concerning a religion is the existence of a supreme being: of God. Once again, jettisoning Euramerican prejudices—and drawing on testimonies from writers from five, seven, or more centuries ago—the Senegalese philosopher emphasizes "the existence of a supreme and unique God within the thought of different African societies."[75] A celestial God all the more supreme because he is not the object of a cult. But what are his attributes?

First, he created the world. This is not to say that he shaped it in the minutest of details by creating raw matter; rather, he transformed it from nonbeing [*non-être*] to being [*être*], leaving up to the spirits [*génies*] the task of organizing it.

The second attribute of God, as an uncreated entity [*incréé*], is to be not only a vital force but the Force of forces, the source of all energy: of all life.

From these two principles flow properly religious acts, that is to say, worship, of which sacrifice is the most effective act. It is rare for humans to address themselves directly to the Supreme Being, who resides in his inaccessible sky. Offerings, prayers, and, generally speaking, ritual ceremonies are addressed to God through the channel of protective spirits, the intermediary forces that are connected to the natural elements that symbolize them.

Alassane Ndaw emphasizes sacrifice. It involves offering, through immolation, a being—a force to *reinforce* the spirits and, through them, the Supreme Being. Sacrifice is, in the etymological and full sense of the word, a communion of the visible and the invisible, of an individual force and the Supreme Force, man and God, a single being and the Being of being. "Thus," concludes Alassane Ndaw, "sacrifice is indeed a union or reunion or reciprocal reinforcement of forces, each feeding the other."[76] Yes, in Negro-African religion, *God needs men*. This is one of the essential originalities of Negro-African philosophy, for we thus find ourselves fully in metaphysics. Let us conclude with ontology.

Citing, at the beginning of chapter VI, a few of my own lines, in which I attempted to define "Negro-African ontology," Alassane Ndaw poses the question: "Is the term *ontology* really suitable for a thought that does not explicitly pose the problem of being?"[77] My emphasis. It is an academic precaution. Indeed, even if Kocc Barma, the Senegalese sage, did not theoretically pose the question, he resolved it with his inquiries, but especially with his answers. In the same way as the diviners, magicians, and other healers; in the same way as the masters of initiates. As Ndaw demonstrates throughout his sixth chapter.

If, in the text cited by Ndaw, I spoke of "ontology," it is because I was referring to Aristotle's physics, even more so to his metaphysics, and, for the last time, to his famous phrase "The science called philosophy is generally conceived as having as its object the first causes and principles of beings."[78] It is in this sense that Marcel Griaule, but also Father Placide Tempels, uses the word. In this sense, *ontology* is the science of being because it concerns first causes.

If there is one point on which all great Africanists agree, it is indeed the Weltanschauung, the Negro-African worldview, which we have sketched several times in this preface and whose essence is constituted by the theory of Vital Force.

Alexis Kagamé aligns here with Placide Tempels and the Griaule school. Thus, Negro-African sages, always and everywhere, as far and as deep as the investigations have gone, have always conceived—because it is a concept—the Universe as set in motion [*mu*] and formed, ultimately, by forces endowed with great vitality and, therefore, capable, as I have said, of being reinforced or *de-forced* [*dé-forcer*]. And in every thing, in every sensible manifestation [*apparence*], from the grain of sand to the cosmos itself, to space and time, including Man, and to God.

It is in metaphysics that one can best compare the two thoughts, Eurameri-can and Negro-African, and thus the two philosophies. For Anaxagoras, we have seen, the first cause of things is the *noûs*, the spirit, that is to say, the mixture of discursive and intuitive reason. For Aristotle—although he recognizes, for the knowledge of truth and action, the cooperation of the *aïsthésis*, of the *noûs* and *oréxis*, that is "sensation," of "reason" and "desire"—his God, Being of beings, is, as we have seen, defined as Intelligence contemplating itself. For the Negro-African sages, on the contrary, before being intelligence, God is forces, better yet, the Force of forces—he is movement, life. It is from Him that all force, all movement, all life emanates; toward Him that all force, all movement, all life moves; and into Him that all force, all movement, all life—better, life fortifying, vivifying itself—is integrated.

Alassane Ndaw draws two consequences from this theory of forces:[79]

The first is that all forces are hierarchized. And that this is to harmonize not only social relations but also the relationships between natural phenomena. There are, first, the demigods or spirits. Next come the primordial, mythical ancestors, then the ordinary ancestors, then living men, in order of *primogeniture*, then animals, plants, and minerals. It is understood that the closer one gets to God, the more vital force one has. It remains that each being, even the humblest, the most apparently inanimate, has a soul, a force. Hence the name "animism" often given to Negro-African philosophy or religion.[80]

It is on this theory that Negro-African ethics [*morale*] rests, which is the second consequence. Thus, for the Negro-African, the good is everything that favors or increases force because it is life; evil is what hinders it, diminishes it. The entire organization of religious ceremonies, the whole ritual, we have seen, is organized with this aim of increasing the Vital Force in mind. It is in this way that Negro Art, beyond aesthetics—and this is what characterizes aesthetics—has as its ultimate goal, in rejoicing the senses and the heart, only to increase, to revitalize life. Negro-African ethics aims, in a word, to make all the forces of the entire universe interact for the Supreme Good, which is the realization, in its fullness, of life: of the Being of beings. "Nothing," says Father Tempels, "moves in this universe without influencing other forces by its movement."[81]

The second consequence of the theory of the vital force is that, as Alassane Ndaw writes, "all creation is centered on man"—that Negro-African philosophy is essentially a "humanist" philosophy, that it is less a philosophy of the subject than a philosophy of the human.[82]

Of course, in the Negro-African universe, as we have seen, every being—even a simple appearance, the slightest sensible sign—is endowed with a singular force. Man, especially the living man, is endowed with the privilege of having the most active, the most dynamic force. This is one of those "secrets," one of those "fissions" that lends its unique character to Negro-African philosophy. The most rational explanation can be given as follows: Man, through the teaching he has received during initiation, through his reflection, through his action, has increased his capacity to act on other forces more than other beings from the animal, plant, and mineral kingdoms. And the living man is more active than the dead ancestors. God Himself, as I have indicated, needs humans to realize His fullness: their actions, their sacrifices, their gatherings, their poetry. It is in this way that, in realizing God and the Universe, Man realizes himself at the same time. God is, indeed, the end of Man, into whom he will enter upon his death in order to identify with God, to become God himself.

I would not want to conclude on the topic of Negro-African ontology without noting an additional convergence between Negro-African thought and modern, even contemporary thought. The theory of the vital force can indeed be compared with the latest discoveries in physics. I refer the reader to the work of Pierre Guaydier entitled *Les grandes découvertes de la physique moderne* [The great discoveries of modern physics].[83]

Like modern physics, Negro-African ontology is an energetics in which nothing is lost, where everything transforms in discontinuity. Like modern physics, it rejects science and classical philosophy—those of Plato and Aristotle but also those of the philosophers of seventeenth-century Europe, for whom everything was immutable, with absolute laws.

Before concluding, I would like to summarize the points of convergence between Negro-African thought and modern thought, as noted by Alassane Ndaw throughout his study, which I will formulate as follows:

1. Negro-African thought is categorical and classificatory.
2. Despite this, it has a global vision of a world that is unified by a dynamic dialectics.
3. Space and time, which belong to the same class, are felt not quantitatively but qualitatively.
4. Despite the coherence of this vision and because Negro-African thought departs from and encroaches on reality, there is a gap, that is to say, a noncoincidence, between the signifier and the signified, the conscious and the unconscious, in short, a discontinuity.
5. Desire, symbolized by femininity, plays a significant role in Negro-African thought and in the Negro-African universe.
6. In this universe, where even God himself needs Man, Man constitutes the center or, better, the dynamic motor: the re-creator.
7. Being, as the first cause, is vital force, and philosophy an energetics.

In his conclusion, Professor Alassane Ndaw invites us, the intellectuals of Black Africa, to develop a new philosophy, which would be "Negro-African."

It is, first, a matter of a philosophy worthy of this name, in the sense that it would be a science of Being or, more precisely, a "conception of the world and of life."

But this philosophy would be Negro-African because it would be rooted in the values of *Negritude* and, primarily, in the power of emotion, of "feeling," expressed through symbolic images, not to mention rhythm, composed of repetitions that do not repeat themselves.

However, this philosophy, as "negro" as it should be, should nevertheless be modern, that is to say, "based on the organization and speculative exploitation of the sensible world."

This means that, assimilating the Euramerican virtues of "thinking," the spirit of organization, and method, the new Negro-African philosophers will develop, within themselves, along with the concept, the spirit of geometry, more precisely, of algebra.

This is to voice my agreement with Alassane Ndaw. Here, at the end of the twentieth century, when all civilizations, and especially the very notion of civilization, are being interrogated, it is essential that each continent, indeed each nation, root itself, in its original virtues, so as to gain vigor, but also open itself up to other virtues, especially those that are most different from its own. Let us not forget that the first and greatest civilizations—from Egypt, Sumer, Greece, Rome, and India—were born in a complementary and exemplary fashion, at the meeting point of Blacks and Whites. Just as *Homo sapiens* before them, through the virtues of biological and cultural *métissage*.

Léopold Sédar Senghor, "Pour une philosophie négro-africaine et moderne," *Liberté 5: Le dialogue des cultures* (Éditions du Seuil, 1983), 211–37. The text appeared first as a preface to Alassane Ndaw, *La pensée africaine: recherches sur les fondements de la pensée négro-africaine* (Nouvelles Éditions Africaines, 1983), 5–47.

1. [Theogonic poetry refers to the tradition of texts following Hesiod's "Theogony," a cosmological work of poetry describing the origins of the cosmos and the genealogies of the Greek gods, composed around 700 BC.—Eds.]

2. [Jean Granier, *Le Discours du monde: Essai sur la destination de la philosophie* (Seuil, 1977).—Eds.]

3. Given that most readers will not read Greek, I have taken to transcribing Greek words with letters from the French alphabet.

4. [While Senghor does not enclose this first sentence in quotation marks, the citation from Aristotle begins here.—Eds.]

5. Aristotle, *Éthique à Nicomaque*, trans. Jules Tricot (Librairie philosophique J. Vrin, 1959), 290.

6. March 1, 1933. [Alain [Émile-Auguste Chartier], "LXXX: Les saints (1 March 1933)," *Propos sur la religion* (Rieder, 1938; reprint, Puf, 1969), 254.—Eds.]

7. Plato, *Œuvres complètes*, tome 1, trans. Joseph Moreau and Léon Robin (Gallimard, Bibliothèque de la Pléiade, 1940), 755.

8. Aristotle, *Éthique à Nicomaque*, 755.

9. Aristotle, *Éthique à Nicomaque*, 276 and 277. [In their English translation of *Nicomachean Ethics*, Robert C. Bartlett and Susan D. Collins translate these lines as follows: "There are three things in the soul that are authoritative over action and truth: sense perception, intellect, and longing." Aristotle, *Nicomachean Ethics*, trans. Robert C. Bartlett and Susan D. Collins (University of Chicago Press, 2011), 117.—Eds.]

10. [*Dianoïa* (Greek: *διάνοια*) refers to "a type of cognition between *doxa* and *noeisis*"; when "opposed to *nous* [= intuitive knowledge], it means discursive, syllogistic reasoning." See F. E. Peters, *Greek Philosophical Terms: A Historical Lexicon* (New York University Press, 1967), 37.—Eds.]

11. More precisely, all "technology" [*technique*].

12. Aristotle, *Éthique à Nicomaque*, 31.

13. Aristotle, *Éthique à Nicomaque*, 80.

14. Aristotle, *Éthique à Nicomaque*, 278.

15. [*Mèden agan* is a Greek phrase meaning "nothing in excess."—Eds.]

16. Aristotle, *Éthique à Nicomaque*, 509.

17. Aristotle, *Éthique à Nicomaque*, 512, 513.

18. [Senghor is paraphrasing Ndaw, in "Introduction," *La pensée africaine*, 51–69.—Eds.]

19. [Ndaw, *La pensée africaine*, 60.—Eds.]

20. [Ndaw, *La pensée africaine*, 60 (emphasis in original).—Eds.]

21. [Ndaw, *La pensée africaine*, 60.—Eds.]

22. [Ndaw, *La pensée africaine*, 60–61.—Eds.]

23. [Ndaw, *La pensée africaine*, 60.—Eds.]

24. [Georges André Malraux (1901–76) was a French writer, art theorist, and minister of cultural affairs. He gave the inaugural speech at the First World Festival of Negro Arts in Dakar (March 30, 1966).—Eds.]

25. [*La philosophie bantoue* was first published in Flemish/Dutch in 1945. Senghor refers to the 1949 edition by Présence Africaine. Placide Tempels, *La philosophie bantoue* (Présence Africaine, 1949).—Eds.]

26. I have preferred here the translation of André Cresson's *Aristote* to the *Métaphysique* of the Librairie Vrin, although both translations are presented as being by J[ules] Tricot. [André Cresson, *Aristote: Sa vie, son œuvre avec un exposé de sa philosophie* (Puf, 1943), 68; Aristotle, *Métaphysique*, trans. Jules Tricot (Librairie Philosophique J. Vrin, 1933), 12.—Eds.]

27. Dominique Zahan, *Religion, spiritualité et pensée africaines* (Payot, 1970), 18. [For an English translation, see Dominique Zahan, *The Religion, Spirituality, and Thought of Traditional Africa*, trans. Kate Ezra Martin and Lawrence M. Martin (University of Chicago Press, 1979).—Eds.]

28. Cf. Aristotle, *Métaphysique*, trans. Jules Tricot, A 2, 78–106.

29. Aristotle, *Métaphysique*, trans. Jules Tricot, A 7, 681.

30. [Lucien Lévy-Bruhl, *Carnets* (Presses Universitaires de France, 1949), 131.—Eds.]

31. Alexis Kagamé, *La philosophie bantu comparée* (Présence Africaine, 1976).

32. Kagamé, *La philosophie bantu comparée*, 48.

33. [Descartes, *Œuvres Complètes*, vol. 3: *Discours de la méthode*, ed. Jean-Marie Beyssade and Denis Kambouchner (Gallimard, 2009), 122.—Eds.]

34. Aristotle, *Métaphysique*, trans. Jules Tricot, A 1, 6.

35. Aristotle, *Métaphysique*, trans. Jules Tricot, A 1, 6.

36. Zahan, *Religion*, 18.

37. Aristotle, *Métaphysique*, trans. Jules Tricot, A 1, 5.

38. Aristotle, *Organon*, vol. V: *Les Topiques*, vol. 2, trans. Jules Tricot (Librairie Vrin, 1939), 29.

39. Aristotle, *Les Topiques*, 29.

40. Cresson, *Aristote*, 82.

41. Kagamé, *La philosophie bantu comparée*, 100.

42. Cf. Henri Gaden, *Le Poular: Dialecte Peul du Fouta sénégalais*, tome 1: *Étude morphologique–Textes* (Librairie Ernest Leroux, 1912), 44–53.

43. Paul Griéger, *La caractérologie ethnique: Approche et compréhension des peuples* (Puf, 1961).

44. C. G. Jung, *Types psychologiques*, trans. Y. Le Lay (Librairie de l'Université, 1950), 392.

45. [Bergson, *Essai sur les données immédiates de la conscience* (Paris: Félix Alcan, 1889).—Eds.]

46. Martin Heidegger, *Introduction à la métaphysique*, trans. Gilbert Kahn (Puf, 1958).

47. Martin Heidegger, *Essais et conférences*, trans. André Préau (Gallimard, 1980).

48. Heidegger, *Introduction à la métaphysique*, 185.

49. Jean Cohen, *Le Haut langage: Théorie de la poéticité* (Flammarion, 1979).

50. Cohen, *Le Haut langage*, 126.

51. Cohen, *Le Haut langage*, 278.

52. [The conference "Négritude et Mathématique" was organized by the Union progressiste sénégalaise and held in Dakar April 12–18, 1971; Niang's contribution was later published as an article in *Présence Africaine* alongside Senghor's essay "Problématique de la Négritude." See Souleymane Niang, "Négritude et Mathématique," *Présence Africaine* 78 (1972): 27–47.—Eds.]

53. Cf. Alexandre Moret, *Histoire de l'Orient* (Puf, 1936).

54. Jean-Marie Durand, *Les plantes bienfaisantes du Rwanda et du Burundi* (Presses du groupe scolaire, 1966).

55. Arthur Lestrade, *La médecine indigène au Ruanda* (Académie royale des sciences d'outre-mer, 1955).

56. Joseph Kerharo and Jacques-Georges Adam, *La pharmacopée sénégalaise traditionnelle: Plantes médicinales et toxiques* (Vigot Frères, 1974).

57. [Roger Garaudy (1913–2012) was a French philosopher and Communist politician who fought in the Resistance under Vichy. Garaudy directed UNESCO's "Dialogue of Civilizations" during the 1970s, a period during which he and Senghor corresponded regularly. In 1972, Garaudy gave a lecture in Dakar, "La contribution de l'Art nègre à la civilisation de l'Universel," and this appears to have been the moment when he and Senghor began discussing the idea of a "Université des mutants," which eventually would be inaugurated at a conference on Gorée Island on October 20, 1978.—Eds.]

58. Jean Granier, *Le discours du monde* (Seuil, 1977), 236.

59. Aristotle, *Métaphysique*, trans. Jules Tricot, tome 1, 348.

60. Granier, *Le discours du monde*, 16, 117.

61. [Henri Grégoire, *De la littérature des nègres* (Paris: Maradan, 1808).—Eds.]

62. Henri Bergson, *La pensée et le Mouvant* (Puf, 1938), 27.

63. Bergson, *La pensée et le Mouvant*, 216.

64. Cf. his lecture titled, "L'Homme africain devant la mort" [The African man before death].

65. [Ndaw, *La pensée africaine*, 95–97, 98–103, 103–8, 108–12.—Eds.]

66. [Ndaw, *La pensée africaine*, 103–4.—Eds.]

67. [Ndaw, *La pensée africaine*, 104.—Eds.]

68. [Here Senghor is playing on the homophony between *connaissance* (knowledge or understanding) and *co-naissance* (literally, cobirth), to suggest a generative process through which one dies to the self in order to be reborn in the Other. This is his "participatory" understanding of knowledge.—Eds.]

69. [Ndaw, *La pensée africaine*, 109.—Eds.]

70. [Ndaw, *La pensée africaine*, 110.—Eds.]

71. And even six, Germaine Dieterlen will tell us, in her *Essai sur la religion bambara* (Puf, 1951).

72. [Ndaw, *La pensée africaine*, 209–35.—Eds.]

73. Madeleine Barthélemy-Madaule, *Bergson et Teilhard de Chardin* (Seuil, 1963).

74. [Barthélemy-Madaule, *Bergson et Teilhard de Chardin*, 644.—Eds.]

75. [Ndaw, *La pensée africaine*, 215.—Eds.]

76. [Ndaw, *La pensée africaine*, 225–26.—Eds.]

77. [Ndaw, *La pensée africaine*, 237.—Eds.]

78. A 1, 10. Once again, I have chosen André Cresson's translation of *Aristote* (p. 68).

79. [In the text published in *Liberté*, this entire paragraph appears within quotation marks, suggesting it is a direct citation from Ndaw, when it is really a paraphrase (of Ndaw, *La pensée africaine*, 240–41); in the original preface to Ndaw's work, there are no such quotation marks. Instead, this paragraph and the one that follows are both set off with bullets. We have removed the quotation marks in translation.—Eds.]

80. [Ndaw, *La pensée africaine*, 240–41.—Eds.]

81. [Ndaw, *La pensée africaine*, 240.—Eds.]

82. [Ndaw, *La pensée africaine*, 241.—Eds.]

83. Pierre Guaydier, *Les Grandes découvertes de la physique moderne* (Corrêa, 1951).

7

As Manatees Go to Drink from the Source

This is not a preface. It is not intended for the readers. As Molière said three centuries ago, the greatest of rules is "to please." It is on the suggestion of some of my critic friends that I am writing these lines, in order to respond to their queries and to the criticisms of a few others who, when they are not accusing negro poets of emulating the great national poets, are exhorting them to feel in *French* simply because they write in French. Some criticize me for imitating Saint-John Perse,[1] when I had not read his work before publishing *Chants d'ombre* [Shadow songs] and *Hosties noires* [Black hosts].[2] Others criticize Césaire for exasperating them with his tam-tam rhythm, as if a zebra could get rid of its stripes. In truth, we are *manatees* who, according to the African myth, return to drink from the source as they once did long ago when they were quadrupedal—or humans.[3] I do not know, exactly, if this is a myth or natural history.

But let us come back to literary history. I have said elsewhere[4] that the endeavor of the poets of the *Anthology*[5] was neither a literary undertaking nor a divertissement; it was pure *passion*. For the poet is like a woman in labor—she must give birth—and the Negro singularly, for he comes from a world where speech is converted spontaneously into rhythm as soon as man is moved [*ému*] and brought back to himself, to his authenticity. Yes, speech [*parole*] is made poem. Must I disclose this? Aimé Césaire's *Cahier d'un retour au pays natal* [Journal of a homecoming] was a painful parturition.[6] The mother quite nearly lost her life in the process—I mean to say, her reason. She remains forever haunted by it, like those clairvoyants Europe locks up in its prison-asylums but whom Africa continues to care for and venerate, as it sees in them the messengers of God.

Of course, since the decree of 16 Pluviôse, Year II,[7] Negroes have *evolved*, to use an ugly expression. They have even terribly evolved; they have remained themselves. Men who *feel* and who do not think. Beauty has always struck them, straight as a spear, at the root of life—catastrophe, too. For me, the *event* makes me sick, my face turns ashen. *She* says that I am an actor! Before the Porte Océane in Havre, before an Île-de-France landscape in autumn, a Florentine palace, a fresco by Giotto, an announcement of a famine in the Indies, a storm in the Antilles, an earthquake at Antananarivo, there they are, Negroes, *seized* to the groin, as though struck by lightning. Think of the *griot* before the Prince, the young woman before the Athlete, her *Lion*. They sing, but not of what they see with their eyes. Of course, they have evolved—courtly love is dead, so, too, are the gymnic games! They no longer have the tam-tam and balafon rhythms, the voice of the koras, the incense of the Lover to inspire them. So here is the modern Poet, gray as winter in a gray hotel room. How would he not think of the Kingdom of Childhood, of the Promised Land of the Future in the midst of the nothingness of the present? How would he not sing his "Negritude standing upright [*debout*]"?[8] And since his instruments have been confiscated, let them be replaced by tobacco, coffee, and grid paper! There he is, just like the griot, with the same tensed throat and stomach, joy in the depths of his anguish. I say: *love and parturition*. Here he is now, the Poet, at the ends of his efforts, a lover alongside his lover, slavering, resting on his side, not sad, ah! but triumphant: light, relaxed and caressing his son, the poem, like God at the end of the Sixth Day.

Why would I deny it? The poets of the *Anthology* have been subject to influences, many influences: they are proud of it. I will even confess—and I learned this from Aragon—that I have much read, from the troubadours to Paul Claudel. And much imitated. I had to write in *French*—I will say why shortly—in a language that was not my own. I will also confess that when I discovered

Saint-John Perse, after the Liberation, I was dazzled like Paul on his way to Damascus. And the *Livre des morts* (Book of the Dead) provoked, in me, the same *rapture*.[9] What is surprising about this? This poetry is not exactly from Europe, and it is not a coincidence if Jean Guéhenno confirms that the texts of *Dogon* cosmogonies "are not without analogy to the poems of Claudel or Alexis Léger (Saint-John Perse)."[10] But I already had, in my drawers, the material for two collections of poetry. The truth is that I read—more accurately, I listened to, transcribed, and analyzed Negro-African poems.[11] And the Antilleans who did not know these poems—Césaire was not among them—would find them naturally by going down into themselves, by letting themselves be carried away by the torrent, a thousand meters underground. If they want to find us masters, it would be wiser to search for them in Africa. For manatees return to drink from the spring of Simal.[12]

Beyond what we deem a fraternal *message*, we would better understand the style of the poets of the *Anthology*: their *Negritude*. Some critics have praised—or bemoaned—our picturesque style, an unintentionally picturesque style, as they would have it. I remember that in elementary school, everything in the French language was picturesque to me, even the musicality of the words. And the women from my village who, during a drought in the rainy season, wore trousers, helmets, and black glasses, and spoke like the French, so as to make God laugh and pour down rain. When we say *kora, balafon, tam-tam*, and not harp, piano, and drum, we do not intend to be picturesque; we are "calling a spade a spade." We write, first, and I do not mean exclusively, for the French of Africa, and if the French of France find something picturesque about it, it will be almost regrettable for us. The message, the image, is not to be found there; it is in the simple naming of things. That is what gives Camara Laye's novel *L'enfant noir* [The Black child] its poetry, just as with Birago Diop's *Contes d'Amadou Coumba* [The tales of Amadou Coumba].[13] This power of the word [*verbe*], as I have tried to show elsewhere,[14] appears already and even more clearly in Negro-African languages, where almost all the words are *descriptive*, whether it is a matter of phonetics, morphology, or semantics. Here, the word is more than an image, it is an analogical image without even the assistance of metaphor. It is enough to name the thing for its *meaning* to emerge from under the *sign*. For everything is, at the same time, sign and meaning for the Negro-African; every being, every thing, but also matter, shape, color, smell and gesture and rhythm and tone and timbre: the color of the pagne, the shape of the kora, the pattern of the lover's sandals, the steps and gestures of the dancer, and the mask, and what not. I remember the reception that my friend Houphouët-Boigny[15] gave in my honor in Yamoussoukro. All the *Baoulé*[16] nobility, dressed in ceremonial attire. Long gold necklaces and plates as large as a hand; fly swatters with gold-plated handles; above all, diadems with Elephants, Spiders, and cornucopia sculpted in gold. This garb, this *regalia* spoke to me in a perfectly clear language. To return to the verbal image, the French have made a habit of underscoring analogy using a second, abstract and moral word. It is not a coincidence if, as André Rousseau has observed recently, Paul Claudel feels the need, in his translations, to make the meaning of biblical images more sensuous [*sensible*].[17] Centuries of rationalism have made a concrete wall out of what was once a transparent veil. It is the merit of surrealism to have revealed that two concrete words sufficed here and that, the more "distant" the "relationship between the two realities brought together," the stronger the image.[18] But the Negro-African poet, as I have said, often makes do with a single sign:

> There are no more young people in the village.
> Dyakhère de Moussa, listen to me.
> The sun is at its zenith, and there is not even a murmur!

This is not a metaphor, but we feel, in these simple words, in the midday peace, the solemn presence of the *Spirits*.

And since I need to justify my poems, I will confess again that almost all beings and things that they evoke are from my canton: a few *Sereer* villages, lost among the *tanns* (marshes), the woods, the *bolongs* (swamps), and the fields.[19] I need only name them to relive the Kingdom of Childhood—the reader along with me, I hope—"through forests of symbols."[20] I once lived there among shepherds and peasants. Evenings, my father would frequently beat me, admonishing me for my wanderings, and, in order to punish and "tame" me, he ended up sending me to the European School [*École des Blancs*], to the great dismay of my mother, who protested that, at seven years old, it was too early. I therefore lived in this Kingdom, saw with my own eyes, heard with my own ears, the fantastical beings beyond ordinary things: the *Kouss* [dwarfs][21] in the tamarin trees, the Crocodiles, guardians of the fountains, the Manatees singing in the river, the Dead of the village, and the Ancestors, who spoke to me, initiating me in the alternating truths of the Night and the Day. Thus, I had only to name the things, the elements of my childhood universe, to prophesy the City of Tomorrow, which will be reborn of the ashes of the City of Yesterday. This is the mission of the Poet.

But the power of the analogical image frees itself only under the effect of *rhythm*. Rhythm alone provokes the poetic short-circuit and transmutes brass into gold, speech [*parole*] into the *Word* [*Verbe*]. We have much abused, between the two world wars, the "narcotic image" [*le 'stupéfiant image'*]; it has even been presented as the essence of poetry. It is fortunate that André Breton himself has reacted against this abuse, and insisted, in *Silence d'or* [Silence is golden], on the sensible—I would say sensual—qualities of words. "Never had so much faith been expressed in the *tonal* value of words," he writes, "as in surrealist writing. The negativist attitudes provoked by instrumental music very well seem, here, to have found a way to make up for each other. In terms of language [*langage*], the surrealist poets were not and are still not enamored with anything so much as with this capacity of words to assemble into singular chains, and thus to shine—and this at the very moment they were least sought after."[22] And again: "The great poets were 'auditives,' not visionaries."[23]

I want to remain faithful to my point, and to avoid making value judgments. The negro poets, those of the *Anthology*, as well as those from the oral tradition, are, before all else, "auditives"; they are *bards*. They are tyrannically subject to "inner music," and first to rhythm. I remember the gymnic poets of my village. The most naïve among them could not compose unless in the trance of the tam-tams—unless sustained, inspired, fed by the rhythm of the tam-tams. For me, it is first an expression, a phrase, a verse that is initially whispered in my ear, as a leitmotiv, and when I start writing, I do not know what the poem will be. This is the state of the negro poet that Henri Hell did not understand when he wrote, about Aimé Césaire: "We appreciate the incantatory power of some of his poems, such as *Batouque*, with its haunting rhythm. However, such brightness, such exaggeration, such provocative excess eventually grow stale. Is such an orgy of rare words (*ramphorinques*, trammel, coalescences, etc.) necessary? This always exacerbated lyricism engenders monotony. *Et les chiens se taisaient* [And the dogs were silent] is no longer a tragedy, but a long lyrical cry the violence of which becomes doleful. The continuous clamor of words is deafening. The incessant flickering of images (no matter how dazzling they are) clouds one's vision. The poem that contents itself with accumulating enumeration after enumeration, cry after cry, is no longer a poem. With no other rhythm than the constant repetition of some incantatory words, it unravels after a while. The incessant and unbridled eruption of images robs them of their efficacy. . . ."[24] Forgive me for citing Henri Hell at such length. He allows us to state the problem by giving the example of a critic who does not want to understand, who resists *sympathy* [*sym-pathie*]. Let us return to images. If the critic speaks of "the incessant and unbridled eruption of images" and their "gratuitousness," it is because he has not penetrated its full meaning.[25] His excuse is that he would have needed to possess the double culture of the Poet, both French and Negro. It is even more concerning that he did not see that, in Césaire's work, images are more than ambivalent, they are *multivalent*, and doubly so. The same *idea-feeling* [*idée-sentiment*] is expressed here by a whole series of images, and each image lives its own life, radiating in all its facets of meaning, like a diamond. Even more serious, Hell did not notice that "the incessant flickering of images" is nothing but one form of rhythm among others. For rhythm remains the issue at stake. Sartre understood this quite well, as he writes in "Orphée noir" [Black Orpheus]: "So one can speak here of *engaged* and even *directed* automatic writing; not because there is any reflective intervention, but because the words and images perpetually translate the same torrid obsession. The White Surrealist finds, within himself, a slackening [*détente*]; Césaire finds the rigid inflexibility of revindication and resentment. [Étienne] Léro's words are organized softly, in decompression, by a loosening of logical ties, around large and vague themes; Césaire's words are pressed against each other and cemented by his furious passion. Between the most hazardous comparisons between the most distant terms runs a secret thread of hate and of hope."[26] This is only possible because the New Negro is animated by a lucid passion, and because the former student of the École Normale Supérieure remains, in his delirium, the magnificent master of his language. I say that rhythm remains the issue at stake. It is to be found not only in the accents of modern French[27] but also in the repetition of the same words and the same grammatical categories, even in the use—an instinctive use—of certain rhetorical alliterations, assonances, homoeoteleutons . . .

helmsman of the night populated with suns and rainbows
helmsman of the sea and of death
freedom o my gawky gal your legs sticky with fresh blood
your cry of a surprised bird, of a fascine
and of a *shabeen* in the depths of the water
of an alburnum and of a trial and of a triumphant litchi
and of a sacrilege
crawl crawl
my gawky one populated with horses and foliage
and with risks and with acquaintances
with heritage and with sources
at the peak of your loves at the peak of your delays
at the peak of your canticles
of your lanterns
on your insect-like and rootlike tips
crawl great drunken spawn of bulldogs of mastiffs of baby wild boars
of lanceolate pit vipers and of fires
in order to rout the scrofulous examples of poultices.[28]

As the navel of the poem, rhythm, which is born of emotion, in turn creates emotion. And *humor*, the other face of Negritude. This is to speak of its multivalence—like that of the image. As it appears in Léon Damas:

All to your needs
all to your joy
all to illusion
all to this Côte-d'Azur
all at last to only you and yourself

but nothing
but nothing again
but still nothing again
and nothing to my hotel drawer
if it is not
poor hangman
the key that swings
the key that does not care[29]

It is not a matter of comparing the poets of the *Anthology* to the great national poets, even though people like Gaétan Picon, Jean-Paul Sartre, and André Breton do not hesitate to rank Césaire at the level of the greatest. Our ambition is a modest one: It is to be the *precursors*, to blaze a trail for an authentic negro poetry that, nonetheless, does not renounce being French. As the painters from Flanders, Holland, and Italy who were called "primitives" once did. In this study, it is a matter, I repeat, of showing the differences of *situation* and that, even if the essence of poetry is the same everywhere, the temperaments and the means of the poets are diverse. To criticize Césaire and other poets for their rhythm, for their "monotony," in a word for their *style*, is to criticize them for being born "Negroes," Antilleans, or Africans and not "French" if not Christians; it is to criticize them for remaining themselves, irreducibly sincere. "Such exaggeration, such provocative excess" can only be explained, in Césaire's case, by his Antillean origins, by centuries of enslavement, by his alienation from Africa and from himself. For centuries, I say, he was snatched from *his* order, thrown into the suffering of exile, the contradictions of *métissage* and capitalism. What is surprising about him making use of his pen just like Louis Armstrong making use of his trumpet? Or, perhaps more precisely, making use of *his* tam-tam like the followers of Voodoo. He needs to lose himself in the verbal dance, in the rhythm of the tam-tam, to find himself in the Cosmos. Henri Hell writes about [Pierre-Jean] Jouve: "Since we are in this world in order to be in total unity with God, and if God is the universal Soul, the poet, like the mystic, must lose the notion of his self to achieve this union. He must free himself from an illusory individuality for the benefit of a superior Self, located *beneath* [*en deçà de*] personality. The Self allows itself to be destroyed in order to expand itself to the ultimate Reality."[30] My emphasis. One should undoubtedly read: *beyond* [*au-delà*]. I fully subscribe to this judgment. It is precisely that Césaire does not do otherwise; he operates only with his own means, which are those of his race and his native island, "Martinique the snake charmer."

Yet another word on this. My friend [Georges-Emmanuel] Clancier[31] advised me: "Let us hope that Senghor manages to create a language for himself with a more diverse rhythm, in which an image, a word will suddenly erect its ridge [*arête*],[32] around which the figure of the poem will organize itself; it is then that he will truly make us penetrate into his poetic universe, which is original and of a rich humanity."[33] This was in 1945. Dear Clancier, I have perhaps succumbed to your advice, which has since been repeated by others. I would regret it if I had been aware of it. Do you not see that you are inviting me to organize the poem in a French style, like a *drama*, whereas, it is for us a *symphony*, like a song, a tale, a play, a negro mask? But the monotony of the tone is what distinguishes poetry from prose. That is the hallmark of Negritude, the incantation that allows access to the truth of essential things: the Forces of the Cosmos.

But, I will be asked: "Why, then, do you write in French?" Because we are cultural *métis*, because, if we feel as Negroes [*en nègres*], we express ourselves in French, because *French* is a language of universal vocation, because our message speaks *also* to the French of France and to others, because French is a language of "gentility and honesty."[34] Who said that it was a gray and lifeless language of engineers and diplomats? Of course, I also said so one day for the purposes of my argument. You'll forgive me for this. For I know its resources for having tasted it, masticated it, taught it, and [know] that it is the language of the gods. Listen to Corneille, Lautréamont, Rimbaud, Péguy, Claudel. Listen to the great Hugo. French is a language of great organs that lend themselves to all timbres, to all effects, from the most exquisite sweetness to the fulgurance of the storm. It is, alternately or at the same time, flute, oboe, trumpet, tam-tam, and even cannon. And French has endowed us with its abstract words—so rare in our mother tongues—through which tears turn to precious stones. For us, words are naturally enveloped in a halo of sap and blood; French words radiate like diamonds. They are flares that light up our night.

We have now arrived at the last question: the *elocution* [*diction*] of the poem. I consider it to be essential. The great lesson I have retained from Marône, the poetess of my village,[35] is that poetry is song, if not music—and this is not a mere literary cliché. The poem is like a jazz score, the execution of which is as important as the text. From one collection of poetry to another, this idea has grown stronger in me; and when, at the head of a poem, I give an instrumental indication, it is not a simple formula. The same poem can thus be recited—I do not mean declaimed—chanted or sung. First of all, one can recite the poem according to the French tradition, by emphasizing the major accent in each group of words. *Expressive* punctuation, which I have made use of in this collection, will help, I hope. One can also recite accompanied by a musical instrument: tam-tam, *tama*,[36] *kora*,[37] *xalam*,[38] as Maurice Sonar Senghor does.[39] It is a matter, then, of emphasizing the final accent of the verse and those of the lyric arêtes in the same way as the town crier in Black villages. One can chant the poem on a musical background with the same instruments or, preferably, with flutes, organs, or a jazz orchestra. Cinema gives us an idea of this method. But, here, the tone is more monotonous. Finally, one can sing the poem to a musical score. The music that Madame Barat-Pepper, the artist behind *Messe des piroguiers* (The *piroguiers'* Mass),[40] has written for "Chant de l'initié" [Song of the initiate][41] on African themes provides an excellent example of this.

I persist in thinking that the poem is completed only when it becomes simultaneously song, speech, and music. The popular so-called expressive elocution, as it is used on the stage and in the streets, is the *antipoem*. As if, beneath its variety, rhythm were not a monotony that translates the *substantial* movement of the cosmic Forces, of the Eternal! . . . It is time that we stopped the process of disaggregating the modern world, and first of poetry. It must be restored to its origins, to the time when it was sung—and danced. As in Greece, in Israel, and above all in the Egypt of the Pharaohs. As in today's Black Africa. "Any house divided against itself," any art divided against itself, can only perish. Poetry must not perish. For then where would the hope of the World be?

NOTES

Léopold Sédar Senghor, "Comme les lamantins vont boire à la source," *Liberté 1: Négritude et humanisme* (Seuil, 1964), 218–27. The text was first published as a postface in Senghor's collection of poetry *Éthiopiques* (Seuil, 1956), 103–23. In our translation of the title, we have preferred to use the term "source" rather than "spring" (another possible translation) to evoke the sense of origins and return suggested by Senghor's imagery.

1. [Saint-John Perse, or Alexis Léger (1887–1975), was a French poet born in Guadeloupe.—Eds.]

2. [Léopold Sédar Senghor, *Chants d'ombre, suivis de Hosties noires: Poèmes* (Seuil, 1948). Both *Chants d'ombre* and *Hosties noires* were originally published in standalone

volumes. Léopold Sédar Senghor, *Chants d'ombre* (Seuil, 1946); Léopold Sédar Senghor, *Hosties noires* (Seuil, 1948).—Eds.]

3. [The image of the manatee is frequently used in Senghor's prose and poetry. This marine mammal, inhabiting the coastal regions of the African continent as well the Americas, is a diasporic figure. It is also especially significant in Sereer mythology. As a mythical creature, part animal and part human, it is considered a bridge between the visible and invisible worlds. The Sereer people hold manatees in such high regard that, in certain instances, they perform funeral rites for them, akin to those reserved for humans. Senghor grew up less than a mile from the Simal River in the Saloum Delta, a habitat where manatees would return to rest in the fresh and calm waters of the Sereer village after their journeys in the ocean. This site is known as the "source de Simal"; the "spring" or "source" of Simal; see also note 12.—Eds.]

4. Cf. Léopold Sédar Senghor, "L'Apport de la poésie nègre au demi-siècle," in *Témoignages sur la poésie du demi-siècle* (Éditions de la Maison du Poète, 1952), 49–65. [The text was written on the occasion of the First International Biennale of Poetry in Knokke-le Zoute, or Knokke-Heist, in Belgium in September 1952 and published the same year in the conference proceedings, *Témoignages*. It was reprinted in *Liberté 1: Négritude et humanisme* (Seuil, 1964), 133–46.—Eds.]

5. Cf. Léopold Sédar Senghor, ed., *Anthologie de la nouvelle poésie nègre et malgache de langue française* (Presses universitaires de France, 1948).

6. [For a bilingual edition of Césaire's text, see Aimé Césaire, *Journal of a Homecoming / Cahier d'un retour au pays natal*, trans. N. Gregson Davis (Duke University Press, 2017).—Eds.]

7. [Senghor is referring to the decree of February 4, 1794, which abolished slavery in French colonies.—Eds.]

8. [In the *Cahier*, Césaire declares Haiti to be the place where Negritude stood up (*debout*) for the first time. Aimé Césaire, *Cahier d'un retour au pays natal* (Présence Africaine, 1956), 44.—Eds.]

9. [Senghor seems to be referring to the Egyptian Book of the Dead. The edition he owned was Grégoire Kolpaktchy, *Livre des morts des anciens Egyptiens* (Editions des Champs-Elysées, 1954).—Eds.]

10. Jean Guéhenno, *La France et les noirs* (Gallimard, 1954), 75.

11. Cf. Léopold Sédar Senghor, "Langage et poésie négro-africaine," in *Poésie et langage* (Éditions de la Maison du Poète, 1954), 93–109. [This text was written on the occasion of the Second International Biennale of Poetry, held in Knokke-le Zoute in Belgium (September 2–6, 1954) and published the same year in the conference proceedings, *Poésie et langage*. It was reprinted in *Babel* 7, no. 4 (1961), 151–59; and in *Liberté 1: Négritude et humanisme* (Seuil, 1964), 159–72.—Eds.]

12. [Simal being a river in the Sine-Saloum region of Senegal. It is also the name of a village along the same river, located just a few miles from Senghor's father's house in the village of Djilor Djidiack, a place to which Senghor often returned as a child. Manatees migrated up the Simal and would feed and rest in its calm waters, including directly in front of Senghor's father's house.—Eds.]

13. [Camara Laye, *L'enfant noir* (Plon, 1953); Birago Diop, *Contes d'Amadou Coumba* (Fasquelle, 1947; reprint, Présence Africaine, 1960).—Eds.]

14. Senghor, "Langage et poésie négro-africaine."

15. [Félix Houphouët-Boigny (1905–93) was an Ivorian politician and the first president of Côte d'Ivoire.—Eds.]

16. [The Baoulé, or Baule, are an Akan people of Côte d'Ivoire.—Eds.]

17. [Between 1918 and 1953, Claudel translated many Psalms from the Latin of the Vulgate; most of the translations were collected and published posthumously. See, for instance, Paul Claudel, *Paul Claudel traduit librement les Sept Psaumes de la Pénitence* (Seuil, 1945); and *Paul Claudel répond les Psaumes* (Ides et Calendes, 1948). It is possible Senghor is referring to one of André Rousseaux's many reviews of Claudel's work, which appeared in the "Les livres" sections of *Le Figaro littéraire*. Reviewing the volumes *Paul Claudel répond les Psaumes* and *Paul Claudel interroge le Cantique des Cantiques* (both L.U.F., 1948), Rousseaux discusses (and criticizes) Claudel's rendering of biblical images through poetic language deemed too worldly and corporeal. André Rousseaux, "Claudel et le 'Cantique des Cantiques,'" *Le Figaro littéraire*, January 15, 1949, 2. In another essay, we find clear resonances with Senghor's notion of rhythm: "The truth is that 'we are music,' that is to say, rhythm associated to the movement of the world the eternal Being." André Rousseaux, "La musique de Claudel," *Le Figaro littéraire*, September 11, 1948, 2 (original emphasis). See also André Rousseaux, *Littérature du vingtième siècle* (Albin Michel, 1949).—Eds.]

18. André Breton, *Premier manifeste du surréalisme* (Éditions du Sagittaire, 1924), 34. [Here Breton is quoting from the poet Pierre Reverdy's March 1918 edition of *Nord–Sud*, a literary review which he edited.—Eds.]

19. Cf. the glossary in *Chants pour Naëtt*. [Léopold Sédar Senghor, *Chants pour Naëtt* (Seghers, 1949), 46–49.—Eds.]

20. [Charles Baudelaire, "Correspondances," in *Œuvres Complètes*, vol. 2, ed. Claude Pichois (Paris: Gallimard, 1975), 11. This is the Pléiade edition, in which the title of the poem is written as "Correspondances" rather than "Correspondences."—Eds.]

21. Spirits that remind us of the first inhabitants of West Africa, the Pygmies, who were extinguished or suppressed by the Tall-Negroes.

22. [André Breton, "Silence d'or," in *André Breton*, ed. Jean-Louis Bédouin (Seghers, 1950), 83–84.—Eds.]

23. [Breton, "Silence d'or," 85.—Eds.]

24. Henri Hell, "Poètes de ce temps: Pierre Jean Jouve, René Char, Aimé Césaire, Jacques Prévert," *Fontaine* 57, no. 10 (1946): 814.—Eds.]

25. [Hell, "Poètes de ce temps," 814.—Eds.]

26. [Étienne Léro (1910–39) was a French poet from Martinique, considered the first poet of African descent to identify as a Surrealist. Jean-Paul Sartre, "Orphée noir," in Senghor, *Anthologie*, xxvii (our translation).—Eds.]

27. Cf. the studies by André Spire and the phoneticians Abbé Rousselot, George Lot, Robert de Souza, and Grammont. [In the former case, Senghor is most likely referring to the poet André Spire's essay *Plaisir poétique et plaisir musculaire: Essai sur l'évolution des techniques poétiques* (José Corti, 1949). In the latter case, Senghor is referring to various

studies on French phonetics, especially applications of experimental phonetics to poetics, by the phoneticians Abbé Pierre-Jean Rousselot (1846–1946) and his student George Lote (1880–1949), and Maurice Grammont (1866–1946). Robert de Souza (1864–1946) was not a linguist but a symbolist poet who wrote several texts on meter and rhythm; Senghor perhaps has in mind his texts *Le Rythme poétique* (Paris: Perrin et Cie., 1892) and *Du rythme en français* (Librairie universitaire, 1912).—Eds.]

28. Aimé Césaire, *Et les chiens se taisaient: Tragédie* (Présence Africaine, 1956), 64–65. [English translation modified from Aimé Césaire, "...... And the Dogs Were Silent," in *Lyric and Dramatic Poetry: 1946–82*, trans. Clayton Eshleman and Annette Smith (University of Virginia Press, 1990), 37. *Shabeen*, a term used in some English-speaking islands of the West Indies, is used in this passage to translate the French *chabin·e* to refer to someone of mixed race. See the note for page 37 in *Lyric and Dramatic Poetry*, 72.—Eds.]

29. Léon Gontran Damas, *Graffiti* (Seghers, 1952), 26–27.

30. [Hell, "Poètes de ce temps," 805.—Eds.]

31. [Senghor is referring to Georges-Emmanuel Clancier (1914–2018). A French poet, novelist, and journalist, Clancier would receive the Prix Goncourt for poetry in 1992.—Eds.]

32. [Clancier's use of the word *arête* also suggests the image of the dorsal ridge of a fish, of a delicate fish bone, of the ribbed or spinelike structure of a vaulted cathedral ceiling.—Eds.]

33. [Senghor is referring to a review of *Chants d'ombre* (1945) by Georges-Emmanuel Clancier in a Sunday issue of the paper *Paysage* (September 2, 1945), cited in Armand Guibert, *Léopold Sédar Senghor* (Présence Africaine, 1962), 156.—Eds.]

34. Guéhenno, *La France et les Noirs* (Gallimard, 1954), 139.

35. I discovered Marône's genius while carrying out a study on Negro-African poetry in the oral tradition. The author of some two thousand gymnic songs, she had extended her glory to the precincts of the ancient kingdom of Sine (Senegal). [Senghor writes *Marôme* but this is a typo; the correct spelling is *Marône*.—Eds.]

36. A little drum hooked under the armpit, most often used by the griots.

37. A kind of harp.

38. A guitar with four strings.

39. [These are all musical instruments that are widespread among different ethnic groups in West Africa.—Eds.]

40. [*Messe des Piroguiers* was a 1958 record composed by Eliane Barat and intended to be a "pure adaptation of the Banda choir"; it featured the Petits chanteurs de Saint-Laurent choir, directed by Abbé Paul Zurfluh, with Félix Maleka on the tam-tam and Abbé Jehan Revert on the organ. Eliane Barat (1915–87) was a French field collector and composer who specialized in Central African music. The *Messe* is available at "Messe des piroguiers," Gallica, Bibliothèque Nationale de France, accessed July 10, 2025, https://gallica.bnf.fr/ark:/12148/bpt6k88106353. Maurice Sonar Senghor (1926–2007) was Senghor's nephew and the founder of the National Ballet of Senegal.—Eds.]

41. Cf. Senghor, *Chants pour Naëtt*. ["Chant de l'initié" was published in *Présence Africaine* 1 (1947): 56–59.—Eds.]

PART II

Negritude, Aesthetics, and Philosophy

8

What the Black Man Offers

Wisdom lies not in reason but in love.
—ANDRÉ GIDE, *Les nouvelles nourritures*, 1935

They (Negroes) disrupt the mechanical rhythm of America, and one must be grateful to them for this; people had forgotten that men can live without bank accounts and bathtubs.
—PAUL MORAND, *New York*, 1930

That the *Negro* is already present in the elaboration of the New World is not proven by African troops serving in Europe; they would prove only that he is participating in the destruction of the previous order, the old order. It is in a number of singular works by contemporary artists and writers that the Negro makes his current presence known, as well as in a few other works—less perfect, perhaps, but moving nonetheless—produced by Black men. It is not about this presence alone that I wish to speak here but also, and foremost, about all the potential presences that the study of the Negro allows us to perceive.

I adopt the word [Negro] following others: It is convenient. Are there Negroes, pure Negroes, *Black* Negroes? Science says no. I know that there is and has been a negro culture, whose sphere included the countries of the Sudan, Guinea, and Congo in the classical senses of these terms. In the words of the German ethnologist [Leo Frobenius]: "The Sudan itself thus possesses an ancient and ardent indigenous civilization as well. It is a fact that explorers in Equatorial Africa encountered fresh and vigorous ancient civilizations everywhere that the predominance of Arabs, Hamite blood, or European civilization had not stripped the dust from the wings of black moths which, long ago, had been so beautiful.[1] Everywhere!"[2] A unified and undivided culture:[3] "I know of no northern people who would be comparable to these primitives in terms of the unity of their civilization."[4] I shall specify. Civilization: a culture that is born of the reciprocal action of race, tradition, and environment, a culture that, having been transported to America, remained intact in style, if not in its ergological elements. This civilization disappeared, was forgotten; its culture has not been extinguished. And slavery, as a matter of fact, compensated for the environment and for the disaggregating effects of *métissage*.[5]

It is of this culture that I wish to speak, though not exactly as an ethnologist. Rather, I will focus on its human flowerings, more precisely, on the new boughs grafted onto the old human trunk. With partiality, of course. The flaws of Black people are known well enough that I will not revisit them here—one, inexcusable among others, is that of not being assimilated in the depths of their personality. I do not mean, "not letting their style to assimilate." What is of interest here are the fertile elements that their culture offers, the elements of the *negro style*. And the latter will endure as long as the negro soul endures. It is perennial, or should I say, eternal?

First, we shall briefly examine the negro soul; then, its conception of the world, from which religious and social life follow; finally, the arts, which are contingent on these last two. All that shall remain for me then is to bring together the riches that we will have gathered during the course of this study into a single sheaf, in a humanistic spirit.

Numerous works have been published on "*the negro soul*." It remains an inscrutable forest, shrouded in mystery. Father [Francis] Libermann used to say to his missionaries: "Be Negroes with the Negroes so as to win them over to Jesus Christ."[6] In other words, rationalist thought, mechanico-materialist explanations, explain nothing. Here less than anywhere else. How many would have fallen prey to the Minotaur had it not been for the help of Ariadne, of Emotion-Femininity? It is precisely a totally rationalist confusionism to explain the Negro by his utilitarianism when he is practical, by his materialism when he is sensual.

Does one wish to understand his soul? Let us create a sensibility like his own. Without literature between subject and object, without imagination in the usual sense of the word, with neither subject nor object. May the colors lose nothing of their intensity, the forms nothing of their weight or volume, the sounds nothing of their carnal singularity. . . . The negro body, the negro soul, are permeable to all the world's solicitations—to even apparently imperceptible rhythms, not only those of the cosmos. This sensibility is moral as well. It is an oft-noted fact that the Negro is sensitive to speech and to ideas, still more to the perceptible—dare I say sensual?—qualities of speech as well as the spiritual, not intellectual, qualities of ideas. Eloquence seduces him, as do the communist theoretician, the hero, and the saint as well. "His voice moved men," they used to say of Father [François-Xavier] Dahin.[7] This gives the impression that the Negro is easily assimilable when it is he who assimilates. Hence the enthusiasm of the Latins in general and missionaries in particular for the ease with which they believe to "convert" and "civilize" Negroes. Hence, often, their sudden discouragement when faced with some irrational and typically negro revelation: "We do not know them . . . we cannot know them," admits the same Father Dahin on his deathbed, after over fifty years in Africa.

Emotive sensibility. *Emotion is negro, as reason Hellenic.*[8] Water rippled by the slightest breeze? "An open-air soul,"[9] battered by winds and whose fruit often falls before ripening? Yes, in a sense. Today, the Negro is richer in gifts than in deeds. But the tree plunges its roots far into the earth, the river runs deep, carrying along flecks of gold. And the Afro-American poet sings:

I've known rivers,
Ancient, dusky rivers,
My soul has grown deep like the rivers.[10]

Let us not digress further. The very nature of the Negro's emotion, his sensibility, explains his attitude before the object that is perceived with such an essential intensity. It is a state of abandon that becomes need, an active attitude of communion—of identification even—no matter how forceful the object's action. Or shall I say, its personality? A *rhythmic* attitude. Let us hold onto that word.

But because the Negro is emotive, the object is perceived both in its morphological features and in its essence. We take for granted the realism of romantics, their lack of imagination. Negro realism, in inhuman situations, will be the human reaction that leads to *humor*. For the moment, I will say that the Negro cannot conceive of an object that is different from himself in its essence. He lends it a sensibility, a will, a human soul—but the soul of a Black man. It has been pointed out that this is not exactly mere anthropomorphism. Spirits, for instance, do not always have a human form. We call it *animism*; I will say anthropopsychism. This is not necessarily negrocentrism, as we will see.

Thus, all of Nature is animated by a human presence. It is humanized in the etymological and current sense of the term. Not only animals and natural phenomena—rain, wind, thunder, mountains, rivers—but also trees and stones become human. Humans who retain their original physical features as instruments and signs of their personal soul. This is the most profound, eternal feature of the negro soul. The feature that, in America, managed to resist all attempts at economic slavery and "moral liberation." "Surely, it is in order to raise taxes, grumbled Madame Vache, who, having hastily caked on a layer of white face powder, slipped on her canary-yellow shoes and her sky-blue chiffon dress with wide embroidered flounces; and, sweating, breathless, but delighted at the chance to sport her hoop earrings and her French gold necklace, she set off for the village, atop a mule."[11] Like a Negress—and like a cow.[12] Even the flowers in *The Green Pastures* adopt, with a negro accent, an altogether negro deference to the Lord's will: "O.K., Lord!"[13]

This is the negro soul, if indeed it is to be defined. I concede that the negro soul is the product of its environment and that Africa is the "Dark Continent" [*Continent noir*]. The effect of the environment is especially perceptible here. The effect of this pristine light on the savanna and at the edges of the forest, where civilizations were born; a stark light that lays bare the essential, the essence of things; this climate whose violence simultaneously crushes and exalts. I grant this, if it will explain things better. In any case, religion and society are, in turn, explained by this soul.

It is often said that the Negro offers nothing new to *religion*. Neither dogma nor ethics [*la morale*], only a certain *religiosity*. But on reflection, does the crux of the matter not lie in this contemptuous word rather than in the thing itself? I nevertheless wish to examine the dogma and ethics of Negroes without being duped.

First of all, these distinctions are not suitable. "Be Negroes with the Negroes"; and they know not how to divide nor count nor discern.

"I believe in God, the Father Almighty, Creator of Heaven and Earth." The beginning of the credo never appalled any Negro. In fact, the Negro is monotheistic, as far back as one goes in history, and across the world. There is only one God, who created all things, who is all power and all might. All the powers, all the wills of the spirits and Ancestors are merely emanations of Him.

But this God, those who are well informed tell us, is vague in his attributes and disinterested in men. As such, we neither worship him nor offer him sacrifices. Indeed, he is love: We need not fear his anger. He is powerful and happy: He eats not, drinks not. But he is no wooden god, no mere piece of timber.[14] My *Sereer* grandmothers, I remember, sought him out in times of hardship. They dressed as men, gear and all, fired their guns, and shot their arrows at the sky.[15] They went so far as to spout crude words . . . in French. And God, smiling, answered them.

Worship concerns the spirits and the Ancestors. It is worth noting, along with Maurice Delafosse, one of the greatest—that is, the most attentive—Africanists in France, that the worship of Ancestors seems to be older than the worship of spirits, and therefore more negro. It is common to all Black Africa. Sacrifices are not the clause of a contract—a "quid pro quo"—any more than an act of magic in the name of a strictly utilitarian purpose, as in secret societies. The latter are of relatively recent origin, and I would see in them a superstitious, all-too-human distortion, as evidenced by the transformation of these magical practices in degenerate negro societies in America. I see three purposes to sacrifices: to *participate* in the power of higher spirits, among which are the Ancestors; to *commune* with them in a kind of identification; finally, to be *charitable* toward the Ancestors. For the Dead, almighty as they are, they do not have *life* and cannot acquire the "earthly fruits"[16] that give living its intense sweetness.

No, neither fear nor material concerns govern the Negroes' religion—though it is not entirely free of these things, for the Negro, too, feels human anguish. But rather *love*, and charity, which is love manifested as action. "What the laborer yearns for when he scans the horizon," says a Tukulor adage, "is the village. It is not the desire to eat but rather the entire past that draws him in this direction."[17]

A similar sentiment animates the son who works for his father, the man who toils for the community. The sentiment of family communion is projected back in time, in the transcendent world, to the Ancestors, to the spirits, and to God. A logic of love.

Henceforth, what is the importance of *ethics*, and what does it matter that there are not any sanctions? But there is an ethics, which is enforced here on earth, by the reprobation of the members of the community and by one's conscience. The feeling of *dignity* among Black people is well known. Ethics consists in not disrupting the communion with the living, the Dead, the spirits, and God, and in maintaining it through *charity*. Whoever ruptures this mystical bond is promptly ostracized.

Let us return to the question of religiosity. What the Negro offers is the ability to perceive the supernatural in the natural, the meaning of the transcendent, and the active surrender that goes along with it—the surrender of love. This element of his ethnic personality is as enduring as animism. The study of the Negro-American proves it. Among the "radical" poets themselves, that is, the communizing poets, religious sentiment surges up suddenly, very high, from the depths of their negritude. *Father Divine*, mocked so extensively by the Paris tabloids,[18] would not have won over the negro masses had he not promised and given his "angels," besides the banquets, the more intoxicating joys of the soul. Negro hysteria? "Nervous postulation," in [Charles] Baudelaire's words, which keeps the New World from peacefully worshiping its Golden Calf.[19]

Here we are at the heart of the humanist problem. It is a matter of knowing "what is man's purpose?" Is it in himself alone that he must find his answer, as [Jean] Guéhenno, following [Jules] Michelet and [Maxime] Gorki, would have it?[20] Or is Man only really a man when he goes beyond himself to find his fulfillment outside the self, and even outside of Man? It is a matter, as [Jacques] Maritain, following [Max] Scheler, says, of "concentrating the world into man" and "expanding man to the world."[21] The Negro answers by negrofying God, by making man—whom he does not deify—part of the supernatural world.

Lord, I fashion dark gods, too,
Daring even to give You
Dark despairing features . . . [22]

The Afro-American poets prefer to speak directly to Christ, to the Man-God.

Now we will consider the natural side of the unitary order of the world: the negro *social order*.

Not only is the family, for Negroes, as elsewhere, the basic social unit, but also society itself is composed of a series of tiered concentric circles, overlapping one another and modeled after the family. Multiple families that share the same dialect and a feeling of common origin form a tribe; multiple tribes that speak the same language and live in the same country can constitute a kingdom; finally, multiple kingdoms may, in turn, become a confederation or an empire. This is why the study of the *Family* is important. We will focus on the elements that must continue to fecundate the negro family and allow it to fuse with and enrich the new humanism. As [Diedrich] Westermann writes, "If

Africans manage to keep [the family] intact during the period of transition, to rid it of its unhealthy elements, and to save it from degeneration, there will be no need for anxiety about their future."[23]

The oneness of the family. It is economic unity, since the wealth [*bien*] of the family is shared and jointly held, as well as ethical unity, since the ultimate purpose of the family is to procreate children who will continue to perpetuate the tradition, piously maintaining and multiplying the spark of life in their bodies and souls.

But this oneness does not ignore individuals, though they are subordinate to the unity of the group. Alongside their shared wealth, women, like children, have their own personal wealth, which they can augment or spend freely. Children receive a liberal education, even though it is harsh around the age of initiation. They are not beaten, and in their age groups [*sociétés d'âge*], they complete their apprenticeship to manhood on their own. And the *Woman* is man's equal, contrary to what most people think. The fiancé is not consulted any more than the fiancée: But they agree and live out their acceptance, which is more important than an impression of choice.[24] Women are not purchased; their families are merely compensated. That is why when they experience some offense from their husbands, they retreat to their parents' homes; and their husbands must come to beg for forgiveness and offer reparation. This, at least, is the Sereer custom. For woman is the *Mother*, the giver of life and the guardian of tradition. Some superficial minds have compared her to a beast of burden. In actual fact, within the division of labor—for there is a division, not a hierarchization—her task is often greater; but so is her responsibility, and thus also her dignity. Paradoxical as it may seem, the Black woman who becomes a "French citizen" loses some of her freedom, and some of her dignity.

The family, limited in this way, is not an autonomous group: It lives within the "square" [*carré*] of the clan family in the sense of *gens*. This is the true Negro-African family. It includes all the descendants of the same ancestor, whether man or woman. It is here that the unitary aspect of the family, as the foundation and prefiguration of the Black social order, appears most clearly. The clan's Ancestor, a spirit himself and a sort of demigod, is the link uniting the divine to the human. Therefore, he created a spark of life and continues to tend to it, to stoke the eternal flame. It is he who obtained from the local spirit of the earth the usufruct of a part of the soil for his descendants, as a shared and inalienable property [*bien*]. The head of the family, the firstborn of the living, is in turn the link uniting the living to the deceased Ancestors. Closer to them, taking part in their knowledge and their power, speaking to them with familiarity, he is more than a chief; he is the priest and the mediator. He is the priest because, in this *community*, no one, and certainly no one holding any power, can act for himself alone. Everyone is benevolent toward others; and each life is deepened and multiplied in this family communion of the Dead and the living.

It is at the level of the tribe, as opposed to the kingdom, that we can most clearly grasp the Negro's solution to social and political problems. It is a solution that responded, in advance, to this "pluralistic unity," which remains an ideal for today's humanists, at least those for whom humanism is not a sort of vain diversion of the *honnête homme*.[25]

The questions related to *property* and *work* are the basis of the whole social problem. For every man, it is a matter of living off his work, considered the essential source of property; liberated precisely by and from his work, it is, above all, a matter of finding a source of joy and dignity. Far from alienating us from ourselves, work should allow us to discover and cultivate our spiritual riches.

The vice of capitalist society is not in the existence of property, a necessary condition for the development of the person; it lies in the fact that property does not reside essentially in work. But, in the negro society, "work, or perhaps more precisely, productive action, is considered to be the sole source of property, but it cannot confer property rights except on the object that it has produced."[26]

However—as critiques of capitalism have often highlighted—property can only ever be theoretical if natural resources and the means of production remain in the hands of a few individuals. In this case as well, the Negro resolved the problem in a humanistic way. The earth, as well as whatever it bears—rivers, streams, forests, animals, fish—, is shared wealth, distributed among families and sometimes even among family members, who have temporary possession or are permanent tenants of it. On the other hand, the means of production in general, the instruments of work, are the shared property of the familial group or the guild [*corporation*].

As a result, the ownership of agricultural and artisanal products is collective, given that the work itself is collective. Hence, this crucial advantage: Each man is materially guaranteed "the vital minimum" based on his needs. "When the harvest is ready," the Wolof say, "it belongs to everyone."[27] And this other advantage, no less important from the standpoint of personal life: The acquisition of excess, of necessary luxury, is made possible by work, since individual ownership is regulated and checked, not eliminated.

For, if Negroes disregarded the individual, they did not subjugate the *person*, as people tend to believe. The person seems to me to be less in need of the singularity that torments our modern individualists, less preoccupied with differentiating himself than with the depths and intensity of spiritual life.

Negroes have not called into question the nature of the person—we know that they converse and hardly debate; they have made individual life possible, even within the collective form of ownership.

"In order for a collective form of ownership to be beneficial to the person," Maritain writes, "it must not have impersonal ownership as its condition."[28] Among Negroes, the human is bound by the juridical bonds of custom and tradition—and above all, by a mystical bond—to the object of collective ownership. Let us leave it at that. The group—family, guild, age group—has its own personality, which is experienced as such by each member. The family, as we have seen, shares the same blood, the same flame; the guild is simply a clan family which holds ownership of a "craft." The human thus retains a sense of individuality—although communitarian—before the object of ownership. But the object itself is, quite often, apprehended as a person. This is the case with natural phenomena: plains, rivers, forests. As has already been said, the Ancestor who occupies the soil is bound to it in the name of the family. For Earth is a female spirit; and the mystical marriage of the group and Mother-Earth is celebrated, "solemnly."

Thus, ownership of the means of production is no longer something theoretical, transient, or illusory. The worker feels that he is a person, not a mere cog in the machine. He knows that his mind and his body toil freely for something good that belongs to him. Even the guildsman, whose profession is inferior to that of the peasant, knows he is irreplaceable. In this way, the basic human needs for true freedom, responsibility, and dignity are met: that is, the needs of the person.[29]

And labor is not a burden but a source of joy. Because it enables the fulfillment and flourishing of the individual. It is worth noting that within the negro social order, working the land is the noblest of occupations. The negro soul remains, tenaciously, a peasant soul. Take, for example, the United States: The negro workers in the North, the active voters, are nostalgic for the plantations of the South, where their brothers live as serfs. And their poets sing:

Of fruit-trees laden by low-singing rills,
And dewy dawns, and mystical blue skies
In benediction over nun-like hills.[30]

Working the land permits the fusion of Man and Creation, which is at the heart of the humanist problem; that it is performed to the world's rhythm: a rhythm not at all mechanical but alive and free, the rhythm of day and night, of the two seasons in Africa, of the plant that grows and dies. And the Negro, sensing that he is in unison with the Universe, rhythms his work through song and the tam-tam. Negro labor, negro rhythm, and negro joy which is liberated through and by means of labor.

Politics, naturally, is closely connected to the *social*. The social is to politics what the artist's hand is to their mind. It is a matter of organizing, maintaining, and perfecting the polis [*Cité*]: of governing and legislating. Governing requires authority; legislating requires wisdom. Both must return to their sources, must strive for the well-being of communities and individuals, that is, for the well-being of the polis. In today's Western democracies, however, these obligations are ignored. The legislator is elected, in the best cases, by a party—an aggregate of material interests—and he legislates under the dictates of a financial oligarchy and for that oligarchy. The legislation is doubly inhumane because it is doubly corrupted. As for the government, despite the ever growing police forces, it lacks authority because authority is based on a spiritual preeminence, and the government is in the hands of shrewd puppets, of *politicians* instead of statesmen.

Things are different in the prototypical negro kingdom, as was the case with the *Sereer* kingdom of the Sine. The legislative assembly is composed of high dignitaries and notables, the chiefs of clan families. Hence, the wisdom that comes with the knowledge of tradition, life experience, and a sense of responsibility. The goal is to reconcile tradition and progress—resistance to progress, often criticized, lies less in the negro genius than in geographic conditions.

The authority of the King, who is an ascendant of the spiritual order,[31] symbolizes the unity of the kingdom. Originally, the King is the descendant of the Shepherd of the people, and he represents the former as well as the latter. Authority of the King. Because the people "take pride in the person of the King himself and his past."[32] Because the King is elected by the people through the heads of the main families. Because electors have the power to suspend or depose him. Efficacy of power, because it is founded on authority and is exercised through numerous ministers whom the sovereign can neither choose nor dismiss.

There is a stark contrast between this harmonious community and the cliché of the "negro tyrant." "Pluralistic unity": a polis modeled after natural communities and built on them. Even the guilds and numerous associations do not remain without influence.

And the *individual*? they will ask me again. And again, I shall answer: The individual is disregarded insofar as his existence is founded on a false notion of liberty and on a separation of personal interests. The case of the *person* is altogether different. The negro social order, I admit, showed little concern for the development of *reason*; and this is a lacuna. Nonetheless, the person still had as many opportunities to develop and impose himself in the associations, the guilds, and the deliberating and *palavering* assemblies. We have not spoken enough about the importance of the *palaver*. Equality reigned there, as did the sense of one's human *dignity*. The same sentiment extended to the servant and the captive. I even knew of people who committed suicide—the act of a free man—because they had been accused of lying or theft.

What the modern world has forgotten—one of the reasons for the current crisis of civilization—is that the development of the person requires a nonindividualistic orientation. It only happens in the land of the Dead,[33] within the sphere of the family, of the group. The need for fraternal communion is more profoundly human than the need for solitude. It is just as human as the need for the supernatural. It has been said that pity is foreign to the negro soul. That may be true for pity, but not for charity, not for hospitality. Wherever one went, there was the commons [*carré*] or the villages reserved to house strangers. It is customary to invite the passerby to share the family meal. The first White people to land were themselves considered divine guests. The greatest praise one can find among the Wolof is: *Bëgg mbok, bëgg nit,* "The one who likes kin, the one who likes people." To those who destroyed his civilization, to the slaver, to the lyncher, the Afro-American poets responded only with words of peace:

I return it loveliness
Having made it so;
For I wore the bitterness
From it long ago.[34]

This is not vain literature. This "humanness" [*humanité*] of the negro soul, this inability to permanently hate helped resolve the racial problem in Latin America, and even in North America. I believe that the contributions of Negroes in the social and political sphere will not end there. This would be the appropriate place to discuss the humanistic role of *Ethnology*. In the development of a more humane world, ethnology should enable us to expect the best from each people. And the Black peoples will not come empty-handed to the meeting of the political and the social, in a world shared between democratic individualism and all-embracing collectivism.

Meanwhile, the negro contributions to the world of the twentieth century have above all been translated into *literature* and *art* in general. As interesting as it may be, the study of African literature and of the nascent Afro-American literature would take us too far afield. I only want to examine the visual arts and music. These should be separated only for practical reasons. Despite what specialists say, we find the same elements in various places, among both Africans and Afro-Americans. The merit of the American experience has been to eliminate everything that was not permanent or human.

But these contributions will have been fruitful for only a few artists. In general, these contributions were turned into fragmented borrowings, devoid of vitality because they lacked spirit. I fear that the surrealists themselves did not have an always discreet—that is to say, enlightened—sympathy for the Negro. How could it have been otherwise in a world enslaved to matter and to reason, where reason is only denounced in order to proclaim the primacy of matter? This is indeed the cause of the decadence of art in the nineteenth century; and the manifestos "for French Art" published by the journal *Les Beaux-Arts* constitute ample evidence. Realism and impressionism are merely two sides of the same error. It is the worship of the real that leads to *photographic art*. Ultimately, the mind is satisfied with analyzing and combining elements of the real, for the sake of a subtle play, of a variation on reality. A natural consequence of Théophile Gautier's position: "My rebellious body does not want to acknowledge the supremacy of the soul, and my flesh does not accept that it is being mortified. . . . Three things please me: gold, marble, and crimson: luster, solidity, color."[35] Preferences may vary, but not the spirit or, rather, the lack thereof. Hence, Baudelaire's attacks against the "Pagan School"; hence, later, those of a Cézanne and a Gauguin, whose disciples ventured toward negro art, to the point of meeting it.

For the merit of negro art is to be neither game nor pure artistic pleasure: It is to signify.

Among the plastic arts, I choose the most representative one—*sculpture*. Even the decoration of the simplest utensils of household furnishings, far from distracting from the object's purpose and being vain ornamentation, underscores this purpose. A practical art, not a utilitarian one; and classical in this original sense. Above all, a *spiritual art*—it has wrongly been described as idealist or intellectual—because it is religious. The essential function of sculptors is to represent the dead Ancestors and the spirits by making statues that are, at one and the same time, symbol and dwelling. The goal is to enable one to grasp, and to feel, the personal soul of the Ancestors and spirits as efficacious will, to grant access to the *surreal*.

This is accomplished by means of a representation of the human and, singularly, through a representation of the human face, the most faithful reflection of the soul. It is a striking fact that anthropomorphic statues and, among these, masks, predominate. A constant preoccupation with the *intermediary Man*.

This spirituality is expressed through the most concrete elements of the real. The negro artist is less a painter than a sculptor, less a draftsman than a model maker, working solid, three-dimensional matter with his hands, like the Creator. He chooses the most concrete material: over bronze, ivory, and gold, he chooses wood, which is common and lends itself to the rawest effects and the most delicate of nuances. He uses few colors, but those he does use are always bold, saturated: white, black, red—African colors. Above all, he uses lines, surfaces, volumes: the most material properties.

However, because this art aims at the *essential* expression of the object, it stands in opposition to *subjective realism*. The artist submits details to a spiritual hierarchy and, consequently, to a technical one. Where many saw only clumsiness of the hands or an inability to observe the real, there is in fact *intention*, or at least a consciousness of ordering—better, of subordinating. I have already mentioned the importance the artist ascribes to the human face.

Rhythm is the organizing force that constitutes the negro style.[36] It is the most perceptible and the least material thing. It is the vital element par excellence. It is the primary condition for and the sign of art, like the breath of life; a breath that quickens or slows, becomes regular or spasmodic, according to the being's tension, to the degree and quality of emotion. Such is rhythm originally, in its purity, as it is found in the masterpieces of negro art, in sculpture in particular. It is composed of one theme—a sculptural form—that contrasts with a parallel theme, like inhalation to exhalation, and that is reprised. It is not symmetry that engenders monotony; rhythm is living, it is free. For reprisal is not mere repetition, nor is it replication. The theme is taken up again in another place, on another plane, in another combination, as a variation; and it acquires another intonation, another timbre, another accent. And the overall effect is intensified, not without nuances. This is how rhythm acts, despotically, on what is least intellectual in us in order to get us to enter into the *spirituality of the object*. And this attitude of abandon of ours is itself rhythmic.

Classical art in the most human sense of the word because it is "controlled romanticism" [*romantisme dominé*], because the artist, mastering the richness of his emotive depths, arouses and guides that emotion toward the Idea. Through the simplest, most direct, and definitive means. Everything converges toward this goal. Here, there is no anecdote, no flourish, no frill. Nothing that distracts. By refusing to seduce us, the artist conquers us. Classical art as Maritain defines it: "Such a subordination of matter to the light of form . . . that no material element derived from things or the subject be admitted into the work unless strictly required as a support or vehicle for that light and which might burden or 'debauch' the eye, the ear, or the mind."[37]

What music at the close of the nineteenth century lacked was neither ideas nor authentic spirituality (it would suffice to mention, for France, César

Franck and Gabriel Fauré), but rather youthful vigor and new means of expression. God, like the mind, is invisible to scientists. Men like Claude Debussy, Darius Milhaud, and Igor Stravinsky felt the need to free themselves from rules that were conventional and had become sterile. And they set out in search of unknown alluvia and "invisible seeds."

Negro music, which we have only recently started studying seriously in Europe, responds to these needs. For, even if people are sensitive to its effects, they have not yet delved deeply into its technique. Music does not exist in Negro-African society as an autonomous art any more than sculpture does. Traditionally, it accompanies ritual songs and dances. Profaned, it does not become independent: It naturally has a place in collective celebrations such as theater, agricultural work, and athletic contests. Even in the nightly tam-tam sessions, music is not a purely aesthetic manifestation but rather allows participants to commune, more intimately, with the rhythm of the dancing community, the dancing World. Much of this has survived among Westernized, Americanized Negroes. Instinctively, they dance their music; *they dance their life*.

This means that negro music, like sculpture and dance, is rooted in the nourishing soil, that it resounds with the rhythms, sounds, and noises of the earth. This does not mean that it is descriptive or impressionistic; it also conveys feelings. Yet it is not sentimental. It provides the vigor needed by impoverished Western music—impoverished because it is based on and developed according to arbitrary rules that are, above all, overly restrictive.

I will not discuss the *melodic* contributions. That goes without saying. This aspect has been the most explored. The same cannot be said for the modal realm. Its richness remains misunderstood. Partly because certain "specialists" have denied the existence of a negro harmony. This is contested by experienced musicians, such as [Julius] Ballanta.[38] Negroes, they point out, sing in chorus. Unlike most of the folk songs of other peoples, which are sung in unison, choruses in *Négritie* are composed of multiple parts. I myself remember how difficult it was for the kind Father who directed our Black children's choir to make us sing in unison without parts or variations. [Maurice] Delafosse, writing about negro choruses, notes that "their harmony is impeccable."[39] "The rhythmic and melodic inventiveness is prodigious and melancholic (as well as somewhat naïve)," [André] Gide writes, for his part, "but what can be said about the harmony! It is here, especially, that my surprise lies. I believed all these songs to be monophonic. And they have gained this reputation because there are never any 'songs in thirds or sixths.' However, this polyphony achieved by the expansion and compression of sound is so disorienting for our septentrional ears that I doubt it can be notated with our graphic methods."[40] Bewildering indeed, and impossible to notate, since the intervals, as well as the melodic and rhythmic patterns, are of the utmost subtlety. "Alongside these," Gide writes earlier, "our own folk songs seem poor, simple, and rudimentary."[41] These alluvial lands await bold and patient pioneers.

It is in the realm of *rhythm* that the negro contribution has been the most significant, the most undisputed. Throughout this study, we have seen that the Negro is a rhythmic being. He embodies rhythm. Music, in this regard, is revealing. We will note the significance of percussion instruments. Often, the only accompaniment to a song is the beating of the tam-tam or the clapping of hands. Sometimes, percussion instruments mark the basic rhythms from which the melody freely emerges. Here, we must revisit what I said above regarding rhythm in sculpture. Let us also add that rhythm enlivens even the melody and lyrics. This is what Americans call *swing*. Characterized by syncopation, it is far from mechanical. It combines uniformity and variety, tyranny and fantasy, anticipation and surprise. This explains why the Negro can find pleasure in the same musical phrase for hours, because the phrase is not exactly the same.

Beyond strictly musical elements, the Negro has demonstrated the potential of certain instruments that were previously ignored or arbitrarily denigrated and relegated to a subordinate role. This was the case with percussion instruments, like the xylophone; and such is the case with the saxophone and brass instruments, like the trumpet and trombone. Thanks to the sharpness, the vigor, and the nobility of their sounds, they were perfectly suited to express the *negro style*. Thanks, also, to the delicately sweet and mysterious effects that the hothouse jazz artists [*hotistes*] have since coaxed out of them.

The negro influence was perceptible and promises to be fruitful not only in musical composition but also in interpretation. Perhaps it is in this realm that Afro-Americans have remained closest to their origins. It is first and foremost a question of style: of *soul*.

Hughes Panassié has brought to light the negro contributions to *hot jazz*,[42] the fundamental aspect of which lies in *interpretation*. But this influence must extend further to classical music. Perhaps more through singers than orchestras. The value of interpretation lies in intonation, as Panassié defines it: "Not only the way the note is attacked but also the way it is held, released, in short, the way it is given its full expression."[43] "It is," he adds, "the expression, the accent the performer imparts to each note and through which he conveys his entire personality." No matter how "faithful" the interpretations of great artists like Roland Hayes or Marian Anderson, there remains always something of negro interpretation. It is this particular way of enveloping the note, the sound, with a halo of flesh and blood that makes it appear so unsettled and unsettling; this "naïve" way of translating the most secret spirituality through the most carnal voice. "The soloist," Gide also writes, "possesses an admirable voice, entirely different from what is expected at the conservatory. It is a voice that at times seems choked with tears—at times, closer to sobbing than to song—with sudden harsh tones that seem out of tune. Then, suddenly, there follows a few very soft, disconcertingly sweet notes."[44]

Limited as they may be these negro contributions have rather profoundly influenced contemporary music. It has become richer and sparer, more muscular and more supple, more dynamic, more generous, and more human, because it is more *natural*. The old myth of Antaeus has not lost any of its truth.[45]

It is with this Greek myth that I wish to conclude. It is not unusual, this encounter of the Negro and the Greek. I fear that, today, many who invoke the Greeks betray Greece. A betrayal of the modern world, which has mutilated man by transforming him into a "rational animal" or even by deifying him as the "God of reason." The negro service will have been to contribute, alongside other peoples, to restoring the unity of Man and the World: to connect flesh to spirit, man to fellow man, the pebble to God. In other words, uniting the real and the surreal—through *Man*, not as center but as hinge, as the navel of the World.

NOTES

Léopold Sédar Senghor, "Ce que l'homme noir apporte," in *Liberté 1: Négritude et humanisme* (Éditions du Seuil, 1964), 22–38. The text first appeared in *L'Homme de couleur* (Plon, 1939), 292–314. An earlier English translation by Mary Beth Mader is included as an appendix to *Race and Racism in Continental Philosophy*, edited by Robert Bernasconi and Sybol Cook Anderson (Indiana University Press, 2003), "Appendix: What the Black Man Contributes," 287–301.

Epigraph 1: André Gide, *Les nouvelles nourritures* (Gallimard, 1935), 22.

Epigraph 2: Paul Morand, *New York* (Flammarion, 1930), 234–36.

1. [Before the industrial revolution, black moths were rare; they gradually replaced pale-colored moths through a process of natural selection. See also Laurent Dubreuil, "Francophone Circulation: Coriolan Ardouin, Charles Baudelaire, and the Black Butterfly Effect," *L'Esprit Créateur* 56, no. 1 (2016): 40–51.—Eds.]

2. Leo Frobenius, *Histoire de la civilisation africaine*, trans. H. Back and D. Ermont (Gallimard, 1936), 16. [For the original, see *Kulturgeschichte Afrikas* (Phaidon, 1933), 15]

3. By "culture," I mean the spirit of the civilization; by "civilization," the works and achievements of the culture. I therefore understand these words rather differently than Daniel-Rops, in *Ce qui meurt et ce qui naît* (Plon, 1937). But this is merely a difference of terminology.

4. Frobenius, *Histoire*, 16. [The original German uses the phrase *Ebenmäßigkeit der Bildung*, which more literally translated as the "evenness/equality of education"; Frobenius, *Kulturgeschichte Afrikas*, 15.—Eds.]

5. [*Métissage* (from *métis*, "mixed-race," and the nominalizing suffix *-age*) literally means the mixing or "cross-breeding" of different races or species. In the contexts of slavery and colonization, it most often referred to mixed-race subjects born of unions between an African or African-descended individual and a European. Senghor expands the notion of *métissage* to reflect a capacious understanding of racial and cultural hybridity, both on the level of the individual and on the level of society. See the discussion of *métis* in the translators' note to this volume.—Eds.]

6. [Senghor approximates the original text. Libermann writes: "Faites-vous nègres avec les nègres, et vous les jugerez comme ils doivent être jugés; faites-vous nègres avec les nègres pour les former comme ils le doivent être, non à la façon de l'Europe, mais laissez-leur ce qui leur est propre" (Make yourselves Negroes with the Negroes and you will judge them the way they should be judged; make yourself Negroes with the Negroes to form them as they should be, not in the manner of Europe, but leave them what is theirs). See François Libermann, *Notes et documents relatifs à la vie et à l'œuvre du vénérable François-Marie-Paul Libermann* (Paris: Maison Mère, 1850), 330.—Eds.]

7. Marcel Sauvage, *Les Secrets de l'Afrique noire* (Grasset, 1981). [This quote does not appear in Sauvage's work.—Eds.]

8. [Senghor's original formulation is an alexandrine, a verse form we have retained in translation.—Eds.]

9. Georges Hardy, *L'Art nègre: l'Art animiste des noirs d'Afrique* (Henri Laurens, 1927), 80.

10. Langston Hughes, "The Negro Speaks of Rivers," in *The Collected Poems of Langston Hughes*, ed. Arnold Rampersad (Knopf, 1994), 23.

11. Lydia Cabrera, *Contes nègres de Cuba* (Gallimard, 1936), 87. With a very interesting preface by Francis de Miomandre.

12. [Madame Vache literally means "Madame Cow."—Eds.]

13. [*The Green Pastures* is a 1930 Pulitzer Prize–winning play by Marc Connelly that retells stories from the Bible in New Orleans. *The Green Pastures* had the first all-Black Broadway cast and featured African American spirituals.—Eds.]

14. [*Soliveau* literally means a small *solive* or "joist." Senghor is perhaps alluding to a fable by La Fontaine (book 3, fable 4, "The Frogs Demand a King") in which a group of frogs ask Jupiter for a king. Jupiter sends the frogs a *soliveau* (in the fable, literally a log) as a substitute. In this case, *soliveau* is used figuratively and could even be a synonym for *fantoche* or "puppet."—Eds.]

15. [The Sereer are a West African ethnic group, found primarily in present-day Senegal, as well as parts of northern Gambia and southern Mauritania. Senghor was Sereer on his mother's side. The Sereer are known for having fought against both jihad and French colonial rule throughout the nineteenth and early twentieth centuries. Their society has aspects of both matrilineality and patrilineality.—Eds.]

16. [Likely a reference to Gide's *Les nourritures terrestres*, the prose poem that preceded *Les nourritures nouvelles*, cited as an epigraph.—Eds.]

17. [The Tukulor (from the French *toutcouleur*) are Pulaar speakers who were traditionally sedentary, as opposed to the Fulɓe, who were itinerant.—Eds.]

18. [Senghor writes, "les *Paris-Soir*," referring to a French newspaper published between 1923 and 1944. The meaning of the plural is something akin to "the tabloids," "the papers," or "the dailies."—Eds.]

19. [Charles Baudelaire, "Notes nouvelles sur Edgar Poe, " in *Nouvelles histoires extraordinaires par Edgar Poe* (Garnier-Flammarion, 1965), 44.—Eds.]

20. Cf. Jean Guéhenno, *Jeunesse de la France* (Bernard Grasset, 1936), 139–40.

21. [Jacques Maritain, *Distinguer pour unir, ou les degrés du savoir*, 5th ed. (Desclée de Brouwer, 1978).—Eds.]

22. Countee Cullen, "Heritage," in *Color* (Harper and Brothers, 1925), 40.

23. Diedrich Westermann, *Noirs et Blancs en Afrique* (Payot, 1937), 114.

24. Cf. Denis de Rougemont, *L'Amour et l'Occident* (Plon, 1939), 302–5.

25. [The *honnête homme* was a masculine social ideal, a gentleman figure that emerged during the seventeenth century as an inheritor of the Greek *kalos kagathos*. He was characterized as being socially adept, cultured, and cultivated, someone who had good taste, avoided excess, and controlled his emotion.—Eds.]

26. Maurice Delafosse, *Les Nègres* (Éditions Rieder, 1927), 44.

27. [Senghor appears to have invented the proverb.—Eds.]

28. Jacques Maritain, *L'Humanisme intégral* (Fernand Aubier, 1936), 202.

29. [Senghor's thinking on the nature of personhood and humanness draws on the Wolof concept of *nité*, "humanness" (from *nit*, "person"), which is based on an altruistic understanding of the person, who is fully human only insofar as they are useful to the community. Usefulness is to be understood here, as Senghor mentions, as pragmatic, not utilitarian.—Eds.]

30. Claude MacKay, "The Tropics in New York," *Liberator* 3 (May 1929): 48, reprinted in *Harlem Shadows: The Poems of Claude McKay* (Harcourt, Brace and Co., 1922), 8. Cf., on the other hand, the poetic works of Jean Toomer, in *Cane* (Boni and Liveright, 1923). Thus, an Antillean student from the École Normale Supérieure, A. Césaire, was able to defend a thesis [*mémoire*] at the Sorbonne on "the theme of the South in Negro-American literature."

31. Cf. Daniel-Rops, *Ce qui meurt et ce qui naît*, 37ff.

32. Westermann, *Noirs et Blancs*, 136.

33. [In a West African worldview, the "land of the Dead" refers to life on Earth, since the dead and the living occupy the same plane of existence, though the former are less visible and less concrete presences than the latter.—Eds.]

34. Lewis Alexander, "Transformation," in *Caroling Dusk: An Anthology of Negro Poets*, ed. Countee Cullen (Harper and Brothers, 1927), 124.

35. Théophile Gautier, *Mademoiselle de Maupin* (Charpentier, 1866), 193.

36. Cf. Paul Guillaume and Thomas Munro, *La sculpture nègre primitive* (Les Éditions G. Cres, 1929), 58–9.

37. Jacques Maritain, *Art et scolastique* (L. Rouart et fils, 1927), 97.

38. Cf. Nicholas George Julius Ballanta, preface to *Saint Helena Spirituals: Recorded and Transcribed at Penn Normal, Industrial and Agricultural School, St. Helena Island,*

Beaufort County, South Carolina (Stirmer, 1924), iv, cited by Alain Locke in *The Negro and His Music* (Associates in Negro Folk Education, 1936), 137–38.

39. [Maurice Delafosse, *Les nègres*, 70.—Eds.]

40. [André] Gide, *Retour du Tchad, suite du voyage au Congo, carnets de route* (Gallimard, 1928), 41.

41. [Gide, *Retour du Tchad*, 40.—Eds.]

42. Cf. Hughes Panassié, *Le Jazz hot* (Éditions R.-A. Corrêa, 1934).

43. [Panassié, *Le Jazz hot*, 79.—Eds.]

44. Panassié, *Le Jazz hot*, 79.

45. [In Greek and Berber mythology, Antaeus or Anti was the half-giant son of Poseidon and Gaia, who lived somewhere in the desert of present-day Libya. According to legend, he was an invincible wrestler as long as he remained in contact with his mother's element, the earth. He was famously defeated by Hercules, who lifted him off the ground.—Eds.]

9

The Contributions of Negro Poetry to the Half Century

First of all, I apologize for limiting my intervention to French-speaking countries, even though I have listened to the voices of Negro-American poets with careful attention for the past twenty-five years. It is true that the *new negro poetry in French* is greatly indebted to these poets, but, given the very paradox of its existence, this poetry may serve as an exceptional testimony.

The paradox was, indeed, to claim to express *Negritude* in French, to express the most concrete being in the most abstract language, the most peasant of all peasant existences in the most elaborate, if not the most artificial, rhetoric. "French poetry," Thierry Maulnier writes, "is the most literary of all literary activities in a country where literature is, so to say, the object of a national cult."[1] And it is no coincidence that Aimé Césaire is a former student of École Normale Supérieure. The birth of an authentic negro poetry of the French language was a response to a kind of vital necessity. A matter of life and death. It is also not a coincidence that this birth occurred during the interwar period.

Put yourself in their skin: wake up, one morning, Black and colonized, Black and naked, "in the shock of being seen" by the corrosive gaze of the White man. They knew, these negro students, between 1925 and 1935, that Europe had for three centuries taught their fathers—the slaves, the colonial subjects [*sujets*], as well as the citizens of 1848[2]—their nothingness. They had no patrimony: They had thought of nothing, built nothing, painted nothing, sung nothing. At the bottom of the abyss, in absolute despair, they were nothing. For how does one draw nothing from nothing?

Marxism offered them a solution: to join the army of the Proletariat. With this army, they would take power, would abolish race and class barriers. After which, Science and Technology would help them dominate nature. Some of them succumbed to the temptation. Not precisely the poets: neither Aimé Césaire nor Léon-Gontran Damas nor Birago Diop. Not because they denied the critical value of Marxism and its power of negation: They knew that only the "socialist" revolution could dismantle Colonialism along with Capitalism. But they knew above all that Science and Technology were White, that the *Nature* in question was matter, the matter of polytechnicians, and not that of farmers. In the "socialist" world of *Reason*, they would be, in the most favorable case, only consumers of White civilization: always colonized, always dependent. They felt in solidarity only with workers, with oppressed Europeans, "for a small stretch of the road." Their own Revolution needed to be *radical*. For, as Sartre writes in "Orphée noir" [Black Orpheus], "even if oppression is singular, its circumstances are tied to historical and geographical conditions: The Black man is its victim, *as a Black man*, whether as a colonized native [*indigène colonisé*] or a deported African. And since he is oppressed in his race and for his race, he must first of all become conscious of his race. . . . The Negro cannot deny that he is negro, nor can he claim to be part of some abstract colorless humanity: He is Black. Thus he is driven back to authenticity: Insulted, subjugated, he draws himself upright, he picks up the word *nègre*, which was thrown at him like a stone, with pride."[3] BARBARIC, Césaire proclaims:

It is the word that supports me
and strikes on my brass carcass
barbaric me the spitting cobra
which awakes me from my rotting flesh

suddenly a flying gecko
suddenly a fringed gecko
and suits me so well in the very places of force

that you will need to forget me
to throw to the dogs the hairy flesh of your chests.[4]

"To claim one's Blackness" [*se revendiquer comme noir*] consisted, before anything else, of turning one's back to the values of the West learned at school: to Technology, to Science, to Reason. This is precisely why, by a stroke of luck, European thinkers, since the beginning of the century, waged war against reason with the "miraculous weapons" of Asia and Africa that Orientalists and ethnologists had patiently discovered, collected. [Pierre-Louis] Flouquet and [Fernand] Verhesen have commended, in Guillaume Apollinaire's poem "Zone," "the great rupture heralding a new age."[5] And it happens that Apollinaire, who, at the end of that very poem, evokes the negro "fetishes" of his house, was one of the first and most passionate evangelists of negro art. But it is mostly with Breton and the surrealists, initiated by Lautréamont and Rimbaud, that the new Negroes find precious allies. Subsequently and with the vehemence he is known for, Césaire proclaims again:

Because we detest you, yes you and your reason,
we repossess ourselves in the name of dementia praecox of
flamboyant madness of inveterate cannibalism

Let us count:
the madness that remembers
the madness that howls
the madness that sees
the madness that bursts its chains
And you know the rest
That two plus two equals five.[6]

And Damas echoes the same message:

For sure I will be
fed up
without even waiting that they take
things the appearance
of a well-made camembert
Then I will stomp my feet
on the plate
or simply grab the collar
of all those who get on my nerves
in bold

colonization
civilization
assimilation and what not

Meanwhile you will hear me
often
slam the door.[7]

But "to claim one's Blackness" is not so much this haughty negation as an authentic self-affirmation. It is a question of the "return to the native land" of "the prodigal Child," of a descent into the depths of the Black soul or, to use the code word, the depths of *Negritude*. Further down, further down, where the river of black wine that brightens the midnight sun flows in uncontrollable rapids. There is the resentment, relying on, rooted in subjectivity. "Thus," Sartre writes, "subjectivity, the relation of oneself with oneself, the source of all poetry with which the (White) worker has had to mutilate himself, reappears."[8] Here we are in the royal domain of the Negro, which is *emotion*. I could have cited [Arthur de] Gobineau: May it suffice for me to recall the Count of Kyserling speaking of the "tempestuous vitality," "of the great emotional heat of Black blood."

In his preface to Césaire's *Cahier d'un retour au pays natal* [Journal of homecoming], André Breton presents "the exceptional intensity of emotion before the spectacle of life (causing the impulsion to act on it in order to change it)"[9] as the common denominator of the conditions of all great poetry. No one has perhaps responded to this demand of contemporary poetry, which Flouquet and Verhesen have strongly underscored at the beginning of their lecture, more than the *New Negroes*. I remember our small group back then and our life: a life of *resistant fighters* and *missionaries* who accepted living their lives—dangerously. I know of a certain work that was morally—what am I saying? physically and metaphysically—lived to the brink of dementia. The doctor ordered: "Complete rest for one year."

The Paradox of Poetry, the magic of Poetry. How do we make other men commune in Negritude, this so particular a thing, and in its abyssal riches? And how to express it in the drab language of engineers and diplomats? Certainly, it is only in the first half of this century that one could have attempted this endeavor, successfully in any case. This century, because it embarked on the quest, and not on the conquest, of continents and of real men, could use the ambivalent myths created by the New Negroes—those of *Exile-Passion* and of *Africa–Kingdom of Childhood*—for the nourishment of Man.

During the interwar period, the Initiates drew dreams from the very marrow of the real, suffering and desire-mingled *passion*—dreams they objectivized, first of all, in the myth of the Exile-Passion. The first outcome of their reflection is *Exile.* They are either Antilleans whose ancestors have been deported from Africa and "enslaved" or African "captives."

of this Paris
where white people are more numerous
than the rice bits of the fields

(Attuly, *Poètes d'expression française*)[10]

Antilleans know that their exile was an abduction through violence and suffering. Their memory of former slaves recites to them:

and the twenty-nine legal lashes of whip
and the four-feet-high dungeons
and the iron collar with spokes
and the severed hamstring of my audacious maroon
and the fleur-de-lis leaching into my shoulder fat from the red-hot
branding iron
and the kennel of Mister Vaultier
Mayencourt, where I barked for six dog months.

(Césaire, *Cahier*)[11]

And many other things still. The African David Diop would say in a more brutal accent:

The White Man has killed my father
My father was proud
The White Man has raped my mother
My mother was beautiful
The White Man has made my brother bend under the sun along the roads
My brother was strong
The White Man turned toward me
His hands red with
Black blood
And with the voice of a Master
"Hey boy, a chair, a napkin, some water!"[12]

But Exile is less about physical pain, less about the abduction from Africa than it is about the abduction from the self. Slavery and Colonization have emptied the Negro of his virtues, of his substance to make of him an "assimilated" [*assimilé*], this negative of the White man, for whom appearance is substituted for being: a void. And Damas laments:

SINCE
how many ME
have died
since they came that night when the
tam
    tam
        flowed from
            rhythm to
                rhythm
        the frenzy
of eyes
the frenzy of the hands the frenzy
of the feet of statues.[13]

What a strange and exiling Exile is that of the man, returned to his native land, to his soul, who does not recognize it anymore and feels like a stranger there. The Antillean administrator sent to Africa confesses:

And then I had to lie on the foreign land
the land that was mine.
A herd of dead stood up in the middle of everything to
lacerate my jacket and curse my name.
(Paul Niger, "Je n'aime pas l'Afrique")[14]

Ladies and Gentlemen, do you not recognize, in this Exile, the cataclysms that have shaken the foundations of the first half of the century? Have you also not smelled the odor of the mass graves and suffered the passion of alienation? In any case, the negro poets have perceived the commonality of our destiny. Like "the Rebel," they accepted the human condition, integrally: "*There is not a poor lynched fellow in the world, a poor tortured man in whom I do not see myself assassinated and humiliated.*"[15] By way of the narrow path of their subjectivity, they joined the crowd of the oppressed, who will be, tomorrow, the army of the Proletariat:

Like the contradiction of features,
resolved through the harmony of the face,
we proclaim the unity of suffering

and of revolt
of all the peoples on the entire surface of the earth.

(Jacques Roumain, "Prélude")[16]

The poets did not fail to draw conclusions—in practice—from this subjective fact, objectivized in this way. From political doubt, they arrived at Marxism. A militant Marxism that would lead some of them to Parliament. It is because they feel doubly proletarian—the proletariats of the proletariats, and not possessed by "a faulty bourgeois conscience," as are the youth in [Paul] Nizan's *La Conspiration* [The conspiracy][17]—that the negro poets raise such a convincing tone. It is, in large part, because they are genuinely *engaged* that the social poems of the greatest among the greatest are so unerring.

Exile-Passion has led us to other men, to *Africa* as well. Thus, the Antillean Paul Niger, in his "pilgrimage to the sources" beyond the native land, returned to Africa. At first, he feels like a stranger there. But, as a seeker with good intentions, he soon discovers that *truth* is not "hiding around the corner" and that, to live it, one must return *to* Africa, which lies at the heart of the Exiled. It is Africa that the New Negroes uncover in their memories by scratching the surface of things. *Africa*, exclaims Jacques Roumain:

Africa, I have preserved your memory Africa
you are within me
Like the splinter in the wound
like a tutelary fetish in the center of the village . . . [18]

And Césaire:

With my heart, I climbed back up to the antique silex,
the old Amadou deposited by Africa
at the bottom of myself . . . [19]

What is this continent for our poets? Guy Tirolien responds: "*The black country where ancestors sleep*."[20] And: "Who, then, were these men torn from their countries, their gods, their families, over the course of the centuries, by an unsurpassed savagery?"[21] Césaire, the professor, responds: "Soft, respectful, polite, courteous men, certainly superior to their butchers, . . . they knew how to build houses, administer empires, build cities, farm, melt minerals, weave cotton, forge iron."[22] But they are not so much men whose civilization can be compared to European civilization as *living beings* [*vivants*]: beings obedient to the rhythm of cosmic forces who are in touch with the sun and the stars, earth, fire, and water, animal, tree, and stone. They are: men of discipline, but also of freedom; men of labor, but also of joy. Here is the myth of *Africa–Kingdom of Childhood*, I mean, the myth of rediscovered *virtues*. This is the endpoint of the pilgrimage to the sources, the nostalgia of all our poets, the Negritude they must live and preach as the Gospel.[23] Damas laments:

> Give me back my Black dolls so that I can play with them
> the naïve games of my instinct.
> Remain in the shadow of its laws
> recover my courage
> my audacity
> feel myself
> a new me of who I was yesterday
>   without complexity
>   yesterday
> when came the time of uprooting[24]

And Césaire's song rises:

> oh friendly light
> oh pristine source of light
> those who have invented neither gunpowder nor compass
> those who have never tamed steam or electricity
> those who have not explored either seas or sky
> but without whom the earth would not be the earth
> excrescence growing more benign even as the earth continues to desert the earth
> grain silo where germinates and ripens what is most earthly upon the earth
> my negritude is not a stone, its deafness heaved
> against the clamor of day
> my negritude is not a film of dead water on the dead eye
> of the earth
> my negritude is neither a tower nor a cathedral
>
> it delves into the red flesh of the soil
> it delves into the burning flesh of the sky
> it digs through the dark accretions that weigh down its righteous patience
>
> Hurray for the majestic Cedrate!
> Hurray for those who have never invented anything
> for those who have never explored anything

for those who have never vanquished anything
but they surrender, possessed, to the essence of every thing
ignorant of surfaces but possessed by the movement
of every thing

unconcerned to vanquish, but playing the game of the world.

Truly the elder sons of the world
permeable to all the breaths of the world
fraternal compass points for all the breaths of the world
deep lake bed for all the waters of the world
spark of the sacred fire of the world
flesh of the very flesh of the world palpitating with the very
movement of the world![25]

This text by Césaire is cited so often only because it is crucial: It opposes the spirit of Negro-African civilization to that of the European West—opposes the *peasant* to the *engineer*, to speak like Sartre. We know that the attitude of Man before Nature is the problem par excellence, the solution of which conditions the fate of men. Man before Nature is the *subject* facing the *object*. For the European, *Homo faber*, it is a matter of knowing Nature in order to make of it the instrument of his will to power: to *utilize* it. He will fix it through analysis, will turn it into a *dead* object in order to dissect it. But how can Life be made out of a dead object? In contrast, it is in his subjectivity that the Negro, "porous to all the breaths of the world," discovers the object in its reality: *rhythm*. And here he abandons himself, surrenders to this living movement, moving from the subject to the object, "playing the game of the world." What is there to say other than that, for the Negro, to know is to live—to live from the life of the Other—by identifying with the object? *Knowing* [*Con-naître*] is to be born to the Other by dying in oneself: it is to make love to the Other, it is to dance the Other. "*I feel therefore I am.*"

By dint of meditating on the Congo
I have become a Congo rustling with
forests and rivers.

(Césaire, *Cahier*)[26]

What about the place of love in this poetry? There is no metaphysical eroticism. It is a carnal love, in lower case. Here, everything is blood and sperm, belly, thigh and genital, rump and hill and fruit. But spiritual love, "spark of the sacred fire of the world." It is the ambivalence of poetry, where spirit uses matter. Negro love. *What*? Paul Niger wonders:

a rhythm
a wave in the night across the forests,
nothing—or a new soul
a timbre
an intonation
a vigor
a dilation
a vibration which de-orbits by degrees
repulses in its march an old heart asleep,
seizes him by the waist and spins
and turns
and vibrates again, in the hands, in the kidneys, the sex
the thighs and the vagina, descend lower
bang the knees, the articulations of the ankle
the adherence of the feet, ah! this frenzy
which oozes onto me from the sky
But also, oh friend, a new pride which designates
in our eyes the people of the desert, a priceless courage
a soul without demand, a gesture without jolt
in a flesh without tiredness.[27]

Here again, Ladies and Gentlemen, you can recognize your quest. If you have embarked in search of continents with Apollinaire, Cendrars, Supervielle, and others, it is not as tourists, is it not, but rather in order to find lost paradises, beyond the factual and thus "superficial" vision of the world. And it is no accident if, among the greatest spiritual explorers of the first half of this century, we count two creoles: Saint-John Perse and Malcolm de Chazal, who, by way of a natural phenomenon of mimicry, have identified their vision with that of dark-skinned men, in the midst of whom they spent their childhood. It is also, as Flouquet and Verhesen have noted, in order to flee "the destruction of the soul that the technical power of modern times . . . seems to imply."[28]

On the ambivalence of art in which the idea makes use of form, and vision makes use of expression. The surrealist revolution alone, as you might guess, will have allowed our poets to express Negritude in French. They did so, after vision, by breaking the sentence apart through the elimination of function words, completing the revolution of the dictionary by granting citizenship to technical and "barbaric" words.

Sartre speaks of weapons "stolen . . . from the oppressor"[29] and used against him. The *method* of negro poets—for there is a method—is, however, less concerted than he seems to think. In truth, these poets had no other choice: Their situation, and above all their heredity, imposed the method on them. It is by beginning from Negro-African languages that one best understands this. These languages are essentially concrete. Their words are always *pregnant* with images, for the roots of words preserve their concrete values. I shall add that the *word-image* is both sign and meaning at the same time, and that the sensual qualities of the word—timbres, tones, rhythms—reinforce the meaning, not the sign. This explains the extreme scarcity of abstract words, even in prose. Finally, in contrast to French, which is an analytical language with a syntax of subordination, based on logic, Negro-African languages express a synthetic thought in a syntax of juxtaposition and coordination, a surrealist syntax.

Following the griots, our troubadours, the negro poets of the French language have received, as a first gift, that of the *image*. Césaire, in his preface to *Végétations de clarté* [Plants of light], praises René Depestre "for filling the gap between the primitive object and the final object of the poem with a real '*equation of metaphor*.'"[30] Mister [André] Davesne, former inspector general of education in Africa, noted a similar phenomenon in the pages he dedicated to the verbal style of Black people who speak French (*Croquis de brousse* [Bush sketches]).[31] It is that, drawing on a language in which practical usage has coated vocables with a sort of fine mist or verdigris, the New Negroes, quite naturally, polish the words, clean the rust from them, use them against the grain, lay them bare; with "their eyes of the before-earth" [*leurs yeux d'avant-terre*], they "perforate" them, or rather endow them with transparent rays. And Césaire reveals:

> My eye sinks like a stone into the object
> no longer being gazed at but gazing[32]

For words cling to things, enlighten things; they are things in their life beyond appearances:

> Words when we handle all corners of the world, when we embrace continents in delirium, when we force our way with doors smoking, words, ah yes, words? but flesh-blooded words, words that are tsunamis and erysipelas and malarias and lava flows and bush fires, and flares of flesh, and blazes of cities . . .
>
> (Césaire, *Cahier*)[33]

It is—besides the fact of living the condition of the Proletariat in one's flesh and in one's heart, "this facility of making things flow into images and ring out in song"—their resentment that allows poets such as Depestre, Roumain, and Césaire to fulfill the ambitions of the former surrealists: to write social poems that remain poems. Listen to [René] Depestre singing of Stalin:

I sing the pure crystal of a man
  a seamless arrow of light
I sing the tumultuous river of that man
  without detours from his source to the sea
I sing his water of benevolence and of anger
  born of mountain snows and which
  drop by drop fills our
  millions of hearts[34]

Depestre the communist is unaware that he is perpetuating the tradition of the griots, major poets, who sing only of Man, the Noble—accompanied by koras, balafons, and tam-tams.

For *song* is the second virtue of our poets. I have said to what extent Negroes were, traditionally, sensitive to the sensual qualities of the word. First to the rhythm, which is the common denominator of all negro arts. Look at them, once again, these poets, listen to them from the abyss of their desire-resentment. Sartre distinguishes Africans from Antilleans, with good reason.

Here are the Africans called upon, seized by the waves of the tam-tam, which Africa has, forever, sent out to the four corners of the world. The tam-tam that sleepless hearts, drowned in the night and the fog, deep in the shacks, hear from afar. Their poems respond to the waves of the tam-tam, espouse them: objectivized, the dreams are tam-tams.

The first draft of the poem is often a word, a phrase, a sentence that is a leitmotiv, the rhythm in which all the words and images of the poem will flow. And this rhythm is tam-tam; this rhythm is ritual because it is binary, repose in the movement, grave solemnity, which can be both joy and sadness. Here, the Senegalese Birago Diop tells us:

Listen more often
to objects than beings.
The voice of the fire can be heard,
listen to the voice of water
listen through the wind
the crying bush.

It is the breath of the ancestors, [. . .]
who did not leave us,
who are not under the ground,
who are not dead.[35]

Here, it is Flavien Ranaivo, the Malagasy, who sings on a Heinteny[36] rhythm:

Do not love me, my kinswoman
like your shadow
for the shadow fades at night
and I must keep you
until the rooster crows
neither like spice
which warms the belly
for then I would not be able
to have my fill
nor like the pillow
. . . . .
nor like rice
. . . . .
nor like sweet words
. . . . .
nor like honey[37]

For the Antilleans, the umbilical cord was cut a long time ago. African rhythm is not, a priori, given; it is not the product of memory, of "the madness that remembers." They must descend into the bottom of the abyss, awaken the volcano of resentment, of "the madness that sees" and "unleashes" itself. Thus, it explodes, the volcano; images burst like fireworks with myriad colors, like rivers of flamboyant lava. It is not the gratuitous play of the surrealists; and it is certainly true that words will freely disintegrate and aggregate according to magical sympathies and repulsions, but they are torn away by the same vertiginous desire, inflexibly oriented toward the same goal. And, at the height of tension, the rhythm of the African tam-tam suddenly bursts forth—the obsessive, monotone, eternal, and despotic rhythm:

It is done: words have lost their ridges [*arêtes*]
words are polished because without need the words
avoid creasing the words play a
harvest where there is place neither for a winner
nor a loser.[38]

And here are the words of Césaire, prince of the Antillean poets, hammering a furious griot rhythm:

right on the river of blood of earth
right on the blood of broken sun
right on the blood of a hundred sun nails
right on the blood of the suicide of glowworms
right on the blood of an ember the blood of salt the blood of the bloods of love
right on the fire bird inflamed blood . . . [39]

Yes, magic of this rhythm that, in Damas's poem-songs as well as in the *blues*, restores life and force to the words:

A taste of blood comes to me
rises up to me
irritates my nose
my throat my eyes

A taste of blood comes to me
fills
my nose
my throat my eyes

A taste of blood comes to me
vertical sacrament like
the pagan obsession with censers.[40]

NOTES

Léopold Sédar Senghor, "L'apport de la poésie nègre au demi-siècle," in *Liberté 1: Négritude et humanisme* (Seuil, 1964) 133–46. The text originally appeared in the proceedings of the First International Biennale of Poetry, held in Knokke-le-Zoute, Belgium, September 1952. Pierre-Louis Flouqet and Arthur Haulot, eds., *Témoignages sur la poésie du demi-siècle* (Éditions de la Poète, 1953), 49–65.

1. [Thierry Maulnier, *Introduction à la poésie française* (Gallimard, 1939), 48.—Eds.]

2. [1848 was the year of the second abolition of slavery in France's colonies.—Eds.]

3. [Jean-Paul Sartre, "Orphée noir," in *Anthologie de la nouvelle poésie nègre et malgache de langue française*, ed. Léopold Sédar Senghor (Presses universitaires de France, 1948), ix–xliv.—Eds.]

4. [This is a quotation of Césaire's poem "Barbare," published in multiple collections, beginning with *Soleil Cou Coupé* (K éditeur, 1948). The poem was published in Senghor's

Anthologie (56) the same year. See also Aimé Césaire, "Barbare," in *Cadastre* (Seuil, 1961), 56–57.—Eds.]

5. [Senghor is referring to Pierre-Louis Flouquet and Fernand Verhesen's opening remarks at the First International Biennale of Poetry in Knokke-le-Zoute, Belgium (1952), later published as Flouqet and Verhesen, "Apport poétique du Demi-Siècle: Rapport établi par MM. P.-L. Flouquet et F. Verhesen pour le 'Journal des poètes,'" in *Témoignages sur la poésie du demi-siècle* (Éditions de la Maison du Poète, 1952), 11–33 (quote on 14).—Eds.]

6. [Aimé Césaire, *Cahier d'un retour au pays natal* (Présence Africaine, 1956), 47–48. In our English translation, we have referred to the bilingual edition Aimé Césaire, *Journal of Homecoming / Cahier d'un retour au pays natal*, trans N. Gregson Davis (Duke University Press, 2017), 100 (translation modified). An excerpt of the *Cahier* was also published in Aimé Césaire, "Cahier d'un retour au pays natal (Fragment)," in Senghor, *Anthologie*, 57–73.—Eds.]

7. [Léon-Gontran Damas, "Pour sûr," in Senghor, *Anthologie*, 12; also published as Léon-Gontran Damas, "Pour sûr," in *Pigments/Névralgies* (Présence Africaine, 1978), 53. We have used the modern Présence Africaine edition throughout, since the original, 1937 edition is not widely available. For the original publication, see Léon-Gontran Damas, *Pigments* (G. L. M. [Guy Lévis Mano], 1937).—Eds.]

8. [Sartre, "Orphée noir," xv. Senghor has added "(*blanc*)" (White).—Eds.]

9. [André Breton, "Un grand poète noir," in Aimé Césaire, *Cahier d'un retour au pays natal* (Bordas, 1947), 18.—Eds.]

10. [The citation begins, "Je suis encore captif de ce Paris. [. . .]" Lionel Attuly, *Poètes d'expression française [d'Afrique noire, Madagascar, Réunion, Guadeloupe, Martinique, Indochine, Guyane], 1900–1945*, ed. Léon-Gontran Damas (Seuil, 1947), 125.—Eds.]

11. [Césaire, *Cahier* (Présence Africaine, 1956), 78.—Eds.]

12. [David Diop, "Le temps du martyre," in Senghor, *Anthologie*, 174–75.—Eds.]

13. [Damas, "Ils sont venus ce soir (Pour Léopold Sédar Senghor)," in Senghor, *Anthologie*, 6; Léon-Gontran Damas, "Ils sont venus ce soir," in Damas, *Pigments*, 13.—Eds.]

14. [Paul Niger, "Je n'aime pas l'Afrique," in Senghor, *Anthologie*, 93–100 (98).—Eds.]

15. [Senghor is quoting Césaire, "Et les chiens se taisaient (Fragment)"; for the full text, see Aimé Césaire, *Et les chiens se taisaient* (Présence Africaine, 1958), 70.—Eds.]

16. [Senghor is citing Jacques Roumain, "Prélude," in Senghor, *Anthologie*, 118. See also Jacques Roumain, "Prélude," in *Bois d'ébène* (Henri Deschamps, 1945), 1–8.—Eds.]

17. [Paul Nizan, *La Conspiration* (Gallimard, 1938).—Eds.]

18. [Roumain, "Prélude," in Senghor, *Anthologie*, 116.—Eds.]

19. [Césaire, *Et les chiens se taisaient*, 77.—Eds.]

20. [Guy Tirolien, "L'âme du noir pays," in Senghor, *Anthologie*, 87. The text was later retitled: Guy Tirolien, "Black Beauty," in *Balles d'or* (Présence Africaine, 1961), 41–42.—Eds.]

21. [Aimé Césaire, "Introduction," in Victor Schoelcher, *Esclavage et Colonisation* (Presses universitaires de France, 1948), 7.—Eds.]

22. [Césaire, "Introduction," 7.—Eds.]

23. [Senghor uses the phrase "Bonne Nouvelle," which has a biblical connotation and refers to the announcement of the Evangelical.—Eds.]

24. [Damas, "Limbé (Pour R.R.)," in Senghor, *Anthologie*, 9. See also Léon-Gontran Damas, "Limbé (Pour Robert Romain)" in Damas, *Pigments*, 44.—Eds.]

25. [Césaire, "Cahier d'un retour au pays natal (Fragment)," 58–59.—Eds.]

26. [Césaire, *Cahier* (Présence Africaine, 1956), 48–49.—Eds.]

27. [Niger, "Je n'aime pas l'Afrique," 100.—Eds.]

28. [Flouqet and Verhesen, "Apport poétique du Demi-Siècle," 20; there is no ellipsis in the original.—Eds.]

29. [Sartre, "Orphée noir," xv.—Eds.]

30. [Aimé Césaire, "Préface," in *Végétations de clarté*, ed. René Depestre (Pierre Seghers, 1951), 10–11.—Eds.]

31. [André Davesne, *Croquis de brousse* (Éditions du Sagittaire, 1943). Davesne (1898–1978) was also the author of the series of primers *Mamadou et Bineta* used to teach French in colonial schools.—Eds.]

32. [Aimé Césaire, "Les pur-sang" in *Les armes miraculeuses* (Gallimard, 1946), 16.—Eds.]

33. [Césaire, *Cahier* (Présence Africaine, 1956), 55.—Eds.]

34. [René Depestre, "Végétations de clarté," in *Rage de vivre: Œuvres poétiques complètes* (Seghers, 2006), 63. The poem was originally published in book form, with a preface by Aimé Césaire, as *Végétations de clarté* (Seghers, 1951).—Eds.]

35. [Birago Diop, "Souffles (À Ch. Cassagne)," in Senghor, *Anthologie*, 145.—Eds.]

36. [Hainteny is a traditional oral literature in Malagasy, characterized by its use of metaphor.—Eds.]

37. [Flavien Ranaivo, "Vulgaire chanson d'amant," in Senghor, *Anthologie*, 208–9; Flavien Ranaivo, "Vulgaire chanson d'amant," in *L'ombre et le vent* (Imprimerie de Tananarive, 1947), 13–14.—Eds.]

38. [Aimé Césaire, "L'irrémédiable," in *Aimé Césaire: Poésie, théâtre, essais et discours*, ed. Albert James Arnold (CNRS Éditions, 2013), 252.—Eds.]

39. [Césaire, *Les armes miraculeuses*, 68. We have used the English translation found in *The Complete Poetry of Aimé Césaire: Bilingual Edition*, ed. and trans. Clayton Eshleman and A. James Arnold (Wesleyan University Press, 2017), 135.—Eds.]

40. [Léon-Gontran Damas, "Obsession" in Damas, *Pigments*, 19.—Eds.]

10

Negro-African Aesthetics

Africa always offers something unique.
—RABELAIS, *Gargantua et Pantagruel*, 1913

The twentieth century will be remembered for the discovery of Black African civilization. When it comes to Black Africa, it was first sculpture that provoked amazement, shock, then admiration. But then Europe discovered, one after the other, storytelling, poetry, music, painting, and philosophy.

It is now, beyond the initial shock, a matter of defining the *spirit of civilization*, I mean, Negro-African *Culture*. Nothing is more revealing, in this respect, than literature and art, particularly when it comes to a "civilization without machines." This "philosophical reflection on Art," which is how we define *Aesthetics*, is all the more necessary given that the admiration felt by certain

European intellectuals for Negro-African literature and art is not without confusion: It is often built on misunderstandings, if not misconceptions.

But before I attempt to define the fundamental laws of Negro-African art, I must speak of the *Black Man* and first sketch out a *psychophysiology* of the Negro, who has developed an original culture.

It has often been said that the Negro is a man of nature. Traditionally, he lives off the land and with the land, in and by the *cosmos*. He is *sensual*, a being of open senses, with no intermediary between subject and object. He is subject and object at the same time. He is sounds, smells, rhythms, shapes, and colors; he is *touch* before he is sight, like the White European. He *feels* more than he sees: He feels himself. It is within himself, in his flesh, that he receives and *feels* the radiations emitted by every existent-object. *Shaken* [*é-branlé*], he responds to the call and abandons himself, moving from subject to object, from I to You, on the waves of the *Other*. He dies to himself to be reborn in the Other. He is not assimilated; he assimilates, he identifies with the Other, which is the best way to get to know the Other.

In other words, the Negro is not devoid of *reason*, as I have been accused of saying. But his reason is not discursive; it is synthetic. It is not antagonistic; it is sympathetic. It is another mode of knowledge. Negro reason does not impoverish things; it does not mold them into rigid schemes, eliminating the juices and the saps; it flows into the heart of things, testing every contour in order to lodge itself in the living heart of reality. *European reason is analytical through use, whereas negro reason is intuitive through participation.*

This shows the sensitivity and *emotive* power of the Black Man. But what captivates the Negro is not so much the appearance of the object but rather its profound reality, its *surreality*; not so much its sign but its *meaning*. Water moves him because it flows, fluid and blue, above all because it washes clean, and even more because it purifies. Sign and meaning express the same ambivalent reality. However, the emphasis is on meaning, which is no longer utilitarian but the moral, mystical meaning of reality: a *symbol*. It is not without interest that contemporary scientists themselves affirm the primacy of intuitive knowledge through *sym-pathy*. "The most beautiful emotion we can experience," writes Einstein, "is the mystical emotion. This is the seed of all art and of all true science."[1]

It is this psychophysiology of the Negro that explains his metaphysics, and hence his social life, of which literature and art are only one aspect. According to Father Placide Tempels, social life in Black Africa is based on a set of logically coordinated and motivated concepts. Those whom Europeans call "primitives," the same missionary declares, "live" more than Europeans "from ideas and according to their ideas."

At the center of the system, enlivening it as the sun does to our world, there is *existence*, that is, *life*. It is the ultimate good, and all human activity tends only toward the growth and expression of vital power. The Negro identifies *being* with life; more precisely, with the *Vital Force*. His metaphysics is an *existential ontology*. As Father Tempels writes, "Being is that which possesses force," or better: "Being IS force." But this force is not static. Being is in an unstable equilibrium, always capable of strengthening or "deforcing" itself. To exist, man must realize his individual essence through the growth and *expression* of his vital force. But this force, the substratum of intellectual and moral, and therefore of immortal, life is only really alive and can grow by coexisting, in man, with the *body* and the vital breath. These elements, made of pure material, are perishable, and disintegrate after death.

But Man is not the only being in the world. A vital force similar to his own animates every object endowed with *sensible* characteristics, from God down to the grain of sand. The Negro has established a rigorous hierarchy of forces. At the top, a unique God, uncreated and creator: "He who has strength, power by his own essence. He gives existence, substance, and growth to the other forces." After him come the Ancestors, first and foremost, the founders of the clans, "the God-like-figures." Then, further down the ladder, come *living beings* who, in turn, are ordered according to custom, but especially according to the order of primogeniture. Finally, at the bottom of the ladder, the animal, vegetal, and mineral classes. There is, in each case, the same hierarchy.

This is a good opportunity to point out that *Man* occupies a notable place at the center of this system, in his quality as a *person*, as an *active existent* capable of increasing his own being. For the Universe is a closed system of forces that are individual, of course, as well as distinct, but also interdependent. The whole of creation is therefore centered on Man. Insofar as being is a vital force, the Ancestors must devote themselves to reinforcing the life of the existent if they do not wish to be *non-existent* [*in-existants*], or "perfectly dead"—to use a Bantu expression. This will enable them to participate in the life of the existent. As for inferior beings—animals, plants, minerals—their only purpose in God's design is to support the action of the Dead. They are instruments, not ends in themselves.

The merit of this existential ontology is that it has, in turn, informed a harmonious civilization and, first and foremost, an authentic *religion*. For what is a religion if not, as its etymology would have it, the link that gives unity to the universe, that unites God with the blade of grass and the grain of sand? This ontology is its dogma. As for worship, which is religion in action, it is expressed in Black Africa through *sacrifice*.

It is the head of the family who offers the sacrifice. He is the priest designated solely by his status as the oldest descendant of the common Ancestor. He is the natural mediator between the Living and the Dead. Closer to them, he lives in their intimacy. His flesh is less flesh-like, his mind more dexterous, his speech more powerfully persuasive; he is already a participant in the nature of the Dead. Sacrifice is, above all, an encounter with the Ancestor, the dialogue between You and Me. We share with him the food whose existential force will give him the feeling of life. And the communion goes so far as identification, so that, by a reverse movement, the strength of the Ancestor flows into the person who offers the sacrifice and the community he embodies. *Sacrifice is the most typical illustration of the general law of interaction between the vital forces of the Universe.*

If we consider *society*, the *natural* aspect of the world's unitary order, we find the *family* to be its most elemental component, its basic cell. Negro-African society is in fact made up of ever widening concentric circles, built one on the other, all interlocking and based on the model of the family itself. The tribe unites several families, the kingdom several tribes. But what is the *family*? It is the *clan*, the group of all people, living or dead, who recognize a common Ancestor. He is the link between God and man, genius himself and "God-like." His life often takes the form of a totemic myth, sometimes linked to an astral myth. Hence the importance of the animal in negro cosmogony. The Ancestor has received a vital force from God, and his vocation is to increase it. As we can see, the aim of the family is to perpetuate a heritage of vital force, which grows and intensifies as it manifests itself in living bodies, in ever more numerous and prosperous existents.[2] The family is a microcosm, an image of the Universe, reflected and enlarged in the tribe and kingdom. The King is merely the father of the larger family; he is the descendant of the Conductor-of-Tribes.

The family, the tribe, and the kingdom are not the only community organizations that simultaneously bind and sustain the Negro. Alongside them, there exists a whole network of organizations whose structures interact with their own. These include *age group fraternities*, a kind of mutual society among which the generations are divided, *trade guilds* and *secret-rite brotherhoods*. The latter have a social, even political role and especially a religious one. In fact, all these organizations have a religious basis, among peoples where the separation of the profane and the sacred, the political and the social, is a recent and rare occurrence. Literature and art fit naturally into the social activities underpinned by religious sensibility.

It is difficult for a Westerner to imagine the place occupied by social activities, including literature and art, in the Negro-African calendar. They occupy not only "Sundays" and "theatrical evenings" but, to take the example of the Sudanese zone, the eight months of the dry season. At this time of year, people are fully occupied with their relations with *Others*: Spirits, Ancestors, members of the family, the tribe, the kingdom, even foreigners. All is Festivity, and Death itself is an occasion for celebration, for the *Festival* par excellence: Harvest and sowing festivals; births, initiations, weddings, funerals; guild festivals and brotherhood celebrations. And every evening, there are tales told around the fire, dances and songs, gymnic games, dramas and comedies illuminated by high flames. And work, which celebrates the marriage of Man and earth, is still relationship and *poetry*. Hence, the work songs: The songs of the peasant, the canoeist, the shepherd. For, as we shall see, all literature and art in Black Africa is poetry.

It is always a matter of entering into relations either with the totemic Ancestors or with the mythical spirits—but the spirit often partakes of the star and the animal, and the legend deepens into myth. Significant in this respect is the festival of *Initiation*, which is opened and accompanied by numerous sacrifices. It is an initiation into the cosmogonic myths, legends, and customs of the tribe; more precisely, a *knowledge* [*con-naissance*], through poem, song, drama, and masked dance, to the primordial rhythm of the drum. It is then that the seed dies in order to blossom, that the child dies to the self in order to be reborn as an adult, in the Initiator of the Ancestor. This is a *religious existentialism*, an *animistic existentialism*. Far from being an obstacle, the Other—adult, Ancestor, genius, or God—is a vehicle, a source of vital force. Far from there being *conflict*, in this confrontation between the *I* and the *You*, there is conciliatory harmony, not derealization, but greater realization of the individual essence.

Literature and *art* are therefore inseparable from man's generic activities, particularly from his artisanal techniques. They are their most effective expression. In *L'enfant noir* [The Black child], [Camara] Laye's father forges a golden piece of jewelry.[3] The prayer, or rather the poem, that he recites, the griot's praise song as he works the gold, the blacksmith's dance at the end of the operation, it is all that—poem, song, dance—which, beyond the craftsman's gestures, *accomplishes* the work and makes it a *masterpiece*. From the same perspective, the arts are interrelated. Thus, sculpture, for example, is fully realized only through dance and the sung poem. Look at the man who embodies Nyamié, the Sun-Spirit of the Baoulé, under the mask of the Bull. Here he is, dancing the gestures of the Bull, to the rhythm of the band, while the chorus sings the poem of the Spirit's epic. Here and there, we have *functional* art. In the last example, the masked dancer identifies with the Sun-Bull-Spirit and, like the sacrificer, makes his force flow over the audience, which participates in the drama.

This is another feature of the *poem*—once again, I call any work of art a *poem*: *it is made by everyone and for everyone*. Of course, there are specialists of literature and art: In the countries of the Sudan, the *Griots*, who are at once historiologists, poets, and storytellers; in the countries of Guinea and the Congo, the civil sculptors of the princely courts, whose shoulder adze is the badge of honor; everywhere, the blacksmith as a polytechnician of magic and art, the first artist according to one Dogon myth, who, by the rhythm of the drum, made rain fall from the sky. But alongside these specialists, there are the people, the anonymous crowd, who sing, dance, sculpt, and paint. Initiation is the school of Black Africa, where man, emerging from childhood, assimilates, along with the sciences of the tribe, the techniques of literature and art. We will have noticed, on the other hand, as these two examples illustrate, that all artistic expression is collective, made for all, with the participation of all.

Because they are functional and collective, Black African literature and art are *engaged*. This is their third general characteristic. They engage the *person*—and not just the individual—through and in the community, in the sense that they are techniques of *essentialization*. They engage him in a future that will henceforth be present to him, an integral part of his self. This is why the Negro-African work of art is not, as has often been said, a copy of an archetype repeated a thousand times. Of course, there are *objects*, each of which expresses a vital force. But what is striking is the variety of execution according to individual temperament and circumstance. Once again, the artisan-poet is situated, and he is engaged with *his* ethnicity, *his* history, *his* geography. He makes use of the materials at hand and the everyday facts that make up the fabric of his life, although he is averse to anecdote, for it fails to engage because it is devoid of *meaning*. As a painter or sculptor, he will occasionally make use of instruments and materials imported from Europe; he will not hesitate to represent the machine, that pride of the West; he will go so far as to dress an ancestral spirit in European style. In the new society, informed by the spirit of the Colonial Monopoly, the storyteller will give money its rightful place, a cardinal one, as the embodiment of Evil. Because he is engaged, the artisan-poet is not concerned with making a work for eternity. A work of art is ephemeral. If the spirit and style are preserved, the old work is hastily replaced—by updating it—as soon as it goes out of fashion or is destroyed. In other words, in Black Africa, "art for art's sake" does not exist; all art is *social*. The griot who sings the praises of the Noble in war makes him stronger and participates in the victory. When he chants the epic of a legendary hero, it is the history of his people that he writes with his language, restoring to it the divine depth of myth. Right down to the fables that, beyond laughter and tears, serve to teach us. Through the dialectic that they express, they are one of the essential factors of social equilibrium. In the guise of the Lion, the Elephant, the Hyena, the Crocodile, the Hare, and the Old Woman, we can clearly read, with our ears, our social structures and passions—both good and bad. At times, it is *negation* in the face of the Great Ones, right against brute force; at other times, *acquiescence* to the order of the Universe: That of the Ancestors and of God. And, concludes the Wolof, "That is how the fable went into the sea. Whoever breathes it first will go to Paradise."[4] The perfume of Black wisdom . . . !

However, one would fail to grasp the essence of Negro-African literature and art by imagining that they are merely utilitarian and that the Negro-African has no sense of *beauty*. Some ethnologists and art critics have gone so far as to claim that the words "beauty" and "beautiful" are absent from Negro-African languages. Quite the opposite is true. The truth is that the Negro-African equates beauty with goodness, especially with efficacy. As is the case in Wolof from Senegal, the words *târ* and *rafet*, "beauty" and "beautiful," are preferably applied to humans.[5] When it comes to works of art, Wolof will use the qualifiers *dyêka, yèm, mat*,[6] which I will translate as that "which is suiting," that "which fits," that "which is perfect." Once again, we are speaking of *functional* beauty. The beautiful mask, the beautiful poem is the one that produces, in the audience, the desired emotion: sadness, joy, hilarity, terror. Significant is the word *ba̧xai*—pronounced *bakhaï* "goodness"—used by young dandies to designate a beautiful girl.[7] For them, beauty is "the promise of happiness." On the other hand, a good deed is often described as "beautiful."

If a poem has an effect, it is because it echoes in the minds and sensibilities of its listeners. That is why the Fulɓe define a poem as "words pleasing to the heart and ear." But if, for the Negro-African as for the European, "the greatest of rules is to please," one and the other do not find pleasure in the same things. In Greco-Latin aesthetics, which survived in the European West, with the exception of the Middle Ages, until the end of the nineteenth century, art is an "imitation of nature"—I mean: a "corrected imitation"; in Black Africa, it is an explanation and knowledge of the world, that is, a *sensitive participation in the reality* underlying the Universe, in the *surreality* or, more precisely, in the Vital Forces that animate the Universe. The European likes to recognize [*reconnaître*] the world through the reproduction of the object, referred to as the "subject"; the Negro-African likes to know it vitally through image and rhythm. For the European, the threads of the senses lead to the heart and to the head; for the Negro-African, to the heart and the belly, to the very root of life. The Baoulé spectators enjoy the Bull mask because it embodies the Sun-Spirit in a formal and rhythmic language.

Image and *Rhythm* are the two fundamental features of Negro-African style.

Image first. But before going any further, we need to pause for a moment to understand the nature and function of language, through a brief analysis of Negro-African languages. This will give us a better grasp of the value of the Negro-African image.

The *Word* [*Parole*] appears to us as the major instrument of thought, emotion, and action. There can be no thought or emotion without a verbal image, and no free action without a thought-out project. And this fact is all the truer for peoples who, for the most part, disdained the written word. The power of the spoken word in Black Africa. *The spoken word, the Word*, is the ultimate expression of the Vital Force, of *being* in its fullness. God created the world through the Word—as we will soon see. For the existent, the Word is the animated, animating breath of the *orant*; it possesses a magical virtue, realizing the law of participation and creating the *named* by its intrinsic virtue. Also, all the other arts are merely specialized aspects of the major art of speech [*parole*]. Before a painting formed of a network of red and white geometric shapes, representing a concert of birds on a tree beneath the rising sun, the artist explained himself as follows: "These are wings, songs; these are birds."[8]

The defining feature of Negro-African languages is first and foremost the richness of their vocabulary. There are ten, sometimes twenty words to designate an object, depending on whether it changes shape, weight, volume, or color; as many words to designate an action, depending on whether it is single or multiple, weak or intense, at its beginning or at its end. In Pulaar, nouns are divided into twenty-one asexual genders, and this classification is based sometimes on their semantic value, sometimes on their phonetic value, and sometimes on the grammatical category to which they belong. But it is the verb that remains the most significant in this respect. In Wolof, more than twenty derived verbs and at least as many derived nouns can be constructed from the same root, using affixes to nuance the meaning. Whereas today's Indo-European languages emphasize the abstract notion of tense, Negro-African languages focus on *aspect*, the concrete way in which the verbal action takes place. In other words, they are essentially *concrete* languages. Words are always pregnant with images; from beneath their value as sign emerges their value as *meaning*.

The Negro-African image is therefore not an equation-image, but an *analogy-image*, a surrealist image. The Negro-African abhors the straight line and the false "proper word." Two and two do not make four, but "five," as the poet Aimé Césaire puts it. The object means not what it represents but what it suggests, what it creates. The Elephant is Strength; the Spider, Caution; the horns are the Moon; and the Moon, Fertility. All representation is image, and image, I repeat, is not equation, but *symbol*, ideogram. Not only image-figuration, but matter—stone, earth, copper, gold, fiber—and even line and color. Any language that is not fabulation is boring. What is more, Negro-Africans do not understand such language. The astonishment of the first Whites when they discovered that the "natives" did not understand their paintings, not even the logic of their discourse . . . !

I have spoken of the surrealist image. But, as you can guess, Negro-African surrealism differs from European surrealism. The latter is empirical; the former mystical, metaphysical. Negro analogy presupposes and manifests the hierarchical universe of vital forces.

Power of the image, power of the Word. So it was in Dahomey, among the Fôn, where the King, at each landmark event during his reign, punctuated a maxim with a major word that served as a new name. "The *Pineapple* that laughs at the drought." And the word and the Pineapple were inscribed everywhere, despotically, becoming an image: in wood, clay, gold, bronze, ivory; on the throne, the headdress, the scepter, and on the palace walls.

In Negro-African poetry, of course, one rarely encounters the abstract word. Here, there is no need to comment on the image; listeners are gifted with double vision. In sculpture, certain masks achieve exemplary suggestion. Among the Baoulé, for example, the Moon-Bull-Spirit mask. A man's face with a goatee, bull's horns and ears—sometimes the horns are replaced by a crescent moon—birds pecking at the forehead or cornucopia: This is the perfect type of image that *creates*, beyond the world of appearances. The more unreal, the more surreal the image, the more powerful it is, to use Breton's expression: "The interdependence of two objects of thought located on different planes, between which the mind's logical functioning cannot build any bridge."[9] Negro-African *painting*, so unjustly overlooked, is no exception to this law. Let us return to "Painting 17" of the *Paredes pintadas da Lunda*. Its power of suggestion comes from the contrasting colors—white and red on a brown-black background—and particularly from the geometric shapes—squares, rhombus, and angles—used to render a concert of birds in the rising sun. Even *music*, which is a fabric of images. For the primary role of music in Black Africa is not to be a concert, an enchantment for the ears, but to accompany the poem or dance, that dynamic sculpture. I saw the Sun-Bull-Spirit dance the other year in Côte d'Ivoire. The dancer expressed the sacred fury of the Bull through his steps, and the orchestra through its musical phrases. Even the story—myth, legend, tale, or fable—even the proverb and the riddle. By the very fact that they are taught, Negro-African stories naturally take the form of parables, images in motion in time and space. "Once upon a time," "It was in very ancient times." And the concept applies not only to myths and legends but also to fables. In fables, the Animal is rarely a totem; it is a so-and-so whom everyone in the village knows well: the tyrannical and stupid or wise and good Chief, the Young Man who rights wrongs, Koumba-the-Orphan.[10] "Once upon a time." And the audience answers: "As usual."[11] It is because Negro-African ontology is existential that the tale and fable are woven from everyday facts. They are not anecdotes or "slices of life." The facts are images, with exemplary value. Hence the pace of the story, its progression by leaps and bounds, its material unlikelihood, the absence of psychological explanations.

However, the image does not produce its effect in the Negro-African if it is not rhythmic. Here, *rhythm* is consubstantial to the image; it is the rhythm that fulfills it by uniting, in a whole, sign and meaning, flesh and spirit. For the sake of clarity, I have artificially distinguished the two elements. In the music that accompanies a poem or a dance, rhythm is as much an image as melody. In the mask of the Moon-Bull-Spirit, it is the rhythm that allows the substitution of the image with the same symbolic value: crescent moon in the place of horns, and cornucopia in the place of birds.

What is rhythm? It is the architecture of being, the inner dynamism that gives it form, the system of waves that it emits toward *Others*, the pure expression of the Vital Force. Rhythm is the vibratory shock, the force that, through the senses, seizes us at the root of *being*. It is expressed by the most material, sensual means: lines, surfaces, colors, volumes in architecture, sculpture, and painting; accents in poetry and music; movements in dance. But in so doing, it orders all this concreteness toward the light of the *Spirit*. In the case of the Negro-African, it is insofar as it is embodied in sensuality that rhythm illuminates the *Spirit*. African dance is averse to the contact of bodies. But look at the dancers. If their lower limbs are agitated by the most sensual vibrations, their heads partake of the serene beauty of masks, of the Dead.

Once again, the primacy of Speech [*Parole*]. It is rhythm that gives it its effective fullness, transforming it into the *Word* [*Verbe*]. It was God's word [*verbe*], that is, *rhythmic speech* [*parole*], that created the world. It is in the poem, then, that we can best grasp the nature of Negro-African rhythm. Here, rhythm arises not from the interplay of long and short syllables but only from the interplay of stressed and unstressed syllables, strong and weak beats. This is rhythmic versification. There is a verse, and therefore a poem, when a stressed syllable recurs in the same time interval. But the essential rhythm is not that of speech but that of the percussion instruments that accompany the human voice or, to be more precise, that mark the basic rhythm. We are dealing with a *polyrhythm*, a kind of rhythmic counterpoint. In this way, speech avoids the mechanical regularity that breeds monotony. The poem thus appears as an architecture, a mathematical formula based on *unity in diversity*. Here is the rhythm of speech in two Wolof poems taken at random:[12]

A) 24 00
24 00

44 00
44 00

43 00
43 00

B) 32 31
32 31
22 31

32 21
32 31
32 21

32 31
32 31

22 31

As one might guess, the basic rhythm is 4444 in the first case, and 3333 in the second. In both cases, the verse is a *tetrameter*. But the audience often participates in the poem. We thus have two groups of rhythms, which allows the two coryphaei—that of the narrators and that of the tam-tams—to give free rein to their inspiration and to multiply offbeats and syncopations, which are firmly grounded in the basic rhythm. For the monotone basic rhythm, far from being an obstacle to inspiration, is its necessary condition. However, the elements of rhythm are not limited to those I have described. In addition to the audience's clapping of hands and the steps and gestures of the narrators and drummers, there are certain rhetorical *figures—alliterations, paronomasia, anaphora*—which, based on the repetition of *phonemes* or sounds, form secondary rhythms and reinforce the overall effect. Finally, the poet makes abundant use of those *descriptive words* the importance of which M[ichel]. de la Vergne de Tressan has revealed.

The "prose narrative" partakes in the grace of rhythm. In Black Africa, there is no fundamental difference between prose and poetry. A poem is simply prose with a stronger, more regular rhythm; in practice, it can be recognized by the fact that it is accompanied by a percussion instrument. The same sentence can be turned into a poem by accentuating its rhythm, expressing thereby the tension of being: the *being* of being. It seems that, "in ancient times," every narrative was strongly rhythmic, was a poem. In less ancient times, the story was still told, in a more monotone voice and in a higher pitch: it was part of a religious ceremony. As it presents itself to us today, even in the form of the fable—the most *desacralized* of all genres—it is still rhythmic, albeit more subtly. First of all, *dramatic interest* is not spared; more precisely, sparing dramatic interest does not mean, as it does today in European storytelling, proscribing repetition; on the contrary, dramatic interest here is born out of repetition: repetition of a fact, a gesture, a song, words that become a leitmotiv. But almost always, a new element is introduced, a variation of the repetition, a *unity in diversity*. It is this new element that underscores dramatic progression. In other words, the prose narrative shies away neither from rhetorical figures based on the repetition of phonemes nor from descriptive words. What's more, Negro-African sentence structure is naturally rhythmic. For, whereas Indo-European languages use a logical syntax of subordination, Negro-African languages tend to use an intuitive syntax of *coordination and juxtaposition*. And, in propositions of roughly equal length, words are arranged in groups, each with a major accent.

In terms of rhythm, *music* is linked to speech and dance, and certainly more to the poem than to dance. For the Negro-African, music is the element that best characterizes the poem. In the languages of Senegal, the same word—*woi* in Wolof, *gim* in Sereer, *yimre* in Pulaar—designates both song and the poem par excellence: the *ode*.[13] In any case, the poem is not complete unless it is sung or at least set to the rhythm of a musical instrument. And the prose of the Town Crier becomes solemn, acquiring authority through the voice of the tam-tam. As has often been remarked, in Negro-African music, rhythm takes precedence over melody. As I said earlier, the purpose of music is less to charm the ears than to *re-inforce* the Word [*Parole*], to make it more effective. Hence the emphasis placed on rhythm, on abrupt falls, on inflections and *vibrati*: the preference for *expression* over harmony.

In recent years, much emphasis has been placed on the ethnological, religious, and social values of Negro-African *sculpture*. And yet the writers and artists who, at the turn of the century, emphasized its aesthetic value—its rhythm—were not wrong. Just take a look at the books that reproduce Negro-African sculpture, such as Carl Kjersmeier's *Centres de style de la sculpture nègre africaine* [Centers of style in negro African sculpture] (Paris, Copenhagen). Consider figure 48, a female Baoulé statuette.[14] Two gentle themes sing in turn. Ripe fruit of the breasts. Chin and knees, rump and calves are also fruits or breasts. The neck, the arms and thighs, columns of black honey. In another volume, this Fang statuette from Gabon also offers us fruits—breasts, navel, knees—, set off by the curved cylinders of the bust, thighs, and calves.[15] Consider now, in the first volume, the top of a Bambara mask depicting an antelope.[16] Strophes of horns and ears; antistrophes of tail and neck, and the hair of a mane sprung from the sculptor's imagination. As André Malraux writes in *La voix du silence* [The voice of silence], "An African mask is not a fixation of a human expression; it is an apparition. Its carver does not impose a geometrical pattern on a phantom of which he knows nothing, but conjures one up by his geometry; the more a mask is like a man, the less effective it is, and the more it is unlike a man, the greater the potency. The animal masks, too, are not animals, the antelope mask is not an antelope but *the* spirit-antelope, and what 'spiritualizes' it is its style."[17] Understand: its rhythm.

Rhythm is even more manifest in Negro-African *painting*. Today's Poto-Poto and Elisabethville painters have begun to persuade attentive observers. They are merely continuing an already ancient tradition. It is well known that Negro-African sculpture is often painting at the same time. But now, over the past twenty-five years, the mural paintings of Black Africa have been discovered, reproduced, and commented on. The rhythm is not marked by the dividing lines of light and shadow, nor is it a form of arabesque, as in classical European painting. Moreover, Negro-Africans paint in flat colors, with no shading. Here, as elsewhere, rhythm is created by the repetition, often at regular intervals, of a line, a color, a figure, a geometric shape, and especially contrasting colors. In general, on a dark background, which creates space or dead time and gives the painting its depth, the painter places figures in light colors, and vice versa. The drawing and coloring of the figures respond less to the appearances of reality than to the profound rhythm of the objects. Two examples will suffice to illustrate this truth. First, "painting 12" in *Paredes pintadas da Lunda*.[18] At the top is a frieze depicting a prince's sumptuous procession. It features six people moving from left to right. From the right: three members of the escort, the two bearers carrying a sort of canopy on their shoulders, in which the prince is lying, then, closing the procession, the fourth member of the escort. The background is light brown; the figures are painted in the three traditional colors of Black Africa: white, black, and red. The six people in the procession all wear white headdresses, black tunics, red sashes, white pants, and black shoes. But the monotony of the basic rhythm must be broken by introducing secondary rhythms. The two bearers have a tunic speckled with white dots, while the members of the escort simply have a row of white buttons on their black tunics, except for the one who opens the procession, whose tunic has no buttons. One of the bearers wears gaiters like the members of the escort, while the second wears low shoes. The two men, one opening and the other closing the procession, each have a staff, but one is white and the other black. Finally, for the two birds painted at the bottom of the frieze, one is black speckled with white dots, like the tunic of the bearers, the other white, like the pants and headdress of the men in the procession. Now let us take a look at "painting 54 A," depicting plants in pots.[19] The two figures are painted in two colors: blue and red on a straw-colored background. Everything is blue and red—stems, leaves, flowers, pots—and arranged symmetrically in quasi-geometric shapes, with secondary rhythms. Decorative paintings, one might say. I would reply: Negro-African paintings, rhythmic paintings. And these facts are all the more significant given that the examples chosen are so strongly influenced by Europe.

It is time to conclude. Thus is the Negro-African, for whom the world *is* a reflexive act upon the self. He does not see that he thinks; he feels that he feels, he feels his *existence*, he feels himself. Because he feels himself, he feels the *Other*; and because he feels the Other, he moves toward the Other, to the rhythm of the Other, in order to be *born with* [*con-naître à*] Him and the world. Thus, the act of knowing [*con-naissance*] is a "conciliatory harmony" with the world, simultaneously consciousness and creation of the world in its indivisible unity. It is this surge of vital force that expresses the religious and social life of the Negro-African, of which literature and art are the most effective instruments. And the poet cries out: "Eia! perfect circle of the world and complete concordance."[20]

Some will say to me that the spirit of Civilization and the laws of Negro-African Culture, as I have outlined them, are not unique to the Negro-African people and that they are shared with other peoples. I do not deny this. Every people combines, in its features, the various aspects of the human condition. But I would argue that nowhere are these traits found together in such balance, in such light; nowhere has rhythm reigned so despotically. Nature has done things well, for it has willed that each people, each race, each continent should cultivate, with particular care, certain virtues of Man, wherein lies its originality. And if it is added that this Negro-African Culture resembles, like a sister, that of ancient Egypt, of the Dravidians, and of the Oceanians, I would reply that ancient Egypt was *African* and that Black blood flows in impetuous streams in the veins of the Dravidians and the Oceanians.

It is not for me to draw a lesson from this study for the Western world. I will only say that to admire negro art in the wrong way is to risk reaping no fruit from it.

In closing, I would like to address the Negroes. The spirit of Negro-African Civilization animates, consciously or unconsciously, the best of today's negro artists and writers, whether they are from Africa or America. Insofar as they are aware of and inspired by Negro-African Culture, they rise to international prominence; insofar as they turn their backs on Mother Africa, they degenerate and become stale. Like Antaeus, who needed to lean on the earth to regain his momentum toward the sky. This does not mean that today's negro artists and writers should turn their backs on reality, refusing to translate the social reality of their milieu: of their race, their nation, their class. Quite the contrary. We have seen that the spirit of Negro-African Civilization is *embodied* in the most everyday reality. But it always transcends it to express the *meaning* of the world.

Europe's literary and artistic history proves that we must remain faithful to this spirit. After the failure of Greco-Latin aesthetics at the end of the nineteenth century, Western writers and artists discovered Asia and, above all, Africa at the end of their quest. Thanks to this, they were able to legitimize their discoveries by conferring on them the value of humanity. This is not the moment we will choose to betray, with Black Africa, our *raisons de vivre.*

NOTES

Léopold Sédar Senghor, "L'esthétique négro-africaine," *Liberté 1: Négritude et humanisme* (Seuil, 1964), 202–17. The text was first published in *Diogène* 16 (1956): 43–61. Much of it overlaps with Senghor's talk, later published as an essay, at the First International Congress of Black Writers and Artists in Paris (September 19–22, 1956). See Léopold Sédar Senghor, "L'esprit de la civilisation ou les lois de la culture négro-africaine," *Présence Africaine* no. 8/10 *Premier congrès international des écrivains et artistes noirs (Paris–Sorbonne: 19–22 Septembre 1956)* (1956), 51–56.

[Epigraph: In the original, the passage reads: "Comme assez savey qu'Afrique apporte toujours quelque chose de nouveau." François Rabelais, *Gargantua et Pantagruel*, ed. Henri Clouzot (Larousse, 1913), 62.—Eds.]

1. [The original quote from Einstein reads: "The most beautiful thing we can experience is the mysterious. It is the source of all true art and science." Albert Einstein, in *Living Philosophies: A Series of Intimate Credos* (Simon and Schuster, 1931), 6.—Eds.]

2. [See chapter 1, note 46, of this volume for a discussion of the term "existent."—Eds.]

3. [Camara Laye, *L'enfant noir* (Plon, 1953).—Eds.]

4. [Senghor is translating one of the traditional formulae used to end Wolof *léébb*, or tales: *Foofu lë léébb jaar tabbi gééj. Ku ko jëkk fóón tàbbi Àjjana.*—Eds.]

5. [The Wolof words related to beauty, in modern transcription, are *taar* (beauty), *am taar* (to be beautiful), *rafet* (to be beautiful), and *rafetaay* (beauty).—Eds.]

6. [In modern transcription, *yéém, mat.*—Eds.]

7. [The more common substantive for *baax* (good) is *mbaax.*—Eds.]

8. José Redinha, print 17, in *Subsídios para a história, arqueologia e etnografia dos Povos da Lunda: Paredes pintadas da Lunda* (Companhia de Diamantes de Angola, Serviços Culturais, Museu do Dundo, 1953). [The original citation reads: "São asas, cantos; são os pássaros." This book is nonpaginated; Senghor refers directly to numbered prints.—Eds.]

9. [André Breton, *Signe ascendant* (Gallimard, 1968), 9. Senghor most likely consulted the version of the text that appeared in *NÉON* 1 (January 1948) or in Breton's *Essais et témoignages* (La Baconnière, 1950).—Eds.]

10. [Kumba amul Ndey ("Kumba without a mother") is a Wolof *léeb*, often compared to the Cinderella narrative.—Eds.]

11. [Senghor is referring to the call-and-response between the storyteller and the audience that opens traditional Wolof *léeb*: *Léébóón / Lippóón; Amoon na fi / Daana am; Bi mu amee yaa fekke? / Yaa wax, ñu dégg.*—Eds.]

12. Cf. Léopold Sédar Senghor, "Langage et poésie négro-africaine," in *Poésie et langage* (Éditions de la Maison du Poète, 1954), 195.—Eds.]

13. [*Wëy wi* or *woy wi* are the modern transcriptions for "song" in Wolof.—Eds.]

14. [Carl Kjersmeier, *Centres de style de la sculpture nègre africaine*, vol. 1 (A. Morancé / Illums bogafelding, 1935–38), n.p. The "Figures" section of this work is nonpaginated.—Eds.]

15. [Kjersmeier, *Centres de style*, vol. 4, n.p.; Senghor seems to be referring to figures 18–19.—Eds.]

16. [Kjersmeier, *Centres de style*, vol. 1, n.p.—Eds.]

17. [André Malraux, *La voix du silence* (Gallimard, 1951), 563. We have used the following English translation: André Malraux, *The Voices of Silence*, trans. Stuart Gilbert (Secker and Warburg, 1954), 565—Eds.]

18. [Print 12 in Redinha, *Subsídios para a história.*—Eds.]

19. [Print 54 A in Redinha, *Subsídios para a história.*—Eds.]

20. Aimé Césaire, *Cahier d'un Retour au pays natal* (Présence Africaine, 1956), 72.

II

The Function and Meaning of the First World Festival of Negro Arts

We are deeply honored to welcome, with the *First World Festival of Negro Arts* [*Premier festival mondial des arts nègres*], so many talents from the four continents: the four horizons of the mind.[1] But what honors us above all, and what is to your greatest credit, is that you will have participated in a project that is far more revolutionary than exploring the cosmos: that is, in the elaboration of a new *humanism* which this time will encompass all men on the whole of planet Earth. Thus, Senegal—and first Dakar—welcomes you as distinguished guests, thereby fulfilling its vocation. For, like the black blade of a plough cutting into the fertile ocean, Dakar has always responded to the call of the trade winds, to the greetings from visitors coming from the seas and the skies. To tie together the dialogues from which civilizations, or at least *Culture*, emerge.

Here we are, here you are, gathered together. Ethnologists and sociologists, historians and linguists, writers and artists, you will have it as your task to locate, to articulate the *function of Negro Art* in the life of Black peoples. The function—in other words, the signs but, essentially, their meaning, that which lies beyond the signs. Today, I would like, more humbly, old militant of Negritude that I am, to tell you not so much the meaning and function of Negro Art—which I have attempted to do elsewhere—but the meaning and function that we Senegalese attribute to the First World Festival of Negro Arts. In a word, if we have taken on the enormous responsibility of organizing this festival, it is *for the defense and illustration of Negritude.*[2]

Defense . . .

Because, here and around the world, people continue to deny Negro Art along with Negritude, that is the *negro values of civilization*. And when they can no longer deny it, this Negro Art, manifest as it is, they try to strip it of its originality: its human truth.

Negro Art has been denied under the pretext that it presented diverse forms. And, in fact, if it is *unified*, it is so in the diversity of its fields, its genres, and even its styles. Just like European art, which in its German, French, Italian, Russian, or Swedish iterations, participates in Greco-Latin civilization: in discursive reason, animated by Christian inspiration. Like European art, which, though subject to frequent revolutions, remains, in its fundamental features, no less identical to itself. To return to Negro Art, it is all the more *unified* if its function is to always actualize its object; its nature on the other hand is to always express this object with the same signs: in the same profound style, that is, precisely to *stylize* it.

It follows that Negro Art cannot be denied for long. All the more because it is Europeans themselves who were the first to discover and define it; Negro-Africans preferred to live it. The most eminent European artists and writers have defended it, from Pablo Picasso to André Malraux, whose presence here I acknowledge as convincing evidence. Not to mention the Black artists and writers from Africa and the Americas who, between the two world wars, and since 1945, have commanded the attention of a world torn apart, but, as such, a world in search of its unity: of its authenticity.

Thus, unable to deny Negro Art, Europeans sought to undermine its originality under the pretext that it had a monopoly neither on *emotion* nor on the *analogical image* nor even on *rhythm*. And it is true that every real artist is endowed with these gifts, regardless of his continent, race, or nation. Nevertheless, it was necessary for Rimbaud to identify with Negritude, for Picasso to be shaken by a Baoulé mask, and for Apollinaire to sing of wooden fetishes in order for Western European art to be willing to abandon, after some twenty-five hundred years, *physéôs mimesis*: the imitation of nature. It is largely by dint of Negro Art—such a fortunate or, at least, fecund chance—that artists from this same West are inspired, today, like [Jean René] Bazaine, by "the most obscure work of the instinct and sensitivity," and that, like [André] Masson, they define a work of art as "a simple play of forms and of legibly organized values."[3] In sum, a simple rhythm. A "play of forces," as my friend [Pierre] Soulages would have said, because rhythm is the harmonious, and thus signifying, movement of forms.

. . . and Illustration of Negro Art

But it is not a matter of defending Negro Art from the past, as it is exhibited today at the *Dynamic Museum*.[4] It is more a matter of illustrating it by showing that it is, in the midst of the twentieth century, an inexhaustible, effervescent source: an essential component of the *Civilization of the Universal*, which is being developed before our very eyes, by us and for us, by all and for all.

And, first of all, by and for Black artists and writers, as evidenced by the *Exhibit of Contemporary Art*, meaningfully entitled: *Tendances et Confrontation* [Tendencies and confrontation]. Thus, after the First, then the Second World War, young Black men and young girls—from Africa, from America, from the very center of Europe—rose up, like young trees shaped by the event. From the depths of their ancestral experiences, from the depths of their more recent experiences as enslaved or colonized peoples or, simply, as men of this century, open to all the contributions, they drew out, with a novel vision of the world, the new words which they offered: the *New Negro*. Their works need not be in anthologies or in museums to be able to fulfill their function, which is: *by expressing life, by signifying it, to help men, all men, live better*.

To help their Black brothers before all others. Consider the former Black slaves of America, deported from Mother-Africa. If they did not surrender to the taedium vitae, if they did not, like other races, allow themselves to act as if they were condemned to death in a dull and doleful torpor, it is because they carried within them a bit of the native land, "the rage to live," *that power of creation which is the original characteristic of art*. For Art is nothing other than the primordial gesture of *Homo sapiens*, who, in signifying life with the image-symbol, intensifies it with rhythm, thereby magnifying it, to give it the value of eternity. Such is, at the very least, Negro Art and, to return to Negro-Americans, the art of *negro spirituals* and the *Blues*. The most banal work of the peasant, the most painful labor of the slave is vivified because magnified with words, with song, with dance: with *rhythm-energy*, which is the very fabric of life.

But slavery is of the past. Today, in Senegal, to take a more current and present example, it is the new national art, which, rooted in the black basalt of Cape Verde, is developing once again at this crossroads of Dakar, where all the grains of pollen of the world blow, along with images and ideas. It is still Negro Art that, saving us from despair, supports us in our efforts of social and economic development, in our *obstinacy to live*. It is our poets, our storytellers and novelists, our singers and dancers, our painters and sculptors, our musicians. Whether they paint violent mystical abstractions or the noble elegance of courtly love, whether they sculpt the national Lion or unheard-of monsters, whether they dance the Development Plan or sing the diversification of cultures, Negro-African artists, today's Senegalese artists help us live longer and better. Live longer, that is, more intensely, by reinforcing the strong tension that characterized the North Sudanese facets of Negro-African civilization; live better to solve the concrete problems that shape our future.

Listening to me one might think that Negro Art is nothing but a *technique*: a set of means at the service of a civilization of comfort, in any case of material production. Hear me well: I have spoken of "development," not of mere economic "growth," that is, the complementary totality of matter and spirit, of the economic and the social, of body and soul; I have spoken of production at the same time, of material and spiritual goods. When I speak of Negritude, I speak of a civilization in which art is, at once, technique and vision, craft and prophecy, a civilization in which art expresses, as Ogotemmêli would confirm, "the identity of material gestures and spiritual forces."[5] It is the same old Negro who, on another occasion, specified that "the weaver sings by throwing his shuttle, and his voice enters the chain, helping and carrying along with it the voice of the ancestors."[6] What is there to say besides that every art—weaving, sculpture, painting, music, dance—is, in Black Africa, speech [*parole*], better *Verb*, I mean, *Poetry*? Indeed, the forms and colors, the timbres and tones, the movements, even the materials used by the artists have the efficacy of the Verb, provided that they are rhythmed. For speech, transformed into Verb, because it rhythms, according to the primordial movement, the forms of named things, re-creates them, rendering them more present, *truer*. It fulfills, in this way, the action of the Creator because, by renewing it, it extends it through art, which, once again, makes eternal the life of things, of beings, by vivifying and magnifying it. Beyond its vital function, such is the meaning of Negro Art: *It makes us participate in the being of God by making us participate in his creation.*

Conclusion

By contributing to the defense and illustration of Negro Art, Senegal is conscious of aiding in the *construction of the Civilization of the Universal.*

Indeed, even before our national independence, for approximately twenty years, we have never ceased building our politics on dialogue. In all areas, but fundamentally in that of *Culture*; for Culture is the first condition and the ultimate aim of all development. But, in order to be in dialogue with others, in order to participate in the collective work of the men of conscience and of will who are rising up all around the world, in order to bring new values to the symbiosis of complementary values through which the Civilization of the Universal is defined, we must, we Negroes, finally, be ourselves in our dignity: our recovered identity.

To be ourselves, by cultivating our own values, as we have found them at the sources of Negro Art: those values that, beyond the profound unity of the human genus, as the product of biological, geographical, and historical facts, are the mark of our originality in thought, in feeling, and in action. To be ourselves, not without borrowings, but not by procuration, I say: through our personal—and at the same time collective—effort and for ourselves. Without which, we would be nothing but bad copies of others in the Dynamic Museum, as the Negroes of America had been under slavery until the end of the nineteenth century, as we ourselves, Negroes of Africa, had been under colonization until the eve of the Second World War.

What, between the two world wars, the young Black men and young girls of my generation wanted was, abandoning the old regime's *spirit of imitation*, to recover, along with the feeling of our dignity, *the spirit of creation* that, for millennia, had been the hallmark of Negritude, as the parietal art of the African continent demonstrates. We intended to become once again producers of civilization, like our Ancestors. For we were conscious that the humanism of the twentieth century, which can only be a Civilization of the Universal, would be impoverished if it was lacking a single value from one people, from one race, from one continent. Once again, the problem presents itself in terms of complementarity: of dialogue and exchange, not opposition or racial hatred. How could we, us Negroes, reject the scientific and technical discoveries of European and North American peoples, thanks to which Man is transforming himself, along with nature?

You, scholars and professors, artists and writers, are the true humanists of our times. *Because Senegal has chosen to be the country of dialogue and exchange, Senegal would like to be your second homeland.* Senegal wishes, in any case, that the great dialogue taking place here today will contribute to the construction of Earth: to the fulfillment of Man.

NOTES

Léopold Sédar Senghor, "Fonction et signification du premier festival mondial des arts nègres," *Liberté 3: Négritude et civilisation de l'universal* (Seuil, 1977), 58–63. The text was originally given as a talk on March 30, 1966, at the colloquium "Fonction et signification de l'Art nègre dans la vie du peuple et pour le peuple" (Function and meaning of Negro Art in the life of the people and for the people) (Dakar, March 30–April 8, 1966) as part of the First World Festival of Negro Arts (1966). An earlier English translation was published in 1995: "The Role and Signification of the First World Festival of Negro Arts, Dakar, 1966," in *Seven Stories About Modern Art in Africa*, ed. Clémentine Deliss and Jane Havell (Flammarion, 1995), 224–26.

1. [The First World Festival of Negro Arts took place in Dakar April 1–24, 1966. The festival highlighted Senegal's recent independence, the philosophy of Negritude, Pan-African unity, and the cultural affinities among African and Afro-descendant cultures. It was attended by luminaries and intellectuals such as Ousmane Sembène, Aimé Césaire, Wole Soyinka, Langston Hughes, Josephine Baker, and Jean Price-Mars.—Eds.]

2. [Senghor is playing on the title of Joachim du Bellay's treatise, *La deffence et illustration de la langue françoyse* (Paris: Arnoul L'Angelier, 1549).—Eds.]

3. [The quotation of Jean René Bazaine (1904–2001) comes from *Notes sur la peinture d'aujourd'hui* (Seuil, 1953), 40–41. Bazaine was a French painter, writer, and designer of stained glass; André Masson (1896–1987) was a French illustrator, painter, and set designer; and Pierre Soulages (1919–2022) a French abstract painter and graphic artist. It is unclear whether Senghor is citing or paraphrasing Masson and Soulages.—Eds.]

4. [The Musée dynamique (Dynamic Museum) in Dakar was inaugurated in March 1966 on the occasion of the festival. It hosted the festival's central exhibit, "L'art nègre: Sources, évolution, expansion." The museum served as a contemporary art museum and, briefly, as a dance center (1976–82), until the space was taken over by the Supreme Court of Senegal in 1988.—Eds.]

5. [Ogotemmêli, cited in Marcel Griaule, *Dieu d'eau, entretiens avec Ogotemmêli* (Fayard, 1975), 25. Ogotemmêli was the Dogon elder who narrated the cosmogony of the Dogon to the French anthropologist Marcel Griaule.—Eds.]

6. [Ogotemmêli, cited in Griaule, *Dieu d'eau*, 69.—Eds.]

12

For a Negro Criticism

I shall be brief. This is a message, not a speech.

Finally, the time has come, in criticism as in other fields of art, to think by ourselves and for ourselves. Especially at a time when, along the banks of the Seine, colloquia are regularly organized where token black lackeys [*petits nègres de service*][1] rail against the values of Negritude—much to the delight of Great White Men, who are thus reassured in their sense of superiority. It is true, as I was informed last month in Paris, that we are in a state of decline.[2] "Values" are no longer in vogue, but rather applause, which is garnered by the servile imitation of Euro-American models.

Since 1960, the year of African independences, and even before that, Negro-African writers and artists have created a new poetry, a new novel, a new painting, a new sculpture. But criticism, at first glance, has not budged from the banks of the Seine, where it continues to make use of methods from the nineteenth century.

We will never be more conscious of the fact that it is time to invent a new, Negro-African criticism, with a new method, a new vocabulary, a new style. But about four years ago, I discovered that this *new criticism* had emerged, timidly, since independence in our African universities, especially at the Federal University of Cameroon. I am certain that this conference will confirm this criticism and, above all, strengthen it.

Of course, it is not a question of ignoring the "new" Euro-American criticism, especially since it owes something to Negro-African epistemology, and chiefly art criticism. Far from ignoring this twentieth-century criticism, we must actively assimilate it.

We must therefore invent, with a new vocabulary and a new style, a new, Negro-African method of criticism, jettisoning once and for all the scientism of the "witless nineteenth century." As if the critic should be omniscient, like God the Father, contemplating the Universe through an objective lens and with a serene gaze. But is it not the nature of lenses to be personal, subjective?

That is to say, in order for criticism to be an expression of truth, it must be human, since it involves man judging a work and, beyond the work, another man. It is the encounter of one sensibility and one imagination with another sensibility and another imagination. It is a reciprocal prehension [*saisie*] of one by the other: the lightning strike of imaginative intuition and the flash of style at the same time.

Prehension of what? Of the writer in his environment, as we say today—his historical and geographical, sociological, but essentially psychological and, as a matter of fact, moral environment. As you well understand, beyond the artist and criticism, there is the people that connects the two, that nourishes them, and that is nourished by them. But, though rooted in a continent, an ethnicity, a society, the artist is first and foremost a human being who, in a human movement of freedom, goes beyond material determinations and even moral ones.

Hence the necessity of an original prehension of one by the other: of the critic by the artist, of the critic by the people, of the people by both, and vice versa. I speak of a thought prehension [*une saisie pensée*], but one that is first temperament to temperament, heart to heart: soul! I say, *soul*, as our Negro-American brothers say.

For there are not ideas on one side and feelings on the other. There are feelings that arise from gestures and images, and ideas that arise from feelings. There are *idea-feelings* [*idées-sentiments*] that are expressed through forms, colors, and movements: through those images that are, in Africa, always analogical, that is to say, symbolic and rhythmic. In Nigritie, every true work of art, whether it be a novel, a riddle, or a caricature, is always a *rhythmic image*.

So let us send the criticism of ideas and their schemes back to the museum of antiquities, along with all the jumble of their pseudoscientific vocabulary and their pedantic style, too.

A work of art—whether poem or story, painting or sculpture, music or dance—is not a set of ideas but a work of beauty. For the critic, it is not a matter of saying what the work means but rather *how and why it is beautiful.* Because the ultimate stupidity, as we have seen from certain aspersers of Negritude, is to try to explain a Negro-African poem using arguments from European philosophy or politics—if only the arguments were to come from mathematics, which is the science of numbers, and therefore of rhythm—when what should have been said is why and how we are moved by this poem. That is why, from the writer, I have turned, naturally, to the *artist.*

The reality is that people want to judge Negro-African works based on outdated European criteria. That too many Negro-African intellectuals suffer from an inferiority complex, and they cling to ideas instead of simply feeling the beauty in a fulgurant intuition.

They forget the lesson of Descartes—but who reads Descartes nowadays?—that "feeling," like "thought" and "desire," is a child of reason. "I want you to feel me," says a certain African notable, while the European specifies: "I want you to know me." African criticism will be the encounter of one person's feeling with another person's feeling, the prehension of the soul by the soul—or it will not be at all.

NOTES

Léopold Sédar Senghor, "Pour une critique nègre," in *Liberté 3: Négritude et civilisation de l'universel* (Seuil, 1977), 427–30. The text was first given as a talk at the conference "Le Critique africain et son peuple, comme producteur de civilisation" (The African critic and his people, as producer of civilization) in Yaoundé, Cameroon, in April 1973.

1. [The term *nègre de service* has a pejorative sense of obsequiousness and groveling and might be translated loosely as "house Negro" or "resident Negro," though here not in the literal sense of someone confined to a domicile.—Eds.]

2. [Senghor uses the unusual expression *les seins ne se portent plus* (literarily, "breasts are no longer worn") in the manner one might say "corsets are out of fashion."—Eds.]

13

From French Poetry to Francophone Poetry; or, The Contributions of Negroes to Francophone Poetry

In their invitations, Pierre Emmanuel and Édouard Maunick have outlined the purpose of this *Meeting* [*Rencontre*] for us. It enables us to move beyond our provincial, national, and continental solitudes. It is a matter of studying the question of creation, together—confronted as we are with the aspirations of our peoples. During the final quarter of this twentieth century in crisis, which we are now entering, they seek to root themselves in their identity but, at the same time, to reach out to one another across the barbed wires of borders. Especially because they speak the same language. It matters little whether this language is maternal or borrowed: It is still a matter of communication. I am speaking of the dialogue that men of this age yearn for.

This dialogue is all the more necessary in that French, the language we use, is, first of all, the least poetic language there is. Thierry Maulnier[1] and Jean-Paul Sartre[2] agree that French was, until Rimbaud's revolution, an analytical and toneless language in which rhythm is barely perceptible, abstract, and lacking color; a language averse to the image. That is why, as a great consumer of raw material, French literature, over the centuries, never ceased welcoming, even seeking out, foreign contributions: Latin and Greek, Italian and Spanish, English and German, Slavic and Arabic, Indian and Chinese, and finally, at the end of the nineteenth century, negro contributions.

That is why, during this meeting and in this time of crisis, which is more cultural than it is economic or political, we would be wise to explore the ways in which the French language, and more specifically Francophone poetry, could continue to enrich itself or, better yet, how it could establish a new *re-naissance* through reciprocal fecundations. Once again, this process began with Rimbaud. At the close of this twentieth century, in which people mingle haphazardly—through boats, railroads, airplanes, and telecommunication satellites—we are exceptionally fortunate, brought together not only by our affinities, such as those that unite us here, but also by our disagreements.

In any case, it is in this vein that I would like to tell you how I see the matter. This will, naturally, be the testimony of a Negro-African. But it may be of some interest. Our values are the furthest apart from, and therefore the most complementary to, French values. And, since the Renaissance, we have been the last to sit at the banquet of the universal. It is true that the Greeks, the civilizers of Europe, did not forget what they owed to "Ethiopians," to Negritude. But still, once again, my address is only one testimony among others. I think of what others could say, especially those from Asia and America. I think of the Lebanese Georges Shehadé's arabesques,[3] of the "Terre-Québec" [Quebec-Earth] and of "l'Homme-Québec" [Quebec-Man] of which the Canadian Gaston Miron[4] sings, and of many others. The features of Negritude that I will define here can be found elsewhere. The specificity of a culture is to focus on certain aspects of the human being and not on others.

Today, we know that *Francophonie* is the set of nations that have French as a national language, an official language, or a language of international communication. There are, notably, forty French-speaking delegations at the United Nations. There are even anthologies of French poetry that feature poets such as Saint-John Perse and Aimé Césaire, who are not from the Hexagon and who may not even be "French." But rare are the commentators who show that these poets enrich the French language, but also the French culture, the Mediterranean and Celtic strains of which they fortify. I will return to this.

It is thus about this enrichment that I wish to speak, beginning with the realm of myth: the imaginary.

Semiology has contributed much to linguistics, and even to criticism, by enabling the latter two disciplines to better decrypt the artistic impulse. But because it is a science from the West, whose privileged tool is discursion, semiology rarely reaches life. Preoccupied with forms and numbers, with quantity, it often fails to grasp life in its sensible qualities. It sees it, measures it: It does not feel it. No one can tell us, even [Pierre] Teilhard de Chardin, that at a certain degree, quantity transforms itself into quality and vice versa. That is theory. The best semiologists are conscious of this, namely Roland Barthes, who, in *L'imagination du signe* [The imagination of the sign] acknowledges that "symbolic consciousness may sometimes mask an unacknowledged determinism."[5]

This is why, in that context, I do not much like the word "symbol," which, to speak like [Jacques] Maritain, is less likely to take us back into the sphere of the imaginary than into that of the "intellect."[6] In the "Kingdom of Childhood," it is through mythical stories that the poets of precolonial Africa lived their poems before they sang them. It is still in that kingdom that the poets and, more generally, the Black artists of today dwell—whether they are from Africa or from the Americas. What struck spectators at the exhibit of Senegalese contemporary art that was held at the Grand Palais in May and June of 1975 was less the forms and the colors that animated the paintings and tapestries than the strange visitors of midnight and also those of midday: the hallucinatory presence of the gods. "Hallucinatory," for the blue eyes of Europeans but not for the African spectators at the Dynamic Museum of Dakar.[7] And especially not for the Senegalese poets, such as Birago Diop, Lamine Diakhaté, Lamine Niang, Malick Fall, Ibrahima Sourang, and Kiné Kirama Fall. All my life I have remained touched by the visions that I had during my Sereer childhood, when I saw the procession of the year's Dead unfold in the *tanns*,[8] while the young herders, my comrades, privileged because they are closer to the source, had seen the Spirits, I mean the gods themselves: They had spoken to them.

The mythical power of Negro-Africans. It is not a coincidence if ethnic characterology writes that Negro-Africans think more readily through analogical images than abstract concepts, making them cousins of both the Mediterranean and the Latino-American peoples. All these gods, all these Ancestors who, as archetypes, live in the depths of memories, are found in Negro-African poems, but also in the poetry of Francophone Negro-Americans: the Antilleans and Guyanese. We find them living in the midst of men, animals, plants, sand and stones, the sun and moon, rains and wind—themselves alive, and present. They live in the images of poets, which semiologists present to us as symbols, reduced to equations: "signifier = signified."

Once again, science here does not prehend—does not exhaust—all of the real. Of course, it reaches forms and colors, and temperature measured in centigrade degrees, but not the texture of the skin, the tone, the heat, neither the sap nor the scent—not life. But let us consider one example. How surprised I was when, conducting research on the "oral poetry" of my village in 1945, I discovered, as we were discussing a different question, that the gymnic songs composed in honor of General de Gaulle, the Royal Air Force, the Americans, and the Russians were, in fact, to honor specific age groups that were initiated during the 1939–45 war. I began, first, in the footsteps of semiologists, by writing equations: "group A = De Gaulle; group B = the Royal Air Force," etc. But I quickly noticed that this method did not help me. Group A resembles General de Gaulle, I told myself, but why does General de Gaulle not resemble group A? The affinities between the two are numerous in the French language and in the French administration. However, one thing identifies them more truly: *honor*. Not an honor that they would possess but an honor that they aspire to and dream of, an honor that they live in their dream. In short, the image, the images of the poem—but also the song, as we will see—make them *participate* in or, better, make them live the same *feeling-idea*, which is the aim of the poem. For Rimbaud, this aim is to "possess truth in a soul and a body."[9] For the Fulɓe of Senegal, poems are "words that are pleasing to the heart and the ear." The two definitions converge, and it is a mistake to insist, as some have, on the "intellectualism" of Rimbaud's poetry. The truth that Rimbaud speaks of is that of the heart, of the "psyche," as we say today, that is, of intuition. To return to the "poem in honor of de Gaulle," the effect of its magic is to introduce the presence of the gods with the force of *Honor* into the heart of the Circumcised, the Initiated. For, in Black Africa, being is force.

Such is the negro image. I, too, have written that it was an "analogical image," a "symbol." It is more than that, even if we pass from oral poetry in Negro-African languages to written poetry in French. Returning to my research, I did not find abstract words in this Sereer poetry—not even the most significant words for the ethnic group, such as "honor" or "beauty," or even "accord" to mean beauty. Only images, and not comparisons; only metaphors or, better yet, the simple naming of being, of the thing, the fact, the gesture:

It is you, being massaged with a vase of oil

. . . .

The indigo flank, measure it with a silver meter

. . . .

I will not sleep, on the arena I will keep a watch
The tam-tam of myself is adorned with a white collar.[10]

Or, to get back to De Gaulle:

The lion's songs,
That is what enrages the young men.
De Gaulle holds the scepter
In France, the knight of Mayé![11]

It can be enough for the poet simply to name, because, in our Negro-African languages, nominal and verbal roots are pregnant with images: they allow us to see, but above all to feel.

Here I am, already in language. Before I move on to this matter, I would like to return to the myth to say how Black poets of the French language have transferred the old myths into the language of Descartes, crafting new ones. Transferred while retaining, along with the values, the ancient style. For style is ethnicity. When Edouard Maunick assimilates Snow, his White wife, to his native island, and even to the slate-gray land of his country, to the Black race, to negro speech, we can wonder, as we have done earlier regarding "De Gaulle's poem," if the semiologists' equations can exhaust the multivalence of negro images. Indeed, in metaphors like Woman-Island-Race and Woman-Earth-Palaver, it is the White woman, the foreigner, who "metamorphosizes into her opposite." But it is by way of the logic of the heart, which "has its reasons," which are not those of science. An attentive study of Césaire's imagery would lead us to the same conclusion. I read, in "Ex-voto pour un naufrage" [Ex-voto for a shipwreck]:

I carry the king's stretcher
I spread out the king's rug
I am the king's rug
I carry the king's scrofula
I am the king's parasol.[12]

As we can see, there are five different ways of expressing submission—or mockery—to the king. The image takes on a life of its own and evolves. I had read, previously, in "La Femme et le Couteau" [The women and the knife]:

Rich flesh with teeth shavings of sure flesh
fly, in bursts of day, in bursts of night, in kisses of wind
in stems of light in stern of silence

fly, hunted entanglements anvils of dark flesh, fly
fly in children's shoes in silver stream
fly, and defy the cataphracts of the night riding on their onagers.[13]

As in the previous verses, the image, more precisely the group of images, evolves powerfully and with a life of its own to explode in a hallucinatory presence that science—the semiological equation—cannot explain. Except for the science of the soul: the heart.

Nothing illustrates this truth better than the following anecdote, with which I will conclude these reflections on the negro image. The day I asked Césaire the sense [*sens*]—I do not mean the "meaning" [*signification*]—of . . . . . . *Et les chiens se taisaient* (. . . . . . *And the Dogs Were Silent*), he hesitated for a second, thought about it, then replied: "It is not simple. . . . It can designate, quite classically, the Chthonic divinities. Perhaps in the sense of the African myth. . . . Several explanations are possible." And I answered: "It is the same thing for me. I feel that an image is true . . . in the sense of the real, not the rational, of course. Then, I welcome it."

In "Orphée noir" [Black Orpheus], Jean-Paul Sartre indicated the major themes of the *New Negro and Malagasy Poetry in French*: "Negritude," "Eros," "Suffering." He showed how the poets of the *Anthology* had created new myths, but in the ancestral style, the Negro-African style, by drawing from the elements of their environment: from natural phenomena, animals, but even more from plants. Leo Frobenius had already signaled the agrarian, that is, the Negro-African, character of the "Ethiopian" race, where the tree is a god. As Aimé Césaire says, "The weakness of many men is that they know how to become neither a stone nor a tree."[14] And he sang in "Les pur-sang" [Purebloods]:

I grow like a plant
with no remorse and with no warping
toward the unknotted hours of the day
pure and sure like a plant
without crucifixion
toward the unknotted hours of the day.[15]

However, David Diop, inclining toward Rama-Kam, the Black woman, whispers to her:

When you love Rama-Kam
It's the tornado that trembles
In the flesh of lightning-night

And leaves me full of the breath of you
O Rama-Kam.[16]

If one browses the entire *Anthology*, one will find that few images, few myths are borrowed from the modern world of the West, except in order to reject this world, a world of inhumanity, as Léon Damas does:

I have the impression of being ridiculous
among them complicit among them a supporter
among them a beheader hands terribly red
with the blood of their civilization.[17]

This is to speak of *Negro Suffering*, on which I would like to dwell rather than on Negro Eros, in which the West has wallowed, seeking to flavor its own erotism. If I had the time, I would have tried to show you that negro sensuality is not erotism and that it is deep within this sensuality that the highest spirituality is incarnated. But let us return to the theme of Suffering.

This is the source of a new mythology, the heroes of which are the old unifying conquerors: the emperor Sundiata Keita; Shaka Zulu, the Black Napoleon; the old resistant fighters to colonization like Lat Dior Diop of Senegal, Samory Touré of Guinea, Béhanzin of Dahomey; and others, less famous.[18] But it is mostly among the Antilleans, severed from their land and their Negro-African languages, that modern heroes sprang up, the most famous of whom are Toussaint-Louverture and Delgrès of Saint-Charles, not to mention "the Rebel" of . . . . . . *Et les chiens se taisaient*, or Negritude, mythicized by the same Césaire, which merges with Mother-Africa. Famous because they incarnate not only negro suffering but also the refusal of humiliation: The negro revolt, present everywhere in the Americas wherever one had to fight and die for freedom. It is their story that Paul *Niger*, the man whose pseudonym is a project in itself, sings:

We must laugh at Soulouque but not ignore Capra-la-mort who attacked Crête-à-Pierrot three times, and three horses were killed under him, and the fourth carried him off; and Delgrès from Saint-Charles, the purest of my brothers, my master and idol, man among men and father of my peers; and the redoubt that explodes with freedom; and Toussaint whose Corsican prevailed only by cunning; and the statute of Josephine the slave owner, which I clearly say will one day explode. . . . [19]

Again, if one browses the *Anthology*: in the Antillean section, it is merely an elegy, interrupted, in offbeats and syncopations, by songs of grave joy. However, suffering is not absent from the African section, as Tchicaya U Tam'si shows, in a remarkable manner, with his oeuvre, which, he tells us, is simply a "synopsis" of his "passion":[20]

How dirty you are, Christ, to be with the bourgeois
. . . .
Christ, I spit at your joy
The sun is black with Negroes who suffer of dead Jews
Who seek their bread's leaven.[21]

Thus, negro suffering, which our poets universalize by transforming it into tenderness. Jacques Roumain has given us, under the title "Madrid," the elegy of the civil war in Spain.[22] In "Bois-d'Ébène" [Ebony wood], he tells us of the fraternity of human suffering:

Like the contradiction of features,
resolved by the harmony of the face,
we proclaim the unity of suffering
and the revolt
of all peoples on the surface of the entire earth.[23]

A race has never suffered as much as the Black race. The slave trade lasted three and a half centuries with 200 million deaths: the largest genocide in history! However, a race has never forgiven so much:

I will not see my blood on their hands anymore
I forget to be a Negro so as to forgive the world for this.[24]

It is Tchicaya speaking, and forgiving. The mythology of suffering is, with a new language, the greatest contribution of contemporary Black poets to universal poetry, and first to Francophone poetry.

It is time to move on to the French language and its transfigurations.

The Charm of Speech

Clearly, alongside the transformations that Negro-American and Negro-African poets have brought to the English language, those that Black poets have brought to French are more reserved. They are no less real, however. To understand them, one must, first, examine Negro-African languages to define their principal characteristics.

The contempt began at the start of the century when we sought an aesthetics in Negro Art—and it is true that it relies on an aesthetics, one that is not unconscious—, whereas what we needed to look for, first, was a *meta-physics*: a *re-ligion* more than an art. The contempt continued with those who seek, in literature, or even in negro poetry in French, a rhetoric when they should discover a *poiesis* [*poïêtique*]: not an art of speech in the objective genitive sense, but an art of speech in the subjective genitive sense, that is, a system of means and processes through which *Speech* creates a world which is new and true at the same time.

One must thus begin from Negro-African languages. Contrary to what the average European thinks, Negro-African languages are not prolix, nor are their literatures verbose. They are agglutinative languages that use affixes, that is, particles, to express morphological or syntactic relations where other language groups employ words or even expressions. On the other hand, if the Negro-African sentence, in its reprises and repetitions, can be long, as we will see presently, the clause that carries only the essential information is, by contrast, grammatically brief and simple.

Hence the force of the Negro-African sentence, and primarily of its "bare words," to borrow Édouard Maunick's expression. Once again, it is that, in Black Africa, even today, words preserve the creative force, the fertile humidity of their roots: They are pregnant with images, as I like to say. The poet does not need other, comparative words; more importantly, he does not need subordinating conjunctions: "like," "thus," "such as," etc. He names things with an abrupt speech, and images and worlds arise. As the poetesses from my village used to say:

Valiant rooster in triumph
Whom I name Faapa Ngoor Diène.
A rainy season-without-rain,
The fortune teller has the power.
The tam-tam breathes smoke,
Women clapping their hands for me.
Men sniggering.
You have told true, Xalis of Téning.

A new but familiar world emerges. It is remarkable that, in the hundreds of poem-songs I have collected—about work, wrestling, dance, festivities—, the poet almost always employs the present tense, regardless of aspect: imperfective, perfective, momentary, habitual. In the absence of the present, one can find the aorist, which is the tense of intemporality. And if it is the future, it is a "near future" or, ad libitum, of a "present future," of an action, of a state that is coming, that will emerge, that is a stronger presence because it is announced.

For Heidegger, as Jean Beaufret tells us in *Twelve Questions*,[25] "all metaphysics is [. . .] a thesis on being," which "is essentially present." Negro-African poetry sings of nothing other than this.

The creative power of the poem, we have seen, does not come from images and roots of words alone, but it also stems from their morphology and their syntax: from the play, within the word, of the morphemes and semantemes, from the play of words within the clause, and of clauses within the sentence. More than prose, negro poetry aims for an economy of means, which suppresses everything that is useless. These are, most frequently, articles and determiners, the absence of which intensifies the dialectic of noun-verb, of essential words, and provokes the poetic short circuit. More than what is said [*le dit*], as I have said, it is eloquence [*le bien dire*] that is the magical charm: that which makes poetry. More than the play of words, the play of phonemes or sounds: of vowels and consonants. For the poem, in Black Africa, once again, consists of "words that are pleasing to the heart and the ear."

Let us reread the poets in the *Anthology*—Césaire, Damas, Niger, Tirolien, Roumain, Brière, Ranaivo, Rabemananjara, Bolamba, the two Diops—, or the younger poets—that is, Édouard Glissant, Georges Desportes, René Depestre, Gérard Chenet, Davertige, Tchicaya U Tam'si, Édouard Maunick, Cheikh Ndaw, Engelbert Mveng, Jean-Paul Nyunai—, we will find, in their poems, the same verbal game, which has led us from images to phonemes, singularly to the very power of naming. Léon Damas sings:

they have looted the space that was mine
the custom the days the life
the song the rhythm the effort
the path the water the hut
the gray smoked earth
the wisdom the words the palavers
the elders
the cadence the hands the tempo the hands
the stamping of feet the soil.[26]

And we see, we hear processing before our eyes three and a half centuries of the slave trade. But, most often, in a convergent assimilation of Negro-African style and French surrealist style, it is the metaphor that is used by our poets: directly, in apposition or with a determiner preceded by the preposition *of*:

freedom oh my great slimy legs
sticky with the fresh blood

your call of a surprised bird and of fascine
and of Chabine[27] at the bottom of the seas
and of sapwood and of triumphant lychee
and of sacrilege
climb climb[28]

We will have noted abstract words among the most concrete words, the most palpitating, which have been transplanted from French: "freedom," "sacrilege." Despite, or even because of, his stated desire to articulate *métissage*, Maunick would like to be—makes himself—more rooted. This explains the frequency of metaphor through the apposition of two, or even three, words joined by one or two dashes: "ISLAND-Woman-Earth," "ISLAND-Evil-Love," "country-you," "smell-darkness." It is one of the tricks that Jacques Rabemananjara is fond of:

Sea of flames and of crimson in the night
the forest where the sky's fire died. My
vivid flesh is no longer anything but incandescence! From
the root to the flower of being, I am burning,
burnt! I shiver vine.[29]

Through the image, we have already entered into grammar: into language. In the preface that I have just written for *Ensoleillé vif* [Sunned alive], Edouard Maunick's most recent collection, and that I entitled "Negritude métisse" [Mixed Negritude], I tried to show what that verbal play, inherited from oral poetry, consisted of.[30]

Of course, we will find in negro poetry of the French language new words to designate the realities of the exotic world: trees and animals, peoples and traditions, and natural phenomena, which are different. I will not stop there: They are exotic only for Western readers. The words forged by negro poets are more significant, namely: "negritude," "koriste," "before nothingness" [*anté-néant*], etc. Still more significant are those among them that follow the dialectic of noun-verb: nouns, adjectives, or participles based on verbal roots, and verbs based on nominal roots. Maunick gives us countless examples: "throbbing" [*lancinance*], "un-sunned" [*désoleillé*], "remembered" [*souvenue*], "landscaped" [*paysager*], "oceanized" [*océaner*]. In the same manner and following the Negro-African tradition, the New Negroes will use an infinitive, an adjective, or a participle as substantives. I mentioned apposition above. One must add the suppression of determiners, which are function words, like articles. This is frequent in Maunick:

anger will be here a game of trespass
. . . .
when distance eats pathways.[31]

All these processes, to which we should add the creation of a nominal phrase through the suppression of the verb, aim at brevity, and thus to the density of expression: to the poetic short circuit.

In comparison to the violence to which Anglophone Negroes have subjected Shakespeare's language, the Francophones' transformations seem benign. Once again, these transformations remain no less real. Even with poets like Césaire and Maunick, Damas and Tchicaya, especially with them, it is still the same language, of course, but in another style: a *negro* style. There are reasons that explain this sense of moderation. The first is that all these poets attended high school and university, where they learned to master the French language in order to bend it to negro genius. The second reason has to do with the genius of the French language itself. Summarizing his theory in *Introduction à la poésie française* [Introduction to French poetry], Thierry Maulnier writes: "The effort of French poetry toward pure poetry is thus not an effort to deprive the poem of any content other than poetry, that would not have any sense, *but to endow the poem with the power of acting poetically on the totality of its content*. It is an effort to deploy poetic means in their greatest vigor and their greatest efficacy. Poetry is not music, but language [*langage*]."[32] I have emphasized the essential here.

However, if poetry is not music, it draws on music, as Rimbaud, the greatest revolutionary of French poetry, so clearly saw. He was the first poet to understand that he needed to renew himself from the sources of Negritude. It is the moment to reiterate that we have misread his famous sentence from *Une saison en enfer* [A season in hell]: "I am a beast, a negro." Indeed, he adds: "But they were able to save me. You are fake negroes." And further: "I invented the *color* of vowels! [. . .] I fixed the form and movement of each consonant, and, with *instinctive rhythms*, I flattered myself for inventing a poetic language [*verbe*], accessible, one day or another, to all the senses."[33] I have emphasized the essential words here, through which Rimbaud's poetics converges with that of the Negroes. This is what brings me to the most sensible qualities, the most sensual of words: to their melody and their rhythm.

As I said above, what provokes the short circuit and exercises a magical charm is, more than images, more than the play of words, the play of sounds: the melodic play of vowels and consonants, of assonances and alliterations, as in the great popular oral poetries of the ancient Celts and Germans, but, before that, of the ancient Egyptians and "Ethiopians." I understand, through this last word, the Negroes of Africa and Asia. In "La Negritude métisse," I have reiterated what alliteration and assonance consist of.[34]

Alliteration is the most frequent form of melody, the most natural to the negro poet, such that we find it, even today, in riddles, sayings, and proverbs.

And it is true that, in ancient times, these were rhythmed like poems. No poet escapes from it today, especially not those poets who, willingly using colloquial language, like Damas and Tchicaya, are averse to all rhetoric: even to all poetics. It is Tchicaya who sings:

from Xamina to Kin three among their squad
make flowers make fires neither fires nor flowers enchant

Though less frequent, because it is more subtle and varied, poets draw more poetic effects from assonance, as in the last verses cited from Césaire:

your call of a bird [. . .] and of a fascine
and of chabine at the bottom of the sea.[35]

You will have felt the opposition *i-eau*.[36] For assonance, more often than alliteration, operates at a distance, and it can enrich itself with rhyme. It is with all of these magical games at once that the most creative, the most poetic of negro poets play: Césaire, Damas, Tchicaya, and Maunick, among others. Combining alliteration and assonance, Maunick affirms:

I no longer say prayer
I no longer say thank you, Missié
. . .
I no longer say, say
I no longer scream, scream.[37]
And Damas:
—you were at the Bar
and me
    among others
at the level of the plastered track
and patinaed with *steps*
with *stomps*
with *slow of swings*
with *sounds*
with *songs*
with blues.[38]

It will be noted that Damas did not hesitate to delight himself wherever he was: even in the English language. This is what explains, more than the exotic intention, our poets' predilection for words transferred, just as they are, from Negro-African languages, from Malagasy, or from the patois "creole." It will equally be noted that with assonance and alliteration we have entered, some time ago, the domain of *negro rhythm* which spread across the entire planet earth, to its extremities in Mongolia, enlivening it in the etymological sense of the word. Rhythm is the major value that Black Africa has brought to the contemporary world: this rhythm which has invaded everything, music and dance, of course, but also painting and sculpture, theater and cinema, but, paradoxically, not yet architecture, where monotonous symmetry still triumphs.

Indeed, as André Gide would observe, speaking of negro song, this rhythm is not monotone.[39] I have defined it as a reprise, which is neither a refrain nor a repetition. In a word, they are asymmetrical parallelisms, such as the painter Léger has illustrated in a colored drawing. It is the reprise of a line, a shape, a color, a tone, an accent, a sound, a word, an expression, a sentence, a stanza. But it is not the same thing, and there is always something new: something different. Nothing illustrates this rhythm better than these four verses, spoken by Césaire's Rebel:

> Beat-me, beat-me, armed scream of my people
> Beat-me warthog and stomp, stomp-me until
> my heart breaks until my veins burst until
> my bones twitter in the midnight of my flesh.[40]

Let us note the words and expressions that punctuate the rhythm: "beat-me," "beat-me," "beat-me," "stomp," "stomp-me," "until," "until," "until." We can number this rhythm: three, two, three. But a minimally careful analysis shows us that the reality is more nuanced. There is only the expression, "beat-me," which is repeated exactly, yet in a different typography.

Rhythm is the fundamental law of all poetry, but above all negro poetry. In Maunick's *Ensoleillé vif*, the speeches[41] appear in series, of which the poems are connected by a verse or an expression, which is a sort of indication that underscores the theme: "love love,"[42] "in the stopped earth,"[43] "invaded invaded."[44] Elsewhere, even in Tchicaya, whose humor often breaks the rhythm, recalls [*rappels*] occur within the same poem: recall of a word, of an expression, or of one or two verses. This is the case in "Viatique" [Viaticum], where the word "sadness" is reprised:

> You are indeed from my country

And

> I forget to be a Negro so as to forgive,
> I will no longer see my blood on their hands.[45]

Naturally, all of this recurs each time with a variant. With Césaire, the process is not brought to its limit but laid out as a foundation: a source and structure at the same time, which provides form and color, melody and rhythm, I say *life*, to the entire poem. This is the case, in *Soleil [cou] coupé*, with poems entitled "La pluie" [The rain], "Ex-Voto pour un naufrage" [Ex-voto for a shipwreck], "À l'Afrique" [To Africa]. And so many others, where the words, magic wands, rhythmic, are respectively "rain," "tam-tam," "peasant," etc.

Let us return, as we did before, to French poetry, to observe that the negro poets have shaken French poetry—like an old woman, wearing hat and gloves, with a necklace around her neck—but without abusing her. Paradoxically, by reintroducing song, melody, and rhythm into French poetry, they have restored it to its primary vocation. One of the most beautiful poems written in French is the sonnet by Ronsard from which I have excerpted this stanza:

> Time is passing, my Lady, time is passing,
> Ah! It is not time, but us who is passing by,
> And we will all be stretched under its blade.[46]

What is admirable, here, is not the image—reprised, repeated, and faded—of time passing, but the play of assonances and rhymes, which play not only toward the ends of verses but within the verses themselves: the play of *a-em* and of *o-on*.[47]

Hence, paradoxically, with an ancestral sense of *accord* and *measure*, two major words in my native language,[48] the negro poets remained faithful not only to the genius of the French language but also to the genius of French poetry, all while contributing the essential values of Negritude. This is summarized by Thierry Maulnier, who writes the following in his *Introduction*:

> The French poet requires materials that he would be able to bring to their supreme incandescence, to subject to an entire poetic transmutation, and which would, for this transmutation, first be freed of the heaviness of their debris and their impurities.[49]

In conclusion, faced with this matter of Francophone poetry, which brings us together today, I will try to define our shared responsibilities: the responsibilities of France and of other Francophone countries, more precisely, of developed European countries, and the developing countries of the Third World.

I have often proclaimed—not only for France but also for other Francophone European and American countries such as Belgium, Switzerland, Luxembourg, and Canada—the necessity of following the example of the United

States of America, where there is, in every major university, a Center for African Studies. It is a matter of creating, as is the case at the Sorbonne, a Center for Francophone Studies in which overseas civilizations will be studied in all their aspects—geographical and historical, but more importantly ethnological and linguistic.

You will say to me: "And you, what have you done?" Indeed, we did not remain inactive. It is in this vein that in Senegal, I prescribed a return to the methodical and rationalized study of French grammar in elementary, middle, and high schools. Not only grammar but literature as well, with its solid and reliable exercises, the *dissertation* and the *explication de texte*. At the University of Dakar, we created a Center for the Study of Civilizations, led by Alain Le Pichon, who, because he is Breton, was ethnically equipped to understand us. But the director might well have been Mediterranean. The objective of the center, of course, is to deepen, through analysis, Negro-African civilization—more precisely negro civilizations—not to mention Negro-Americans or the Dravidians of India, in order to determine its essential values. It also is a matter of exploring these values in correlation with and in comparison to the values of other, different civilizations. The research agenda of the Center for the Study of Civilizations in Dakar proposes to:

- Study the symbolic and imagological content of oral African literature;
- Determine the dynamism of the traditional imaginary universe, individual and collective, to study its sources, its functioning, and its possibilities of reactivation;
- Promote the development of methods in the human sciences with the aim of applying them to education, science, culture, and information programs;
- Study in depth our national languages, considered as instruments of cultural development and education, by positioning French as a "language of external communication" in relation to "languages of internal culture";
- Support artistic creation and collective cultural action within the framework of the national politics of cultural development;
- Determine the psychological obstacles in individuals from different milieus (infants, adolescents, adults, urbanites, country folk) and the resistances or the permeability of certain social categories when faced with the cultural phenomenon and that of the development through a psycho-pedagogical, sociological, historical, economic approach, etc.;

- Study, finally, the adequacy and inadequacy of operating concepts used thus far in the fields of the human and social sciences, as well as produce, if need be, by way of a necessary semantic critique, new conceptual and methodological elaborations capable of objectively apprehending the Negro-African condition in its statistical and evolutive dimensions.

I have come to the end. Once more, what I have told you concerning the negro poetry of the French language, it would be necessary for others to say for Arabic and Indochinese poetry in French, but also for the other, Eurameri-can poetries: Belgian, Swiss, Luxembourgian, above all Canadian. Alongside *Africa portensa*, there is, indeed, America, and the prodigious Canada. That is precisely what French poetry needs: charm and magic. In order to be *Poetry*, all while remaining French.

NOTES

Léopold Sédar Senghor, "De la poésie française à la poésie francophone; ou, apports des nègres à la poésie francophone," in *Liberté 5: Le dialogue des cultures* (Seuil, 1993), 68–84. Originally given as a talk at the "Rencontre des poètes francophones" (Hautvilliers, October 3, 1975).

1. [Thierry Maulnier, *Introduction à la poésie française* (Gallimard, 1939), 100–101.—Eds.]

2. [Jean-Paul Sartre, "Orphée noir," in *Anthologie de la nouvelle poésie nègre et malgache de langue française*, ed. Léopold Sédar Senghor (Presses universitaires de France, 1948), xviii.—Eds.]

3. [Georges Shehadé (1905–89) was a Lebanese poet and playwright. A self-declared Francophile, he is often presented as the "poet of the two banks" of the Mediterranean, in reference to his engagement with the Arab world and his contribution to the French language. In 1986, he received the Grand Prix de la Francophonie. Shehadé is an example of Senghor's understanding of Francophonie as a celebration of diversity that can be found across the French-speaking world.—Eds.]

4. [Gaston Miron (1928–96) was a Canadian writer, an avid Francophile, and arguably the most important literary figure of Quebec's nationalist movement.—Eds.]

5. Roland Barthes, *Essais critiques* (Seuil, 1964), 208.

6. [Jacques Maritain, "Signe et symbole," *Revue Thomiste* 44, no. 2 (1938): 299–330.—Eds.]

7. [On the Musée dynamique (Dynamic Museum) in Dakar, see chapter 11, note 4, of this volume.—Eds.]

8. [The *tanns* are swampy marshlands that surround Sereer villages such as Palmarin and Joal and are believed to be supernatural spaces where the gods and spirits live; as such, they are also sites for ritual sacrifice.—Eds.]

9. [Arthur Rimbaud, *Une saison en enfer* (Bruxelles: Alliance Typographique, 1873), 53.—Eds.]

10. [These are verses from Sereer gymnic songs typically sung during wrestling (*bakk* in Sereer; *làmb* in Wolof). Elsewhere, Senghor provides the original Sereer for some of these verses: *Wo naa montee mbaar fo neew* (It is you, being massaged with a vase of oil) / *Daankiim, ngel ne mfeeka* (I will not sleep, on the arena I will keep a watch) / *Lam laa mi xaala a yuube* (The tam-tam of myself is adorned with a white collar).—Eds.]

11. [This is one of the Sereer praise poems composed in honor of De Gaulle and mentioned previously by Senghor.—Eds.]

12. [Aimé Césaire, "Ex-voto pour un naufrage," in Senghor, *Anthologie*, 79. See also Aimé Césaire, *Soleil cou coupé* (K éditeur, 1948), 63.—Eds.]

13. [Aimé Césaire, "La femme et le couteau," in Senghor, *Anthologie*, 65; Aimé Césaire, *Les armes miraculeuses* (Gallimard, 1946), 94.—Eds.]

14. [Césaire, "Question Préalable," in *Soleil cou coupé*, 88.—Eds.]

15. [Césaire, *Les armes miraculeuses*, 21.—Eds.]

16. [David Diop, *Coups de Pilon* (1956; reprint, Présence Africaine, 1980), 27.—Eds.]

17. [Léon-Gontran Damas, "Solde," in Senghor, *Anthologie*, 12. The original edition of *Pigments* (GLM, 1937) is not easily accessible, so we have used a modern edition: Léon-Gontran Damas, "Solde" in *Pigments/Névralgies* (Présence Africaine, 1978), 42. In this edition, the final word of the quotation is interspersed with dashes ("ci-vi-li-sa-tion").—Eds.]

18. [Sundiata Keita was a prince and founder of the Mali Empire during the thirteenth century; Shaka Zulu, (also called Chaka kaSenzangakhona) was a nineteenth-century Zulu king; Lat Dior Diop (Lat Jor Jóób) was a nineteenth-century *damel* (king) of Cayor in Senegal and today is celebrated as a national hero for his role in the resistance to French colonization; Samory Touré (Samori Ture) was a nineteenth-century Malinke and Soninke Muslim cleric and military leader who founded an empire that stretched across present-day Guinea, Sierra Leone, Mali, Côte d'Ivoire and Burkina Faso; Béhanzin was a nineteenth-century king of Danxomè and led the resistance to French colonization.—Eds.]

19. [Paul Niger, "Lune," in Senghor, *Anthologie*, 102.—Eds.]

20. [An allusion to "Au sommaire d'une passion," Tchicaya U Tam'si, *L'Arc musical* (P.-J. Oswald, 1970), 33–50.

21. ["Le contempteur," in U Tam'si, *L'Arc musical*, 62, 64.—Eds.]

22. [Jacques Roumain, "Madrid," in Senghor, *Anthologie*, 112–13.—Eds.]

23. [Jacques Roumain, "Bois-d'Ébène," in Senghor, *Anthologie*, 118.—Eds.]

24. U Tam'si, "Viatique," *L'Arc musical*, 57.—Eds.]

25. Jean Beaufret, *Douze questions posées à Jean Beaufret à propos de Heidegger* (Lettres Nouvelles, 1975; reprint, Éditions Aubier-Montaigne, 1983), 20–21.

26. [Léon-Gontran Damas, "Limbé (Pour R.R.)," in Senghor, *Anthologie*, 9. See also Léon-Gontran Damas, "Limbé (Pour Robert Romain)" in Damas, *Pigments*, 44–45.—Eds.]

27. [*Chabin*—*chabine* in the feminine—refers to a mixed-race person in the French Caribbean, specifically the child of two *métis* parents (as opposed to the term *mulâtre*, which refers to the child of a European and a Black Caribbean or African person).—Eds.]

28. [Aimé Césaire, "Et les chiens se taisaient (Fragment)," in Senghor, *Anthologie*, 68; Aimé Césaire, *Et les chiens se taisaient: Tragédie (arrangement théâtral)* (1956; reprint, Présence Africaine, 1958), 64. Césaire's text appeared in multiple editions and substantially different versions, beginning in 1946 as part of Césaire's first collection of poetry, *Les Armes miraculeuses* (Gallimard, 1946), and later in book form by Présence Africaine. For simplicity, we have cited directly from the Senghor's *Anthologie* and the 1958 Présence Africaine edition. See also the corresponding passage in a bilingual version of the 1943 "lost" typescript, Aimé Césaire, ... *Et les chiens se taisaient*, ed. Alex Gil (Duke University Press, 2024), 287.—Eds.]

29. [Jacques Rabemananjara, "Lyre à sept cordes," in Senghor, *Anthologie*, 198.—Eds.]

30. [Léopold Sédar Senghor, "La Négritude métisse," in Édouard Maunick, *Ensoleillé vif: 50 paroles et une parabase* (Éditions Saint-Germain-Des-Près / Nouvelles Éditions Africaines, 1976), 11–38. Maunick's title is a play on words and could be translated as "brightly sunny" or "sunned alive," in the sense of *brûlé vif*, "burned alive."—Eds.]

31. [Maunick, *Ensoleillé vif*, 71–92.—Eds.]

32. [Thierry Maulnier, *Introduction à la poésie française* (Gallimard, 1939), 56.—Eds.]

33. [Rimbaud, *Une saison en enfer*, 30.—Eds.]

34. [Senghor is referring to his preface to Maunick's volume; see note 30 to this chapter.—Eds.]

35. [Césaire, "Et les chiens se taisaient (Fragment)," 68.—Eds.]

36. [In the original lines, there is a contrasting assonance between the vowels [i] and [o], which Senghor highlights by unitalicizing the relevant syllables: cri/*oi*seau/*fas*cine/*chab*ine/eaux.—Eds.]

37. [Maunick, *Ensoleillé vif*, 110. In his citation, Senghor highlights the assonance in [i] (*prière, merci, missié, dis, dire, crie, crie*) and alliteration in [m], [d], and [kr] (*merci/missié, dis/dire, crie/cri*).—Eds.]

38. [Léon-Gontran Damas, *Black-Label* (Gallimard, 1956), 57.—Eds.]

39. [Gide writes with admiration of "la musique nègre" in various texts, including *Le retour du Tchad* (Gallimard, 1928) and *Voyage au Congo* (Gallimard, 1927). In *Le retour*, for instance, he shares an anecdote regarding African songs with harmonies so elaborate that they make French popular songs appear "crude, poor, simplistic, and rudimentary" (40). Gide writes: "The precise notes are not given (which makes it extremely difficult to notate the melody). [. . .] Here, the voice is never in tune. Moreover, when one sings *do ré*, another sings *ré do*. Others create variations" (40).—Eds.]

40. [Césaire, "Et les chiens se taisaient (Fragment)," 66–67.—Eds.]

41. [Maunick's text, as its title suggests, is composed of fifty *paroles* and one *parabase*.—Eds.]

42. [Maunick, *Ensoleillé vif*, 66, 70.—Eds.]

43. [Maunick, *Ensoleillé vif*, 80.—Eds.]

44. [Maunick, *Ensoleillé vif*, 95, 101.—Eds.]

45. [U Tam'si, "Viatique," 60.—Eds.]

46. [Pierre de Ronsard, "Sonnet à Marie," in *Œuvres complètes*, tome VII, ed. Paul Laumonier (Gallimard, 1950), 152–53 (our translation).—Eds.]

47. [This is evident in the original: "Le temps s'en va, le temps s'en va, ma Dame, / Las! le temps non, mais nous nous en allons, / Et tous seront étendus sous la lame."—Eds.]

48. [Senghor is perhaps referring to the Wolof term *ànd* (literally "to walk or go together"), which can express accord, harmony, to be harmonious.—Eds.]

49. [Maulnier, *Introduction*, 45.—Eds.]

14

Oral Tradition and Modernity

This conference, organized by the International Pen Club and the African Cultural Institute, is timely. Contrary to popular belief, oral tradition is not an obstacle to modernity. Indeed, in order for the civilization of the third millennium—which the *Dialogue of Cultures* is preparing—to be the Civilization of the Universal, it will need to be fecundated by the values expressed by oral tradition. And in fact, these values have been fecundating what will be the civilization of the year 2000 since the early days of colonization.

But how should we understand the phrase "oral tradition"? By this, we mean, of course, oral literature as we still live it in Africa: myths, legends and tales, poems sung or chanted, sometimes danced, total theater with masks, songs, and dances. However, one must go further to encompass, within this phrase, philosophy, music, singing, and dance as autonomous disciplines, not to mention the visual arts, namely painting and engraving, sculpture, and even weaving.

By focusing on Black Africa, and without going as far back as Abbé Grégoire and his *De la littérature des nègres* [On the literature of Negroes],[1] I would like to show you, in the first part of my talk, how oral tradition has fecundated the "cultural revolution" in certain arts during the twentieth century. In the second part of my talk, by drawing on personal experience, I will try to show how Negro-African oral poetry can inspire a "modern poetry." Not in the original sense of these words, which corresponds to the period between 1453 (the fall of Constantinople to the Turks) and 1789 (the French Revolution), but in their current sense, referring to the nineteenth and especially the twentieth century. In truth, when we use the words "modernity" and "modern" today, we often think of the period following what I call the "Revolution of 1889." Indeed, it is from this moment that Europe began to turn away from Cartesian rationalism, but above all from positivism, inherited indirectly from Greco-Roman antiquity. Most significantly, it was at this moment that Rimbaud, one of the revolutionaries of 1889, proclaimed himself "negro."

However, it was not until 1906 that Pablo Picasso—*seized* [*saisi*], in Leo Frobenius's sense, by the style of the [African] mask—drew inspiration from "negro art" in his *Nu sur fond rouge* [Nude on a red background].

As we know, it was the School of Paris, composed largely of foreign artists, beginning with Picasso, that best defined and realized this aesthetic, which, mutatis mutandis, has every chance of being the very aesthetic of the civilization of the third millennium. Yet it will essentially be the aesthetic of the twentieth century, which I have defined as "an image or a set of analogous, melodious, and rhythmic images."

This is to say that the art of the twentieth century is neither realistic nor gratuitous. It is even opposed to realism. As André Malraux, following Élie Faure, the greatest French art critic of the twentieth century, said: Unlike Greek art, which was *physeôs mimésis*, or "imitation of nature," negro art turns its back on the real. More precisely, it penetrates it with its intuition, like invisible rays, to express, beyond ephemeral appearances, its *sub-* or *sur-reality*: In any case, its life, both palpitant and permanent.

After the visual arts, it was negro music which, at the beginning of the twentieth century, invaded Europe, then the world, but by way of the Americas, first the United States: through *jazz*. Jazz itself, a creation of the "Black race," if we are to believe Hugues Panassié,[2] was born out of the songs of slaves—*Blues*, and *negro spirituals*, but also from the offbeat and syncopated music of *ragtime*. This is confirmed in the work of Guy-Claude Balmir, entitled *Du chant au poème* [From the song to the poem], which has recently been published by Payot.[3] Its merit is to deepen and, at the same time, broaden the question of tradition. And yet, despite the use of Euro-American instruments, such as the clarinet, the trombone, the cornet, the banjo, and the double bass, one finds in jazz the characteristic features of Negro-African music. And, first, its integral character, of total art, which unites, in a single manifestation, music, singing, and dance. There is also—and this is a second major characteristic—the fact that the interpretation of a musical text is as important as, if not more so than, its writing. I do not mean its *creation*, for creation is precisely the symbiosis of writing and interpretation. And, then, Negro-African music also has these essential characteristics, which are the offbeat and syncopations, not to mention, in interpretation, the inflection, the glissando, the vibrato. And, in Black Africa, music and singing is, once again, danced, transformed into a "total spectacle," as Maurice Béjart would say.[4]

This brings us to dance, considered as an autonomous, primary art, at least in Africa, if we refer to the prehistoric paintings and engravings of the Sahara. Indeed, dance here seems to be the first language of art, of the soul, and it remains so to this day. I still remember a high school student who came to announce to his mother that he had passed the baccalaureate exam. Instead of congratulating and hugging him, as a European mother would, she began to dance in front of her son, softly and with solemn grace, to express her joy.

Allow me to return to Maurice Béjart, the son of our compatriot, the philosopher Gaston Berger. Seeking to provoke a renaissance of classical dance, the great choreographer fecundated it by adding to the forty or so steps of European dance other steps borrowed from Asia, from America, but especially, returning to the source, from Africa. Hence, dance conceived as a total spectacle, with the movements of the body expressing those of the soul through sung poems, as in precolonial [*anté-coloniale*] Africa. But the bodies are either naked or painted, adorned or, better, sculpted. And it is known that Black skin enrobes the body. As for the dance itself, it relies firmly on a battery of tam-tams playing at a continuous rhythm. It is precisely this *tempo* that allows the dancers to indulge freely in all expressive fantasies under the influence of inspiration: from the quivering of the shoulders to the powerful *yëngël ndigë*,[5] that is to say, the tornadoes of the hips.

We have seen, with the visual arts, music and singing, and finally dance, how negro art in general has renewed Euro-American arts. Concerning literature, including philosophy, more specifically, I will abandon Euramerican experiences for African ones.

If I speak of philosophy, it is because, for a long time, it was denied that there existed a Negro-African philosophy, even though Leo Frobenius and the Griaule School had proven otherwise with works like those of Mmes

Calame-Griaule and Dieterlen, not to mention that of Dominique Zahan.[6] What is new are the remarkable studies that Negro-Africans have made of Negro-African philosophy. I will mention here only *La philosophie bantu comparée* [Comparative Bantu philosophy], the work of Alexis Kagamé, a Rwandan, and the doctoral thesis of Professor Alassane Ndaw, *La pensée africaine* [African thought].[7] As is known, this thesis, defended at the Sorbonne, received distinction [*la mention très honorable*] at the time. In our struggles for the cultural renaissance of Black Africa, it is a matter, in philosophy, of starting from these two works, and a few others, to construct a modern Negro-African philosophy, as we have done for other literary genres.[8]

Regarding literature itself, I will take the example of poetry. First, this is because it remains the major art form, even today; it is also because, with respect to French, one of our languages of international communication, poetry requires a perfect mastery of the language. If, despite this difficulty, poetry enjoys the favor it does among young people, it is because it suits the African temperament and soul. For all these reasons, more so than in other genres, we must begin with oral tradition.

So, at thirty years old, or more precisely, at the age of twenty-nine, fresh out of the Sorbonne and convinced by these arguments, I burned all the poems I had written in French up to that point:[9] They were too influenced by French poetry. It is true that at the Paris Institute of Ethnology, I had read translations of Negro-African poems. However, I needed to do better by going to the source: by translating poems myself from Senegalese languages. This is what I began doing during the vacations of 1937, advocating, moreover, and to the great scandal of intellectuals, a return to "national languages."[10] And my discovery was, for me, a revelation, and above all a lesson.

Indeed, Negro-African poetry, as I discovered it then, was more complex, richer, more poetic—I mean to say more *creative*—than contemporary European poetry. It too participates—I am using the *present* tense—in this aspect of manifestation, this aspect of total play [*jeu total*] that, as we have seen, characterizes Negro-African art. The words are sometimes sung, sometimes chanted, most often with the accompaniment of one or several musical instruments, but primarily a percussion instrument that marks the basic rhythm.

To be more concrete, and to advance my analysis, I will focus on the *kim njom*, the "gymnic songs" (literally, "wrestling songs"), that enchanted my Sereer childhood. It is by beginning from these poem-songs [*poèmes-chants*] that I gradually came to define the Negro-African aesthetic.

I have said "poem-songs" because, in Sereer, as in the other languages of the Senegalo-Guinean group that I know, the same word designates both song and poem. In my native language, Sereer, it is *gim* in the singular and *kim* in the plural. Indeed, the *kim njom* are always sung, in several voices, by young girls and women, with an accompaniment in thirds and fifths. One finds here, as we might guess, all the traits of negro song that we have observed in the *Blues* and *negro spirituals*. As for the texts and their style, nothing resembles them more than Japanese *haikus*. Like haikus, Sereer *kim* are short poems of two to four lines, each animated by one or more symbolic images. Here are two gymnic songs among the ones I prefer:

Daan*kîm*, ngel *ne* m'fee*ka*.
Lam *la mi* caa*la* a yuu*be*.

I shall not sleep, on the square I will keep watch.
My tam-tam is adorned with a white collar.

Lan *Sar a* lip*wa* pay *baal*.
O fes *o* ge*noox*, *nan fo* soo*rom*.

Lang Sar is draped in a black pagne.
A young man rose up, like a Filao tree.

The *kim njom* are generally composed by young girls to sing about the qualities and other virtues of their fiancés: of their "slender Black men." In the first of the two poems, the fiancée expresses her joy at seeing her champion triumph. In the second poem, she sings about her "slender Black man." For, naturally, among the Sereer people, to be beautiful, one must be tall, slender, and ebony Black.

The *kim njom* can also be recited rather than sung. I have noticed, in this case, that each line carries the same number of accents of intensity. I have noted them above by not italicizing the accented syllables. Here, there are three accented syllables in each verse.

However, given that the *kim njom* are sung, one rarely finds the alliterations and assonances that, among other things, characterize the poetry of the Senegalo-Guinean languages, including Sereer, Wolof, and Pulaar. We know the famous *tagg* of the wrestling champion Mbaye Diop, which begins with:

yaa*ganaa*, yaa*ganaa*, yaa*ganaa*—Dëgë *lë*.

It's been a long time, a long time, a long time—It is true!

This is a tetrameter with four accents, which, as is the rule in Wolof and Sereer, though not always in Pulaar, fall on the first syllable of the word. It is precisely on this privileged syllable that the alliteration plays out, as in the verse:

Ndë*ndë jib*, ndaa*ré jib*, ta*ma jib*—Dë*gë lë*.

The *ndeundeu* resounds, the *ndaré* resounds, the *tama* resounds.[11]

Here, the accent is on syllables starting with dentals: *nd, nd, t*, and *d*. Occasionally, the alliteration is more subtle, involving not precisely the first consonant but rather the first vowel of the word. Here is an example, still in the same *tagg*:

Ku*luxum* lu *jigeen* su*ke jur*—Dë*gë lë*!

Blessed be what the woman on her knees gives birth to!

It is by beginning with traditional Negro-African poetry, of which I have highlighted only a few characteristics, that French-speaking Black poets, both African and Caribbean, have created, in this twentieth century, either unconsciously or, among the greatest, consciously, a new poetry. Its merit, among the best of these poets, is to be simultaneously rooted in *Negritude* and open to modernity: to the idea-feelings and the style of the twentieth century. To be, already, a *symbiosis* because it is cultural *métissage*, as the civilization of the third millennium will also be. Before concluding, I refer you to Aimé Césaire's latest collection of poems, entitled *Moi, Laminaire* [Me, Laminaria]. It is still Césaire, but the best of Césaire. It is "the great negro cry": his revolt, but also his fraternity. In terms of style—analogical images, alliterations, assonances, and repetitions that do not repeat—the great Caribbean poet has never been so *negro*: so creative.

I would like to conclude by making some concrete suggestions. The cultural facts presented here prove two truths about this twentieth century of ours, which is a century of transition, of parturition. The first is that Afro-Americans have only realized their cultural renaissance, in all fields, by returning to African sources. I have said: "Afro-Americans" even though I have chosen my examples from "negro art" in the general sense of the expression: in the sense of the depths of Africa, of *Ur-Afrika*, to borrow [Leo] Frobenius's phrase, of that Africa which is common to both Arab-Berbers and Negro-Africans. The other truth is that, even for *Albo-Europeans*, the cultural renaissance that began in 1889 also had to draw from African sources.

It is true that we, too, Africans of the twentieth century, have come to admit the necessity of the *Pilgrimage to the Source*. In almost all nations and continents, we have even taken the first steps. But how slow the progress is! . . .

To take the example of my country, Senegal, we had decided, over ten years ago, to bring our people back to our cultural tradition: *oral tradition*. The government even developed a phonetic alphabet that allows us to transcribe our six national languages, all of which were supposed to be taught in primary schools, according to the region and district. Well, like tortoises, we are still at the stage of a few experimental classes. There is something more serious: For each of the six languages, we would need to write about ten doctoral theses: on nouns, nominal classes (for Pulaar, Sereer, Wolof, and Jola), determiners, verbs, etc.—if we want to master them scientifically, at least. We are far from achieving this goal! . . . Yet language is simultaneously the vehicle and the principal instrument of any culture.

It is understood that *African Studies* in schools, from primary to higher education, will not confine itself to languages and literature, including Philosophy, the importance of which I need not emphasize. It will naturally extend to the Visual Arts, to Music and Singing, to Dance, and to Drama. I know that Theater draws from literature; Music, Singing, and Dance as well. However, let us be wary of the dichotomies and other artificial divisions of Euramerica. Africa has always believed in the virtue of symbiosis and has realized it.

This is why the L. S. Senghor Foundation has decided to entrust the State with the granting of scholarships, except in exceptional cases in higher education at the doctoral level, to focus on research into African oral tradition. More precisely, it is a matter of encouraging scholars writing doctoral theses—not only in their research but also, and especially, in publishing their theses and other studies.

I will conclude with a wish: that in all countries with universities, a similar foundation may assist the State in fulfilling its major task, which is to achieve a cultural renaissance rooted in the still-fertile soil of oral tradition.

NOTES

Léopold Sédar Senghor, "Tradition orale et modernité," in *Liberté 5: Le dialogue des cultures* (Seuil, 1993), 185–91. The text was originally given as a lecture at a symposium organized by the International Pen Club and the African Cultural Institute (January 24, 1983).

1. [Abbé Henri Grégoire, *De la littérature des nègres* (Maradan, 1808).—Eds.]

2. Cf. Hugues Panassié, *La véritable musique de jazz* (Robert Laffont, 1952).

3. [Guy-Claude Balmir, *Du chant au poème: Essai de littérature sur le chant et la poésie populaires des Noirs américains* (Payot, 1982).—Eds.]

4. [Maurice Béjart was the stage name of Maurice-Jean Berger (1927–2007), a French dancer, choreographer, and opera director.—Eds.]

5. [*Yëngël ndigg* in Wolof means "to shake the hips."—Eds.]

6. [The linguist and anthropologist Geneviève Calame-Griaule, the anthropologist Germaine Dieterlen, and the ethnologist Dominique Zahan were leading French Africanists who focused especially on the Dogon and Bambara.—Eds.]

7. [Alexis Kagamé, *La philosophie bantu comparée* (Présence Africaine, 1976); Alassane Ndaw, *La pensée africaine: Recherches sur les fondements de la pensée négro-africaine* (Nouvelles Éditions Africaines, 1983).—Eds.]

8. [See Senghor's essay "For a Modern and Negro-African Philosophy," chapter 6 of this volume.—Eds.]

9. See the note on page 27. [The note appears on the first page of Senghor's essay "L'inspiration poétique, ses sources, ses caprices" (in *Liberté 5: Le dialogue des cultures* [Seuil, 1993], 27–37), and is a correction to Senghor's claim that identifies 1936 (not 1937) as "the year [he] burned all [his] early poems." The note reads: "They were, in fact, put aside and published, in 1990, in *L'Œuvre poétique*, Éditions du Seuil [Editor's note]."—Eds.]

10. [Senghor is alluding to his argument for a new bilingualism and the use of national languages such as Wolof and Sereer in Senegalese schools, articulated as early as 1937 in the speech that would later be published as "Le problème culturel en A.O.F." ("The Problem of Culture in French West Africa," chapter 15 of this volume) and developed throughout his career. Léopold Sédar Senghor, "Le problème culturel en A.O.F.," in *Liberté 1: Négritude et humanisme* (Seuil, 1964), 11–20.—Eds.]

11. [The *ndënd*, *ndaré* (not to confuse with *ndaare* literally "the last one"), and *tama* are types of drum, listed in order of largest to smallest.—Eds.]

PART III

Negritude, *Métissage*, and the Dialogue of Cultures

15

The Problem of Culture in French West Africa

Shall I admit this, even if it disappoints you? The prominence and distinction of my audience remind me that it is as a peasant from the Sine that I intended to speak to you tonight.

I had imagined an informal conversation—and this will be a conversation—before the members of the Association and a few friends. I even considered proceeding dialectically, in the form of question and answer, in the style of good old Socrates and our sage Kocc Barma. My intention is not to convince you of my opinions but rather to lead you to frame the problem of culture in French West Africa clearly. It is the most pressing issue of our time—the matter to which the Association has dedicated itself[1]—and its solution presses down on us with urgency. My intention is to lead you along with me to free yourselves from—and bring forth—this spirit of truth that you contain within you or, rather, free it from the shackles that still encumber it: opinion, interest, and passion.

First, we will attempt to squeeze [*presser*] the word "culture" in order to extract [*exprimer*] its substantial meaning. Once culture has thus been defined, both in terms of its essence and its aims, we will finish clarifying the term in light of race and milieu. From there, we will need only to deduce the general principle that must guide any cultural politics in French West Africa—so as to study a few aspects of its application at various levels of the education system. In so doing, I am sure, we will not have saved its dramatic interest for last.

The time of seduction has passed, it is high time that we hang the seducers.

"A big word, your *Culture*," Samba Sène said to me.

I responded: "Sène, I do not think it is so much a big word as it is a big thing, for Sène also cultivates his field and feeds his family with it."

If you do not mind, we will attempt to define the word with respect to Education and Civilization. We will say that Culture is to Education what the artist is to the worker. It is imagination, an active mind, for there is in the word the idea of a creative dynamism. I will propose the following definition: *a racial reaction of Man to his milieu, aiming for an intellectual and moral equilibrium between Man and this milieu.* Since the milieu is never immutable, no more so than race, culture becomes an endless effort toward a perfect equilibrium, a divine equilibrium. Education is both the laborer and the tool of Culture. For the child, education consists of the acquisition of the cumulated experiences of previous generations, in the form of concepts, ideas, methods, and techniques. The set of concepts and techniques of a given people at a given moment in its history constitutes its civilization. This is also what we call the set of successive civilizations of a people.

In a word, to realize its ideal, *Culture* uses *Education*, which is the study of the civilizations of a given people. Thus, if education programs in France reserve a more and more significant place for the study of foreign civilizations, especially for economic and social facts, the reason is that our idea of Man has changed with the expansive development of international relations as well as economic and social sciences.

I will thus say to my interlocutors:

What will we make of the *Black Man*, more precisely, with the West African?

–A Frenchman, Demba N'Diaye replies.

–N'Diaye, did you attend the Olympics in Berlin?

–Only to get lynched! . . . In any case, I read the reviews.

–I do not think that Hitler holds you in high enough esteem to have you lynched. Tell me, in what events did Negroes excel?

–In track and field, which required: flexibility, agility, and elasticity.

–Very good.

He continued: "By the way, they did well to abstain from the other sporting events; they would have been defeated and ridiculed."

–Worse. Say instead that, in the other events, they had already been defeated in America. You see, one must understand and not force one's genius, even, or above all, in matters of the soul and the mind. Do you believe that we will ever be able to defeat Europeans in Mathematics, with the exception of remarkable men, who would confirm that we are not an abstract race? "It is not enough to want to go; one must be able to go":

Bega dèm tahoul
a dèm, men
a dèm a
di tah a dèm.[2]

Race is a reality; I do not mean racial purity. There is a form of difference which is neither inferiority nor antagonism. As [Robert] Delavignette wrote: "We tasted the sweetness of being different and together."[3] If you treat me like a reactionary, I will protest and, distinguishing politics from culture, I will propose: "Let us work to make of the West African a French citizen, politically: but culturally?"

A second interlocutor said to me, "We will give him a profession: he will be a peasant, a worker, a civil servant." I fear, indeed, that my friend takes the means as an *end*. . . . One is not born to be a lawyer or a street cleaner, one works in such a profession only to earn a living.

The *Profession*, even if it can be considered one of the objectives of Education, is only an accessory to it, at least insofar as it is not a social function; it could not be the end goal of Education, even less that of Culture. For why would a future engineer take Spanish literature, the future district commissioner use the pull-up bar? And do we not see students who would have made excellent professors of Greek rejected at the baccalaureate? All in the name of the principle of scientific equality, which, as you know, is a principle of culture.

My neighbor in my village Silmang Faye responded to me: "We will make of the West African a *man of honor*."

—Faye, Kor Yandé, that feeling of honor is very noble. But I remember that a servant from our community threw himself in the river—he was fortunately rescued—because his "boss" called him a liar and he, a servant, was conscience of telling the truth. What should we think of a feeling that robs our society of the best among us?

It therefore will not suffice for our man to be a man of honor, but he must also be well educated, of an open mind, in a word, a *Man* in the full sense of the term, a *Samba-Linguer* as Wolof N'Diaye says.[4] And here we align with the Greek *Kalos-kagathos*, the Latin *Vir bonus*, and the French *honnête homme* of the seventeenth century.[5]

If you take, for instance, our ideal of Man in West Africa—and I am conscious of the element of arbitrariness in this definition—our conception of the *Samba-Linguer*, two remarks become necessary. The first is that this ideal corresponds to something specific: a sense of honor, a not unrefined politeness, a mindset that is more astute than erudite. The second is that this ideal is becoming outdated; it was marred by a certain disdain of novelty, of economy, and of exact sciences, to name just a few lacunae. Lacunae that become more and more serious because here we stand connected to the five parts of the world through bonds that are stronger than the cables connecting us to those parts—namely, to France.

We are engaged in the same destiny; they are our formidable competitors, in economic struggles as well as political contests. If we want to *survive*, we cannot escape the necessity of adaptation, of *assimilation*. Our milieu is no longer West African; it is also French. It is international. To put it simply, it is *Afro-French*.

We can now lay out this general principle: that the study of West Africa and of France should constitute the two poles of Education in French West Africa and that this *bicephalism* will be found at all levels. As we move forward, the African side will lose its force of attraction to the advantage of the French side. It is a matter of beginning from the Negro-African milieu and the civilizations in which the child is immersed. The child must learn to explore and express the basics in his native language, then in French. Little by little, he will expand the circle of the universe around himself—the universe in which, as a man, he will be engaged tomorrow. With his race, he will need a richer and more nuanced knowledge of French. That is to say, bicephalism desires *bilingualism*. In other words, our general principle takes several forms in its application to the various levels of the Education system.

If primary education [*enseignement du premier degré*], elementary school, has a cultural objective, it could not be a uniform one, as you might guess: It will have to be adapted to the region, the milieu, to the degree of evolution of the people. A certain flexibility of programs, a certain freedom in the choice of textbooks will be necessary, a greater spirit of initiative will be required of the teacher.

A few examples will serve as illustrations for our general principle as well as for our definition of Culture. The most recent course selection [*orientation de l'enseignement*] in French West Africa—cultural in this case—has generated a certain number of innovations: among them, the proscription of metropolitan textbooks in primary school education and, in rural schools, the addition of hours for manual and agricultural labor. Normally, it should also have had the effect of implementing *bilingualism*. I would like you to consider these measures and the fact that they cannot be applied uniformly.

Some people only see, in bilingualism, a theoretical interest, and they reject it for practical reasons, objecting that general education would suffer from it, particularly the teaching of French. It would be quite the opposite, according to the opinion of certain distinguished minds. For the latter, practical considerations would stand in favor of bilingualism, as a principle of culture. At the beginning of his studies, the Black child must concentrate his efforts on three major points, which is to disperse them: to learn to read, to learn French, and to acquire certain common scientific notions. Teaching in the native language, vernacular teaching, would solve the problems of this system. The pupil would start school at five years old instead of eight or even ten. For one, two, or three years, he would be taught, in his language, the basics of geography, of history, of science, and of indigenous ethics. At six or eight years old, the soul immersed in our old renovated ideal, the mind exercised and already well furnished, the child would begin his elementary studies with greater ability. He would need five or six years to finish them, provided that classes and sections are not multiplied, as they are in the cities, where the average student takes seven, eight years and more to complete his certificate of primary education.

I have not changed my perspective. The length and format of vernacular education will not be the same everywhere. Perhaps, in certain cities, in certain neighborhoods, where the Black child speaks French at home, we will be able to go so far as to eliminate it, which does not imply that there is a cultural advantage for a native [*indigène*] to ignore his mother tongue. Far from it, as we will see.

People are even more divided when it comes to the hours of manual and agricultural labor in rural and regional schools. People wondered whether Medina was an urban or a suburban district and whether the Black peasant knew how to cultivate the land. It would have been better to ask if the Black peasant was a peasant, and if the inhabitant of Medina had the mindset and the profession of an urban citizen.

It is a question of training neither model farmers nor qualified workers—the learning of a profession is an added benefit. We want *agri-culture*, as well as the professions, to lead to culture. It is a matter of having an integralist conception of Culture and of developing one's *character*. Morality, which should not be confused with Anglo-Saxon puritanism and petit bourgeois moralism, is in constant decline among the "*evolués*." The cause lies in abandoning the moral traditions of our forefathers; what is most serious is that the evolution of customs has outpaced the evolution of minds, and that the former was not governed by the latter. Yet the activities formerly considered to be servile and that, today, give the majority of men their sense of dignity, develop, besides manual agility, self-control and a *taste of perseverance*. And even of *thrift*, for students have their school account, which they learn to manage.

Shall I speak of *agricultural labor*, in this mystical sense of the *Land*, which was that of our peasants? Shall I inform you that the healthiest, strongest, peoples are those among whom the *sense of the Land* is strongest?

I know the little success that these activities would have in cities. I am no longer surprised by this hostility of the petit bourgeoisie. It is natural as well as universal, and there is real harm from our cultural viewpoint. Physical education, sports, and scouting have the same moral effects as manual labor. Moreover, team sports develop the taste of emulation, the sense of solidarity, and the spirit of sacrifice to the group.

I will not dwell long on *textbooks*; I will not belabor demonstrating that they must respond to our principle of bicephalism as well as to the diversity of environments. It would be easy to prove—rural educators have proved it to me—that the famous *Mamadou and Bineta* works wonders in rural areas.[6] But it is not designed for students from Dakar: It does not tell them about the myriad things with which urbanites are familiar. I dream of a textbook for each school and even, thinking of Telemachus, of a textbook for each student. I await—I no longer dream of—the Citizen's *Mamadou and Bineta*, and a book for primary schools that will gather the best pages from colonial writers, Black as well as White, and of metropolitan writers, some of whom will enlighten and complement the others.

It is here that I will distinguish *level of culture* from *level of instruction*. Level of culture would be a certain degree of vigor and intellectual acuity, which would allow the student to lucidly evaluate events and men while being in harmony with his regional milieu. Level of instruction would be a certain sum of knowledge to be recognized with a diploma. The ideal case is that the level of culture perpetually increases without the deterioration of the level of instruction. It is natural that the latter is more sophisticated in the city than in the countryside; this is not of importance. Students from my village, if they attend EPS[7] or High School, will have a mind nimble enough to adapt quickly. It is the quality of the level of culture that matters.

I have always felt uncomfortable with *upper primary education*. I have the sense that it is a sort of bastard genre and that it contains a contradiction even in its appellation. Until this year, we have pretended to be preparing students for the profession and offering a disinterested education in equal measure. One has been detrimental to the other. This explains the most recent reform of the education system. We wanted to integrate upper primary education into secondary education, thereby prioritizing Culture. I am surprised that we have chosen this moment to introduce, at the high school of Dakar, upper primary education, in its most old-fashioned form, its most questionable form. One will respond that it is at the request of my peers. It is not a reason for me to think that they are right.

The transformation of upper primary schools into schools for professional aims, as is happening elsewhere in French West Africa, is more logical. Truth be told—and this is not a paradox—, the next goal of these schools is to provide the cultural training necessary for entry into federal schools. This formation can be found, in the first year, at Ponty[8] where future educators, future doctors, and future administrators all brush elbows.

How can one deny, on the other hand, the cultural role of *craftsmen's houses*? We seek to train not mere workers who follow a blueprint but inspired craftsmen who draw upon old Black techniques, by fecundating them through the study of European techniques.

I retain, among the *professional schools*, only those that present a cultural interest: EPS, teacher training schools, and craftsmen's houses. If we refer to our primary principle, general education, these institutions must reach a harmonious equilibrium, not a *compromise*, between primary and secondary education. Many students will become instructors; even the others will have an educational role and serve as role models. Their primary quality will be to be Africans by way of their knowledge of Africa, more importantly by way of their *sense of Africa*. It is my understanding that they are not lacking this quality. Its acquisition, I insist, remains essential, as does—and one stems from the other—the study and practice of an indigenous language.

But it is not enough to know. The educator must be able to judge and, to do so, compare. It would be enough to require a more thorough teaching of History and of French letters. We reacted against "our ancestors the Gauls." This is common sense. But the singularity of every reaction is to be frenetic. It would perhaps be time to react against the reaction. It is a matter of pedagogy. We will no longer amuse ourselves with the "Vase of Soissons"[9] or with Napoleonic swashbuckling; they will explain to us how a nation, from their ancestors the Gauls and from the darkness of their forests, rises, slowly, through failure and trial and error, toward the light and toward freedom. How else can we explain colonial humanism: the work of [Louis] Faidherbe and the spirit of [Cornelius van] Vollenhoven?[10]

The organization of *secondary education* in French West Africa seems perfect at first glance. I could deny neither the excellence of the teachers, of my former teachers at least, nor the positive results that they achieve. In addition, French programs and regulations are applied. Yes and no; they must and must not.

Our definition of Culture, as you might recall, requires that the student be oriented according to his abilities, which are, at the same time, hereditary and a result of the milieu. I heard moderate people saying that *orientation* is practiced with assurance in our high schools, in only a few minutes, but with neither counselors nor counseling classes, with neither appeal nor revision unless it goes in one direction, which gives us food for thought.[11] We did not familiarize ourselves with the student, we did not observe his reactions daily in front of a poem, a problem, or an instrument. And we evaluate his gifts, not in terms of his interests and abilities, but his age! Thus, the child is set on a path that is not his own. Someone who would have made a delightful regional poet becomes an engineer of agronomy who yawns all day long. To be precise, I have the impression that the natives in French West Africa, *exceptis excipiendis*, are more gifted in the humanities than in the sciences; I fear that we do not make access to the literary sections easy enough, although we need to surround our science students with particular care, because they are rare. We may wish to avoid discussing classical heredity. The Greeks and, especially, the Latins were more intelligent than learned. Old Cato would not have felt like a stranger in the Sine, and sometimes, I wonder if the wily Ulyssess did not leave offspring in the Baol during his long peregrinations. One can only hope that the counselor, if there is an orientation, serve as an adviser and that he give his advice fearfully; one can only hope that placement errors can easily be fixed. As in France, where selection determines placement, which determines freedom. Such is the letter and the spirit of the Jean Zay reform, which is democratic and cultural in its objectives.[12]

After the principle of orientation, let us now turn to *bilingualism*. The teaching of general culture, professed in high school, does not exclude knowledge of one's country; it presupposes and supposes it. Hence the preponderance of *French* in secondary education. For us Afro-French people, this implies the teaching of French and of an indigenous language, which will serve as a second living language, as in Indochina and in Madagascar. Which language among the multiplicity of languages and dialects? There are mother tongues and dynamic languages, languages of prey: *Mandingo*, *Hausa*, *Yoruba*, *Pulaar*, and *Wolof*. And, I understand, by grammar, history, geography, folklore, the civilization of the people in question.

First of all, there is, in such an education, a *social interest*. The elite is called on to serve as model and mediator. What credibility would they have if cut off from the roots of their race? What competence, if they do not know their people?

The *cultural interest* is greater still. The mission of the intellectuals is to restore *Black values* in their truth and their excellence, to awaken their people to the taste of bread and to intellectual pursuits, by which we are *Men*. Above all through Letters. There is no civilization without a literature to express and illustrate its values, just as the jeweler bejewels a crown. And without written literature, no civilization would go beyond mere ethnographic curiosity.[13] Yet, how can we conceive of an indigenous literature that is not written in an indigenous language? A Black literature in French seems possible to me, it is true. Haiti has proven it, and other Black literatures have borrowed a European language and emerged: a Negro-American literature, a Negro-Spanish literature, and a Negro-Portuguese literature. To articulate my entire line of thought, I would deem this to be a little premature. Our people, in its entirety, have not yet tasted all the beauties of the French language; and our writers should have been able to distinguish and utilize all its resources. Finally, such a literature would not be able to express all our soul. There is a certain taste, a certain odor, a certain accent, a certain Black timbre [*timbre noir*] inexpressible with European instruments. The inventors of *hot jazz*, who use a stuffed trumpet and other instruments that appear strange to the man of the streets, have understood this.

Bilingualism, specifically, would enable an *integral expression* of the *New Negro*—I deliberately use this word; it must be restored to its dignity. Scientific works, among others, would be written in French. We would make use of an indigenous language in literary genres that expresses the genius of the race: poetry, theater, and storytelling.[14]

One might object that indigenous languages are neither rich nor beautiful enough. I could respond that this is not at all important, that they ask only to be handled and fixed by talented writers. Malagasy is, today, a literary language;

yesterday, it did not have a written grammar. Paul Laurence Dunbar, Claude McKay, Langston Hughes, Sterling Brown have turned Negro-American patois from a mere stuttering of uprooted slaves into a marvel of beauty: *a thing of beauty*. But I refer you to the griots of ancient royal African courts, or simply to the peasants of the Kayor. I have always admired their language and the fact that they transformed bargaining over a Kola nut into a literary work, a delightful and rich mix of subtlety and humor. I will say further that linguists love to cite languages such as Mandingo for their prodigious capacity of verbal invention. No, it is not the instruments that are lacking; I am only waiting for the talents that they will have *cultivated*.

I hear whispering. Many peers would have wanted to hear me take a side regarding one practical detail or another: the age limit, for example, or teaching scholarship. This was not precisely my topic; that is not what is essential. Once again, I merely wanted to try to distinguish, along with you, the elements of the problem and how they are ordered. Agreement on practical aspects, on details, will be reached without difficulty: *Wax ci njëlbéén, mujj ga rafet*.[15] My opinions are debatable, I know: Each time I study the application of our principles to teaching, I venture beyond those principles. You will debate them; you would be right to. I will be pleased if I have been able to raise, in you, some doubts—especially in you, the youth—, to give you the idea that the problem is not simple, that it does not require a brutal solution, but must be considered with a cool and clear head.

Perhaps, doubt will not be enough, and you would like to take something positive away with you, some viaticum according to our custom of *yóóbël*.[16] In the guise of conclusion and as counterevidence, I would like to draw on an example that some will think of using against me: the example of the former colonies, where diplomas abound, where teaching standards are replicas of those from the Metropole.

I will question the French-Antilleans of my generation: someone like [Pierre] Aliker, an intern in the Paris hospitals; [Aimé] Césaire, a student of the École Normale Supérieure; [Jules] Monnerot, an essayist and critic; [René] Sauphanor, professor *agrégé* of Physics. What do they tell us? That in the French Antilles, they have many diplomas and little culture, despite their fierce intelligence; that they do have a literature, but that it is only the photographic negative, a pale copy of the metropolitan one; that at the assembly of peoples "at the gathering of giving and receiving,"[17] according to Césaire's phrase, they have no other choice but to show up empty-handed; that this is due to how they are taught, since they have never been taught the history or the civilization of their ancestors from Africa. Listen rather to Léon Damas, the young Guyanese poet, who presents himself as a "negro poet" and who sings, in an instinctively rediscovered tam-tam rhythm, his spiritual nudity following the austerity that came with exile:

They came that night when the tam-
tam
        flowed
            from rhythm
        to
    rhythm
the frenzy of the eyes,
the frenzy of the hands, the frenzy of the feet
of the statue
Since then
how many ME,
how many ME, how many ME, ME, ME
have died
since that night when the
    tam-
    tam
flowed
        from rhythm
          to rhythm
the frenzy of the eyes,
the frenzy of the hands, the frenzy of the feet
of the statue.[18]

It is late and you are about to depart. Allow me to walk with you a good way back along the path. Accept this viaticum, young men and young girls, my comrades. You will meditate on these words by Claude McKay, the Negro-American poet and novelist, a native of Jamaica. In *Banjo*, he tells us through the character of Ray: "Getting down to our native roots and building up from our own people it is not savagery: It is culture."[19]

NOTES

Léopold Sédar Senghor, "Le problème culturel en A.O.F.," in *Liberté 1: Négritude et humanisme* (Seuil, 1964), 11–20. The text was first given as a lecture to the Dakar Chamber of Commerce for the Foyer France-Senegal (September 10, 1937).

[Chapter title: In Senghor's original title, "A.O.F." stands for Afrique Occidentale Française, the federation of French colonies established in West Africa between 1895 and 1958. The capital was Saint-Louis, in Senegal, until 1902, then Dakar.—Eds.]

1. [Senghor is referring to the Foyer France-Sénégal, a cultural and sporting association founded in 1933 by Papa Guèye Fall.—Eds.]

2. [In modern transcription: *Bëgg dem taxula dem, mëna dema di taxa dem*. (Senghor has separated the postposed "*-a* linker" on auxiliary verbs for the purposes of versification).—Eds.]

3. [Robert Delavignette (1897–1976) was a colonial administrator and the director of the École coloniale from 1937 to 1946. The quotation comes from Robert Delavignette, *Soudan–Paris–Bourgogne* (Grasset, 1935), 25.—Eds.]

4. [Samba Lingeer (or Samba Linguère), from *samba* (a first name) and *lingeer* (royal princess) is a Wolof concept that means "a man worthy of a princess," that is, a gentleman.—Eds.]

5. [These are all virtuous or ethical masculine ideals that denote gentlemanly, honorable, or moral personal conduct.—Eds.]

6. [*Mamadou et Bineta* was a textbook series by the French schoolteacher André Davesne (1898–1978), who taught in Mali, Senegal, and Congo. The books were used to teach French in primary schools throughout West Africa from 1929 onward. For an overview of the series, see Nicole Biagioli, "Interculturalité et colonisation dans la série *Mamadou et Bineta*, d'André Davesne: Méthode d'apprentissage du français pour l'Afrique noire française," *Cahiers de Narratologie* 40 (2021), http://journals.openedition.org/narratologie/12649.—Eds.]

7. [EPS stands for Enseignement primaire supérieure (upper primary education), which may be something like "junior high" in English.—Eds.]

8. [The William Ponty School (École Normale William Ponty) was a teacher-training college created in Saint-Louis in 1903, initially intended to train the colonial elite for teaching and administration in French West Africa.—Eds.]

9. [The Vase of Soissons was a sacred vessel stolen in the Battle of Soissons of 486, won by Clovis I. A disgruntled soldier smashed the vase with his axe, and it was returned, broken, to Saint Remigius. A year later, Clovis smashed the soldier's skull, supposedly saying, "Souviens-toi du vase de Soissons!" (Remember the Vase of Soissons!).—Eds.]

10. [Louis Faidherbe (1818–89) was a French general and colonial official; as governor of Senegal, he created the *tirailleurs sénégalais*. Though presented as a humanist, he is known to have terrorized entire communities in the northern part of Senegal by setting entire villages on fire in the colonial effort. Cornelis van Vollenhoven (1874–1933) was a Dutch legal scholar of the East Indies.—Eds.

11. ["Orientation" refers to the advice students receive in their selection of courses or curriculum of study.—Eds.]

12. [Senghor is referring to the education reform proposal made by Jean Zay (1904–44), then minister of national education, to the Chamber of Deputies on March 5, 1937. Because of political opposition, the ambitious reform was never realized, but some of its recommendations, such as *classes d'orientation* (a class designed to test student aptitude

and interest in order to improve student placement), were implemented on an experimental basis.—Eds.]

13. Since, I have revised this perhaps too summary of a claim (1963). [Senghor seems to be referring to his text "La littérature africaine d'expression française," based on a 1963 speech and published in Senghor, *Liberté 1: Négritude et humanisme* (Seuil, 1964), 398–402.—Eds.]

14. I have also revised this claim (1963). [See Senghor, "La littérature africaine d'expression française."—Eds.]

15. [Senghor writes: *Wah tyi nydyèlbèn, moudy ga rafèt*. The more common version of this proverb is *Wax teel, mujj ga rafet*. Senghor uses the term *ci njëlbéén*, which means "in the beginning," instead of *teel*, "early."—Eds.]

16. [*Yóóbël* refers to the tradition of giving gifts to visitors when they leave.—Eds.]

17. [The phrase, popularized by Senghor, is originally Césaire's. It appears in Césaire's 1935 article "Nègreries: Conscience raciale et révolution sociale," in which the word *Négritude* first appears in print, published in the May–June issue of *L'Étudiant noir*.—Eds.]

18. [This is the poem "Ils sont venus ce soir," which Léon-Gontran Damas dedicated to Senghor; Léon-Gontran Damas, "Ils sont venus ce soir (Pour Léopold-Sédar Senghor)," in *Pigments-Névralgies* (G. L. M. [Guy Lévis Mano], 1937), 13.—Eds.]

19. [Senghor was likely consulting the first French translation, published in 1931. Claude McKay, *Banjo*, trans. Ida Treat and Paul Vaillant-Couturier (Éditions Rieder, 1931). We have cited the original, English version. Claude McKay, *Banjo: A Story Without a Plot* (Harper and Brothers, 1929), 200.—Eds.]

16

Perspectives on Black Africa; or, To Assimilate, Not Be Assimilated

To Robert Delavignette

My dream is that it (Morocco) may offer the sight of a *human collective* in which men, so diverse in origin, in clothing, professions, and races, pursue the search for a common ideal, a *common reason for living*, without giving up any of their individual ideas.
—HUBERT LYAUTEY, *Paroles d'action*, 1927

Our setbacks in 1940 will have had the most fruitful result of having led metropolitans and natives [*indigènes*] from the Colonies not to restate the problem of colonization but to rethink it. Its solution—as everyone senses—is at the very basis of the French renaissance. Since 1940, the word "Empire" has acquired an almost magical prestige: It has been one of the poles of French political thought. And people have not failed to speak of "the loyalty of Empire." Many have been surprised, amazed, and pleased by this.

Such loyalty was—is—natural, however. At least for French Black Africa, which I know and about which I wish to speak here. If the events of 1940 have come as a surprise to Africa, I do not believe that they have created a crisis of conscience there. Indeed, in Black Africa, we were not unaware of French inferiority in terms of equipment and training, and even of the inferiority of the High Command. But the idea of French courage was not questioned. The soldiers who had returned from the frontlines and who had witnessed the heroism of their officers could testify to it. It is not that Black loyalty had not been tested. I will not insist on some of the errors that were committed by the local Administration, and which also wounded the dignity of the Native [*Indigène*]. But the Native would have found it particularly disgraceful to abandon the defeated Nation; especially since he knew, as always, how to distinguish the error of the local Administration from the *spirit* of the Metropole. And Black Africa did not budge.

This is what transcends the problem of the colonial conquest, I mean its legitimacy. Undoubtedly, colonization may be—and must be—a boon for the natives [*indigènes*], but to justify it by its benefits is to confuse its outcome for its goal. There is not a single French citizen who does not think that the Roman conquest was ultimately a benefit for the Gauls. Yet Vercingetorix is a national hero, and nothing can legitimize the massacres such as that of the Avaricum during which 39,200 out of 40,000 inhabitants perished. No, good cannot justify evil. Moreover, historically, Caesar, like modern colonizers, gave as the reason for his expeditions, the defense of "borders," "trading posts," and "interests." That is the word. Conquerors cannot be expected to be saints. France does not need to justify its colonial conquests, no more than the invasion of Brittany or the Basque Country. It simply must align its interests to those of the natives. *The colonial problem is, ultimately, nothing other than a provincial problem, a human problem.* I am not the first one to notice this. [Hubert] Lyautey had already said so and, closer to us, Delavignette, this imperial humanist, in his book, so suggestively titled *Soudan–Paris–Bourgogne* [Sudan–Paris–Burgundy].[1] Paris uniting the two provinces!

I. Contacts

Thus, here we are before the colonial *fact*. It is from this standpoint that the question must be posed: What does France do with its colonies? What must France do with the natives [*indigènes*]? One of my metropolitan friends, who was surprised that I did not wish to think of Negro-Africans as "primitives," adorned as they were with the Homeric epithet of *sympathetic*,[2] thought he could end the discussion by saying to me: "Admit, finally, that we have brought you civilization." And I said: "Not precisely." You brought us *your* civilization. Let us take what is best, what is fecundating from it, and allow us to give the rest back." Contact between *two civilizations*, this seems to me the best definition of the problem. In any case, it is from this angle that we wish to examine it.

Colonization is not only a *fact*; it is a *historical fact*. We will resolve the problem all the more successfully if we examine how we attempted to resolve it in the past. Criticisms of the theories already expressed, of the methods already employed, as well as of the solutions to be proposed must begin from this analysis. And in fact, the currents dividing theorists of colonization today—*assimilation* or *association*—did not crop up yesterday. They can be traced back to the very beginnings of the contacts between the French and non-Europeans. They date back to the Age of Discovery or even beyond, to the Crusades. One can trace their respective evolution and their interaction in Mister André Sidobre's remarkable article published in *L'Homme de couleur* [The man of color].[3]

First, the doctrine of *Assimilation*, which seems to have particularly fallen out of favor today. Yet it is a quintessential Latin and French doctrine; for it is in France that it was formulated with the greatest clarity and refinement. Above all, it is the expression of French rationalism, of this rationalism, which originated from *Cartesianism* and still governs the minds, despite the assaults against it.

If Descartes sets *passions* aside, more precisely if he wishes to conquer or control them by way of "firm and determined judgments pertaining to the knowledge of good and evil,"[4] that is to say by way of *reason*, it is, ultimately, because he thinks they are less essential to human nature. Do they not partake of the body, and is Man not, in his essence, a thinking being, a "thinking reed," as Pascal would put it? For, while the passions vary among different men, reason remains identical to itself everywhere. In practice, common sense is "the most evenly distributed thing in the world."[5] And, in actual fact, contemporaries will see, in the "exotics"—beneath differences in clothing, beliefs, and customs—men who are like them. This was already the opinion of the precursors of Cartesianism, of Montaigne, of Rabelais, who, if they saw the native [*indigène*] as "a new-born child," believed him, for this reason, to be educable. We know the famous words of the Sun King to his godson, the Black prince Aniaba. As the prince was about to leave him, on the eve of sailing for his new States, Louis XIV apparently told him: "Prince, between you and me, there is only the difference between Black and White."[6] One understands: As a result of the education offered to you in our court, you have now become a Black-skinned Frenchman. This is the very formula of assimilation.

As we know, the eighteenth century of the *philosophes* would push Cartesianism to its extreme conclusions. The *Declaration of Human Rights* is the political expression of this.[7] French universalism speaks of *Man*, not of men. And, if it speaks of men, it adds the epithet "all" to the word. The *Société des Amis des Noirs* [Society of the friends of the Blacks], to which the most prominent philosophes belonged, transposed the principle of universalism into the colonial and practical domain. Ultimately, this Society facilitated the passing of the law for the abolition of slavery, voted on February 4, 1794. The doctrine of assimilation triumphed. Napoleon was to reinstate slavery eight years later. He bitterly regretted it after the fact. But, as early as the Restoration, the assimilationist current, deaf to such changes, reemerged—and the monarchy was not uninvolved. It would triumph a second time, in 1848, by way of the union between revolutionaries and Catholics. There was nothing strange about this coalition. For, let us note, Catholicism, as the name suggests, is universalist in its essence, and, by the same token, it aims for assimilation "since it embraces," as the encyclical *Maximum illud* says, "all who worship God in spirit and in truth."[8] Abbé Grégoire, who was the heart of the Société des Amis des Noirs, wrote: "The Christian religion is an infallible means of spreading and preserving civilization."[9] Today, we would write "Civilization," in uppercase.

The doctrine—perhaps we should say, the practice—of *Association* is that of old France, the France of the Middle Ages. The King of France was the king of the "States" and provinces, which preserved their "customs" and their regional life. This is why as early as the Crusades—the first colonial conquests, and the only ones without material interests as their goal—association imposed itself as a model. Catholics, schismatics, and Muslims, to name but a few, lived side by side, with each group maintaining its particular status, so long as each one was able to have access to the same ranks and professions. Mister Sidobre writes: "In the midst of the theocratic Middle Ages, legislation respected the status given to each person by their religion: 'three thoughts, three races, three aesthetics' were thus able to simultaneously leave their mark on the same soil."[10]

We would have to wait until the nineteenth century to return to the practice of association and for the doctrine to be formulated with clarity. Several reasons can be invoked in this respect. First, it is that the facts had shown the disadvantages of assimilation. Or rather, the disadvantages of its hasty and overly reckless practice; for, in fact, uprooted and Christianized slaves had been assimilated regardless of whatever might have been said. On the other hand, the conquest of Algeria and of the Senegalese "hinterland" brought in Muslim populations that were uneasily, if not impossibly, assimilated. Finally—and this is undoubtedly the main reason—, mindsets had evolved. The nineteenth century saw the extraordinary development of the historical, philological, biological, and, later, ethnological sciences. We realize that, even in Europe, men are different from one another, that there is not one *Civilization*, but civilizations, born from the intermingling of several influences: history, language, race, geography. . . . France itself, fallen from its earlier preeminence, recovered from its revolutionary and Cartesian intoxication, and wonders, too, "whether God is French." Let us not forget, the nineteenth century was that of nations and nationalism. The twentieth century has received this inheritance.

And theoreticians of association emerged. They were, at the same time, realists, and deeply generous and humane ones at that, from [Thomas Robert] Bugeaud to Robert Delavignette, by way of Napoleon III, [Louis] Faidherbe, and Lyautey. This theory can be summarized in the words from Lyautey that I have cited as an epigraph. Delavignette joined Lyautey by going further, it seems to me, in the sense of a "conciliatory" and humanist accord. In *Soudan–Paris–Bourgogne*, he writes: "The twenty thousand Sudanese schoolchildren of my time will soon reach one hundred thousand. They will return to the school of their Sudan. *They will restore it to its proper values* at the same time *as they will reform it by associating it with France.*"[11]

As natives [*indigènes*] of Black Africa, we make these words our own. We have a temperament, a deeply original soul. This is reflected in our customs and our beliefs. We can transfer, as is, into our own territories, the political and social organization of the Metropole, with its departments and deputies, proletariat and parties, unions and secular education. We can be made to lose our virtues, and perhaps our failings. The Metropolitans' flaws will be inoculated in us; I doubt that their virtues can be transmitted to us in this way. The only risk is that we will become pale French copies, consumers rather than producers of culture. For the vine, which is one example among a thousand, cannot acclimate in Black Africa; it grows there, but the grapes will not ripen. The soil is different, and so is the climate.

Does this mean that the anti-assimilationists are right? Far from it: They are too quick to triumph. We have a different temperament, a different soul, of course. But aren't differences found more in the relation between elements than in the nature of those elements? Beneath the differences, are there not more essential similarities? But above all, is *reason* not *the same* in all men? I do not believe in the "prelogical mentality." The mind cannot be prelogical, even less a-logical. *I am afraid that the word "assimilation" might lead to confusion, that it might create uncertainty*. As it is said in the *Littré*, "To assimilate is to convert to similarity: civilization assimilates different peoples."[12] The concept of civilization seems to me to be too narrow here; however, the definition is not bad. For, while it is not quite true that a civilization can assimilate a given people—and it must be remembered, from the definition, that to assimilate is not to identify, to "make identical"—a people can, by contrast, assimilate a civilization. As evidenced by the different European nations with respect to Greco-Latin civilization, or Japan with respect to the West. Some will object that "you can only assimilate what is similar." Is that not contradictory? If "to assimilate" indeed means "to make similar," the similar need not be assimilated.

Certainly, we Negro-Africans are against this false assimilation, which is only identification. But we remain nonetheless wary of the anti-assimilationist current, in which the best men mingle with the worst—alongside Lyautey, the *colonist*, for whom colonization is synonymous with the use of "sweated labor"; alongside Delavignette, the "creole," who thinks that "Negro sweat fertilizes the sugarcane plantations."[13] It is, as Mister Sidobre so aptly puts it, "the tradition of evil."[14] Its masterpieces were Le Pacte colonial [the colonial monopoly], Le Code noir [the Black code], and, in 1802, the reestablishment of slavery and of the slave trade, which, in the case of France, led to the loss of Haiti, its most beautiful colony at the time.[15] Here and there, the principle is the same: the only aim of colonization, a planned economy, is to enrich the Colonizer. We understand, therefore, that assimilation, which implies a certain intellectual and political emancipation, presents itself as the great enemy, even in its Christian form. Some planters "claim," as [Victor] Schœlcher wrote in 1842, "that the more enlightened a slave, the more inclined to *reason* and to *unruliness*."[16] Even closer to us, in 1929, Mister [Albert] Bessières wrote in *La Vie intellectuelle* [Intellectual life]: "How do you expect our colonists, an Algerian priest told me, to desire the conversion of the natives? They would no longer be able to kick them in the rear."[17] It is Mister Sidobre who cites these lines. I readily acknowledge that these are extreme cases, and specifically "colonial" ones. But the *paternalism* of our Capitalism, the fear of a certain metropolitan bourgeoisie at the idea of a native [*indigène*] elite and the fear of the political expression of seventy million French subjects [*sujets*] or *protégés* seem to me to derive from the same current. This explains our wariness and why we feel the need to pierce through the *anti-assimilationist equivocation*, to separate the wheat from the chaff. Without surprise or indignation, for that matter. It is human that the privileged do not willingly renounce their privileges, even if they are from a generous nation by definition and by nature.

Reasoning on a general level, we arrive at the following conclusion: that we must *transcend the false antinomy, "association or assimilation," and say, "assimilation and association."* Lyautey wrote: "The Cooperation demands that we be dual."[18] In this, he understood that the authority of the Sultan of Morocco had to be restored. We must be dual! Not two abstractions nor simply two material presences, but two persons in the moral and judicial sense of the word. Thus, master and slave, nor even the employer and the worker, within a purely capitalist regime, cannot be two partners [*associés*]. On the other hand, partners may have different, I do not say opposing, conceptions and temperaments. It is even good that this be the case. They must, however, mutually assimilate each other's ideas since they must work *with common outlooks and shared interests*, each one having, at the same time, to adapt to the nature and the habits of their coassociate [*co-associé*]. For "a house divided against itself," to use the Gospel's expression, "is bound to perish."

In the case of the Metropole, it is not a matter of adopting native customs and institutions. The Metropole must, nevertheless, understand their *spirit*: and perhaps—as we will see—it will be able to benefit from them when the time to return to the old French tradition arrives. For the Colony, it is, above all, a question of assimilating the spirit of French civilization. It is an active and judicious assimilation, which fecundates the autochthonous civilizations and brings them out of their stagnation or makes them reemerge from their decline. *It is about an assimilation that allows for association*. It is only on this condition that there will be "a common ideal" and "a common reason for living," only on this condition will there be a French Empire.

II. The Black Community

From these preliminary remarks, we must now examine—and outline—the political and social organization of Negro-Africans. This will enable us to grasp its *meaning* and to mask out its moribund elements, so as to retain only the living forms, which the French genius must fecundate. Naturally, it cannot be a matter of delving into the particularities of different peoples.

It is Pierre Mille, I believe, who marveled at the "clean slate" of the *Black soul* and the fact that it could be freely built upon.[19] This is the moment to regret the lack of ethnological and historical culture among numerous "colonial" writers. Unfortunately, it is they who form the opinion not only of the layman but also of most intellectuals. It is also necessary to affirm the existence of a *Negro-African Civilization* and its character of originality. A character that is all the more distinct by virtue of the fact that this civilization, for thousands of years, received few contributions from the outside, incubating, as it were, in a vacuum protected by hostile coasts and deserts.

This is to say that, here, originality and antiquity go hand in hand. One writer, even recently, has maintained the thesis of *negro anarchy*; he wanted to see, in our great States of the Middle Ages and of Modern Times, only a creation of Islam. I like to acknowledge the intellectual contributions of Islam; I even say, often, that Arab-Berber civilization was to the "Sudanese" countries what Greco-Latin civilization was to Europe. But, once again, *fecundating is not creating*. I will oppose our writer's opinion to that of two great ethnologists, two Africanists. Maurice Delafosse, speaking of the political organization of the Ghana Empire, writes in *Les nègres* [The Negroes]: "This is very important, for we find proof that before the introduction of Islam—there were Muslims in Ghana in the 10th century, but they were all foreigners, and the King and his subjects were pagan Blacks—and, even more so, before any European intervention, Negroes had achieved a sufficient degree of culture to form stable States, perfectly comparable in many respects to the Eastern and European States of the same period."[20] [Leo] Frobenius aligns with Delafosse. He writes: "We also know that the particular organization of the States of the Sudan existed long before Islam, that the refined [*réfléchis*] arts of the cultivation of fields and of politeness, and that the bourgeois orders and the systems of corporations in negro Africa are thousands of years older."[21]

Precolonial Black Africa presented the most diverse political regimes, from the "Empire," which, theoretically, encompassed all of the western Sudan over an area of two thousand kilometers, to the "extended family" of the tropical or equatorial forest, by way of the kingdom or tribe. It is still the small kingdom, the size of a French province, that seems to me to be the most typical, such as the three Sereer kingdoms of *Baol*, *Sine*, and *Saloum* in Senegal.

Some have denied that there are "peoples" and "nations" in Black Africa. I fear that these words are given an overly modern meaning; that they are confused with the "fatherland," which results from a growing *consciousness* of the nation, the latter having become the "object of a kind of secular cult"; that they are confused above all with the modern State, which Mister Lucien Febvre presents in the *French Encyclopedia* as "centralized, based on identical legislation for all, impartial administration for all, and equal taxation for all."[22] But, if the nation is indeed a *social* fact, as Professor [Louis] Le Fur would have it, and if it is made up of the following elements—one of which, moreover, may be more pronounced—race, language, religion, shared customs and traditions, and a "desire for a shared life," then it can be said that there were nations in Black Africa.[23] I must specify that the "desire for a shared life" was stronger at the level of the village and the canton than at the level of the State. What is, in any case, indisputable, is the feeling of a shared language and culture, hence the attachment to that language and culture. Sometimes, this feeling goes beyond the nation properly speaking. The Wolof, for example, do not generally apply the contemptuous term *lakakat*, "barbarian" (literally: "one who speaks a foreign language"), to other Senegalese peoples—Haalpulaaren, Sereers, and Jolas—whom they consider to be their brothers in race and in language.

To give a vivid idea of the political and social organization of a Negro-African kingdom, I can do no better than to retrace, fairly briefly, that of the ancient Sereer kingdom of the Sine, from which I come.[24]

The political and social order in the Sine was essentially based on the *caste hierarchy*. There were:

1 At the head, the King or *Bour*;[25]
2 The *Guelwârs*, or Nobility, who theoretically represented the ancient *Malinke* conquerors;
3 The free men, divided into *Dyâmbours* and *Bâdolas*. This is the majority, the mass of Sereer peasants;
4 The *Nyênis*, or Craftsmen, themselves divided into subcastes: blacksmiths, doctors, shoemakers, weavers, *laobés* or woodworkers, griots;
5 The *Fâd* (singular: *pâd*), or Captives. I say "captives" rather than "slaves."[26]

The King is assisted by ministers, military governors, and civil "officers." Among the first, let us mention the three principal ones: first, the *Dyarâf-bourey*, or Great Dyarâf.[27] He is the representative of the freemen. As such, he fulfills the duties of Prime Minister and Minister of Justice. Next, the *Farba-bourey*, or Great Farba, chief and representative of the Captives.[28] He is Minister of War. Finally, the *Farba-bir-Keur*, or Farba of the Court.[29] A sort of Master of Ceremonies, he fulfills functions similar to those of the Minister of the Interior and Minister of Finance. Alongside the ministers are the lower *bours*, who govern the provinces and border regions of the kingdom. Below them, the *sâkh-sâkhs*,[30] *guelwârs* or *dyâmbours* who administer the villages organized into cantons, and the *dyâligués*,[31] captives of the Crown, who administer the villages of the Fulɓe foreigners.

The King is elected. The choice is, moreover, made by the representatives of all the castes, in principle by the Great Dyarâf, among a few *guelwâr* families. The King is the political, civil, and religious head of the State. The governors, a hereditary position, as well as the ministers and officers, appointed by the King, all serve directly under his orders. However, he cannot make any important decision without the approval of the Council of the Throne, composed of *guelwârs* whose office is hereditary.

The King was a mystical figure: He represented the unity of the kingdom, the religious bond that connected the community of the living to the Ancestors and to the Divinity. About fifty years ago, the majority of royal dynasties in Black Africa were dynasties of conquerors. This was the case for the Sine. This explains the singularity of the religious remit of the *Bour*.[32] His person is sacred, and he is the Head of the official religion. But he is not the Priest, because sacerdotal dignity is not the result of conquest. He does not perform sacrifices himself; he merely is in high command of the clergy of the "national" shrines.

The Great Dyarâf is chosen by the King on recommendation of the *bours*.[33] He may be a *bour*; most often he is a *sâkh-sâkh*, a *dyâmbour*. Holding rank immediately after the King, Prime Counsellor as Prime Minister, he is the Supreme Judge, who alone can mete out the death sentence.

The Great Farba is chosen from among the *dyâligués*. He is the Head of the Crown's army of captives. It is important that he be of serf origin and that the bulk of the troops be constituted by the captives he represents. The Army is, thus, entirely devoted to the person of the King and removed from the intrigues of a rather turbulent nobility. The *Farba-bir-Keur* is also a former *dyâligué*. He collects the taxes gathered by the *bours*, *sâkh-sâkhs*, and *dyâligués* and, generally, manages the kingdom's finances.

The lower *bours* are the most typical expression of the *Guelwâr* nobility. Moreover, some were *dyâmbours*, for there was constant intermingling between the two castes, between which mixed marriages were not prohibited. As representatives of a tradition of the utmost sensitivity and honor, the *guelwârs*, and singularly the *bours*, were the most beautiful, if not the most authentic, expression of Sudanese Africa. At the head of the provinces, namely the border regions, they fulfilled both civilian and military functions.

The *sâkh-sâkhs*, we have said, are chosen from among the *dyâmbours*, from among the families of notables that are the most influential thanks to their seniority, their wealth, their clientele, in a word, their experience. These are prefects of sorts whose administrative districts extend throughout the kingdom, including to the border regions. Their essential role is to transmit the King's decisions and to ensure their execution, and also tithe the crops and herds, which is the regular tax.

The *dyâligués*, of serf origin, fulfill the same functions among the Fulɓe minorities, whose rights, limited as they may be, are recognized and respected.

In this way, what characterizes this political organization is *equilibrium*. All the castes, from the *guelwârs* to the *captives*, participate in the life of the State, support the edifice, the cornerstone, the King, while the latter ensures their unity beyond their diversities, beyond even their antagonisms.

The *bâdolas*, the poor of the caste of free men, as well as the *nyênis*, the craftsmen, may seem to us to be categories somewhat sacrificed in this system. Let us note that the difference between the *dyâmbours* and the *bâdolas* is a difference of class, and therefore of wealth, and not of caste. On the other hand, though despised, the *nyênis* nevertheless exercised a real, though occult, influence.

It is at the level of the village that the social organization of Negro-Africans in general, and that of the Sereer in particular, is most apparent.[34] More than a political grouping, the village is a community that is based on religion and economic realities.

At the head of the village, there is the village leader [*chef de village*] or *Dyarâf.* Of course, he has a political function, which is to convey the orders of the Central Power, and to ensure their execution. He is above all the justice of the peace and the manager of the village community's possessions. And these latter functions are explained by his religious character. He is the Priest. Before French colonization, *he was the descendant of the Founder*—who often gave his name to the village—*of the one who bound, in a contract, the Jinn of the Earth and the other Spirits of the land.*[35] In this capacity, he is responsible for their worship and also for the cult of the Founder, promoted to the rank of beneficent spirit. Thus, the village appears, first of all, as *a community of believers organized around the same cult*, like a parish.

The village also appears as a *community of possessions* [*biens*]. We should pause here for a moment and expand on this idea in depth; in other words, we should outline the regime of *property*.

The word is somewhat inappropriate, as ethnologists have already pointed out; or rather, it is ambiguous. Indeed, strictly speaking, one can designate with this term only the products of labor: things manufactured for individual use. The rest is collective property. We cannot even say that there is "land ownership." For the land, rivers, lakes, and other features of the earth are the property of the *Spirits*. Rather, they are indistinguishable from them. *Mother-Earth* is a jinn. Thus, in the soil, we can have rights only of use, of cultivation. It is these rights that the Founder acquires over a circumscribed area, which forms the commune. Hence the name *Lamane*, "Master of the Land," which is given to the head of the village, his descendant and successor.[36]

The King bears a similar title. He refers to himself as "the Eminent Master of the Land." Such is the case with most Negro-African kings. This matter merits an explanation. The King bears this title only under the guise of a juridico-religious fiction. It is assumed that the ancient Sereer dynasty ceded its rights to the new, *Malinke* conquerors; the Sereer dynasty, whose first king, above the *lamanes*, would have taken possession of the country in the name of his people. In fact, the title would better suit the Great Dyarâf, who represents the *lamanes* to the King. It is he who is responsible for defending the possessions of the village communities against the possible arbitrariness of the chiefs and even of the *Bour*. Is this to say that the King's land rights are illusory? Hardly. They extend across all the vacant lands not owned by the communities.

But let us come back to the village and its leader, the Lamane. As we have said, he is the *manager of the village community's possessions*. These possessions consist of fields, pastures, forests, waterways, springs, wells, etc. Their first character is that they are *inalienable*. The Lamane cannot sell anything. He cannot even rent anything without the approval of the Council of Notables, a kind of municipal council formed by the heads of the "compound" [*carré*], that is to say the "extended families." The village property is *undivided*: it belongs, en bloc, to all members of the community. No parcel may be definitively ceded. In the past, the Lamane regularly carried out a redistribution of land between the different families. This was the essence of his role as manager. He was also generally responsible for ensuring the integrity and maintenance of the community property and for indicating and overseeing the necessary public works.

We have spoken of families, among whom the land of the village was distributed. Now is the time to examine the essential features of the *Sereer family*, which, as elsewhere in Black Africa and in the world, forms the "social cell."

First, there is the *immediate family*, the family in the European sense of the word, which includes the father, mother, and children. It is the paternal family, which has only legal value.

The true Sereer family is the maternal family, the *extended family*, which includes all the descendants, within a maternal lineage, of a single woman who is the common Ancestor. For the bonds of blood are established by the mother, and by her alone. The Sereer say that "it is the womb that ennobles."

In principle, all members of the extended family live in the same *compound*, formed by several households. However, founded on a religious and economic basis, like the village and even more so than the village, it has a deep sense of unity. At the top is the Head of the family, who is essentially the oldest man from the oldest generation. He is assisted by a Family Council composed of all major family members of both genders. They may depose him in the case of senility, madness, or serious misconduct.

Firstly, *the Head of the family is the priest responsible for the worship of the Ancestors*. He alone can speak to them, and he can do so only in the interest of the family community. As such, he is responsible for the supervision and moral oversight of all family members, especially children and young people.

Second, *the Head of the family is the manager of the family possessions*. These have the same characteristics of inalienability and indivisibility as the village possessions. The remits of the Head of the family can, in turn, be compared to those of the Head of the village. They are very extensive, but can be grouped under three headings: distribution, conservation, administration. In particular, the Head of the family receives, in the family granaries, a share of the product of the work of each man, the rest being left to the needs of the household or the individual; within the family, the *dowries* paid for the young women he gives in marriage. During all important life events—birth, marriage, death—he assists members of the community both materially and morally.

Between the family and the village, which are the two poles of social activity, we can distinguish a series of groups whose interaction animates and balances this activity. Africanists have often noted and described them: they are the societies of women and men, age classes, classes of initiates, brotherhoods with secret rites, and castes.

I will dwell only on the groups that are most characteristic and most alive and well in the Sine.

The village is divided into a *society of men and a society of women*, whose action is apparent only on special occasions. One should not think that the role of the woman was negligible. Just as women's labor is different, the role of their society is different; and, while it is true that the society of women specializes in defending women's interests, it also has a say in the major issues of interest to the village.

In the Kingdom of the Sine and, in general, among the Sereer, the *classes of initiates* have replaced age classes, in accordance with the natural evolution of Negro-African societies. These classes are formed at the time of circumcision, a ceremony that occurs around puberty. In reality, circumcision is merely an opportunity for a veritable education. It is a matter of preparing young people for their role as men. Rather, it is a true religious initiation, with hardship, asceticism, rites, and ceremonies, an initiation based on the mystery of *Death-Rebirth*.

This initiation, led by a kind of specialized clergy, takes place in the *sacred woods*. In practical terms, it includes instruction, the main subjects of which are Religion—in connection to Ethics—History, Politics, Custom, and even Hygiene and the Aesthetics of the community. It is a matter of maintaining and perpetuating the tradition, therefore the life of the community. On emerging, within their respective class, functioning as a kind of political party, men will make the voice of their generation heard.

Concerning the life of the castes and their relations in the village, we will not revisit the *guelwârs*. At the head of the cantons, provinces, and border regions, they occupy command posts or live at the court of the King and the *bours*.

In the villages, the first rank therefore belongs to the "free men," to the peasants, who are *dyâmbours* or *bâdolas* according to their wealth. Let us emphasize, here, that in Black Africa, working the land is the noblest work, and that *Negro-African civilizations are above all peasant civilizations*. It is the free men who form the classes of initiates we have just mentioned, and it is from among them the Head of the village and the Council of Notables are recruited.

The *nyênis* or craftsmen live apart and marry among one another within their subcastes. These include, in descending order, jewelers, blacksmiths, weavers, shoemakers, *laobés* or woodworkers, and griots.[37] The craftsmen—especially the griots—live in the entourage of the King and the *bours*; but they are also rather widespread in the villages. Like the other castes, they are organized and hierarchical. They are subjected to an apprenticeship, which is in part an initiation, since technology is made of secrets and is accompanied by magical rites. Then they undertake the various steps that must lead them to mastery.

Of course, the craftsmen are despised, especially the griots, who are poets, musicians, actors, and dancers, because, dependent on the generosity of the nobles, they must necessarily flatter them. However, they are still esteemed for their art and for the services they provide to the village. And they are also feared, because of the secrets they hold. It is from among them that healers and doctors of all kinds are recruited. So, occult as it may be, their influence is no less real.

At the bottom of the social ladder, there are the *captives*. They are divided into *captives of the Crown* and captives of private individuals. The second group is further divided into *trade captives* [*captifs de traite*] and *domestic captives* [*captifs de case*].

The captives of the Crown are the privileged ones. We have seen that they furnish the King with his high officials: *farbas* and *dyâligués*. Most are *tyedos*, that is to say, soldiers.[38] As such, they have the benefits granted to military everywhere.

Captives who have been purchased or conquered form the subcaste of the trade captives: They are the most unfortunate. They can be beaten; women are given as concubines to free men or as wives to other captives—without their consent. However, the captive, even the trade captive, cannot be sold. He can purchase his freedom [*racheter*], even against the will of his master; and he cannot be put to death arbitrarily.

Domestic captives, the most numerous kind, include the mass of freed men [*affranchis*] and the sons of trade captives born in the master's home. They are more servants than slaves in the old sense of the word. They are part of the family whose name they bear. They work only in part for the master. The master, however, must provide them with a field, food, clothing, and a wife.

If we wish to summarize, we readily notice the essential characteristics of Sereer society. What is striking is its *unity* and *harmony*. *On the one hand, it is, in effect, based on hierarchy and, on the other hand, on the equilibrium of castes, genders, and generations*. These are the permanent characteristics of all Negro-African societies: their qualities. We also see its shortcomings or inadequacies: contempt for craftwork; castes in the place of classes; serfdom, tempered as it may be; finally, generally speaking, *a too absolute subordination of the person to the community*.

This overview, it seems, has been lengthy enough. However, in order to be exhaustive, we would have needed to deepen the features of Negro-African religion and make a study of the psychophysiology of the Black man, which would have allowed us to identify the significant place of art in his life.[39] Here too, his qualities would have appeared to us: *religious mysticism, preponderance up to the point of excluding all which, in the work of art, is not purely artistic*. And also, his defects: *contempt for reason and moral speculations*; I do not mean practical morality.

III. Modifications: The French Graft

Colonization was meant to change this Negro-African political and social organization. This was even the proclaimed goal: Colonization was intended to work for the benefit of the natives [*indigènes*]. What were, in reality, the deeds of the Colonizer? Have they been carried out in the way we have outlined above: elimination of *the elements of death and fecundation of the elements of life*? That is the issue we must address now. The following pages will be the *presentation of a program based on the Negro-African reality* and, at the same time, a critique—which we intend to be objective—of the colonial methods of the Third Republic.

One may be surprised that I am beginning with the matter of *religion* and proclaim it to be fundamental while I have only attempted to give a systematic outline of the Negro-African religion. Here religion is everywhere, permeates everything, and it is less important to know what it was than to know that it was the cornerstone of the State and society, namely, that of the village and of family communities.

What was the attitude of the Third Republic before the religious question? Let us confess that, most often, when it did not deny religion, it ignored it. Some "distinguished" minds went about denying that there was, in Black Africa, anything other than "crude fetishism." It was in vain that Delafosse and other great Africanists rose up against this ignorant contempt. Too often, the Priest was taken for a sorcerer, and when they were not collecting religious objects, they were destroying "idols." In instances when the Republic protected Religion it was non-negro religions, Christianity and Islam, that benefited. But, most often, Religion was ignored, at least in school. The primacy of the intellect was proclaimed, intelligence was nurtured. And the Black youth, through taking tests and passing exams, by competently performing delicate functions and engaging in scientific research, proved that it was not lacking in intelligence. But, at the same time, to consider two examples, theft and crime increased in countries where there were no police, and the number of teenage mothers—which is a remnant of naivety—grew in countries where the girl's integrity was a condition of marriage. For the cold categorical imperative cannot replace the warmth of the Ancestors. Reason has unknotted the bonds of love.

I am a Catholic. However, I can speak only about imported religions from my Negro-African perspective, that is from the outside. For, how can we judge religions here if not by their political and social effects?

It is undeniable that the Arabo-Berber and *Islam* have leavened Black blood: the Negro-African Civilization. They brought to us martial fervor and intellectual curiosity, a religion and an ethics [*morale*] that are more founded on reason—and the idea of God was purified as it was refined. The Sudanese civilization of the Middle Ages, which North Africans and Portuguese people considered as equal to theirs, proved that there could be a "conciliatory agreement" between Islam and the Negro. Two observations arise, however. The first is that, *far from being assimilated to it, the Negroes assimilated Islam*; in other words, *Sudanese humanism* was not the result of conquest. In fact, if Arabo-Berbers played an important role in higher education, the political framework of the State was historically Negro; this is what constituted its strength and its stability. The second observation is that the Arabo-Berbers fomented the wars that led to the decline of this Sudanese humanism. The Empire of Ghana fell under the blows of the Almoravids, the Empire of Gao under the blows of the Moroccans.

And here is the danger that the Arabo-Berber and Islam pose to Negro-African Civilization. The restlessness of souls becomes belligerent anarchy. But this danger belongs to the past. More dreadful is the alluring Arab intellectualism that delights in the games of the mind and leads to abstraction, that is to say, to the death of sensuality: to the death of negro art. Even more dreadful is this materialism, the offspring of intellect, which reserves for the layman earthly pleasures in paradise.

An abstract and formalist Islam, a degenerate Islam, is therefore a danger to us. Muslim Negroes must work to restore to it its mystical and humanistic leaven by according it with our soul. This is what West African Islam began to do.

I cannot address the *issue of Catholicism* without referring to the fascinating debate this year between Reverend Father [Francis] Aupiais and Mister [Marcel] Griaule at the Foyer des étudiants coloniaux de Paris [Association of colonial students of Paris]; a debate that could not reach a resolution, for it opposed a man of faith and a man of science. As both a Catholic and a Black man, what more could I have asked for? I can at least offer a synthesis.

I believe that asking whether Negroes should be evangelized is the wrong way of framing the question. Let us keep in mind that we are facing the *fact of colonization*, which I have defined as "a contact of civilizations." Whether we like it or not, it is necessary that Religion, as well as the entire Negro-African Civilization, be transformed. Mister Griaule wants the "natives" themselves to transform it. But these Frenchified Negroes, are they not, thereby, also Christianized? For how can we deny that Western civilization, particularly French civilization, is entirely leavened by Christianity?

Just as French colonization, in its "civilizing" action, cannot ignore Negro-African Civilization, Catholicism cannot ignore *Animism* without risking serious failure. Nothing solid, sustainable, can be built in the sandy plains of these countries if it does not rest on the stony foundations of Animism. Father [Francis] Libermann, the founder of the Congregation of the Fathers of the Holy Spirit, already had this intuition, as he wrote to his missionaries: "*Be Negroes with the Negroes so as to win them over to Jesus Christ.*"[40] And, interpreting the last missionary encyclicals of the popes, Father Aupiais writes: "*Black Churches will be African, or they will not be at all.*"[41]

For the missionary, it is thus a matter of studying indigenous religions, before anything else. What hinders the debate is that Father Aupiais uses the terms "religious aspirations" and "fetishism." We have no doubt that these terms do not match the complexity of his thought, for elsewhere he uses, more than once, the term "religion." And he acknowledges that there is in this religion a belief system, a cult with a ceremonial that is rich in symbolism, and an ethics based on the observance of positive laws.

What, then, is the role of the Catholic missionary? Father Aupiais states it clearly: "The Missionary would radically harm his work . . . if he did not introduce the *graft* [*greffe*] that would improve—would completely transform—its leaves, its flowers, its fruits, its very essence, on a trunk that he would leave firmly anchored and richly sustained by roots as ancient as itself."[42] Yes, it is a matter of performing a graft. This is the same image that we have long enjoyed using to speak of colonization. It is a matter of enlightening the negro sense of the divine, its religious fervor, these arduous practices—including asceticism—that presuppose a long education of the will. *The role of Catholicism is to more clearly distinguish the individual from the family, and God from the spirits and Ancestors. It is to provide a more conscious unity of feelings, which are all the stronger in that they are more intertwined. It is to impart a universal character to the familial and "national" religion.* Through Christ, God made flesh, who thus prevents Catholicism from falling into formalist abstraction. Mister Griaule will say that I speak as a believer, and he would not be wrong.

Catholicism, as we can see, should remain close to its evangelical sources. It cannot flourish in the African soil if it appears—as it too often does in the Metropole—as a recipe for good manners for self-righteous bourgeois, an instrument of subjugation in the hands of a paternalistic capitalism. I fear that, in the administrative centers of French West Africa (A.O.F.), it has already begun to take on this appearance. It is high time to sound the alarm.

We have studied one type of *Negro-African political organization* above. What has been done with this system? Was it merely transformed? No, it was destroyed, with the best of intentions. This was certainly necessary in the case of religious empires formed recently and artificially, such as those of Samory and Elhadj Omar, although the grand intentions of the latter should not be ignored.[43] Even in the case of other people who were tenacious adversaries, I believe that it would have been better to practice Lyautey's policy after he subdued the Malagasy leader Rabezavana. As Mister [Raymond] Postal states, "He set him free and brought him under his command. . . . It's a roll of the dice. . . . And he was right, the future would prove it."[44] But what about the abolition of royalty in the Sine after the Great War and the death of Koumba Ndôfène Dyouf?[45] The answer is that the progress of colonization allowed, even demanded, "direct rule." Has enough thought been given to the fact that the pact of *association*, which the *protectorate* constitutes, was thereby broken and that the *Code de l'indigénat* [Indigenous code] was a denial of *assimilation* itself?[46] *For the paradox is that direct rule, which had been instituted, quite sincerely, in the name of progress, was, in reality, a political regression.* We have seen that in the old system, all castes participated in the election of the King and in the administration of the State, that the individual, the person—a notion that Islam and Catholicism would deepen but that they did not create—is protected by the customs and the family community. On the other hand, the Code de l'indigénat gives us an absolute administrator, who receives his orders from Dakar and Paris and pronounces, "without judgment," sentences "ranging from one to fifteen days in jail, and fines of 1 to 100 francs." I quote Mister [Henri]

Labouret, who finds that "between French citizenship and the status of our nationals . . . there may be degrees, steps to overcome," and who considers that if, "indeed, we have embarked on this path," we have done so "timidly."[47]

Yes, the political status of the Native [*Indigène*] is a paradox in most cases. It responds neither to the principles of association nor to those of assimilation. All great theoreticians of colonization have, at least implicitly and frequently unambiguously, condemned it. It is on the basis of our opening remarks and from the perspective of the African reality that, once again, we must seek the solution to the problem. We shall say that the *political expression of Black Africa desires leaders who represent the People, leaders chosen by the People*. This principle stems from the French tradition and the Negro-African tradition at the same time.

"Black Chiefs" [*Chefs noirs*] is the title of one of the most beautiful chapters of *Soudan–Paris–Bourgogne*. Delavignette notes that *Nigritie* is "a country of chiefs" and that this is one of its eternal features. He writes, "In Sudan, under colonial rule, in the vicinities of the governor's Residence, there still is a country of chiefs, a country where the chief emerges among the people as visibly and naturally as a tree grows in a field."[48] In the first days of captivity in the *Frontstalags*, chiefs emerged from the masses of *tirailleurs sénégalais* [Senegalese riflemen] to speak to the occupying authorities on behalf of the rank-and-file soldiers, as if they wanted to confirm Delavignette's word. The soldiers called them "chiefs." They were often mere soldiers, but they had succeeded in imposing themselves by their character and their knowledge; in comparison, many officers had only a nominal function.

However, today there is a crisis of chiefs that is affecting the health of the Colony; I would rather say, the health of Colonization. The fact of the matter is, almost everywhere, princes were disbanded and transformed into minor officials of a *subprefecture*. Delavignette adds: "We have let warrant officers and middlemen transform these chiefs into neighborhood dogs and lowly business couriers."[49] I personally fear they have been debased. Already, in the evolved colonies, the people no longer consider them their representatives. In the Colonial Council of Senegal, for instance, they represent only the Administration that appoints them and are in permanent conflict with the councilors elected by the citizens. Skepticism has crept into the minds. The natives know that the administrators who appoint the canton chiefs derive their power neither from their religious character nor from their family tradition, but from their knowledge. Spontaneously, they turn to their peers who have acquired science, to the intellectuals who form the new elite. This had already happened in Islamized countries. It is a common mistake among colonizers to believe that the native elite is cut off from the People. Yet the results of the Senegalese elections send a very clear message. For years, we have always elected, as a Member of Parliament, an intellectual of the country, whether he was *métis* or a pure Negro.[50]

Once again, the Chief must represent the masses; which implies the accession of the masses to citizenship. It is not a matter of drowning the representatives of the Metropolitans, in some run-of-the-mill Palais Bourbon,[51] under waves of colonial deputies, who would rely on seventy million individuals. It is a matter of the *citizenship of Empire* [*la citoyeneté d'Empire*], an idea that has been gaining ground in France for several years. It is even the title of an article by Professor Labouret, published in *L'Homme de couleur*. In this article, the author writes, speaking of the aspirations of the native elite: "These legitimate satisfactions cannot be denied without injustice. *It would be easy to do so by creating, in each of our territories, a local citizenship that would give to each local citizen a set of rights that are more or less equal to those of French citizens*, but which would be valid only in the colony or group of colonies where those who benefit from those rights are from."[52] My emphasis.

We agree with Professor Labouret on almost all points. It is normal that we do not agree on all of them. I do not see why the rights of the citizens of the Empire would cease to be valid in the other territories of the Empire. Are they not still *men*? And are we expected to relieve a Caribbean official appointed in Senegal or an Indian worker who earns a living in Indochina of their duties? The exercise of these citizens' rights seems to me all the more legitimate in that the Caribbean or the Indian in question belong to a minority. On the other hand, if Mister Labouret wishes to grant citizenship indiscriminately to all Indochinese, he nonetheless wishes to create in A.O.F., in A.E.F. (Francophone Equatorial Africa), and in Madagascar, a group of privileged people whose privileges are acquired through instruction and services rendered to France. Will we be allowed to doubt that the intellect—and instruction in general—is the best criterion for the establishment of a scale of values? Let us note, precisely, that this opinion has long been outdated in Europe. As for services rendered to France, and singularly to military service [*service de sang*], were these not asked most heavily of A.O.F.? I am not implying that A.O.F. should receive preferential treatment; I am merely asking that it be treated justly. And if we get back to our principles, has A.O.F. not always shown its profound political awareness?

How would the representatives of colonial peoples be elected, and what would be their remit? I can only stick to generalities. I am not a ballot fanatic. That is a European mode of election. Nor do I wish that the vote be individual. I rather want it to be family-based in Black Africa—which would be in the tradition of the country—*provided that women could make their voices heard*.[53]

There would be several degrees of elections: The village chiefs would appoint the representatives of the circles, who would appoint the representatives of the Colonies; the latter would, in turn, choose the members of the *Federal Assembly*. The "colonial nations" would, indeed, be constituted on the basis of the existing federations: North Africa, A.E.F, A.O.F., the Antilles, Indochina, and Madagascar. Only the Governor General, appointed by the Metropole, would have the executive power and the right to take initiatives when it comes to legislative matters, but he would need the support of the Federal Assembly for his projects to be legally binding. There would be, in the Metropole, an "Imperial Parliament," which would be composed of the representatives of the Metropole and those of the Colonies. This Parliament would be responsible for all issues of general interest: Imperial Defense, External Affairs, etc.

This system, as we can see, far from weakening the authority of the Metropole, would only strengthen it, *since it would be based on the consent and love of freed men—of free men*. Far from weakening the unity of the Empire, it would weld it together, since the bandleader's mission would not be to stifle the voices of the various instruments, by drowning them out with his own voice, but to lead them, in unison, and to allow the most delicate bush flute to play its role.

Politics is merely an instrument in service of the social. Lyautey clearly saw this, as he never ceased affirming the *primacy of the social*. For him, the action of the State should strive to establish economic prosperity and social peace. But these, in turn, are only means in service of the ultimate goal, which is the fulfillment of spiritual life. Indeed, they are not the requisite conditions for the flourishing of minds in the various fields of arts and letters. It appears, however, that the People, the masses—and ultimately it is about the masses—cannot live an authentic, intense, spiritual life in the midst of poverty, social struggles, and insecurity of the minds. Hence the need to *overcome poverty*, to create a new social order based on the foundations of the old one.

I will not insist on the creation and organization of a *modern economic infrastructure*, on roads and railways, ports and large-scale projects that would lead to the industrial, or simply commercial, development of the Colony. Indeed, the Metropole is too invested in this to neglect it; it is all too prone to view it as the sole colonial reality. From [Jean-Baptiste] Colbert to Mister [Émile] Bélime, there is an entire intellectual lineage that has focused on this topic.[54]

I will not insist on the organization and development of the *Health Service* either. Although the funds allocated to this service are far from being sufficient, it is still one of the best organized services. The Medical Corps, in the Colony, comprises the men who have the highest sense of their mission, those who are the most devoted. The great endemics have almost disappeared: plague, yellow fever, sleeping sickness. However, much progress remains to be made in this area. The recruitment of colonial doctors must be intensified. And it comes as a surprise that there is serious talk of limiting the number of medical students, and that such talk had begun when the Colonies—and even the French countryside—were asking for ten times, a hundred times, more medical doctors. It is truly surprising that we have so easily heeded the selfishness of the authorities. Moreover, it is within the Colonies themselves and among the native populations that this recruitment should be intensified. It would be a matter of increasing the number of students admitted annually to the School of Medicine and of elevating the level of medical studies through the creation of a University.

But let us discuss the more serious matters, or rather one of the most serious matters. *The agrarian question has always been the basis of all reform and social progress.*

The *Grandes Compagnies* [Trading companies] bankrupted A.E.F. at the beginning of Colonization. The French Government had to abolish them after resounding scandals and courageous campaigns, which are to the credit of French intelligence and valor. Since then, in A.O.F., we have attempted to create large enterprises sparked by grand intentions. My African and peasant sense is suspicious of large enterprises. Millions, if not billions, go into them. Once again, these "large-scale projects" leave me wary. It is the people who always bear the brunt of prestige politics—of the politics that partly inspires these projects—for it is not based in reality and crushes the human. Peasants first deserted the "polytechnic villages" of the STIN (Société des Travaux des Irrigations du Niger) [Niger Irrigation Works Company]. This is because official speeches had presided over their foundation, not libations of milk, not the sacrifices of white chickens; because they were based only on science, not on the tombs of the Ancestors; because their life was punctuated by the bugle, not the traditional tam-tam. I was told that, since then, we have begun to learn from Africa, that peasants have come back, bringing with them their "Paternal gods." I want to reassure myself that by issuing a primary school diploma in Africa, we do not stop halfway.

It is true that the development of concessions and *colonial settlements* [*colonat*] in certain regions—Guinea and especially Côte d'Ivoire—is not meant to reassure us. To speak like Sidobre, Colonists have always represented "the tradition of evil." Alongside the large trading companies, they are likely to represent colonial capitalism; they already represent it. It is difficult to see any progress from the old Negro-African social organization. Indeed, it would be a regression—not even a reaction—to replace collective property with large-scale individual property, even if it were in the form of a *concession*; to replace family work and the work of the age group performed to the sound of the tam-tam with that of groups of agricultural workers toiling under the baton of a foreman, even if he is a native; to replace the free commitment of the *navétanes*[55] with "compulsory volunteering," as the Blacks themselves call it. Once again, we must return to inalienable family property and to the farming of the land by the owner himself, I mean by usufructuary. I fear that after having freed the domestic captive, we are in the process of creating, with the colonial settlements, a proletariat, which would, in the future, lead to social conflicts and unspeakable hatred. Do we wish to increase production? If the native is interested in his work, if he receives appropriate rural instruction, he will not fail to produce more. The role of rural schools and agricultural cooperatives or *welfare companies*, created by the General Government, is precisely to provide this education.

We thus arrive at the ultimate goal of Colonization, or rather its ultimate instrument, *Education*, for the *goal is the search for and improvement of Man*. In the case of Education, there is a dual objective: preparation for the social function and, above all, the formation of the will, heart, and intelligence—in a word, an *education* of the soul. "*There is only one civilization: that of the soul.*"

In other words, if we return to our opening remarks, it is a matter of preparing for an active assimilation that, in turn, will prepare the ground for a fecund association. That is, on the one hand, Assimilation of European technologies, of French techniques of work and thought; and association, on the other hand, to the work of the Imperial Community by the contributions of the Black soul, Black workers, and Black land.

The current organization and methods of Education in A.O.F. and, to some extent, in A.E.F. largely respond to these principles. Yet it is obvious, as one might guess, this service is far from perfect when it is not even so in the Metropole. This is evidenced by the perpetual changes of curricula and schedules, if not of method.

First, a general observation. In Black Africa, the number of schools and the funds allocated to Education are still very low. A few years ago, only one boy in ten could attend school, and one girl in two hundred. I do not wish to criticize; I simply wish to point out the most urgent measure to take and to draw the attention of the Metropole to the great pity of schools in Black Africa.

I remind you that there are three levels of Education: the first level of Education [*l'Enseignement du premier degré*] with the rural schools, regional schools, and urban schools; the second level of Education [*l'Enseignement du second degré*] with vocational and craft schools, teachers' colleges, and high schools;

and Higher Education [*l'Enseignement supérieur*] with the Veterinary School and the School of Medicine and Pharmacy. I only wish to focus on those schools that raise the critical issues.

The *Popular Rural School* is the most recent, and this is why the issue it raises has not yet been resolved. We have not yet made a distinction between what is preparation for the profession and what is education. Indeed, I even fear that a hierarchy has been established in the wrong direction, giving the professional precedence over Man. Yes, I fear that too much importance has been attached to *facts*, to the detriment of *spirit* and method; quite frankly, I fear that there is a tendency to turn village schools into farm-schools. It was intended that School, as preparation for life, should have its windows wide open to the life of the village, that teaching should come out of its abstract ivory tower, that the Instructor's lesson should be given in the face of things, that, in any case, it should find its application in African and peasant realities. And we were the first to applaud this *revolutionary education*, which took off from life in order to come back to life and transform it. But, to do so, it was thought beneficial to increase the hours of manual labor, to reduce the hours of class, and to lighten the curricula—which were already not exactly hefty. Have we not gone so far as to denigrate books? It seems to me that this is where the error lies. *The rural school should not be a farm-school, but simply a rural school—with the emphasis on "school."* It is less a matter of teaching children to handle the plough or other tools, which are intended for adults, than of familiarizing them with the idea of new agricultural techniques and instruments; it is less a matter of proscribing books than introducing, in school, the new books that speak of Africa—and there are some excellent ones; it is a matter, especially, of learning to read them, so that these books may teach one to better judge men and things. In short, *it is not about learning less but learning better; it is not about lowering the level of instruction but raising the level of culture.* For preparation for the profession itself will be in vain if it is not, simultaneously, education through the development of mind, heart, and hands at the same time.

I have said: hands. I do not wish to be taken for a denigrator of manual labor. I know its educational value. The work of the hands is a natural activity of Man, and responsible for the health of the body. The health of the soul, too. Not only because the health of the soul is conditioned by the health of the body, but also because such work has its own virtues: It develops the taste for effort, the sense of the real and the honest, the sense of the true, for its results are proportional to the amount and quality of the effort. And this is why the Indian sage Mahatma Gandhi considers it to be the most effective instrument of spiritual liberation. By emphasizing the intellectual aspect of scholastic education, I wish only to restore, between the hands and the head, the necessary equilibrium, the human equilibrium, that some overzealous protagonists of the Popular Rural School tend to disrupt.

Although the *Professional Schools* were not created recently, the *Houses of the Craftsmen*, which have been added to them, are. I will not dwell on the Professional Schools, especially not on the sector from which office workers will emerge: secretaries and accountants. . . . More interesting is the school that forms wood or iron workers: carpenters, blacksmiths, etc. It is true that, here, students must assimilate European techniques and instruments, but it is also, for them, a matter of highlighting a hereditary manual skill and, as the occasion arises, of *creating*, or rather of reclaiming, the Negro-African style.

But the need to reclaim, and maintain, the style of Black Africa must impose itself, even more so, on those who enter into the House of Craftsmen. For here it is a matter of preserving and renewing, if not the instruments and technologies, then at least the old crafts of the Black country: shoemaking and leather work, weaving, basketry, pottery, jewelry. . . . The new craftsmen will meet new needs by making new objects; but they will do so in the Negro-African style. Otherwise, their art is debased into a mere technology of comfort, a kind of graceless grocer's art. But *this style, because it is spirit more than technology, feeds in the depths of the Black soul.* Hence the need to maintain its traditional qualities: its tension, its warmth, its rhythm. We break the barriers of castes—provided that we do not erect, in their place, the barriers of classes!—; we ennoble craftwork. We can only applaud these advances. But we should refrain from severing the bonds of material and moral solidarity that made the strength and unity, the life of the caste-corporation and of the family. It would be the death of the soul, the death of Negro-African art.

The *"William-Ponty" Teachers' College*, transferred from Gorée to Sébikotane, is undoubtedly the most important in A.O.F.[56] The "rural teachers' colleges" should be tied to it. William-Ponty trains future public servants—doctors, pharmacists, and veterinarians—and, above all, future indigenous schoolteachers. If it is true that Civilization, as the French would have it, is primarily of an intellectual and moral nature; one can say that schoolteachers are the most active agents of French Civilization in A.O.F. The General Government, which gives all its care to the "William-Ponty" Teachers' College, knows this well. It is here that the scholastic revolution took place; it is here that it is carried out the most methodically.

All subjects have been transformed not only in their curriculum but also and mostly in their spirit. In this regard, Mister [Roger] Dumargue has written an article shedding light on the matter: "Teaching French at the William-Ponty

School" in *L'Information d'Outre-mer* [Overseas news].[57] There, we see that assignments are closely linked to the lesson, the *dissertation* to the *explication de texte*, knowledge of Africa to that of France, through French writers.[58] Here, the *dissertation* is, before all else, a commentary on the analyzed reading, but a commentary in light of the African experience.

Let us be more specific. The purpose of the teaching of French has as its aims:

1) The acquisition of general ideas, which shape the spirit of the "*honnête homme*";[59]
2) The learning of the language as well as training in style.

It is based on these principles that the authors of the curriculum have been chosen from among those writers who are at once the most "human" and the most "artistic": Corneille, Racine, Molière, and Hugo. Some colonial writers have been added to them: [Pierre] Loti, [André] Demaison, and Delavignette. For the former, it is a matter of verifying the human truth of their work by seeking whether the characters they paint, whether the feelings they express are found in the Black world and, if so, under what singular aspect they are presented. Regarding the colonial writers, it is a matter of knowing what is true and false in the White's portrait of the Black Man. But French writers are not only masters of thought; they are also masters of writing. After the study of ideas, the study of language and style. The study of the latter will enable the elaboration of the most essentially French qualities—clarity, order, and harmony—qualities that the student will need to demonstrate in the expression of feelings, in the painting of Negro-African types.

We have accomplished much at William-Ponty. However, there is still much to be done; the scholastic revolution must go on. At William-Ponty, teachers ruthlessly hound everything that smacks of exaggeration, obscurity, verbiage, what they call "Black defects," which are merely student defects; I refer them to the copies of the high school examination [*bachot*]. I fear that the wheat has been taken away with the chaff; in other words, the qualities of Negro-African style have been stifled, because the Black man is, above all, a lyrical mind, who has a profound sense of the verbal image at the same time as that of the rhythm and the music of the words assembled. Why not require students to read René Maran? But we continue to steer clear of Maran—because of the preface to *Batouala*.[60] Meanwhile, the language of the schoolteachers trained at William-Ponty retains something stiff and dull in its wisdom, its correctness: *it is a language without style*.

If we wish to get to the crux of the matter, we will say the following. In order for the teaching of French to be fruitful, it would be necessary to add the teaching of *Ethnology*. Schoolteachers should not merely achieve the ideal of the *"honnête homme."* On the one hand, their task is to know Africa and transform it within themselves and, on the other hand, it is to make Africa known to their peers and to help it advance along its own course. Yet, however alive and well the teaching of French may be at William-Ponty, when applied to African things, it does not offer the best introduction to knowledge about Africa. It postulates another discipline, with a more rigorous, more scientific, method: Ethnology, and, especially, its two main branches, *Ethnography* and *Linguistics*. Teachers of Ethnology would thus complete the personal experience that each student of Africa has by illuminating that experience in the light of others; above all, they would provide the student with a solid method of research, allowing him to contribute new, firsthand material, which scholars will use for their analyses. And these analyses, in turn, would be new points of departure for future explorers. The Old Africa is dying. Customs and languages are changing with incredible speed. Yes, now is the time to photograph her face as it appears today, a face whose eternal features are still so pronounced. *Tomorrow, it will be too late.*

The scholastic revolution in A.O.F. has stopped at the *high school* gates. These remain bastions, not so much of reactionism—reactionism can be salutary when it is, for someone who has lost their way, a step back in the right direction—but of a fixed tradition, which is not even that of Africa.

No doubt, we are dealing here with elite subjects, and we believe that we can introduce them to disciplines and forms of knowledge that have formed today's most advanced nations. This is true for Mathematics and for the hard Sciences, which, by definition, have no borders and concern reason, itself universal. On the other hand, History and Geography have developed on a world scale. I am thinking above all of languages, especially the so-called classical languages: Greek, Latin, and French. I know the benefits of such languages, having been nurtured by them. I know that the Latins and especially the Greeks discovered "general ideas"; earlier and better than others, they brought these ideas to light thanks to an art in which the economy of means contributed to their effectiveness. I know that, for Negro-African peoples, there is no better school, for, if education means developing the native qualities, it also means correcting hereditary defects while acquiring the opposite virtues.

However, it should be noted that this teaching of classical languages is not an end itself. It is an instrument to aid in the discovery, within the self, of human truths, and in their expression in the singular form that they assume here and there. Underlying the Greek fables, for instance, Racine and the French discovered French truths, and the study of the Greek technique of expression merely served to forge a French style. For Negro-Africans, the matter is the same today, particularly in their study of French letters. We have seen this with respect to teachers' colleges. *I would like for exercises and dissertations in high school to also be a constant confrontation, a continuous exchange of perspectives between Europe and Africa.* The Mediterranean Sea has never played such an interesting role. An inland sea, a connecting sea, it has never had the opportunity for such fecund exchanges, for it is a matter of intellectual exchanges, better: of spiritual exchanges.

But just as, in the Metropole, the teaching of French accompanies that of classical languages, it would be good if, in the high schools of Black Africa, *a native language was the necessary companion of French.* For several decades, people have been advocating for the "modern humanities." Why would there not be "Negro-African humanities"? Every language, I mean every civilization, can be the subject of the "humanities" because *each civilization is the singularly pronounced expression of certain features of Humanity.* How else could the Black elite play its role and, thanks to French ferment, spark a revival of indigenous civilization when it started out unaware of the latter? And where can we find a more authentic expression of this civilization if not in indigenous languages and literatures?

One might object, perhaps, with the theory of the Negro-African "clean slate," of the primitiveness of our languages. Once again, I will refer you to the great Africanists. They will tell you that Black Africa has flexible, rich languages, capable of expressing even abstractions, albeit in a purely African, imagistic and poetic way. They will tell you that Africa possesses a certain number of written languages. However, to its written literature—which is, most of the time, influenced by Arabic, and thus imbued with rhetoric—I prefer the oral literature of the *griots*, our troubadours, which does not allow itself to become pedantic because it expresses "the emotional warmth" of the Black soul. But I prefer, quite simply, the popular literature, in which the features of our soul are even more accentuated. These riches are merely awaiting linguists who wish to fix them and preserve them in writing. The future high schooler will find in them the face of eternal Africa; he will find in them a proper means of expression, which the *New Negro* will need to study. If the New Negro must have his literature, as in America, he will go to draw it from these sources. *With new instruments, imported from Europe, from France, it is the very land of Africa that he will cultivate.*

Once again, this is the ultimate goal of Colonization: intellectual fecundation, spiritual grafting. In other words, to return to the conclusion of my opening remarks: *an assimilation that allows for association; but an assimilation by the native.*

It is with this idea of association that I wish to close. The Colony is a source and opportunity for exchange. The Metropole is, and has been for some time now, exporting machinery and manufactured products to her Colonies and importing raw materials. But, tomorrow, for her reconstruction, she will need not only raw materials; she will also require spiritual forces. Thus, she will need to rebuild, along with her factories, her fleet, her ports, the spiritual patrimony that has been sapped and ruined, little by little, by a brand of materialism that claims to be intellectual. To do so, she will not have to return to the civilization of some irrevocably bygone Middle Ages, but to look on her ancient traditions with a new gaze in order to discover in them the sources and conditions of her rebirth.

The Metropole has already begun doing so. We do not think ourselves too presumptuous in asserting that, in addition to her provinces, her colonies and, among them, Black Africa, can help the Metropole uncover, in her own traditions, the most fecundating elements: a sense of community, a sense of hierarchy, a sense of the divine—at least of the spiritual—, a sense of an art that plunges its roots into life, which is as much a *game of the soul* as of the spirit, if not more. May we be heard. It is not a matter of enrolling France in the school of Africa; it is not even a matter of this assimilation of African elements that French writers and artists have begun to implement. Frobenius, wishing, in the *Destin des civilisations* [Destiny of civilizations], to identify the essential features of the European complex, addresses Africa, where these features appear with more simplicity, more force in the opposition of the *Hamite* and the *Ethiopian*. It is a similar service that Black Africa can provide to France: Africa can help France rediscover her ancient face, which is the authentic one, beneath the distortions to which its modern evolution has subjected it.

Increasingly, it is a question of an *Imperial Community*. What Lyautey dreamed of for Morocco is in the process of becoming reality. Is not the Empire, today, *a grouping of humanity in search of a common ideal, a common purpose in life*? This common ideal, the Colonies say to the Metropole, can be found in her very tradition, and it is this tradition that will constitute the unity of the French Empire.

NOTES

Léopold Sédar Senghor, "Vues sur l'Afrique noire ou assimiler, non être assimilés," in *Liberté 1: Négritude et humanisme* (Seuil, 1964), 39–69. The text was first published in Robert Lemaignen, Léopold Sédar Senghor, and Prince Sisowath Youtévong, *La Communauté impériale française* (Éditions Alsatia, 1945), 57–98.

[Epigraph: Hubert Lyautey, *Paroles d'action: Madagascar–Sud-Oranais–Oran–Maroc* (Librairie Armand Colin, 1927), 340–41 (Senghor's emphasis). Senghor adapts the original citation, which reads: "Ce que je rêve [...] c'est qu['il] [...] s'élabore au Maroc un édifice solide, ordonné et harmonieux; qu'il offre le spectacle d'un groupement d'humanité où des hommes si divers d'origine, d'habits, de professions et de races, poursuivent, sans rien abdiquer de leurs conceptions individuelles, la recherche d'un idéal commun, d'une raison de vivre."—Eds.]

1. [Robert Delavignette, *Soudan–Paris–Bourgogne* (Grasset, 1935).—Eds.]

2. [In the *Iliad*, Homer presents the Ethiopians as a morally blameless people, whom gods visit when they leave Olympus. Homer uses the word *ἀμύμων*, an honorific that connotes blamelessness, excellence, nobility. He declares: "For Zeus went yesterday to Oceanus, to the blameless Ethiopians for a feast, and all the gods followed with him." *The Iliad* (London: Gilbert and Rivington, 1841), 423–24.—Eds.]

3. [André Sidobre, "La vraie tradition française," in *L'Homme de couleur*, ed. Jean Verdier (Plon, 1939), 315–46.—Eds.]

4. [Descartes, *Les passions de l'âme, précédé de la pathétique cartésienne par Jean-Maurice Monnoyer* (Gallimard, 1988), 185.—Eds.]

5. [Descartes, *Œuvres Complètes*, vol. 3: *Discours de la méthode*, ed. Jean-Marie Beyssade and Denis Kambouchner (Gallimard, 2009), 81.—Eds.]

6. [This famous citation recounts the Sun King's encounter with Aniaba, a prince of Assini, in modern day Cote d'Ivoire, who traveled to France in 1688.—Eds.]

7. [Senghor refers to the Declaration des Droits de l'Homme et du Citoyen of the eighteenth century, which laid out the major principles of the future French Republic (*liberté, égalité, fraternité*) and the decree of abolition of slavery by the Convention in 1794 in the wake of the revolutions in France and Saint-Domingue/Haiti.—Eds.]

8. [Senghor refers here to the papal letter from Pope Benoît XV addressed to the missionaries to spread the word of God in the entire planet.—Eds.]

9. [Henri Grégoire, *De la littérature des nègres* (Paris: Maradan, 1808), 41.—Eds.]

10. [Sidobre, "La vraie tradition française," 317.—Eds.]

11. [Delavignette, *Soudan–Paris–Bourgogne*, 244.—Eds.]

12. [Émile Littré, *Dictionnaire de la langue française* (Paris: Hachette, 1873–74), 218.—Eds.]

13. [A similar formulation occurs in Senghor's "Prière de Paix": "Pour engraisser ses terres à canne et coton, car la sueur nègre est fumier" (Negro sweat is manure). Senghor, *Poésie complète* (CNRS Éditions, 2007), 167.—Eds.]

14. [Sidobre, "La vraie tradition française," 324.—Eds.]

15. [The "Pacte colonial," also called the "régime de l'exclusif," established a trade monopoly between metropolitan France and its colonies; the "Code noir" was the legal document governing the conditions of French slavery.—Eds.]

16. [This is originally a citation from the report of the Procureur du Roi in Basse-Terre Guadeloupe (September 26, 1841), cited in Ministère secrétaire d'état de la marine et des colonies, "Colonies françaises: Exécution de l'ordonnance royale du 5 janvier 1840, relative à l'instruction religieuse, à l'instruction primaire, et au patronage des esclaves. Exposé sommaire (Seconde Partie: 1840–1841)" (Paris: Imprimerie royale, 1842) 18 (Senghor's emphasis).—Eds.]

17. [Albert Bessières, "Problèmes de morale coloniale," *La vie intellectuelle* (February 1929): 316–29. Also cited in Sidobre, "La vraie tradition française," in Verdier, *L'Homme de couleur*, 338.—Eds.]

18. [Hubert Lyautey, *Paroles d'action: Madagascar–Sud-Oranais–Oran–Maroc* (Librairie Armand Colin, 1927), 68.—Eds.]

19. [Pierre Mille (1864–1941) was a French journalist and writer known for his colonial fictions and reporting in Madagascar and West Africa.—Eds.]

20. [Maurice Delafosse, *Les nègres* (Rieder, 1927), 21.—Eds.]

21. [Léo Frobenius, *Histoire de la civilisation africaine* (Gallimard, 1936), 16.—Eds.]

22. [Lucien Febvre, "De l'état historique à l'état vivant," in *L'Encyclopédie française*, vol. 10: *L'État moderne: Aménagement, crise, transformations*, ed. Anatole de Monzie, Henri Puget, and Pierre Tissier, eds. (Société de gestion de l'encyclopédie française, 1936), n.p. (10°08–14).—Eds.]

23. [Louis Le Fur (1870–1943) was a French jurist. Senghor is perhaps alluding to his *État fédéral et confédération d'états* (Paris: Marchal et Billard, 1896).—Eds.]

24. Cf. Louis Aujias, "Les Sérères du Sénégal," in *Bulletin d'Études historiques et scientifiques de l'A.O.F.* 8 (1931): 293–333.

25. *Bour* is a Wolof word, as is the case for most functions or caste names. Indeed, the country between Senegal and Saloum was once under the suzerainty of the Wolof King of Jolof. [*Buur* in modern transcription. The "Wolof King of Jolof" was the Buur-ba Jolof, the founder of the Wolof empire, Niadiane Ndiaye.—Eds.]

26. [These are all terms from the Wolof caste system. In modern transcription: *buur, gelwaar, jàmbur, baadoolo, ñeeño, lawbe, faad* (pl.) or *paad* (sg.). The Wolof term for griot, which Senghor does not use, is *géwël*. On the caste system, see Abdoulaye Bara Diop, *La société wolof: Tradition et changement; les systèmes d'inégalité et de domination* (Karthala, 1981).—Eds.]

27. [*jaraaf bu rëy* in modern transcription.—Eds.]

28. [*farba bu rëy* in modern transcription.—Eds.]

29. [*farba bir kër* in modern transcription.—Eds.]

30. [*sax-sax* in modern transcription.—Eds.]

31. [*jaalige* in modern transcription.—Eds.]

32. [The Wolof word *buur*, which translates roughly to "king" or perhaps "royal authority," was a political, spiritual, and military leader. Here, where "Bour" is capitalized, Senghor is referring to the supreme leader of a kingdom, who held ultimate authority, not to lower-level local rulers, whom he calls *petits bours*, the "little" or lower *buur*.—Eds.]

33. [Here Senghor appears to be referring to the "lower" *buur*.—Eds.]

34. [Jean Ortoli and Alfred Aubert, eds., *Coutumiers juridiques de l'A.O.F.*, vol. 1: *Le Sénégal* (Larose, 1939).—Eds.]

35. [For a more developed explanation of this, see chapter 1 of this volume.—Eds.]

36. [*laamaan* in modern transcription.—Eds.]

37. [Cheikh Anta Diop suggests the stability of the caste system is perpetuated by the heredity of social status. For an alternative discussion of the caste system in precolonial Africa, see Cheikh Anta Diop, *L'Afrique noire précoloniale* (Présence Africaine, 1960).—Eds.]

38. [*ceddo* in modern transcription.—Eds.]

39. Cf. Léopold Sédar Senghor, "Pour un humanisme: Ce que l'Homme noir apporte," in Verdier, *L'Homme de couleur*, 291–313.

40. [In Libermann: "Faites-vous nègres avec les nègres, et vous les jugerez comme ils doivent être jugés; faites-vous nègres avec les nègres pour les former comme ils le doivent être, non à la façon de l'Europe, mais laissez-leur ce qui leur est propre" (Make yourselves Negroes with the Negroes and you will judge them the way they should be judged; make yourself Negroes with the Negroes to form them as they should be, not in the manner of Europe, but leave them what is theirs); François Libermann, *Notes et documents relatifs à la vie et à l'œuvre du vénérable François-Marie-Paul Libermann* (Paris: Maison Mère, 1850), 330.—Eds.]

41. [Cf. note 42 of this chapter. This expression was taken up later by the Beninese theologian Julien Pénoukou, in *Églises d'Afrique: Propositions pour l'avenir* (Karthala, 1984), 43.—Eds.]

42. [We were unable to find the published source of this quotation, but Michael McCabe has found the text at the Archives des Missions Africaines. Although the text bears no title and is not dated, it was probably written between 1926 and 1928. See Michael McCabe, "L'évolution de la théologie de la mission dans la Société des Missions Africaines de Marion Brésillac à nos jours," *Histoire et missions chrétiennes* 2, no. 2 (2007): 128.—Eds.]

43. [Samory Touré and Elhadj Omar Tall are well-known West African Muslim clerics who resisted French colonization and participated in the propagation of Islam in West Africa.—Eds.]

44. It is from this book, written with such lucid fervor, that I take everything I say about Lyautey in this study. [Raymond Postal, *Présence de Lyautey* (Alsatia, 1941) 128–29.—Eds.]

45. [Senghor probably is referencing the death of Maad Mbacke Ndepp Ndiaye in 1898, when the Council of the Kingdom of the Sine designated Koumba Ndoffene Diouf as his successor. Diouf ruled from 1898 to 1924. He is also known as Coumba Ndoffène Fandepp, not to be confused with the first Coumba Ndoffène Diouf, Coumba Ndoffene Famaag, who was king from 1853 to 1871. The council's decision was rejected by the colonial administration, which instead divided the Sine into two main cantons, with two different chiefs, and effected the de facto abolition of the monarchy. This led to the rebellion of the population, which refused to pay taxes.—Eds.]

46. [The Code de l'indigénat, also called the *régime de l'indigénat*, was a penal administrative system adopted in 1881 in Algeria and Cochinchina and generalized to all French colonies in 1887. These regulations, officially intended to administer French colonial possessions, allowed the differentiation between nationality and citizenship, thereby institutionalizing inequality between French citizens (*citoyens*) and French colonial subjects (*sujets*). The Code de l'indigénat subjected the latter to forced labor, restrictions of movement, requisitions without warrant, and hefty taxes, among other degrading rules and laws. Forced labor, one of the most significant aspects of the Code de l'indigénat, enabled France to undertake large-scale projects, such as the construction of railroads, as documented by André Gide in *Voyage au Congo* (Gallimard, 1927). The Code de l'indigénat was officially abolished in 1946, though it was only in 1956 that legal equality between all citizens of the French Empire was finally established.—Eds.]

47. [Henri Labouret, "Citoyenneté d'Empire," in Verdier, *L'Homme de couleur*, 356.—Eds.]

48. [Delavignette, *Soudan–Paris–Bourgogne*, 72.—Eds.]

49. [Delavignette, *Soudan–Paris–Bourgogne*, 48.—Eds.]

50. [Senghor is referencing his own election to the French National Assembly, in October 1945, the same year he made this speech. The young *agrégé* won the votes of the peasants who not only saw him as one of them but also appreciated his new stature as the first Black man to hold an *agrégation.*—Eds.]

51. [The Palais Bourbon is the seat of the Assemblée nationale (National Assembly).—Eds]

52. [Labouret, "Citoyenneté d'Empire," 357.—Eds.]

53. [Senghor's text was originally published in 1945, less than a year after the granting of women's suffrage in France on April 21, 1944.—Eds.]

54. [Jean-Baptiste Colbert (1619–83) was a French statesman and comptroller general of finance under King Louis XIV. Émile Bélime (1883–1969) was a French public works engineer and colonial official in Niger; he authored several studies of colonial agriculture, infrastructure, and economics, including *La production du coton en Afrique occidentale française* (Publications du Comité du Niger, 1925).—Eds.]

55. [*Nawetaan* are seasonal agricultural workers.—Eds.]

56. [École William-Ponty is a teachers' college based in Senegal. The alma mater of most of the first generation of African leaders, it was founded in Saint-Louis, in 1903, before it moved to Gorée in 1913, and then to Sébikotane, a town and commune near Dakar, in 1938. William-Ponty resettled in Thiès in 1970, and finally in Kolda in 1984.—Eds.]

57. [Roger Dumargue, "L'Enseignement du français à l'École W. Ponty (AOF)," *L'Information d'Outre-mer* 1 (1939): 27–32.—Eds.]

58. [The *dissertation and explication de texte* are French academic, namely scholastic, genres of argumentation or commentary and literary analysis, respectively.—Eds.]

59. [The *honnête homme* was a seventeenth-century model gentleman—a social, intellectual, and moral ideal.—Eds.]

60. [René Maran, *Batouala: Véritable roman nègre* (Albin Michel, 1921). Maran won the Prix Goncourt the year of the novel's publication, making him the first Black writer to do so. Famously, the novel was banned in 1928 in France's colonies for the critiques of colonialism contained in the novel's preface.—Eds.]

17

Why an Indo-African Department at the University of Dakar?

The *Institut fondamental d'Afrique noire* [IFAN; Fundamental Institute of Black Africa], as its name suggests, is an institute of the University of Dakar focusing, above all, on fundamental research with a particular emphasis on the humanities and natural sciences.

From this perspective, its essential mission is to study the *Black Man* of Africa: his prehistory as well as his history, his languages, his arts, and, generally, the society in which this man has lived. In other words, the aims of IFAN's activities are the systematic inventory of the physical, biological, and social environment in which the Negro-African dwells as well as the constitution, conservation, and enrichment of foundational collections that are indispensable to a profound knowledge of Black Africa. In short, IFAN is an organization whose main role is to encourage, promote, and publish academic works pertaining to Black Africa in general, West Africa in particular.

That is to say that Senegal finds, in this academic institution, a privileged instrument for the implementation of its cultural politics, which is, first of all, a commitment to being rooted in Negro-African values or, in a word, in *Negritude*.

However, although its mission has been to work toward the cultural renaissance of Black Africa in particular, IFAN has recently expanded its field of action to the Indian subcontinent with the creation of an *Indo-African Department*. Why such an innovation? That is, precisely, what I would like to discuss with you today.

Before going any further, I must thank my compatriot Cheikh Tidiane Ndiaye, who is working on a doctoral thesis on *Wolof* (one of the languages of the Senegalo-Guinean group) *and Dravidian languages*. Indeed, thanks to his research, he has confirmed to me what Miss Lilias Homburger, my professor at the École pratique des hautes études, suggested: the kinship of Negro-African and Dravidian languages. This conference owes much to Ndiaye.

If I have decided that the Fundamental Institute of Black Africa should draw a parallel between India and Africa by studying the two together, in the same department of research, it is for many reasons: subjective reasons, of course, but also objective reasons.

Among these subjective reasons, the first is that, with respect to geography, Indians are neighbors to us, Sudano-Sahelian people. On the other hand, in the 1950s, I knew Mister Malcolm Adiseshiah, then deputy general director of UNESCO, who, having become my friend, introduced me to Dravidian realities, which, since then, I feel are so close to Negro-African realities.

Geographical and Prehistorical Reasons

To come back to geography, the south of India is on the same latitude as Senegal, Mali, Niger, Tchad, Soudan, Ethiopia, and Somalia. Even better, there is only the Indian Ocean between the eastern coast of Africa and the south of India. Moreover, geologists claim that the Indian subcontinent was, in the past, attached to East Africa. The evidence revealed by marine biology is of paramount importance for this question.

Thus, were prehistorians able to work in the underwater depths, they would discover ancient lithic industries—if not human fossil skeletons—in this area located between eastern Africa and the south of India, unless the Indian Ocean had formed before the emergence of the human species. In any case, the *Tamil* legends speak of existence, in an immemorial time, of flourishing cities that have been engulfed by the ocean.

That is, perhaps, an allusion to the land that would have connected India to Africa and would have been invaded by the ocean during the great neolithic revolution, that is, the period of prehistory when *Homo sapiens* accomplished his "first revolution" by laying the foundations of a historic civilization thanks to the new techniques he had invented. I note, in passing, that it is certainly not a coincidence if these first civilizations, born in the valleys of the Nile, the Tigris, and the Euphrates, and finally the Indus, have borne the marks of the Black Man. But perhaps it is, simply, about a vague souvenir of a universal deluge, which the *Sangami* have attempted to give a poetic interpretation in their old literary monuments such as the *Cilappatikāram*?[1]

Furthermore, it is remarkable that the Pithecanthropus—proconsuls and Australopithecus—who, without being the ancestors of the human species, are zoologically its neighbors, like the *infra-* and *parahominiens*, have flourished, at the same time, in eastern Africa and in the south of India. This is what Pierre Teilhard de Chardin noted in the *Apparition de l'homme* [Appearance of man]. "It is," he wrote, "on a tropical and subtropical land of the Ancient World—an area extending, in fact, throughout India, up to Malaysia, but singularly centered on the African continent—that the evolution of higher primates became more and more concentrated."[2]

Thus, if it has been proven that eastern Africa and the Indian subcontinent were linked, we would need to nuance the thesis that considers East Africa to be the cradle of humanity, a thesis defended by many of the leading prehistorians and anthropologists, such as Camille Arambourg, Henri Breuil, Louis S. B. Leake, Van Riet Lowe, Marcelin Boule, and Pierre Teilhard de Chardin. In other words, we could consider not only East Africa to be the cradle of humanity but rather the entire area located between eastern Africa and the south of India.

The thesis, reformulated in this way would no longer have many contradictions with Islamic thought, according to which Adam, the father of humanity, appeared in India and Awa, our maternal ancestor, in southern Arabia, the two having met in Harafat. What a curious coincidence that *attan* is the word designating "father" in Tamil (given that *n* can be replaced with *m* in this language), and *ava* the word designating "mother" in Kannada (*avai* in Tamil, *av* in Kota, *avë* in Kodagu).[3]

Historical and Racial Reasons

But, beyond geography and prehistory, there are *historical* links.

In fact, since they were located on both sides of Arabia and the Semitic world, it was natural that, as soon as the beginning of the Arabic incursion into foreign countries, India and Black Africa became the first and the most profoundly affected by the Islamic movement. This is such that the influences of Arabo-Islamic civilization—in a word, of Arabness [*Arabité*]—on *Indianness* [*Indianité*] and *Negritude* are considerable and more or less of equal value. These contributions are, moreover, reciprocal because Black people were already there when the Semites arrived in the Middle East, as well as in India.

On the other hand, because both are located at the crossroads of the major trade routes that colonial powers used to discover new lands from the fifteenth to the seventeenth centuries, India and Black Africa were well suited to sustain, one after the other, the influence of the Portuguese, the English, and the French. That is why, to this day, we have in India and in Black Africa, the same vestiges of European colonization in diverse areas, especially in that of linguistics. For example, I have just discovered that the Portuguese word *saboola*, "onion," has given the Sereer *sibola* and the Wolof *soble*, and the word *saboola* in Malayalam, a language spoken in the center of the State of Kerala. In the same way, the word designating "key" in Wolof, *caabi*, and the same word in many Indian languages come from the Portuguese *caavi*.

The anthropological links, I mean, the links that exist between the Dravidians and the Blacks of Africa, the *Negro-Africans*, are even stronger than the affective links of colonial history. It is, in fact, unquestionable that the Dravidians share the same Black blood with their brothers from Africa and the diaspora. The ancient Greeks, who called all Blacks *Aithiopes*, were not mistaken. They only differentiated between "Eastern Ethiopians," or Blacks from Asia, and "Western Ethiopians," or Blacks from Africa. Keen observers, they divided them between "straight hair," "curly hair," and "wooly hair." I suggest you read Snowden Junior's book entitled *Blacks in Antiquity*.[4]

We know that attempts have been made by anthropologists to identify the Dravidians with what has been called the "Mediterranean race." This appellation is confusing since it can suggest an interpretation of the notion of *race* based on geographical delimitation. Yet, if the notion of race is stripped of certain superfluous details, it is essentially—though not exclusively—reduced to the color of the epidermis. It is in this sense that we speak of a "Black race," a "White race," and a "Yellow race."

Therefore, it would have been more appropriate to call this Mediterranean race a "Negroid race," as certain scholars do, because its characteristic features are, precisely, those of the Black race in general: dolichocephaly and dark and brown skin—the two last adjectives being, most often, only euphemisms for

"Black." I refer you to the description that Alexandre Moret gave of the ancient Mediterranean.[5] It is worth recalling that the ancient Greeks did not consider the ancient inhabitants of the North-West of Africa, known today as the Maghreb—Morocco, Algeria, Tunisia—to be "White" since they called their inhabitants *Mauroi*, "Moors," that is, "men with dark [*sombre*] skin." And Herodotus, in the fifth century BC, teaches us that the Colchians, a people of the Middle East, were "Black like Egyptians."[6]

Furthermore, as I have said in a lecture on the "Foundations of Africanity or Negritude and Arabism" given at the University of Cairo in February 1967,[7] my professor at the Institute of Ethnology of Paris, Dr. Paul Rivet, used to say that "there is 4 to 20 percent of Black blood around the Mediterranean." He was, thus, alluding to the Negroids of the upper Paleolithic and the Mesolithic periods—Grimaldi man and Caspian man who had been an important element of the Mediterranean up to the Neolithic period.

Must we mention the other tendency that prevails in the works of several anthropologists and ethnologists, which consist of designating Dravidians and Ethiopians, Somalis and Sudanese, Nilotics and Fulɓe and Tutsis, and even Berbers, with the appellation of "Hamitic race"? In this instance, too, I will say that the appellation is confusing, because even if the Ethiopians and the latter groups are marginal, they are incontestably Black, in the way that the Berbers, in general, are marginal Whites. In reality, the word "Hamite," which ultimately designates nothing other than Black peoples—call them "marginal" if you prefer—is a political pretext. How, in fact, can we speak of men with "black skin" who are not "Black," if not "Negroes," and, at the same time, designate White Americans as "Negroes" because they have a drop of Black blood?

We will ignore all the theories relating to the origins of the Dravidians, for the problem is far from being resolved. We will only retain this one: *There is a Black subrace in the population of the south of India.* This granted, it is important not to underestimate the blood links that unite Dravidians and Blacks from Africa. Especially since the Black Dravidian subrace is the same as the Black subrace of eastern Africa that lives along the same latitude. During my last stay in Addis Ababa, I was struck by the significant number of Ethiopians who, with their refined features, their Black skin, and their straight hair, resembled Dravidians. I mentioned this to the Emperor, who, with a knowing look, merely smiled, royal.

In summary, the similarity between India and Black Africa, as we see it, finds its foundations in geography, anthropology, prehistory, and history.

It is this similarity that I would like to develop now by examining the cultural facts, that is, the values of civilization.

First, in *Ethnology*, there are the facts revealed by several authors, German ethnologists, in particular.

The first among them, Leo Frobenius,[8] defined an "Eritrean culture" that would be the remnant of an *ancient culture common to meridional Asia—particularly India—and Black Africa*. This culture would have entered Africa through the north and the south—through the Red Sea and Ethiopia, on the one hand, and through the coast of Mozambique, on the other.

Among the characteristic features of this cultural cycle, I will recall *metallurgy* and *cotton spinning*, in particular. This will allow me to show that, in effect, this "Eritrean culture" is the remnant of an ancient *Indo-African culture*. Indeed, the vocabulary related to metallurgy, on the one hand, and cotton spinning, on the other, happens to be exactly the same in Negro-African languages and in the Dravidian languages of India.

With respect to metallurgy, we can draw the following connections: Wolof *xanjar*, "bronze"; Pulaar [*poular*] *xanjara*, "bronze"; Telugu *xancara*, "a work of bronze"; Bambara *numu*, "forge," and Telugu *inumu*, "iron"; Wolof *kamara*, "name of the blacksmith caste"; and Telugu *kamara*, "name of the blacksmith caste." *Kamara* is found in other Dravidian and several Indo-Arian languages. As for cotton spinning, Wolof uses the verb *ëc*, "work on raw cotton to transform it," which can be compared to the Pengo verb *ec*, "to card cotton."

Following Leo Frobenius, G[eorge]. Montandon[9] defined *seven cultural cycles in Black Africa, four of which would be in relation with certain sectors in India, Malaysia, and the Oceanic islands*. Based on the list of the elements of these four cultural cycles made by D[enis].-P[ierre]. de Pedrals,[10] we identify the following elements:

1 For the *totemic cycle*: *totemism*, patriarchal exogamic clans, initiation rites with genital mutilation, the round hut with a conical roof, the penile or phallic sheath, and the *use of assegai*.[11]
2 For the *paleo-matriarchal cycle*: the matriarchate, exogamic matrimonial classes, feminine initiation ceremonies, masculine secret societies with masks, worship of ancestors, lunar mythology, magic, wooden drums, with *hoe-farming* and square gabled huts.
3 For the *neomatriarchal cycle*: matriarchy, monogamy, a ceremony for the first menstruation, worship of ancestors, magic, twilled basketry, ceramics, *hoe farming, domestication of dogs and fowl*, stilt houses.
4 For the *pastoral cycle*: *breeding livestock*, milk-based food, metallurgy, social classes, dome-shaped huts.

As we will have noticed, for each of these cultural cycles, we have, by design, noted one or two elements because we would like, thereby, to focus on these elements.

Regarding *totemism*, it is important to note that the word *cubbaa* (DED, 2203),[12] designating the "peacock" in Kurukh, is also found in the proper name *joob* in Wolof, borne by all the members of the clan who have the peacock as a totem. As a matter of fact, we say *jambë joob*, which means that "the peacock's name is *Diob*." Or again, *Jooba Juba*, which is the hypocoristic formula to call any individual from this group who has the peacock as a totem. Furthermore, Mister Cheikh Tidiane Ndiaye, has told me that he has discovered, among other things, the following rule of phonological correspondence: the voiced palatal *j* in Wolof = the voiceless palatal *c* in Dravidian.

As for the *use of the assegai*, we can equate the Wolof word *xeej*, "assegai," and the Gondi Muria *kac*, "assegai." Note, by the way, the following morphophonological rule: Wolof CVVC and Dravidian CVCC.[13]

As for *hoe farming*, the Wolof have the word *konko* "curved hoe," which is exactly the same as the Naiki word *konki*, "curved hoe." I refer you to entry 1689 in the *Dravidian Etymological Dictionary*.

As for *domestication of dogs and fowl*, it is easy to connect, on the one hand, the Wolof word *kuti*, "young dog," to the Tamil word *kutti*, "young dog" (DED, 1390); and, on the other hand, to connect the Wolof word *kur*, most often used to name fowl, to the Kui word *kuur*, used to name fowl, as W[alter Warren] Winfield notes.[14]

Finally, regarding *livestock breeding*, the following comparisons are quite noteworthy: Wolof *xar*, "sheep," and Brahui *xar*, "ram" (DED 943); Wolof *nag*, "cow," Sereer *nask*, Pulaar [*poular*] *nagge* and Tamil *naaku*, "female buffalo," Tulu *naaki*, "heifer," Kota *nag*, "young female buffalo between two and three years old" (DED, 3010); Pulaar [*poular*] *mbeewa*, "goat," and Parji *meeva*, "goat" (DED, 4174); Sereer *bir*, "to draw milk," Pulaar [*poular*] *birde*, and Konda *piir*.

In addition to Leo Frobenius and G[eorge]. Montandon, H[ermann]. Baumann and D[iedrich]. Westermann also have said a word or two about the cultural relationship between India and Black Africa. In fact, in their book entitled *Les peuples et les civilisations de l'Afrique* [Peoples and civilizations of Africa],[15] they consider that *certain agricultural methods in the "neo-Sudanese cultural cycle" (soil fertilization, terraced farming, irrigation canals, etc.) began with a wave of men coming from the south of India* through Abyssinia or Ethiopia. It seemed that their route, from the Nile to Senegal, was scattered with certain agricultural tools as well as megalithic monuments corresponding to agrarian cults.

Still on the topic of the cultural kinship between southern India and sub-Saharan Africa, it is important to mention the work of André Leroi-Gourhan and Jean Poirier. In their book on the *Ethnology of the French Union*,[16] they noted the resemblance of various objects found in Togo to Indian objects: war axes, daggers with ring-shaped handles, ankle rings, and more. These are, moreover, the same objects that D. P. de Pedrals had inventoried as being elements of Montandon's "Sudanoid" cultural cycle, to which he added *jewelries with replicas in India*.

In short, it is in the context of all these cultural correspondences that we must situate [Friedrich] Ratzel's famous formula: "Almost all of Africa appears as a single great ensemble of more or less faint echoes of Asia."[17]

Linguistic Reasons

We have just touched on linguistics by way of ethnology. We shall now return to linguistics by saying one or two things about the *kinship between Dravidian languages and Negro-African languages*.

In the nineteenth century, Alfredo Trombetti was one of the first to suspect that Dravidian languages and Negro-African languages represented a common language, related to Sumerian.[18] Recently, in a letter addressed to a Cameroonian friend, Father Engelbert Mveng, on the process of deciphering the writing of the first historical civilization of the Indus valley, I said to him: "Like me, you would have thought to show the link between Egyptian writing, Dravidian writing, and Sumerian writing. I have the impression that there is, at the origin of the three civilizations, a Black blood and, better, a Black spirit." In any case, the Negroids were the first to occupy the valleys of Egypt, Mesopotamia, and the North-West of India, and to establish the first agrarian civilizations there during the Neolithic period. "These first colonizers of the eastern valleys," Alexandre Moret writes, "are Negroids, originally from Indo-African regions, chased northward by the transformation of forests and savannas into steppes."[19]

Allow me a brief digression on the relationship between the Sumerians and the Dravidians. We will note that A[rumugam]. Sathasivam of the University of Colombo, has clearly taken sides. For him, Sumerian writing has a Dravidian origin. Better, Sumerian is a Dravidian language. I encourage you to read his two books: *Sumerian, a Dravidian Language*[20] and *The Dravidian Origin of Sumerian Writing*.[21] This thesis, which is difficult to refute given the clarity and depth of its argument, confirms the conclusion that Father H[enry]. Heras from Bombay[22] had reached: that Mohenjo-Daro and Harappa culture precede Sumerian culture, and it is most likely that the former has engendered the latter.

The only difficulty regarding the question of the anteriority of this civilization of the Indus Valley to Sumerian civilization is that, according to archeologists, Sir John Marshall and Sir Mortimer Wheeler, for example, Mohenjo-Daro and Harappa civilization must have emerged over the course of the third millennium before our era (2800 BC), while Sumerian civilization already existed during the fourth millennium BC. But, according to Father Heras, the proto-Indian people, namely, the Dravidian people, had spread their Zodiac and perfected its division of time around 4980 BC. This point of view was confirmed by Father A[ntonio]. Romaña, then director of the *Observatorio del Ebro, Tortosa* [Ebre Observatory in Tortosa, Spain], when he claimed that "the beginning of the constellation of the Bull in Mohenjo-Darian society coincided with the winter solstice that year (4980 BC). It is thus that Father Heras, basing his argument on this claim and on his own reading of three inscriptions, asserted that "Mohenjo-Daro belongs to the fifth millennium before our era."[23]

Having come to the end of my digression, let us return to the kinship between Dravidian and African languages, through a review of authors that have studied the question.

Thus, Miss Lilias Homburger identified, in Jules Bloch's *Structure grammaticale des langues dravidiennes* [Grammatical structure of Dravidian languages],[24] a certain number of morphemes that can be found in many Sudano-Sahelian languages. Since, the idea of a kinship between Dravidian languages and certain Negro-African languages became dear to her. Thus, she began to study, successively, Senegalo-Guinean languages, Mande languages, Bantu languages, and Ancient Egyptian by comparing them to Dravidian languages. This is what led her to publish, in turn, the following articles: "Eléments dravidiens en peul" [Dravidian elements in Pulaar],[25] "Le télougou et les dialectes mandés" [Telugu and Mande dialects],[26] "Canara-Bantu,"[27] "De quelques éléments communs à l'égyptien et aux langues dravidiennes" [On several elements shared by Egyptian and Dravidian languages],[28] and, finally, "Les sonantes en sindo-africain" [The sonorous consonants in Sindo-African].[29]

We need to keep in mind that Miss Homburger was convinced of two things: on the one hand, she was convinced that "Dravidian languages allowed us to explain the morphology of the Senegalese group and, in particular, that of the Pulaar-Sereer."[30] On the other, she was certain that there was a kinship between Kannada and Bantu languages.[31] In fact, the Bantu infinitive form ending in *-a*, its subjunctive in *-e*, preterit in *-i* or in *-idi*, and nominal agents in *-i* can be found, with the same values in Kannada and other Dravidian languages. The suffix of the Bantu causative is *-is*, while, in Kannada, the suffix *-is/u* plays a similar role. The dative *-ku* is characteristic in the Bantu and Kannada groups (and in other Dravidian languages): It is pre-posed in Bantu and post-posed in Kannada.

Unfortunately, Miss Homburger has passed away without having the time to deepen her theories.

We must also note an article by Edwin H. Tuttle on the *Nubian and the Dravidian*.[32] This article of ten or so pages is a brief inventory of facts rather than a detailed study. Yet he does not provide us with indications of the nature of the kinship between the Nubian and the Dravidian.

The dissertation currently being written by the Senegalese Cheikh Tidiane Ndiaye, "The Kinship between Wolof and Dravidian Languages," is the only complete study that has been undertaken at this point.[33] This dissertation, which I consider particularly important, addresses, simultaneously, phonology, morpho-phonology, grammar (morphology and syntax), and lexicology. We hope that Ndiaye will take full advantage of his three-year stay at the University of Annamalai as a *Senior Research Fellow*.

Conclusion

If I have attempted to present here the reasons why the Fundamental Institute of Black Africa (IFAN) has opened an *Indo-African Department*; it was, as you might guess, to arrive at the conclusion that Dravidians and Blacks from Africa have great interest in collaborating in the field of fundamental research in order to examine together the points of convergence—better, of kinship—in the values of civilization belonging to both Black worlds, I mean the Black Dravidian World and the Black African World.

By way of conclusion, I would like to go back to Lilias Homburger, that is, to the time when, as a young teacher of French, Latin, and Greek, I was also taking courses in prehistory and linguistics at the Institut d'Ethonologie de Paris on the one hand, and at the École pratique des hautes études on the other.

It was during this period that there began to emerge in me a certain vision of the past of Black peoples. During the Neolithic period, they occupied our *Fertile Crescent* and laid the foundations of *Civilization*. By "Fertile Crescent," I mean the arc stretching from the Straits of Gibraltar to the north of the Indochinese peninsula. And yet Black people occupied the Mediterranean Basin and all of South Asia, along with the Middle East, the Indian subcontinent, and the Indochinese peninsula. They are the ones who laid the foundations of the first historical civilizations: Egyptian, Sumerian, and Dravidian.

The poetic stories of ancient Greeks were not, therefore, far-fetched, since they were *poiêsis*, that is, an expression of human realities. Thus, for the ancient

Greeks, *Ethiopians*, that is, Blacks, were the most ancient inhabitants of the earth, and they had invented religion and law, art and writing.

When during these years, I examined, the images, I mean, the potteries and sculptures, of the first civilization of the Indus Valley reprinted in books, I was struck by the resemblance between their style and that of Black Africa. And I was not surprised when a bulletin [*flash*] from UNESCO announced, in 1969, that the writing of this first civilization translated a Dravidian language.

I managed to acquire the pamphlet in which Mister Asko Parpola, of the Scandinavian Institute of Asiatic Studies told the story of the deciphering of that writing.[34] This scholar reveals to us that the language was a Dravidian language, that Hinduism was nothing other than the religion of the ancient Dravidians, and, moreover, that it was close to that of the ancient Egyptians with its animal gods, but also that it was a religion rethought by Arian minds.

There we had it, the confirmation of the thesis that, as a militant of Negritude in the 1930s, I defended along with my friends Aimé Césaire and Léon Damas. This thesis was, still is, that, far from being ashamed of our Black skin and of our original civilizational values, we must be proud of them. For, as Césaire—who invented the word "Negritude"—says, we are "veritably the firstborn children of the world." And I say that before we became consumers, we had been, for millennia, the first producers of civilization.

However—and this point is important—, it is *métissage* that made the flourishing of historical civilizations, be it Egypt, Sumer, or India, possible. A civilization without mixture is a cultural ghetto. As the French anthropologist Paul Rivet noted, all historical civilizations born along the latitudes of the Mediterranean come from the *métissage* of Blacks and Whites or Blacks and East Asians [*Jaunes*]. The merit of these civilizations and, first, of Indian civilization is to have incarnated the dichotomous reason of Whites in the intuitive reason of Blacks—and it is said that the East Asians [*Jaunes*] participate in both—the purest spirit in the most rhythmic, most alive flesh. This is the ideal of any great civilization. In any case, that is the ideal of the *panhuman Civilization* that is being developed, during this second half of the twentieth century, with the participation of all nations but more importantly of the three great ethnicities—and their *métis*.

[Please note that I had to standardize the transcription of the Dravidian languages and the languages of the Senegalo-Guinean group in the text. This has led me to use Senegalese transcription for Dravidian languages.

Here are some precisions that will allow the reader not to get lost:

1 Implosives of the Senegalo-Guinean group are rendered with a circumflex accent. Examples: Sereer *ɓ̂ir*, "to draw milk."
2 Palatals are noted *j, c, ñ, y*.
3 Long vowels are indicated by doubling the vowel.
4 The nasalized consonants are noted in a very simple way. For example, *nc* and not *ñc, [ñ]k*.]

NOTES

Léopold Sédar Senghor, "Pourquoi un département indo-africain à l'Université de Dakar," in *Liberté 3: Négritude et civilisation de l'universel* (Seuil, 1977), 480–92. The text was first given as a talk at the Annamalai University in Chidambaram, Tamil Nadu, India, May 24, 1974.

1. [The *Cilappatikāram* is the earliest Tamil epic, a tragic love poem of 5,730 lines composed mostly in *akaval* (*aciriyam*) meter.—Eds.]

2. [Pierre Teilhard de Chardin, *L'apparition de l'homme* (Seuil, 1956), 279. The original reads slightly differently: "[C]'est (à partir de l'Oligocène) sur une aire tropicale et subtropicale de l'Ancien Monde,—aire se prolongeant en fait, à travers l'Inde, jusqu'en Malaisie (Orangs, Gibbons), mais principalement axée sur le continent Africain (Chimpanzés, Gorilles),—que s'est peu à peu concentrée l'évolution des Primates supérieurs."—Eds.]

3. Thomas Burrow and Murray B. Emmeneau, *Dravidian Etymological Dictionary* (Clarendon Press, 1961), entries 121 and 232, pages 12 and 20.

4. Frank M. Snowden Jr., *Blacks in Antiquity: Ethiopians in Greco-Roman Experience* (Harvard University Press, 1970).

5. Alexandre Moret, *Histoire de l'Orient*, tome 1 (Presses universitaires de France, 1941), 29.

6. [Senghor is referring to Book 2, section 104, where Herodotus writes, "For it is plain to see that the Colchians are Egyptians; and this that I say I myself noted before I heard it from others. [. . .] I myself guessed it to be so, partly because they are dark-skinned and woolly-haired." Herodotus, *The Histories*, trans. A. D. Godley (Harvard University Press, 1920), 391–92.—Eds.]

7. [Léopold Sédar Senghor, *Les fondements culturels de l'Africanité ou Négritude et Arabité* (Présence Africaine, 1969). The text was first given as a talk at the University of Cairo in 1967 and republished in *Liberté 3: Négritude et civilisation de l'universel* (Seuil, 1977), 105–50.—Eds.]

8. Leo Frobenius, *Der Ursprung der afrikanischen Kulturen* (Berlin: Verlag Von Gebrüder Borntraeger, 1897–99).

9. Georges Montandon, *L'Ologénèse culturelle: Traité d'éthnologie cyclo-culturelle et d'ergologie systématique* (Payot, 1934).

10. Cf. Denis-Pierre de Pedrals, *Manuel scientifique de l'Afrique noire* ([Payot] 1949).

11. [An assegai is a type of light wooden spear or javelin, usually with a wooden tip. In Wolof, it would be called a *xeej*.—Eds.]

12. [DED refers to entries in Burrow and Emmeneau, *Dravidian Etymological Dictionary*.—Eds.]

13. [CVVC refers to the syllable structure consonant-vowel-vowel-consonant; CVCC, to a syllable structure consonant-vowel-consonant-consonant.—Eds.]

14. Walter Warren Winfield, *A Vocabulary of the Kui Language* (Asiatic Society of Bengal, 1929).

15. Hermann Baumann and Diedrich Westermann, *Les peuples et les civilisations de l'Afrique*, trans. Lilias Homburger (Payot, 1948).

16. André Leroi-Gourhan and Jean Poirier, *Ethnologie de l'Union Française*, vol. 1: *Afrique* (Presses Universitaires de France, 1953).

17. ["The population of Africa has undoubted affinities with that of Asia." See Friedrich Ratzel, *The History of Mankind*, trans. A. J. Butler (Macmillan, 1986), 6.—Eds.]

18. [Alfredo Trombetti (1866–1929) was an Italian linguist renowned for his work in comparative linguistics and his advocacy of the monogenesis theory, which hypothesized that all human languages originated from a single ancestral language. His research encompassed a wide range of languages, including those of the Caucasus, Semitic languages, and others, as he sought to identify connections supporting his monogenesis theory.—Eds.]

19. [Moret, *Histoire de l'Orient*, 38.—Eds.]

20. Abumugam Sathasivam, *Sumerian: A Dravidian Language* (Berkeley, 1965).

21. Abumugam Sathasivam, "The Dravidian Origin of Sumerian Writing," *Proceedings of the First International Conference Seminar of Tamil Studies, Kuala Lumpur, Malaysia, 1966*, vol. 2 (International Association of Tamil Research, 1969), 673–78.

22. Henry Heras, *Studies in Proto-Indo-Mediterranean Culture*, vol. 1 (Indian Historical Research Institute, 1953).

23. ["Mohenjo-Daro therefore must belong to the beginning of this millennium or to the fifth millennium B.C." Heras, *Studies in Proto-Indo-Mediterranean Culture*, 230.—Eds.]

24. [Jules Bloch, *Structure grammaticale des langues dravidiennes* (Adrien-Maisonneuve, 1946).—Eds.]

25. Lilias Homburger, "Eléments dravidiens en peul," *Journal des Africanistes* 18, no. 2 (1948): 135–43.

26. Lilias Homburger, "Le télougou et les dialectes mandés," *Journal des Africanistes* 21, no. 2 (1951): 113–26.

27. This article constitutes a chapter in Lilias Homburger, *Les langues négro-africaines et les peuples qui les parlent* (Payot, 1957). [Lilias Homburger, "Annexe I: Le canara-bantou," in *Les langues négro-africaines et les peuples qui les parlent*, 2nd ed. (1940; reprint Payot, 1957), 324–29.—Eds.]

28. Lilias Homburger, "De quelques éléments communs à l'égyptien et aux langues dravidiennes," *Kêmi: Revue de philologie et d'archéologie égyptiennes et coptes* 14 (1957): 26–33.

29. Lilias Homburger, "Les sonantes en indo-africain," *Journal des Africanistes* 34, no. 2 (1964): 281–98.

30. [On these affinities, see Homburger, "Le sindo-africain," in *Les langues négro-africaines*, 302–23, esp. 322, regarding Pulaar. See also Homburger, "Annexe I: Le canara-bantou."—Eds.]

31. [See Homburger, "Annexe I: Le canara-bantou."—Eds.]

32. [Edwin H. Tuttle, "Dravidian and Nubian," *Journal of the American Oriental Society* 52, no. 2 (1932): 133–44.

33. [See, for instance, Cheikh Tidiane Ndiaye, " À propos des morphèmes aux signifiés comitatif, instrumental, ablatif et locatif en wolof et dravidien," *Bulletin de l'Institut Fondamental d'Afrique Noire* 43, nos. 1–2 (1981): 162–67.—Eds.]

34. Cf. *The Indus Script Decipherment* (Madras, 1970). [We have been able to locate only the following publication for 1970: Asko Parpola, Seppo Koskenniemi, Simo Parpola, and Pentti Aalto, *Further Progress in the Indus Script Decipherment* (Scandinavian Institute of Asian Studies, 1970). This study was preceded by Parpola et al., *Decipherment of the Proto-Dravidian Inscriptions of the Indus Civilization: A First Announcement* (Scandinavian Institute of Asian Studies, 1969), and Parpola et al., *Progress in the Decipherment of the Proto-Dravidian Indus Script* (Scandinavian Institute of Asian Studies, 1969).—Eds.]

18

Negritude and Mediterranean Civilization

This conference, "Black Africa and the Mediterranean World in Antiquity," seems to me one of the most important conferences ever held in our capital since Independence. It is not a coincidence that I titled my talk, "Negritude and Mediterranean Civilizations." Indeed, I would like to examine a major matter of civilization in the spirit of the *Dakar School*, that is, in relation to Black Africa.

In the first instance, no perspective could be more productive than the historical perspective, since this perspective encompasses—in the concrete sense of time—prehistory along with history, and—in the mental sense—Culture along with Politics and the Economy.

If I have correctly understood Mister Louis Lonis, the head of the Department of Ancient History, who, under the authority of Dean [Jean-Paul] Morel, has organized this conference, it is a matter of studying the presence and influence of Negro-Africans in the first Mediterranean civilizations from the triple perspectives of settlement, contacts, and relations: the influence of Negro-Africans, but also the influences to which they have been subject. This is what I translate as "Anthropology and Civilization," without, of course, forgetting History and Prehistory. But I know that the latter two disciplines will not be overlooked since, once again, the Department of History is the principal organizer of this event.

You can imagine that, if I accepted the invitation to open this conference, it is because it resonates with the Senegalese project of a new civilization and, more precisely, with the humanism of Negritude. It is always a matter of rooting ourselves in our multimillennial values of civilization while also opening ourselves to the fecundating values of other races, ethnicities, or peoples because they are complementary. That is why we should define and, in order to do so, study both civilizations as well as their mutual influences. In this perspective, we have begun training Senegalese specialists in the neighboring languages and civilizations of Berbery, Ancient Egypt, Sumer, and Dravidian India, among others. I have said "India." It is because the Negro in question is not solely from Africa. By exploring this avenue of research, we are merely confirming the direction taken by several Black intellectuals who began defining the contributions of Negroes to Mediterranean civilizations many years ago. Among these intellectuals, the most renowned are Cheikh Anta Diop, Frank M. Snowden Jr., Engelbert Mveng, and Théophile Obenga.

It is within this framework that I would like to situate my reflections, as they have developed since the 1930s, when I took courses at the Institute of Ethnology in Paris and at the École pratique des hautes études, with professors such as Marcel Mauss, Paul Rivet, Marcel Cohen, and Lilias Homburger, among others.

I remember Paul Rivet affirming, during the rise of Nazism, that there was about "4 to 20 percent of Black blood around the Mediterranean." Leaning over to my neighbor, I added, with a smile: "At least!" Indeed, I knew that with 25 percent of Black blood, one can pass as White, and vice versa. But it was later—after the disaster of 1940—when, as a prisoner of war, I had the time to reflect for two years on Mediterranean languages and civilizations, which, since 1935, I had taught without seeking to penetrate their meaning, if not their intimate sense. I went on to discover that the "Mediterranean miracle," from the Egyptians to the Arabs, but first the "Greek miracle," was the miracle of cultural *métissage*.

I will begin my reflections from this idea.

The first question that presents itself to us is that of settlement. It could be formulated as follows: "What races and what peoples inhabited Mediterranean countries before the arrival of the Semites, but particularly the Indo-Europeans, that is, the Celts, the Greeks, the Latins, the Germans, and the Slavs?" "What peoples," I have said, while thinking, in particular, of those who, with writing, founded History in the valleys of the Nile, the Euphrates, and the Indus.

Before History, we must turn to Prehistory, keeping in mind two major facts on which prehistorians and anthropologists rely to establish two fundamental principles of their sciences. The first fact, as Professor Paul Rivet would tell us, is that before the upper Paleolithic period, when two races met, they often fought, and one would destroy the other. Since the upper Paleolithic period, and this is one of the features of *Homo sapiens*, they often fought, but they always mixed. It is this *métissage* that constitutes, precisely, the second fact.

From the facts presented here, we have deduced the following two principles:

- Since the emergence of *Homo sapiens*, two races or two peoples in contact always mix.
- Every major civilization is a cultural *métissage*.

Guided by these two major principles, we will study the Negro-African contributions, more specifically the *Negroid* contributions, in the settlement of Mediterranean countries.

There are numerous prehistorians and anthropologists who attribute Aurignacian civilization, the first civilization of the upper Paleolithic period, to the Negroids of the Grimaldi race. I will mention Paul Rivet, René Verneau, Henri Breuil and Raymond Lantier, Marcelin Boule, and Pierre Teilhard de Chardin, among others. In his *Histoire de l'orient* [History of the Orient],[1] Alexandre Moret clarifies, regarding the upper Paleolithic period, that "the Mediterranean zone and Europe were first inhabited by short-statured Negroids of the type of the Hottentots and the current Bochiman. [. . .] Negroids, before entering Europe through the Sicilian and Egea bridges, which fell apart shortly after their passage, [. . .] had inhabited North Africa. Until the Neolithic period and protohistorical times, their influence remains persistent in Egypt, in Tunisia, and in the Mediterranean basin."[2] But Professor René Verneau, the leading expert in Anthropology, corrects him: "Grimaldi Negroids are tall in stature and their skull is extremely advanced in height: Bochimans are dwarfs whose skull is remarkably flat from top to bottom."[3]

Regardless, other Negroids, namely the famous Capsians who, according to Tunisian scholars, had preceded the Berbers in their country, left Africa, in turn, to invade Europe. Moret writes: "What is important is that the genuine center of Capsian civilization is located at the median tip of North Africa.

From there, this Capsian art extended, on the one hand, to Iberia and Sicily, in Southern Italy; and, on the other hand, to Libya, Egypt, Syria-Palestine."[4]

According to prehistorian anthropologists, these Negroids, who intermixed with White Cro-Magnon men and, to a lesser extent, with individuals from the Chancelade culture, of the yellow race [*de race jaune*], evolved into *Homo mediterraneus*: dolichocephalic individuals, brown-skinned with long faces and of medium height, as described by Moret. They resemble the pre-Hellenic people depicted in Egyptian and Cretan frescoes, according to Jean Vercoutter.[5] Let us keep in mind that Vercoutter employs the phrase "red-brown," without mentioning "curly hair," which we will encounter later among North Africans [*Maghrébins*].[6]

If, from southern Europe and the islands, we orient our analysis toward North Africa and the Middle East, Moret distinguishes four races there: Capsian Negroids, Kushite Hamites, Semites, and Brachycephalics from the Alpes. The problem seems to me to be even more complex, and you will, no doubt, ask yourselves about the men who, during the African upper Paleolithic period, founded *Aterian* civilizations in the Maghreb and *Sibilian* civilizations in Egypt, alongside *Capsian* civilization. If, "during the Upper Paleolithic period," as Breuil and Lantier concluded, "there is evidence," in southern Europe, "of Negroid, Ethiopian, white, and probably yellow human strains,"[7] we need to underscore the persistence of negroid elements in North Africa, the Middle East, and India up to the historical era. It was even the Negroids themselves who, in the valleys of the Nile, the Euphrates, and the Indus, founded the first agrarian civilizations. "These first settlers in the Eastern valleys," argues Moret, "are Negroids originally from Indo-African regions, pushed toward the North by the transformation of forests into savannahs and then into steppes."[8] Their descendants would not be strangers to the invention of the first writing systems.

This presence of Black people in the historical era is confirmed by the following facts, among others. In Raymond Roget and Stéphane Gsell's anthology, *Le Maroc chez les auteurs anciens* [Morocco among the ancient authors],[9] I note that the Latin and Greek writers cited in the volume speak of the presence of Moorish people along with that of the Ethiopians, that is, of Black people.[10] And we know that ancient Greeks did not consider Moorish people White since *mauros* in Greek means "of a dark color," like the word "Sarrasin," in French, which refers to the Almoravid Berbers, given, as stated in the *Robert*, "the dark color of the grain" of the cereal. On the other hand, Herodotus informs us that the Colchians, in the south of Caucasia, were Black, while Lucan informs us that the Garamantes of Libya were *perusti*, "completely burnt," which is the translation of the Greek *aithiopès*. Finally, Asko Parpola, the linguist who deciphered the writing system of the first Indus civilization, revealed to us that it was the language of Dravidian Blacks and that this particular script dates to about 2500 BC, that is to say, a thousand years before the arrival of the Aryans.[11] I imagine that there must have been a moment, during the upper Paleolithic period or during the Neolithic period, when Negroids were discontinuously spread around the Mediterranean, particularly in the Middle East and in the entire southern part of Asia up to the islands of Oceania.

You will have noticed that, in the passages I have cited just above, Moret speaks to us of "Kushite-Hamites" along with "Negroids." Once again, the question of the *Hamites* is raised, and I would like to share my thoughts on this.

If I focus on Negro-Africans, without mentioning Blacks from Asia, Oceania, and the Americas, we tend to distinguish four subraces: *Ethiopians*, *Sudanese*, *Bantus*, and *Khoisans*. "Ethiopians," that is to say, the current Ethiopians from the North, the Somalis, the Nubians, and the Fulɓe are "marginal Negroes," while "marginal Whites" would be represented by North Africans today, namely, the Moors and the Tuaregs. As a Mauritanian intellectual told me, "The Moors are Arabic-speaking Berbers with a strong mixture of Black blood." To which could correspond the following definition of the Fulɓe: "Black people with a mixture of Berber blood who speak a Negro-African language."

To return to the Hamite question, European geographers, historians, prehistorians, and even anthropologists—and, even more so, politicians—have often fallen into the Europocentric trap that consists of labeling the same people "White" or "Black" depending on the interests of the moment. Before Mussolini, Ethiopians were "White"; since then, they have become again what they were according to the Greeks: "Black." And even Henri Gaden, who was, during his time, the leading French specialist of the Fulɓe, falls into what I call *Albocentrism*. Thus, in his book *Le Poular* [Pulaar], we find the following definition for the word *wode*: "qualifying theme: red. *Bodeejo*, pl. *wodeebe*: that which is of the white race in opposition to Blacks (*Baleebe*)."[12] In reality, the nomadic Fulɓe have three colors with which they designate the "black" color of the majority of Senegalese people (*Baleebe*), the "red" color of the Fulɓe (*Wodeebe*), and the white color of the Europeans (*Daneebe*). The best evidence that they do not disparage Blacks is in a story reproduced by Gaden himself and entitled "The Two Fulɓe Chiefs," where it is Hamadi the Black man who beats Hamadi the Red-skinned man.[13] One will have remarked, in passing, that the Fulɓe use the same word "red" as Jean Vercoutter, who went so far as to employ the expression of a "red-brown skin, often dark" to indicate the color of the Pre-Hellenics.

To conclude on the question of settlement, it is a matter of studying, by relying on facts, the progressive *albisation*, that is, the whitening of Mediterranean countries: from the upper Paleolithic period to the historical era.

Speaking of the Senegalese project, I specified that this was a matter of building a "new civilization." That is to say, the study of settlement is not the essence of the matter. It is merely a necessary prerequisite, it is true, to the study of the contacts and relations: of exchanges, and therefore, of reciprocal influences, I mean of cultural *métissages*.

We will thus have to explore this phenomenon, characteristic of *Homo sapiens*, at the dual levels of language and art, for it is in these areas that a civilization best defines itself. I will begin with language, which seems to me, despite appearances, the least characteristic phenomenon. Indeed, it is easily borrowed.

I will begin with Paul Rivet's article "The Oceanian Group."[14] He, indeed, had the gift of discovering Black presence everywhere in the world and not solely in Africa. In this article, he postulates "that the Sumerian world, whose contact with India is attested as early as three thousand years before our era, has played, in a certain age, an important role as an agent of transmission of cultural elements between the Oceanian group, Europe, and Africa."[15] Returning to this idea in a minor work entitled *Sumérien et Océanien* [Sumerian and Oceanian] where he points out a certain number of common roots to Oceanian, Semitic, and Indo-European languages, Rivet concludes: "I am more and more convinced that there has been, in the entire Mediterranean basin and in a more or less vast area of Africa, an Oceanian substrate that has exerted an influence over the populations of diverse origins who invaded these regions over the ages."[16]

To simplify, the Oceanian influence of which Professor Rivet speaks is nothing other than the influence of the Negroids in general, as it expressed itself during the prehistorical and protohistorical eras. What one should retain from his thesis is that, before the arrival of Indo-Europeans and Semites, Negroids had exercised a certain influence—a reciprocal one—on the languages of the brown Mediterranean peoples. This influence can be observed by every careful reader of *Les langues du monde* [The languages of the world], the seminal text published "by a group of linguists and edited by Antoine Meillet and Marcel Cohen."[17] It remains that, to perceive this influence, one must, in opposition to the geographical distribution adopted by my two former professors, and which has, I am aware of it, the merit of underscoring the reciprocal borrowings, put aside, on the one hand, Indo-European languages and, on the other hand, Semitic languages. This would, under our framework, juxtapose Mediterranean languages and Negro-African languages. By Mediterranean languages, I mean Basque, Berber, Coptic, Ancient Egyptian, Caucasian languages, and, among

Asiatic [*asianiques*] languages, Sumerian and Elamite. By "Negro-African languages," I mean, in addition to the Sudano-Guinean and Bantu groups, the Cushitic groups in the North and the Khoin in the South. I would have liked to classify the Eteo-Cretan, the Eteo-Cypriot, and the Etruscan among Mediterranean languages but these dialects remain little known despite the progress made in the past twenty years.

As I was saying earlier, it is in morphology that linguistic kinship can best be identified. From this standpoint, what characterizes Negro-African languages are the following common characteristics:

- Primitive biconsonantal roots
- Lack of a fundamental distinction between the noun and the verb
- Nominal classes
- Lack of nominal or verbal inflection and, consequently, an abundance of affixes
- The importance of aspect over tense, namely of perfect and imperfect aspects above all others

What is remarkable, once again, is that each of the Mediterranean languages mentioned earlier has, at least, two of these five common characteristics. Naturally, given their anthropological kinship, we find the same similarities in Dravidian and Oceanian languages, and even in certain languages of Pre-Colombian America, if we are to believe Paul Rivet and Alexander von Wuthenau.

That said, among Mediterranean languages, we should begin with those closest to Negro-African languages: with Berber but, before that, with ancient Egyptian and Coptic, as Lilias Homburger recommended to us in her courses. This is the moment to mention Théophile Obenga's insightful article entitled, "The Ancient Egyptian and the Negro African."[18]

It remains, once again, that among cultural phenomena, linguistic facts appear to me less convincing than artistic facts, insofar as we can collect them from prehistory onward. When, in the course of my official visits, I explore the prehistorical galleries in museums, I immediately recognize the negroid art objects without the need of any explanation. These objects bear the sign of negro rhythm like a seal. In anterior Europe and Asia, namely in Mediterranean countries, these works are almost always from the upper Paleolithic (Aurignacian) period, the Meso- or Neolithic periods, when not from the historical era. Nothing is surprising about this, for, as Élie Faure writes in "Incarnation du rythme noir" [Incarnation of Black rhythm]: "It is in the Black man that the interior meaning of rhythm has maintained itself in its purest form."[19]

However, negro rhythm is not the monotonous "repetition" denounced by the European petit bourgeois. Whether it is about sounds or colors, forms or gestures, it is a matter of reproducing the same sound, the same color, the same form, the same gesture, but in a different context, a different environment. Often—and here rhythm is of a superior quality—it is not a question of sameness but of similitude, not a question of the same color, for example, but of one of its shades.

However, negro rhythm cannot be reduced to this reproduction: to this reprise that is not repetition. It is not a simple movement of sensuality, as many have claimed: The rhythmic flesh is, through the act itself and at the same time, spiritualized. For the Black man, rhythm is one of the elements of language and it is not separate from the symbol. This is why I have defined the object in negro art as "a symbolic and rhythmic image." This is to say that it is the antithesis of realism or of naturalism, if you will. As Élie Faure puts it in the same article, "it is constantly a symbolic equivalent and not a representation of the universe."[20]

It is thus these two elements, rhythm and symbol, that fundamentally characterize negro art and allow us to detect its presence in prehistoric art objects. These objects are the most eloquent evidence of *Homo sapiens* and his Neolithic offspring.

And, first, the symbol or the analogical image, always in use and, spontaneously, in the popular art of Black Africa. The Black artist emphasizes the most significant parts of the object that, in Man, are at once the most carnal and the most sensual: the hair, the eyes, the nose, the mouth, the navel, above all the breasts, the genitals, and the curves of the hips. He not only does so by emphasizing them, enlarging them to a hypertrophic level, but also by endowing them with rhythm: giving them correspondents. These are, in some cases, echoes on the level of form or color; in other cases, responses—the concave responding to the convex, for example—; still in other cases, they are contretemps, that is asymmetrical parallelisms. Such is negro rhythm, which always offers responses but not where and when they are most expected. It is the surprise that unsettles confident expectation, diversity within unity.

From this point of view, nothing is more emblematic than the art of statuary. We will take this as the most significant example of Aurignacian art. Among the forty statues inventoried in Europe and Siberia in 1959, almost all of them were female. We found in them the characteristic features of negro art; that is, in addition to the symbolism of fertility, the stylization of negro rhythm with the lumbar curves or "steatopygia,"[21] Nubian hairstyles, and geometric tattoos. One will find this symbolism—though not always of fertility—and this stylization here and there around the Mediterranean up until the Neolithic period, and even up to the historical era. Besides Egypt, I am thinking, in particular, of Pre-Hellenic statuary—of the "little man from the Cyclades," for example—, of the statuary of the prehistoric Middle East or even of Carthage, which I examined with curiosity last year in Tunis in the company of Mister Bachaouche, Director of Antiquities.[22]

I have chosen the example of the art of statuary because it is the most significant, the genius of the Black artist being tectonic before all else. I could have chosen painting. The major point of my talk has been to draw your attention to the question of method. In the areas of art, linguistics, as well as anthropology, it is a matter of beginning by defining the features of Negritude before exploring its expression or, perhaps more exactly, its realization.

This brings me to my conclusion. Ultimately we must avoid two pitfalls: On the one hand, the prejudices of the Albo-Europeans, of which we have seen an example related to the Fulɓe; on the other hand, those of Negro-Africans that, from time to time, make their way into the heads of our scholars and, I admit, from which I myself have not always been exempt. But since it is easier to point fingers at the prejudices of others as opposed to one's own, I will point out, in conclusion, the challenges that confront African scholars in the study of Mediterranean antiquity.

One of my Ethiopian friends, who is preparing a doctoral thesis on the relationships between the theater of ancient Greece and that of Black Africa, told me about the revulsion expressed by conservators of Greek museums who were showing him Pre-Hellenic art objects that presented certain affinities with negro art. I believe I have found, in a different vein, echoes of this revulsion in *Le Nouvel Observateur* of August 12, 1975, where Mister Bernard Teyssèdre, speaking about the mural paintings of Thera temporarily exhibited at the archeological museum of Athens, writes: "The subjects painted at Thera are, in this context, unexpected: today, at Santorini, these swallows are no longer alive, [. . .] let alone the blue monkeys and Oryx antelopes (which, undoubtedly, have never lived there); the African-style earring, but also one of the pugilist children, are foreign to the Creto-Myceneans, but familiar to the Nubians. These paintings, let us not forget, had a religious dimension; in no way did they pretend to express daily life."[23] And so on! Fortunately, common sense and, even better, scientific objectivity ultimately triumph. And Mister Teyssèdre concludes: "The African themes of Thera, for us difficult to decipher, bear witness to the intense intermingling of peoples who, in the middle of the second millennium, traveled across the Aegean sea, the Near East and Egypt, at a time when the Cretans were landing in Libya, when European chariots descended upon the Sahara, when Hyksos, coming from the sea, reigned upon the Pharaohs' throne."[24]

If I have cited the art critic at such length, it is because his conclusion is similar to the one I intended to give, although it was necessary to insist here less on themes than on style. Thus, in addition to method, my conclusion will be a reminder of the two principles announced at the beginning of my talk: (1) Two peoples that enter into contact always mix; (2) every great civilization is a cultural *métissage*. To which I would add, for the researcher, the necessity of scientific objectivity. This does not exactly exclude a "sharpness of the mind," but what is better is the vision born of sensible intuition. It is on this basis, in any case, that the Senegalese government, after consultation, intends to make the theme of your conference one of the aspects of the research program at the Senegalese University.

Now, I have only to wish you the success that your conference deserves at this moment when the *Civilization of the Universal*, of which Senegal remains an active militant, appears on the eve of the twenty-first century.

NOTES

Léopold Sédar Senghor, "Négritude et civilisation méditerranéennes [*sic*]," in *Liberté 5: Le dialogue des cultures* (Seuil, 1993), 85–94. The text was first given as a talk at the conference "Afrique noire et monde méditerranéen dans l'Antiquité" (Black Africa and the Mediterranean World in Antiquity) in Dakar, January 19, 1976.

1. Alexandre Moret, *Histoire de l'Orient*, tome 1 (Presses universitaires de France, 1941), 19.

2. [Moret, *Histoire de l'Orient*, 19.—Eds.]

3. Cited in Henri Neuville, "Peuples ou races," in *Encyclopédie française*, tome 8, article 7, ed. Lucien Febvre (Société de Gestion de l'Encyclopédie Française, 1935), 52–58.

4. Moret, *Histoire de l'Orient*, 29.

5. Cf. Jean Vercoutter, *Essai sur les relations entre Égyptiens et Préhellènes* (A. Maisonneuve, 1954), 86.

6. I have since learned that when the Greeks arrived in what today is Greece, it was inhabited by Black people. Moreover, today's Greeks have 45 percent blood-type O, that is to say, African blood.

7. [Henri Breuil and Raymond Lantier, *Les hommes de la pierre ancienne (paléolithique et mésolithique), nouvelle édition revue et augmentée* (Payot, 1959), 167. See also Henri Breuil and Raymond Lantier, *The Men of the Old Stone Age (Paleolithic and Mesolithic)*, trans. B. B. Rafter (George G. Harrap, 1965), 132.—Eds.]

8. Moret, *Histoire de l'Orient*, 38.

9. Raymond Roget, *Le Maroc chez les auteurs anciens* (Les Belles Lettres, 1924) [Stéphane Gsell wrote the preface to the volume.—Eds.].

10. In the etymological sense of the word in Greek, *aithiops*, "ethiopian," means "a burnt, black face."

11. [See, for instance, Asko Parpola, Seppo Koskenniemi, Simo Parpola, and Pentti Aalto, *Decipherment of the Proto-Dravidian Inscriptions of the Indus Civilization: A First Announcement* (Scandinavian Institute of Asian Studies, 1969); Asko Parpola et al., *Progress in the Decipherment of the Proto-Dravidian Indus Script* (Scandinavian Institute of Asian Studies, 1969); and Asko Parpola et al., *Further Progress in the Indus Script Decipherment* (Scandinavian Institute of Asian Studies, 1970).—Eds.]

12. [Henri Gaden, *Le Poular: Dialecte peul du Fouta sénégalais*, vol. 2: *Lexique poular-français* (Ernest Leroux, 1914), 223–24.—Eds.]

13. [Henri Gaden, "Les deux chefs peuls," in *Le Poular: Dialecte peul du Fouta sénégalais*, vol. 1: *Étude morphologique; Textes* (Ernest Leroux, 1912), 120–29.—Eds.]

14. Paul Rivet, "Le Groupe Océanien," *Bulletin de la Société Linguistique de Paris* 27, fasc. 3 [nos. 81–83] (1926–27): 141–68.

15. [Rivet, "Le Groupe Océanien," 159.—Eds.]

16. Paul Rivet, *Sumérien et Océanien* (H. Champion, 1929), 8.

17. Centre National de la Recherche Scientifique [National Center of Scientific Research].

18. Théophile Obenga, "Égyptien ancien et Négro-Africain," *Cahiers Ferdinand de Saussure* 27 (1971–72): 65–92.

19. Élie Faure, *L'homme et la danse* (Pierre Fanlac, 1975), 37 [Senghor has misquoted the chapter title, which is "Incarnations du rythme noir" (Incarnations of Black rhythm), *L'homme et la danse*, 35–43.

20. [Faure, *L'homme et la danse*, 40. Senghor has elided the original slightly, which reads: "It is constantly a radical transposition of the object or of objects interrogated by the artist, a symbolic equivalent and not a representation of the universe."—Eds.]

21. Cf. Luce Passemard, *Les statuettes féminines paléolithiques dites 'Vénus stéatopyges'* (Teissier, 1938).

22. [Cycladic art, known especially for its small marble figurines, is one of the branches of Aegean art that flourished c. 3300 to 1100 BCE.—Eds.]

23. [Senghor has miscited the article; it is from the August 12, 1974, not 1975, issue. Bernard Teyssèdre, "Passant par Athènes: Sous les laves d'un volcan grec, une ville morte, deux fois plus vieille que Pompéi," *Le Nouvel Observateur*, August 12, 1974, 54.—Eds.]

24. [Teyssèdre, "Passant par Athènes," 54.—Eds.]

19

French and African Languages

Mister Pierre Dumont's doctoral thesis, titled *Les relations entre le français et les langues africaines au Sénégal* [The relations between French and African languages in Senegal], is timely.[1] It is no coincidence that, throughout my careful reading of his thesis during the summer of 1982, I thought of the debates at *Mondiacult*, that is, the *Conférence mondiale de l'UNESCO sur les politiques culturelles* (UNESCO World Conference on Cultural Policies), in which I had participated as president of the *Association des amis de Miguel Angel Asturias* [Association of Friends of Miguel Angel Asturias], which brings together Latin American and African intellectuals. As is known, this organization of the United Nations, led by the Senegalese Amadou Mahtar Mbow—a man of culture if ever there was one—has made the *dialogue of cultures* the primary objective of its activities. In this last quarter of the twentieth century, it is a matter of preparing, methodically, and with the help of all continents, races, and nations, the *Civilization of the Universal*: a fully human civilization because it is composed of the complementary contributions of all social groups.

A politician, after stating the problem at hand, would have begun by defining his policy—at least, the principles on which it is based—to solve all the economic and financial, social and cultural issues his nation faces. The professor that he is, Mister Pierre Dumont prefers, instead of this deductive, abstract method, to induce his cultural policy—for that is what is at stake—from the concrete situation that manifests itself in a country like Senegal. This is all the more effective given that my country, being the longest colonized and assimilated, is more readily convertible to a "cultural revolution." It remains that, paradoxically, dialectically, and by that very fact, it is easier both to analyze the situation and to find, at least theoretically, appropriate solutions.

However, before going further, I would like to tell you in a few words who Mister Dumont is. His father, a man of culture and experience, was my adviser on Muslim Affairs when I was president of the Republic of Senegal. One can judge the importance of this function by recalling that Muslims represent 85 percent of the population in Senegal. During this time, his son Pierre was, first, both an assistant and a researcher at the University of Dakar, before leading the *Centre de linguistique appliquée de Dakar* [Center for Applied Linguistics of Dakar], or CLAD, for several years. It was after the Senegalization of this position, and with his agreement, that he returned to France, where he now teaches African linguistics in Nice.[2]

What characterizes this book, which goes beyond linguistic science to discuss cultural and even political problems, is not only the breadth of knowledge in the various fields addressed but also the relevance of the judgments and the realism of the proposed solutions. This does not mean that I am always in agreement with respect to the details. It is precisely this diversity in nuances that enriches our dialogue: between a European, a Frenchman, and an African, a Senegalese man.

Agreeing, thus, with Mister Pierre Dumont on his conclusions and propositions, as well as his analyses, I would like to clarify certain points and respond, in passing, to some questions, even criticisms, however minimal they may be.

After defining his goal and objectives, Mister Dumont has drawn on a solid and comprehensive bibliography to carry out his research. The references include, on the one hand, the founders of grammar and, consequently, of modern linguistics; on the other hand, there are specialists in Negro-African languages. Among the former, I noted my former professors at the Sorbonne—J[oseph] Vendryès and F[erdinand] Brunot—alongside F[erdinand] de Saussure and R[oman] Jakobson; among the latter, J[oseph] H[arold] Greenberg, W[illiam]

F[rancis] Mackey, and, more specifically, the French and Senegalese linguists of CLAD. I only regret that Dumont did not include in his bibliography Lilias Homburger, this remarkable woman at the École pratique des hautes études who, beyond the study of African languages, introduced me to the study of agglutinative languages, which span across Africa, Asia, and pre-Columbian America.

Thus, drawing on the theories of the greatest linguists and, concretely, on the work of specialists in French and African languages, particularly Wolof, Mister Dumont has divided his thesis into two parts. In volume I, he deals with "linguistic problems" properly speaking, while in the second volume, he addresses "pedagogical problems." He does not even hesitate to discuss "political problems," as his subject demands.

The first two chapters were the most enjoyable for me to read. Indeed, beyond the phonological, morpho-syntactic, formal, and semantic differences, our researcher understood the need to attend to, if not emphasize, psycholinguistic factors. He has gone further: by pointing out the "insufficiencies" of contrastive studies, he implicitly highlights the pitfalls of studies on Senegalese languages, particularly Wolof. But as my own research on noun classes and verbs has confirmed, these two grammatical categories are the most important ones in numerous African languages, especially those in the "Senegalo-Guinean groups" and the Bantu group. And yet these are the categories where Mister Dumont finds the existing research to be lacking.

I will cite just a few examples, beginning with the pronouns.

First, there is confusion between *léén*, "you" (second person plural of the personal object pronoun), and *leen* (third person). There is also confusion between *nu*, "we" (first person plural of the subject pronoun), and *nyu* [*ñu*], "they" (third person).

This confusion, which is frequent among speakers in Senegal today, even among Wolof speakers, mainly stems from the fact that it was first introduced by Senegalese people from other ethnicities that adopted Wolof later.

With respect to noun classes, one cannot fully understand them in Wolof without also studying them in Sereer, but especially in Pulaar, where their triple semantic, morpho-syntactic, and phonological function becomes clearest.

As for verbs, with which Mister Dumont concludes chapter 2 of volume I, he rightly emphasizes their specificities, which are more differential than contrastive, and which exist in both French and Wolof.

What characterizes the genius of the French language is its rationality and, consequently, its power of abstraction. Careful to distinguish between causes and effects, Pierre Dumont judiciously classifies facts in temporal order, where the cause always precedes the effect. That is why, in each verbal mode, he multiplies the tenses. Thus, he has created eight indicative tenses, not counting the compound tenses.

The genius of African languages, especially Negro-African languages, is different. It is that of life, of the concrete, of the image. The Negro-African does not ignore tense—that is to say, the precise moment in time when the speaker situates the action or state—but he privileges aspect,[3] which consists of either the concrete manner in which the action is carried out or the way in which the state expressed by the verb is presented. For instance, to consider only the action, it is a matter of knowing if it is single or multiple, momentary or lasting, at its beginning or end, light or intense, etc. Thus, in the preterit of the imperfective indicative [*prétérit de l'imperfectif de l'indicatif*], I noted a dozen or so forms corresponding to the imperfect indicative [*l'imperfait de l'indicatif*] in French. In the Senegalo-Guinean languages I have studied—*Sereer, Pulaar, Wolof*—, there are five sub-moods of the indicative, which, inspired by Lilias Homburger, I have called *enunciative, verbative, demonstrative, subjective*, and *objective*.

As we saw above, chapters 3 and 4 of volume I are dedicated to mutual borrowings between Wolof and French. What strikes the reader here is the equal plasticity of these two languages, each borrowing or assimilating according to its genius. Precisely because of the difference in their respective geniuses, the two languages do not borrow the same words or categories of words, but above all, they do not assimilate them in the same way. Each accomplishes one or the other process according to its own genius and sociocultural situation.

As our author puts it in his conclusion to chapter 3, "The study of borrowings from Wolof to French reveals tendencies of the Wolof language itself." Noting the borrowings of technical words, which most often express aspects of modern industrial civilization, what is striking is, on the one hand, the need for rationality, as demonstrated by certain borrowed words, and, on the other hand, and more generally, the simplification that arises, whether in terms of etymology or morpho-syntax.

I will begin with the second phenomenon. From the earliest grammars written in the nineteenth century, Wolof appears as a simpler, more rational language than Sereer and Pulaar. This can be explained if all three, along with other languages, are descended from *proto-Sereer*, which would play the same role for these languages as the prehistoric *Indo-European*, which is theoretically reconstructed from the oldest and most significant European languages.

In this regard, among Wolof borrowings, nothing is more characteristic than the trend toward simplification because of lexical rationalization. This is confirmed by the borrowing from French of conjunctions of subordination such as *paskë* (*parce que*, "because"), *kom* (*comme*, "like"), and now *komkë* (*comme que*, "like that") and *piskë* (*puisque*, "since"). This is because, emphasizing intuition as well as synthesis, African languages employ a syntax of juxtaposition and coordination, while European languages use a syntax of subordination.

If we now turn to the borrowings that French has made from Wolof, we find, first and naturally, words designating African realities, such as *kora*, *balafong*, etc., on which I will not dwell.[4] More interesting are the words borrowed from the genius of Wolof. The most significant ones here are those testifying to an extension or a restriction of meaning, but above all words that create images by means of metaphor or metonymy.

Thus, volume II is entitled "Problèmes politiques et pédagogiques" [Political and pedagogical problems]. This explains why, in the same chapter, Mister Dumont discusses both "linguistic policy and instruction in Senegal."

In a brief introduction to this chapter, after condemning the "traditional methods" of the colonial regime that were "modeled on those used in the former metropole," he presents a new method. This new method is in reference to Jean Dard, the French schoolteacher who, while serving in Senegal, was the first to recommend in 1821 that primary school should begin with "the study of the mother tongue."[5] And the researcher then elaborates on his ideas about this new method. Essentially, for him, it is a matter of reducing French to its secondary role as a *language of international communication* by restoring to Senegalese languages, especially to Wolof, the role they should never have lost as mother tongues, and thus today, as national languages in their own right, without any limitation of time or space.

This requires some explanation, which our author provides by opposing both purism and creolization as well as a certain Francophone elitism. This attitude leads him, naturally, to a new bilingualism, which, in his view, does not come without raising delicate questions, including the choice of one or more national languages, whether or not to eliminate the Senegalese languages not retained as national languages, and finally, the regionalization of education. Incidentally, he seems to favor "trilingual instruction."

Mister Dumont concludes this first chapter of volume II by raising the major problem underlying the linguistic debate: the confrontation between tradition and modernity, where the respective situations of Zaire and Senegal are significant, if not exemplary. This, he argues in conclusion, is the problem ultimately raised by the project of a *Francophone Community*.

Speaking of the Senegalese situation, our author has noted what he believes to be "the absence of a definition of Senegalese language policy." Having come to know the consciousness and dedication of the former director of the Center for Applied Linguistics in Dakar, I owe him, as well as his readers, a response. Indeed, he alludes to the former President of the Republic of Senegal. I will therefore begin with a brief history of the *Negritude* movement.

"Negritude" is, on the one hand and objectively, *the sum total of the civilizational values of the Black world*. It is, on the other hand and subjectively, *for Negroes, the way* of living these values. The movement was launched in France, as we know, in the early 1930s. The group we formed—Césaire, Damas, Birago Diop, Ousmane Socé Diop, and a few others—opposed the group of Marxist-Leninists, most of whom were anti-French. For them, political independence conditioned all other forms of independence—economic, social, and cultural—whereas, for us, it was cultural independence through rootedness in Negritude.

And we fulfilled the movement by living it. Thus, alongside my studies in literature and grammar at the Sorbonne, I attended courses in ethnology and linguistics at the Institute of Ethnology in Paris and at the École pratique des hautes études. Moreover, here and there, we began to offer, in our presentations or dissertations, a *Negro-African reinterpretation* of the authors on the curriculum, or even of our professors. This amused some, such as the philosopher André Cresson from Lycée Louis-le-Grand, while scandalizing others, naturally at the Sorbonne, including Daniel Mornet, Professor of French. I mention Lycée Louis-le-Grand because it was there, in the second year of preparatory classes [*première supérieure*] before entering the Sorbonne, that we began to react as Negroes.

One can find the presentation of my thesis in the famous issue of *L'Étudiant noir*. I shall summarize it. Before sitting down at the banquet of the Universal, at the "the gathering of giving and receiving"—the expression is Césaire's—we must return to drink from the sources of Negritude. In truth, far from abruptly and foolishly rejecting the values of the European West, we needed to sift through them to select only those we could assimilate and from which we could benefit. Hence my formula: "To assimilate, not be assimilated." In short, it is a matter of rooting ourselves in the values of Negritude and, at the same time, opening ourselves up to the values of other civilizations.

However, we did not content ourselves with theorizing. We intended to put our theses into practice, in all domains: whether it be literature or the visual arts, music or dance, philosophy, or even science. Regarding science, in particular, linguistics was not overlooked. And it is no coincidence that on my return to Senegal, after having completed my higher education, my first public lecture, given at the Chamber of Commerce, was titled "The Problem of Culture in French West Africa."[6] To the scandalized stupefaction of Senegalese intellectuals, I advocated a return to Senegalese languages with the implementation of bilingualism in education. I specified: "It is a matter of beginning from the

Negro-African milieu and the civilizations in which the child is immersed. The child must learn to explore and express the basics in his native language, then in French. Little by little, he will expand, around himself, the circle of the universe in which, as a man, he will be engaged tomorrow."[7] Incredible but true: not one of the intellectuals present supported me then in my fight for the teaching of Negro-African languages. It was said here and there: "After learning Latin and Greek, he wants to bring us back to Negro-African languages."

To overcome the opposition of the Senegalese intelligentsia, not to mention the fiercely assimilationist Metropole, we would have to wait for *Independence*—that is, twenty-three years of struggle in all areas but, foremost, and once again, for the triumph of Negritude in the mind of the Senegalese bourgeoisie. It remains that, once independence had been gained, the head of state and his government were required to start from scratch. Thus, they had to lead the struggle on the three fronts of Politics, Economy, and Culture in order to overcome two attempted coups, the deterioration of the terms of exchange, which had replaced "the trade economy," and finally, the student revolt of 1968, inspired, if not masterminded, by a spirit of mimicry, coming straight from Paris.[8] It was only from 1969 onward, with the reopening of the University of Dakar and the revision of the Constitution, that the head of state and his government could effectively tackle a fundamental reform of Education. Moreover, the decade of Independence had not been wasted, as the ministers responsible for Education had taken advantage of it to preserve its quality.

Therefore, with respect to cultural policy and, more specifically, the pedagogy of the Senegalese state, I will discuss the guiding principles of these two areas before moving on to their applications.

As head of state, I have always, in the same way as I have done once again above, clearly defined the principles that should guide our cultural and, consequently, pedagogical action in the long term. It was, and still is, as we will see, about an ultimate goal and the objectives that will allow us to achieve that goal as fully as possible. The ultimate goal is the self-fulfillment [*épanouissement*] of every Senegalese and, collectively, all Senegalese as *integral human beings*, as bodies, souls, and spirits. The objectives are, in a word, the respective and reciprocal developments of these three major elements of the human person through a double movement of rooting in Negritude and an opening up to the fecundating contributions of other continents, races, and nations.

I have reiterated these declarations on the principles before and after Independence. I have often been reproached for advancing them, but especially for remaining faithful to them—sometimes going so far as to be accused of *stubbornness*. So, having defined the principles, what will their practical, pedagogical applications be? It is here that we consciously have chosen bilingualism as the preferred means, among others, of education, training, and culture, in our case, that of Franco-Senegalese bilingualism. I say "consciously" because this choice was not self-evident, for having been "colonized, despised," we were tempted by one or the other extreme solution: the choice, to the exclusion of all other languages, of either French or *Wolof.*

As head of state in a presidential regime, I did not choose French for two reasons: first on principle, second on the basis of experience. It is, on the one hand, out of fidelity to the principle, defined above, of the rootedness, foremost, in Negritude. On the other hand, having taught French for ten years, I knew well its virtues of rationality but also its limitations, if not its impossibility, in expressing the mysteries of the Black soul.

I did not choose Wolof, for various reasons grounded in factual evidence. First, the statistics cited on the number of Wolof speakers are inaccurate. Out of some six million Senegalese, the Wolof ethnic group accounts for no more than one and a half million, whereas the Fulɓe ethnic group, in the broad sense of the term, counts just as much if one includes immigrants from Guinea-Conakry. The second, more decisive reason is that if one were to choose the richest and most nuanced language, spoken over a larger area and by a greater number of people, it would be Pulaar, with its twenty-one nominal classes, not to mention other morpho-syntactic features. The third reason is that I made my choice while being all the more conscious given that I had, for fifteen years, been a professor at the École nationale de la France d'outre-mer, where I had taught "Negro-African Languages and Civilizations," essentially the languages of the "Senegalo-Guinean" group, to speak like Maurice Delafosse. Ultimately, and in my name, the Senegalese state chose, in its time, a bilingual instruction or, better, a *bilingual education* comprising, on the one hand, French, and on the other hand, six Senegalese languages, including four from the Senegalo-Guinean group—*Wolof, Pulaar, Sereer, Jola*—and two from the Mande group—*Malinke* and *Soninke.*

Why eliminate, from teaching, seventeen of the twenty-three languages spoken in Senegal? In a word, it was to be more effective because more realistic. Indeed, it is clear that, in the long term, the other seventeen languages, even if they are taught, will struggle to survive because, in political, social, and especially cultural relations, they will appear useless. Which is already the case. These languages can be classified into three families: that of the Senegalo-Guinean group, such as *Mandjak* and *Mancagne*; that of the Mande group, such as *Bambara,* which is a dialect of *Manding* just like *Malinke.* I will not forget that of the paleonegritics, or "primitive Senegambians," such as, on the one hand, the *Tendra* and *Gnougne* languages of eastern Senegal, not to mention those of Casamance, such as *Bassari, Cognagut,* and *Bainouk*; and, on the other hand, the languages of the Thiès massif falsely called "Sereer," such as *None, Ndoute,* and *Safene.*

Finally, some worried that the Senegalese State had not been more precise regarding the role it assigned to the six national languages, not only in primary, secondary, and higher education but also in scientific and technical life, as well as artistic and literary life, not to mention politics and the economy. My response is that here there is a double question of method.

First and foremost, we must start at the beginning. Once the principles have been clearly defined, it is a matter of applying them within the framework of the long-term *Economic and Social Development Plan,* which we were the first to develop in Francophone Black Africa, even before independence. As we know, this plan is divided into quadrennial plans, which are revised every two years. Thus, it is at the time of each revision as well as each elaboration that, in every sector, ministry, department, etc., we delve into the details of programming.

To come back to the teaching of national languages, as Mister Dumont puts it, we began by creating ad hoc commissions of specialists, which I myself chaired. Thus, after having elaborated a transcription that was rational, because it was phonetic, for the national languages, in reference, moreover, to international standards, we established, for each of the six languages, the rules governing the segmentation of words within the sentence. All of these practical provisions were enacted by decree and in application of the Loi d'orientation de l'Éducation nationale [National Education Policy Law], signed on June 3, 1971.[9]

The most difficult step to overcome, I admit, remained, and still remains, the transition from declarations of principle, as well as from laws and decrees, to concrete, dynamic language teaching. And Mister Dumont is right to remind us of this. It is the most difficult stage to overcome, I acknowledge, because it involves turning words into action. This requires funding, which has been granted in Senegal, but above all, dedicated and competent teachers and, even before that, researchers. It is precisely to promote research and teacher training that the Senegalese state created the *Center for Applied Linguistics in Dakar* (CLAD). Mister Dumont details, without exhausting the subject, the remarkable work that has made it possible to create experimental classes for the teaching of *Wolof.* I did not hesitate, at the time, to support the project developed for Sereer. In fact, I have inquired several times about the status of the project.

Here is where the problem lies. For Mister Dumont, "while the majority of the Senegalese teaching staff is convinced of the necessity of introducing *at least one African language* into the official programs of the Senegalese school, there remains a minority that considers this measure harmful to Senegal's development." And he continues: "Among the parents of students, *many* are also opposed to the use of African languages."[10] I am less optimistic than our author. Indeed, from experience, I know that, without even mentioning the parents of students, the majority of teachers, even in primary education, are opposed to it. Especially since they are required to use the CLAD method, which demands greater intellectual effort. The most obvious evidence of this are the delays, noted by Mister Dumont himself, in the establishment of experimental classes for Sereer teaching as well as in the training of teachers in the new bilingual pedagogy.

It is with awareness of these difficulties in the application of the principles and of the National Education Policy Law that the Senegalese state proceeded slowly, cautiously, decree by decree, experiment by experiment, revealing the next stage only just before having completed the previous one. This is once again a matter of a *grand design*, which, in my mind, cannot be fully realized before the year 2050. The major objective, to be clearer, must then have been achieved; it is—as is also the aspiration of the Maghrebi States, to take this example—to think, speak, write, and teach in the six national languages, and especially to act effectively in all areas, whether it be politics or the economy, sciences or technology, and naturally, literature or art.

After providing these responses to the concerns of some and the inquiries of others, I would like to return to Mister Dumont's argument: to chapter 2 of volume II, entitled, "Teaching in French." Without revisiting the pedagogical principles that have been clearly and pertinently presented here, I prefer to focus on the teaching of Phonetics and the instruction of writing.

I will focus first on Phonetics, because, paradoxically, Morpho-syntax, not even the agreement of tenses, does not present our students with major difficulties. In my opinion, the greatest difficulties lie in the specificities of French phonetics, particularly the openness and closeness of vowels, the use of the silent *e*, and word stress.

In the first case, the difficulty was exacerbated by the influence of Southern pronunciation, as French officials in Senegal before independence were largely composed of Southerners. Thus, in the Senegalese pronunciation of French, many closed vowels are open, as in *autre*, *rose*, etc. As for the silent *e*, whose pronunciation is more or less clear, which can even lead to elision, even within the body of the word, its use is very delicate. That is why—though it is a personal opinion—I would prefer for the model pronunciation given by the scholastic radio to be "that of a bourgeois from Paris." As we were taught, at the Sorbonne, it is an *ideal*. As for word stress, it is fortunate that this is the same in French and in the languages of the Senegalo-Guinean group. The only difference, though it is an important one, is that in Senegalo-Guinean languages, stress is on the first and not on the last syllable. While you hear "*Madam*" from a French mouth, you hear "*Madem*" from the Senegalese mouth. It is this shift in accent that often prevents the newly arrived Frenchman from understanding the Senegalese.

With respect to writing, it is the best way to instill in the Senegalese student that *spirit of organization and method* that is the major contribution of *Euramerican* civilization to the Dialogue of Cultures. This is what Professor Mohamadou Kane, head of the French Department at the University of Dakar, told me: "I prefer young French *agrégés*, who base their teaching on *la dissertation* and *explication de texte*, to the assistants, who are typically doctoral candidates."[11] In short, *explication de texte* leads to *dissertation*: to reasoning rationally while also maintaining dramatic interest, but also to employing words more for the precision and density of their meaning than for their sonority and, consequently, their incantatory power, as is too often the case in Africa.

As for the method itself of the manual *Pour parler français* [For speaking French],[12] the leaders of the CLAD, after reflecting on the various criticisms that had been addressed to this work, took the initiative of making proposals for reform. I will reiterate only the most important proposals, focusing more on the spirit than the letter—once again, on the principles, rather than the details of their application.

It is true, as the leaders of CLAD acknowledge, that too much emphasis was placed on oral proficiency, on dialogue, to the detriment of writing and composition; it is also true that the manuals were written, and the teachers trained, too hastily. Such weaknesses are easily remedied, as evidenced by the provisional but fundamental proposals submitted by the CLAD to the Senegalese authorities. Among these, I have retained not only the teaching of traditional values but also the creation of a *Pedagogical Institute*. Allow me to emphasize that, in the case of the Institute, the issue is less about creating a new École normale than it is about teaching, in schools that already exist, the improved CLAD method. I will come back to this in my conclusion, as well as to linguistic planning.

At the end of chapter 2 of volume II, following the methodological questions, comes "The Teaching of French," in its concrete realities and, first, in the choice of a linguistic norm. Here, too, CLAD has put forward the idea of a *Standardization Committee*, bringing together French and Senegalese linguists, which would base its work on some principles of contemporary linguistics. Especially since it is a matter of defining, little by little, the "French of Senegal," as it presents itself face to face with, and as a province of, "metropolitan French" [*le français central*]. This means that we must achieve a balance or, better, a symbiosis between the "creative imagination," so to speak, of Senegalese French and the rational rigor of metropolitan French. I believe, as suggested in a footnote, that the ideal "French of Senegal" should be sought among "the good Senegalese authors of French expression."[13] I am thinking of novelists and storytellers, philosophers and essayists, even poets, especially when it comes to words and expressions designating the new realities of the real country: those of nature and society, but also of the negro heart and spirit.

The third and final chapter of volume II, the most important one, is dedicated to "Teaching in African Languages." "The most important," I have said. Not that this final form of teaching has been undertaken more recently; it is that it is more fundamental, but also more difficult, since it involves teaching the mother tongue. As Mister Dumont reminds us, Jean Dard, who was the true founder of the Senegalese school, wanted, first, to start at the beginning: by teaching Senegalese languages. This is what Catholic missionaries have continued to do so far, even though their pedagogy has not always kept pace with the progress of grammar and linguistics, as Father [Francis] Libermann advised them, saying: "Make yourselves Negroes with the Negroes in order to win them over to Jesus Christ."[14] This is what Dard, turning his back on colonialism, already believed. But Dard did not convince the Governor, and it would take the Fourth, but especially the Fifth, Republic and Independence for the ideas of the Negritude movement to be accepted.

As I often do, I will address only the questions that are the most important and, at the same time, the most difficult to resolve. This is the case with the national language or languages to be taught. I will not revisit this, having already addressed the issue. Thus, the problem of orthography now presents itself to us, along with the questions of the "determiner-head relationship" [*déterminant-déterminé*], "verbal inflectional affixes" [*modalités verbales*], and "consonant gemination."

Regarding the *determiner-head relationship*, I will recall the two principles that I set forth while presiding, one after the other, over the six ad hoc commissions tasked with defining orthography and word segmentation in national languages. For agglutinative languages, it was a matter of facilitating their teaching and writing by segmenting everything that is separable. For this, it is necessary to resort not only to synchrony but also to diachrony, that is to say, to historical grammar. It is in this vein that, about forty years ago, while in captivity, I collected texts from Wolof speakers. The most interesting ones are texts in which the speaker imitates the style and speech of the elderly. This gave me, among other things, the opportunity to collect expressions such as *as ndaw as tubaab, as sancal as Waalo*, which I translate, word for word: "a little one, a toubab," "a flour, a Waalo woman," that is to say, "a little toubabesse," "flour from Waalo."

To understand the grammatical phenomenon well, one must start with the system of nominal classes in the Senegalo-Guinean group, of which Pulaar offers the best example. To focus on Wolof, let us first consider the series of morphemes that correspond to the French definite article, taking up the two examples above. We can have the two forms *ndaw si* and *ndaw sa*, each of which can have two meanings, one spatial and the other temporal: "the small one here" or "the one that is now in question" and "the small one there" or "the one that was in question." But we can find the phrase *ndaw su rafet*, which means: "a beautiful small one," that is, word for word, "(a) small one that is beautiful." Thus, in contrast to *si*, "there, here," and *sa*, "there, over there," which express *overdetermination*, we have *su*, which expresses indeterminacy. I will go further by noting that the spatiotemporal values of the vowels *i, a*, and *u* are found in contexts other than in the morphemes of the nominal classes. This is the case with the conjunctions *bi* and *ba*, which mean "when" or "whenever" and introduce temporal subordinate clauses. It is also the case with the conjunctions *su* and *bu*, which mean "if" and introduce conditionals. Finally, it is the case with morphemes like *di* and *na*, which, in verbal forms, express imperfective aspect in the case of *di* and perfective aspect in the case of *na*.

To conclude this grammatical problem, if one seeks to explain the rules of grammar to students, even those in primary school, rationally, one must not hesitate to make use of historical grammar. At the time, I did so with my students, not only from the École nationale de la France d'outre-mer but also with Year Six [*classe sixième*] students. And it yielded good results.

With respect to *verbal inflectional affixes*, I owe readers a correction as well as an explanation.

The correction is as follows: Diachronically and to stick with the same example, *gisna ma* becomes *gisnâ*, with a long *a*, and not *gisna*, with a short *a*; this is evident. If one has read otherwise in my text, it is simply a typo. In contrast, for *gis (na) nga* and *gis (na) ngéén*, I believe, without claiming infallibility, that *na* has disappeared in the second person of the singular and the plural. The best proof of this is that we find the forms *nu* and *ngéén* in the aorist of the *expeditive*.

To continue with Wolof, the *expeditive* is a mood that I have discovered and defined, alongside the *indicative* with its sub-moods, the *injunctive*, the *conditional* or *suppositive*, the *imperative*, and the *infinitive*. The *expeditive* is the absence of mood, just as the aorist, the narrative tense par excellence, is the absence of tense, but not necessarily of aspect.

Furthermore, I have identified several tenses. Here are some examples with the verb *gis* "to see," to stick with the same verb:

- present of the imperfective: *ma di gis, nga di gis, ngéén di gis* ("I see, you see, you [pl.] see");
- momentary preterite of the imperfective: *ma doon gis, nga doon gis, ngéén doon gis* ("I was seeing, you were seeing, you [pl.] were seeing");
- habitual preterite of the imperfective: *ma daan gis, nga daan gis, ngéén daan gis* ("I used to see, you used to see, you [pl.] used to see");
- aorist: *ma gis, nga gis, ngéén gis* ("I see" or "I saw," "you see" or "you saw," "you [pl.] see" or "you [pl.] saw");[15]
- pluperfect: *ma gisoon, nga gisoon, ngéén gisoon* ("I had seen, you had seen, you [pl.] had seen").

As for *consonant gemination*, I confess that I have not been convinced, even by S[erge]. Sauvageot's study.[16] First, there is the fact that I have studied Wolof phonology in the phonetics laboratory of the Collège de France, with the assistance of the head of the laboratory and using a kymograph.[17] I found fewer geminate consonants than the researchers at CLAD. I know, moreover, and from experience, that too often researchers believe they have found what they have decided to seek. The issue of geminate consonants has always seemed to me to be a matter of "politicking." That is why I have maintained the decree in question, especially since initially we wanted to simplify spelling as much as possible.[18] Contrary to French tradition and in accordance with the latest reforms.

I will not dwell for long on paragraphs B and C of chapter 3, dedicated to "theoretical and applied research on African languages," nor on paragraph D, dedicated to "pedagogical instruments." Especially since, in the lengthy parenthesis just now, I have preemptively addressed certain questions raised here, as well as certain remarks made, by Mister Dumont. Regarding the "training of future teachers" of national languages, in particular, he is right to emphasize this. I would even go further by proposing that courses in general linguistics and Negro-African linguistics be introduced in teacher-training colleges for primary school instructors. The same goes for when Dumont proposes a "realistic solution" to the methodological problem of bilingual education in French and African languages, especially when he suggests extending this to all national languages.

The reader may have noticed that my *preface* deviates from the usual model, in which a professor presents the work of their student, as I have done for a former student of the École nationale de la France d'outre-mer. This is a different scenario: that of a technical assistant loaned by France to the Republic of

Senegal. Hence the necessary *dialogue* established between the head of state and him, particularly facilitated by their shared background as educators in the same discipline. It is this *dialogue*, characterized by its friendly candor, that I am extending in this preface.

What can I say in terms of a general conclusion, except that I agree with Dumont when he titles his conclusion "For a New Francophonie"? Because this new Francophonie turns its back on the old Francophonie of colonial assimilation, but also because it aims, in advocating for a bilingualism based on contrastive studies of languages and cultures, for the symbiosis, not the confrontation, of values that are complementary because they are different. In each case, it is a matter of rooting oneself in one's motherland in order to open oneself up to the fecundating pollens of the Other.

It remains the case that the magnificent work carried out at the Center for Applied Linguistics in Dakar, for several years, by a fraternal team of French and Senegalese linguists under the direction of Pierre Dumont risks collapsing. Indeed, and to be frank, after his departure, Senegalese teaching unions, united for the first time, pressured and succeeded in *abolishing the CLAD method*. Of course, this method was not perfect, any more than the *living Latin* method I practiced in my youth; however, it was effective and required only refinement.[19] The truth is that this method, which turned its back on rote learning, on *Psittacism*, demands a double effort—a triple effort, in reality: with respect to the specificity of French, that of the Senegalese language, and the relationship between the two languages.

This is the real problem blocking the future of Black Africa. I say "Black Africa" because the Maghrebians, who successfully practice Franco-Arabic bilingualism, have largely solved the problem. Some even advocate for a trilingualism in which Berber, an authentically African language, would have its place. Therefore, to return to Senegal, if we want the endpoint—and the Senegalese State wants this—that is to say, the *renaissance*, with languages, of *Negro-African culture*, we must return to a contrastive, differential, or comparative method, ad libitum, which, unlike the prevailing laxness, demands a maximum effort in terms of method, organization, and work. It is precisely here that Francophonie can best assist us.

However, if we want to achieve the "national awakening" [*sursaut national*], to use President Abdou Diouf's phrase, the effort will not only be demanded of teachers but also of researchers, and especially Senegalese linguists. Too often, the latter lack both ambition and modesty. They settle for a master's degree all while proclaiming themselves "linguists," instead of competing for the CAPES and aggregation in Grammar, on the way to earning a doctorate, which would allow them to be fully *professors*, that is, both teachers and researchers.[20]

It is this model of consciousness and work, of method and organization, but also of confidence in the creative genius of Black Africa, as evidenced by Senegalese languages, that Mister Pierre Dumont exemplified during the years he led the CLAD. It is this model that his thesis teaches us. This is why I recommend it to the youth, as well as to teachers in Senegal and Black Africa, not to mention the French who take an interest in our continent.

NOTES

Léopold Sédar Senghor, "Le français et les langues africaines," in *Liberté 5: Le dialogue des cultures* (Seuil, 1983), 238–53. The text was first published as a preface to Pierre Dumont, *Les relations entre le français et les langues africaines du Sénégal* (A.C.C.T [Agence de Coopération Culturelle et Technique] and Éditions Karthala, 1983), 7–20.

1. [Pierre Dumont's book *Les relations entre le français et les langues africaines du Sénégal* was based on his 1981 doctoral thesis, of the same title, at Université de Paris III.—Eds.]

2. [Senghor is referring to the fact that a Senegalese linguist took over Dumont's post.—Eds.]

3. [Whereas *tense* refers to the time when an action or event occurs, or when a state or process holds, *aspect* refers to the internal makeup of an action, event, state, process, or situation—for instance, with respective to completion or perfectiveness (perfective aspect). See Friedrich Hamm and Oliver Bott, "Tense and Aspect," in *The Stanford Encyclopedia of Philosophy*, ed. Edward N. Zalta and Uri Nodelman 2024, https://plato.stanford.edu/entries/tense-aspect/. See also Stéphane Robert, "Tense and Aspect in the Wolof Verb System," in *Aspectuality and Temporality: Descriptive and Theoretical Issues*, ed. Zlatka Guentchéva (John Benjamins, 2016), 171–230.—Eds.]

4. [The *kora* is a string instrument; the *balafoŋ* is a gourd-resonated xylophone.—Eds.]

5. [Jean Dard was appointed to serve in Saint-Louis in northern Senegal as a colonial teacher and was among the educators who founded the "École mutuelle" in 1817, which began with instruction in Wolof. As a linguist, he conducted research on Senegalese languages, especially Wolof, as well as Bambara, authoring several lexicographic and grammatical studies. Dard recommended instruction in Wolof as early as 1817, when the first schools were established, writing that "Black people [*les noirs*] must be instructed in their mother tongue" ("Rapport de Jean Dard au colonel Schmaltz," December 18, 1817 (ANSOM, Affaires Politiques, 2796/1), cited in Pierre Gomis, "Scolarisation et promotion féminines au Sénégal: différenciation sexuelle et disparités sociales devant l'école" (PhD thesis, Université Aix-Marseille I, 1999), 47.—Eds.]

6. [Later published as Léopold Sédar Senghor, "Le problème culturel en A.O.F.," in *Liberté 1: Négritude et Humanisme* (Seuil, 1964), 11–21. See chapter 15 of this volume.—Eds.]

7. [Senghor, "Le problème culturel en A.O.F.," 14.—Eds.]

8. [In May 1968, Senghor deployed the Senegalese military to brutally repress student strikes and protests, initially led by leaders of the Student Union (Union des étudiants sénégalais) at Université Cheikh Anta Diop, but which quickly spread throughout Dakar. For an overview, see Abdoulaye Bathily, *Mai 1968 à Dakar ou la révolte universitaire et la démocratie: Le Sénégal cinquante ans après* (L'Harmattan-Sénégal, 2018; revised and expanded second edition).—Eds.]

9. [Loi n° 71-36 du 3 juin 1971 d'Orientation de l'Éducation nationale.—Eds.]

10. [Dumont, *Les relations entre le français et les langues africaines*, 205 (Senghor's emphasis).—Eds.]

11. [*Dissertation* and *explication de texte* are French academic, namely scholastic, genres of argumentation and literary analysis, respectively.—Eds.]

12. [*Pour parler français* was a textbook series developed by the CLAD and the Bureau Pédagogique de Dakar and published by Istra (Paris) from the late 1960s onward.—Eds.]

13. [Dumont, *Les relations entre le français et les langues africaines*, 256.—Eds.]

14. [In Libermann: "Faites vous nègres avec les nègres, et vous les jugerez comme ils doivent être jugés" (Make yourselves Negroes with Negroes and you will judge them the way they should be judged); François Libermann, *Notes et documents relatifs à la vie et à l'œuvre du vénérable François-Marie-Paul Libermann* (Paris: Maison Mère, 1850), 330.—Eds.]

15. [The aorist, when used to indicate past actions, corresponds to the *passé simple*, a literary past tense, in French, which is how Senghor translates the Wolof examples.—Eds.]

16. [Serge Sauvageot, "Description synchronique d'un Dialecte wolof: Le Parler du Dyolof" (PhD thesis, Institut Fondamental d'Afrique Noire, 1965). Consonant gemination was a major political, not just theoretical, issue for Senghor; he famously had Ousmane Sembène's film *Ceddo* (1977) banned on the basis that Wolof did not permit geminate consonants.—Eds.]

17. [A kymograph was an instrument used in early experimental phonetics to mechanically record articulatory movements.—Eds.]

18. [Senghor is referring to the "Décret n° 71-566 du 21 mai 1971 relatif à la transcription des langues nationales" (1972). Other relevant decrees include n° 71-1025 and n° 71-1026 (1975), which determined segmenting rules for writing Wolof and Sereer, and Law n° 77-55 (1977), which introduced sanctions for failing to respect standard orthography in the publication of national language materials.—Eds.]

19. [The "Living Latin" method is an approach to language acquisition that considers Latin a natural human language rather than a purely written "dead" language.—Eds.]

20. [CAPES stands for Certificat d'aptitude au professorat de l'enseignement du secondaire (Certificate of aptitude for secondary school teaching), a certification for teaching in secondary schools.—Eds.]

20

The Dialogue of Cultures

I would like to begin by expressing to Professor Luise Abramowski, Dean of the School of Protestant Theology, in very simple terms, how moved I am by this honor that the *Doctor Leopold Lucas Foundation* has bestowed upon me.[1] The Foundation has, for the year 1983, granted me its prize, which it awards each year for the work of a writer who has distinguished himself in the realm of "promoting relations between men and peoples." I am even more moved because the reputation of your school has transcended German borders.

Please allow me, dear Dean, to place this ceremony under the aegis of Friedrich Hölderlin, whom I consider, along with Johann Wolfgang von Goethe, the greatest German poet of all time. Besides, as we know, he studied at the Tübingen protestant seminary and passed away in this city. He also championed the dialogue of cultures. Moreover, as I was writing my speech, I could not help but be guided by his words: "Like springtime, genius emigrates from country to country."[2]

And so, today, I would like to speak to you about the central problem that calls on us with the greatest urgency, but above all about the necessity of this *Dialogue of Cultures* to which UNESCO has already dedicated two international conferences.

First, what is at stake? Before trying to respond to this question, we must situate it in what the United Nations calls the "North-South dialogue." As we know, this is, in theory, a general dialogue, both economic and cultural, between all members of the United Nations; more precisely, it is a wide-ranging discussion, on an equal footing, between developed and developing peoples, between Euramerica and the Third World. In his *Défi mondial* [World challenge], Jean-Jacques Servan-Schreiber notes that since the first conference was organized in 1974, on the theme of "North-South" relations, two thousand conferences, symposia, and other colloquia have been held.[3] All, alas!, have resulted in a failure or semifailure. Including the conference in Cancún, which had recommended a general conference where "global negotiations" would be organized. Today, in May 1983, we speak less and less of "global negotiations." *Hic jacet* the root of the problem, which we will now examine in order to identify a solution that is effective because it is human. But, before going any further, I will say a word about the issue of economic problems, which are the most difficult to resolve, precisely due to a certain "cultural contempt."

Regarding economic issues, the heart of the problem lies, in theory, in the deterioration of the terms of trade following the Colonial Monopoly in the wake of the broadscale independence movements of the 1960s.[4] But what is, exactly, this "deterioration"? "Deterioration" means that, each year, the prices of goods and services sold by developed countries, located for the most part in Euramerica, increase at best or stagnate at worst, while those of developing countries decrease or stagnate. According to the World Bank, between 1952 and 1972, the rate of deterioration has been, annually and on average, 2.5 percent. Since the second oil shock, from 1979, experts have calculated it as follows. For industrial countries, inflation would be, annually and at a maximum, 15 percent; but for Third World countries, it would range between 30 and 200 percent.

In order to rectify this situation, which is so detrimental to the Third World and to Africa above all, but also to industrialized countries, from which poor countries buy fewer and fewer goods and services, we have made different propositions, one of which is that developed countries would keep their promise of devoting 0.7 percent of their GNP to development aid. At the UN's first extraordinary session dedicated to disarmament, I proposed a 5 percent tax on all war budgets. If some two thousand meetings, organized by the UN over the course of eight years, have all resulted in a more or less complete failure, this is not the result of chance. For lucid minds who have been attentive to this issue, the cause of this failure has a name. It is called "cultural disdain." It is thought that some ten thousand dollars of income per capita is not enough for the population of Euramerica while four hundred dollars is more than enough for an African peasant. Indeed, it is still believed that it is enough for those people without civilization. It is precisely here that the real debate lies between the North and the South, between the Great Whites and other peoples.

We will begin by evoking certain facts concerning Prehistory that demonstrate the central role of Africa, the Black Continent, so to speak, in the development of the first civilization worthy of its name. Moreover, the latest conference on Human Paleontology, held last year in Nice, in France, confirmed that it is indeed in Africa that Man had emerged from animal and that this continent stood at the forefront of civilization until the appearance of *Homo sapiens* about forty thousand years ago. I will add that it remained so until the emergence of Egyptian civilization.

A dual question arises here: both cultural and biological. Some historians have denied the Egyptians the honor of inventing the first form of writing. On the other hand, I recall that at the "White man's school," in Africa, we were taught that Egyptians were White or, modestly, that they were "Mediterranean."

We will begin with race. Herodotus, in his second book of *Histories*, informs us, without insistence, and by way of a single sentence, so natural was it for him, that Egyptians "are Black-skinned and curly-haired."[5] As we all know, since then, a good amount of mixing between Blacks, Whites, and even East Asians [*Jaunes*] has been happening, all around the Mediterranean. And yet, despite all the White blood received by the Egyptians, the numerical table of blood groups that defines race or, more precisely, *métissage* is approximately similar to that of the Senegalese, who are usually presented as the prototypical "Negroes."

With respect to culture, most Egyptologists acknowledge that, whether it is a question of philosophy or religion, literature, science or art, the first principles or intuitions were articulated by the Egyptians, who transmitted them to the Greeks, who came to learn from them. It is in this way that philosophers like Plato and Pythagoras, scholars like Thales and Eudoxus, the physician Hippocrates, and the historian Herodotus himself felt the need, during their time, to go to Egypt to seek education in the temples. I know that Sumerologists, and even certain Egyptologists, argue that Sumerians invented the first form of writing. This serves, in my opinion, to uselessly divert the debate. Indeed, Sumerians have often been compared to Dravidian Blacks in India in both the domains of biology and culture. Moreover, I note that Sumerian is an agglutinative language, just like all African languages, except those of the Khoisans, and like the languages of the Indo-Malaysian subcontinent, not to mention Oceanian languages. I refer you to a book by one of my former professors, Paul Rivet, entitled *Sumériens et Océaniens* [*sic*] [Sumerians and Oceanians].[6]

However, before the Greeks had passed the torch to the Romans, the Semites of the Near East had, for more than two thousand years, been developing their civilization at the same time as, and often in competition with, the Egyptians. They were, of course, as Alexandre Moret puts it in his *Histoire de l'Orient* [History of the Orient],[7] mixed Indo-European peoples but also, before that, Black people who had previously been the "first colonizers" of the Mesopotamian valleys. These Semites developed, on the basis of Sumerian culture, the Assyro-Babylonian civilization, one of the most brilliant civilizations of antiquity. However, I will retain only the three major monotheistic religions that, as much as Greco-Roman civilization, would transform the world: Judaism, Christianity, and Islam. Today, these religions include, among their followers, close to half of the population of the globe. What distinguishes them as purveyors of civilization is not so much the practice of monotheism, which is not exclusive to them, as the symbiosis of spirit and soul that they realize in Man or, more precisely, to speak like the Greeks, between *dianoïa* and *thumos*, that is discursive reason and intuitive reason.

That is to say that Greece, which founded civilization, not Indo- but Albo-European, remained faithful to the lessons drawn from the contact with the Near East, more importantly with Africa. Moreover, it is toward a Greco-African symbiosis, integrating Persian and Indian thought, that philosophers like Plato and Origen have worked. To take the example of ancient Greek literature, which I taught along with their language, nothing reminded me more than their theater of the "total spectacle" that makes up traditional African drama, which, in my days in the "Kingdom of Childhood," was at the same time drama, music, song, often polyphonic, dance, even sculpture and painting with the mask and the tattoos on the ebony bodies. It is that the sources of Greek theater have the old mysteries of Osiris as their ancient sources.

As you know, it is in 86 BC, with the fall of Athens, that the Greeks, in turn, passed the torch to the Romans. Rome—that is, above all, the spirit of discursion and practical sense. This military and judicial spirit would enable the Romans to swiftly form an empire around the Mediterranean Sea. Here, I would like to dwell on only two features that characterize Romanness [*romanité*], better, Latinness [*latanité*]. As always, I will draw my examples from the domains of arts and letters, philosophy, and religion.

Moving from Athens to Rome, theater, the African origins of which we have noted, would soon mitigate its lyrical dimension by eliminating choirs and by reducing the *canticum* to two actors: the singer and the flutist. And nothing to underscore the rhythm. And we would end up dedicating all the space to the *diverbium*, I mean to conversation, to prose, even when written in verse.

Concerning the contributions of Semites to the field of religion, Rome, following the language and literature of the Greeks, integrated the Christian religion into its culture, albeit with difficulty. This is evidenced by the persecutions of which Christians were victim until the fourth century AD. However, Roman Christianity, even before it was acknowledged, or at least tolerated, by Emperor Constantine, had been Romanized, that is rationalized, juridicized. It is, precisely, against this deviation that Saint Augustine, the African, would react. He did so by restoring Christianity to its origins of mystical revelation: by Africanizing it in a certain sense. I am aware that, in wanting to increase the role of discursion in Augustine, his act of faith has been assimilated to the Cartesian *cogito*. Wrongfully, because, here, it is a matter of a *cogito* of the soul. Thus, Augustine, in the etymological sense of the word, *reanimated* [*ranimé*] Catholic faith by reintroducing intuition and, better, faith.

This is a properly African reaction, the effects of which would, to a certain extent, be reinforced by the Middle Ages. The Middle Ages would do so thanks to the biological and cultural symbiosis of Celts and Germans, following the invasions of the Germans, who descended from Scandinavia. Since the disputes that erupted, right before the Second World War, concerning "race," "ethnicity," or "civilization," it is surprising we have not underscored more the fact that Europeans from the North-West are essentially the product of a *métissage* between Celts and Germans.

Of course, we must not deny the contributions of Mediterranean cultures within medieval Christian civilization, if only because Christianity comes from them. It remains that, except for Iberia, Mediterranean contributions during this period had become less active. Moreover, we will examine them cursorily. Indeed, what are the principal factors of medieval civilization? We are in the habit of saying that it is characterized by Feudalism, the Cathedral, and the University.

First, let us begin with Feudalism. About fifty years ago, when economics prevailed in History, emphasis was placed on the desegregation of the State and the decline of medieval trade. But we did not emphasize enough the fact that the feudal regime had been instituted precisely to combat such desegregation by connecting the peasant to his master, his protector, by means of a social contract. I would like to begin by returning to the fact that, today, historians ascribe as much, if not more, importance to civilization, or even to religion. This will explain both the Cathedral and the University.

More so than any pope, one figure dominates the Christian Middle Ages. This is the "Angelic Doctor," Saint Thomas of Aquinas, an Italian born in the Kingdom of Naples, but—this detail is important—to a Norman mother. It is ultimately he, and not Saint Augustine, who gave the Catholic Church its doctrinal foundation. As you know, Thomism, still taught in the seminaries, is a new symbiosis: that of theology and philosophy, faith and reason, and more precisely, of the two reasons. It is a kind of dialogue of cultures between Aristotle the Greek and Saint Augustine the African.

If Thomism, as symbiosis, has survived, in Catholicism, all the cultural revolutions, it is, essentially, because it embodies the Indo-European spirit in its entirety by associating its two essential components, which are Greco-Latin culture and Celto-Germanic culture. It remains that during the Middle Ages, the two reasons were still in equilibrium even though, in Thomism, intuitive faith predominated in principle. I say "in principle," for, for an African reader like me, Saint Thomas of Aquinas, in fact, puts emphasis on discursive reason. The ambivalence, or even ambiguity here, was the result of the biological and cultural predominance of Celto-Germans in North-Western Europe.

To return to the Cathedral, it is the expression of the Christian faith spread throughout Europe by the Roman conquest. But it is, in North-Western Europe, in Gaul and in Germanic countries, the expression of a Christian faith even more restored in its original fervor, for it found fertile terrain in Celtic and Germanic souls, and more specifically in the Celto-German symbiosis that followed the invasions originating from Scandinavia. Paradoxically, this symbiosis would, despite Saint Thomas of Aquinas, strengthen the fervor of the Christian faith originating from Africa with Saint Augustine. I have said "paradoxically," for Germanness [*Germanité*], and for me the word is laudatory, is closer to Africanness [*Africanité*] than has been thought. It is the German philosopher and ethnologist Leo Frobenius, not I, who demonstrated the affinities existing between the German and the African, each one being endowed with a rich and profound sensibility. It is merely that the sensibility of the German reacts slowly, whereas that of the African reacts quickly, in an explosive manner, as is shown in characterology today.

The Cathedral, I have said, but also the University. The University, in the Middle Ages, combined, under the high authority of the Church, the institutions of secondary and higher education. Contrary to what we were taught previously, in the secular school, the Middle Ages was not an era of intellectual regression, because it was a period of religious blossoming. In the literary, scientific, and even technical fields, universities had preserved everything they could from Greco-Roman civilization. And not only did they add African and Near

Eastern cultural contributions, but also Celtic and Germanic civilizations, as is evidenced by Thomism and mystical, symbolic art, cathedrals, not to mention their technological achievements. Without this original civilization of the Christian Middle Ages, the Renaissance would not have occurred.

The Renaissance is generally defined as a movement of arts and ideas that, begun in Italy in the fifteenth century, spread across all of Europe. It was characterized by a return to antique, that is Greco-Roman, ideas and art. In truth, the movement came from afar; and goes farther still: toward the *Civilization of the Universal*, to speak like Father Pierre Teilhard de Chardin.

One must go back to the Carolingian empire: to Charlemagne, the organizer, who introduced Italy into his empire and reinforced, in schools, the teaching and study of classical languages and letters. Moreover, it was the Carolingians who encouraged, on the other hand, Roman art, which, contrary to its name, attests to a new influence from the Near East, conveyed by Christian monks. One must also not forget the Arabic influences exerted on medieval Europe through Iberia: through Spain and Portugal.

Italy was better positioned than any other country to be the first to herald, while initiating, the *Renaissance* of Greco-Roman civilization: the renaissance, moreover, not so much of its ideas as of its intellectual dynamism, its spirit of discursion, which, in practice, transforms into a spirit of method and organization; not so much of its literatures and arts as of its science and techniques. It is, in a word, the technological revolution, with the invention of the compass, of gunpowder and of printing, which has led historians to fix the end of the Middle Ages, not at the fall of Constantinople to the Turks in 1453 but with the discovery of the Americas and to the end of the *Reconquista* in 1492.

In the realm of Letters, I am thinking not so much of Italy, once again the initiator, as of the great countries of the North-West such as France, Germany, and England, the Celto-Germanic countries to which I will add the Netherlands, Belgium, and Luxembourg. I am thinking less of poetry, regardless of what has been said about it, than of theater and above all of philosophy. Here, moreover, it is only in the seventeenth and eighteenth centuries that the seeds of the Renaissance would bear fruit. In theater, this would be, in France, the rule of the three unities. In philosophy, the idealist rationalism of Descartes, Leibniz, Kant, not to mention Locke's empiricism.

In the realm of visual arts, I will return to Italy, which, as early as the twelfth and fourteenth centuries, as early as the *Pre-Renaissance*, had initiated the new classicism. It is, in architecture, a geometry characterized by equilibrium and symmetry; in sculpture, anthropocentrism with an emphasis on the human body; in painting, realism, whether regarding Man or his natural environment.

In a word, we had returned to the aesthetics of *physéôs mimésis*, the imitation of nature, to which African, Asian, American, but also Oceanian aesthetics will be opposed, and which they will transform little by little with other ideas. Allow me to remind you that the aesthetics of the cathedral was symbolic, in the sense that it focused less on man than on God, but through the sensible appearances of nature.

Let us begin with pre-Columbian America and with the fifteenth, sixteenth, seventeenth, and eighteenth centuries. It is on this continent, more than anywhere else, that Europe lost the opportunity to assimilate the fecundating values of Amerindian civilization. "Lost opportunities" is the title of the third chapter of Roger Garaudy's essay *Pour un dialogue des civilisations* [Toward a dialogue of civilizations].[8] Indeed, when the Europeans arrived in the Americas, they began by decimating millions of Native Americans. Not only men but also their artworks, even their writings, were destroyed: temples, sculptures, and manuscripts. Despite this, Amerindian culture did not fail to somewhat influence, in South America, Latin-American literature and the arts. Not to mention European travel writings, but above all the reflections of the *philosophes*, who not only condemned colonization but also presented Amerindians as the authentic children of this human nature on which a new humanism could be built.

After the Americas, the Near East and North Africa, where the Semites, but above all the Arabs among them, would continue to play a major role. It is no chance if, last year, the city of Marseille organized a series of exhibitions entitled *L'Orient des Provençaux* [The Orient of the Provençaux].[9] Let us specify, straightaway, that the Arabs in question have mixed with Blacks and Indo-Europeans in North Africa as in the Near East. This has been proven, today, by the numerical tables of their blood groups as well as by their arts and literatures. The Arabs who conquered North African countries one after the other were less numerous than has been said, and above all believed. Let us take the example of Almoravids, who built an empire encompassing the Western Maghreb and Spain: They were a symbiosis, once again both biological and cultural, of Berbers and Blacks, more specifically of the Fulɓe.

Contrary to common belief, and far from provoking the regression of civilization in South-Western Europe, the Arab conquest, which, from the eighth century onward, extended to North Africa and Iberia, was, in contrast, a fecundating catalyst of civilization. These Arabo-African contributions constituted, in their own way, one of the important factors of the Renaissance and, before that, of Roman civilization, as we have previously noted.

Indeed, Arabo-Africans brought, among other fertilizing elements, the suppression of serfdom as well as new techniques in the major domains of Mathematics, Medicine, Agriculture, and Craft. In truth, it is the Arabs who transmitted to Western Europe not only a part of ancient Greek thought and culture, but also the sciences and technologies of ancient Greece.

From the Near East, we will now move on to the Far East. Original and rich as their civilizations may be, Persia and India will contribute less to the period we are discussing—from the fifteenth to the eighteenth century—than Japan, but above all China. It is the Chinese who would invent gunpowder and the printing press.

In the realm of visual arts, it is painting and ceramics, singularly Japanese landscape printing, that will have the greatest influence on European art, and as early as the Italian Pre-Renaissance. I am thinking of the painters, but above all of the Italian, French, and English ceramists: of this new style, in which neither Man nor or even Dragons are the center of nature, but rather the landscape. It is a matter of a symbolic landscape, no longer rhythmed by geometrical lines, but by curves, curls, and other spirals. A landscape animated by Taoism, the dialectic of *yin* and *yang*, of the male and the female. It is here a vitalism that we will find, or rather *re-discover*, in Africa.

But let us go back to the Renaissance. In order to better understand its spirit, one must, as always, return to Aristotle, who is the true founder of European philosophy. One must return to *Nicomachean Ethics*, in which he writes: "Yet there are, in the soul, three dominant factors which determine action and truth: sensation, spirit [*esprit*], and desire."[10] It is a sentence that Descartes would not forget, for in one of his *Meditations*, he translates these three factors as "thinking" [*penser*], "will" [*vouloir*], and "feeling" [*sentir*].[11] No translation better renders the Albo-European spirit in which sensibility [*sensibilité*] comes last, turns "desire" into "will," and above all "spirit" into "thinking." Indeed, the Greek *noûs* cannot be reduced to thought. It is the symbiosis of *dianoïa*, or discursive reason, and *thumos*, or intuitive reason. What is interesting here is to see that the *noûs* is the essence of Cartesian philosophy, that is, of the European spirit, pushed to the height of its solely discursive, "unidimensional" reason, as the philosopher Roger Garaudy presents it: "Idealism, by which it is designated, leads, paradoxically, to a mechanical and soulless materialism because it is mathematical."[12]

It is, indeed, against Cartesianism that the majority of German philosophers and, more generally, those from the North reacted, for about two centuries, as I tried to show in a lecture that I gave in Francfort-sur-le-Main last year and that I entitled, "The Revolution of 1889 and Leo Frobenius."[13] For Descartes,

Leibniz, and Kant were idealists: they started from the subject. But, while Descartes had reduced the man-subject to discursive reason, the two German philosophers re-instilled not only spirituality alongside intuitive reason in him but also practice alongside theory.

Friedrich Hegel, Johann Gottlieb Fichte, and Ludwig Feuerbach will, in turn, react against Leibniz and Kant, but always in a German spirit. Hegel also begins from the Idea, but it is in order to arrive at the practice of the real, spirit and matter, even flesh, with all its contradictions. Following Fichte, who laid out the principles of a modern humanism, rooted in the free subject, it is Feuerbach who will overturn the Hegelian dialectic by substituting spirit with matter, a sensible matter, and God with Man. It is during this cultural revolution, in its infancy, it is true, that Karl Marx—less atheistic, in any case, more spiritualist than has been said—came onto the scene. Even more so given that his dialectic, as he specified it, was driven by a "vital spirit," which I underscored at Trier, on March 13, during the conference organized to celebrate the centenary of his death.

On Germany's central role in the Revolution of 1889, although the Revolution was initiated in France. In truth, the Renaissance only grazed the Northern European peoples, the Germanic peoples, singularly the German peoples, and not for long. In France, Cartesianism would extend throughout the eighteenth century, namely with encyclopedists. And Romanticism would only last a few decades. In Germany, it is at the height of the eighteenth century that Romanticism would be born, I mean would be reborn, with writers such as Friedrich Novalis, as a return to the eternal intuitions of the German soul: the *Ur-Deutschland*.

Nineteenth-century French positivism, as a new form of Cartesianism, would have little influence in Germany, even in the form of "realism." Indeed, the German soul would continue its march forward, its resurrection, in the philosophies of Arthur Schopenhauer and Friedrich Nietzsche. For Nietzsche, man's vocation, his self-fulfillment, resides less in the truth than in life: in the free will of man who makes himself *superhuman*, by inventing new values, drawn from his will, certainly but, profoundly, from his intuitions, his sensibility. Nietzsche also preaches the "eternal return" to the symbiosis of the Apollonian spirit and the Dionysian soul, but with an emphasis on the latter. The Revolution of 1889 was ripe. Let us not forget that it is between 1883 and 1885 that *Thus Spoke Zarathustra* was published.[14]

What is the meaning of what I call "the Revolution of 1889?" First, let me remind you that 1889 was the year in which the French philosopher Henri Bergson published *Essai sur les données immédiates de la conscience* [Essay on the immediate data of consciousness] and Paul Claudel, his first play, *Tête d'Or* [Golden head].[15] Not to mention that, a few years before, the poet Arthur Rimbaud had published his masterpiece: *Une saison en enfer* [*A Season in Hell*].[16] What is the meaning of these three works? They mean that French writers and philosophers were turning away from intellectualist positivism to return to the same positions as the Germans: toward a symbiosis that prioritized sensible intuition over unidimensional rationalism. Indeed, *Tête d'Or* is Claudel's first and most romantic play, whereas in *Une saison en enfer*, Rimbaud, while singing a new aesthetics, writes his greatest poem: the most beautiful one. Let us listen to him: "Yes, I've shut my eyes to your light. I am a beast, a Negro. But I can be saved. You are fake Negroes. [. . .] I enter the true kingdom of the children of Cham. [. . .] I invented the color of vowels. [. . .] I fixed the form and movement of every consonant, and I flattered myself for inventing, with instinctive rhythms, a poetic language [*un verbe poétique*] that would be, sooner or later, accessible to all the senses. I alone would be its translator."[17]

Let us dwell on this new aesthetic so as to define it. Its most important expression is "a poetic language [*verbe*], accessible [. . .] to all the senses." This means not only that the sensible signs, perceived by the five senses through symbolic images, translate the realities of the spirit and the soul, of the invisible universe, but also that they are interchangeable. This aesthetic of Rimbaud is exactly the Negro-African aesthetic, which I define as such: "an image or a set of analogical melodious and rhythmed images." I specify that it is always a living rhythm, made of asymmetrical parallelisms or, better, of repetitions that do not repeat.

Thus, here is Africa coming, coming back within this "dialogue of cultures," which it had been the first to establish, through Egypt. The same Africa, Black Africa. It was indeed she who arrived last to the circle, called on by the Revolution of 1889. It is she who marked with her seal the School of Paris, as well as German expressionism, better, *Germanic* expressionism, for I am thinking of the Flemish and other Dutch communities. Moreover, this influence of Negritude had been encouraged by the recourse, during the second half of the nineteenth century, to visual influences, but also literary ones, from the Far East, which were accompanied by those of India and Persia.

Thus, today, if Europe has remained at the forefront of sciences and technologies, of which I have barely spoken, all the arts bear the mark of this aesthetic, whether in India, China and Japan, the United States of America and Latin America, as well as Europe. It is the case of the new music and the new songs from the Americas, which, among other things, are characterized, here, by polyphony and, there, by contrast, offbeat, and syncopation. It is also the case of the new dance—I am thinking of Maurice Béjart—which aims less for technical or physical prowess than for an analogical language in a total spectacle. And it is, then and at the same time, often with mask, dance and painting, song and poetry.

I will conclude briefly.

It is a fact, and a global one, that all cultures from all continents, races, and nations are, today, cultures of symbiosis in which the four fundamental factors—sensibility, will, intuition, and discursion—play, more and more, equal roles. All continents—from the oldest, Africa, as well as to the youngest, America—have contributed to this vast dialogue, which unfolds on the level of the Universal.

Today, the major issue for humanity is that each continent, race, or nation, each man or woman, finally become conscious of this cultural Revolution and, above all, that, burying their cultural contempt, they bring their active contribution to it.

NOTES

Léopold Sédar Senghor, "Le Dialogue des cultures," *Liberté 5: Le dialogue des cultures* (Seuil, 1993), 199–210. The text was first given as an address at the University of Tübingen in Germany where Senghor was awarded the Dr. Leopold Lucas Prize (May 27, 1983).

1. [Senghor was the 1983 recipient of the prize, which recognizes "outstanding achievements in the fields of theology, intellectual history, historical research and philosophy" and, in particular, "personalities who have made a significant contribution to the promotion of relations between people and peoples and who have rendered outstanding services to the dissemination of the idea of tolerance through their publications." Previous laureates include Paul Ricœur, René Girard, and Giorgio Agamben. "Dr. Leopold Lucas Prize," Faculty of Protestant Theology, Eberhard Karls Universität, Tübingen, accessed July 14, 2025, https://uni-tuebingen.de/en/faculties/protestant-theology/faculty/lucas-prize/.—Eds.]

2. [Friedrich Hölderlin (1770–1843) was a poet and philosopher of German Romanticism. Senghor is citing Hölderlin's "Gesang des Deutschen" (Song of the German) (1799). The stanza reads: "Doch, wie der Frühling, wandelt der Genius / Von Land zu Land [. . .]" (Yet, like spring, genius wanders / from land to land). Most likely, Senghor had access to the French edition of Hölderin's verse. Friedrich Hölderlin, *Poèmes (Gedichte)*, trans. Geneviève Bianquis (Éditions Montaigne, 1943), 257.—Eds.]

3. [Jean-Jacques Servan-Schreiber, *Le Défi mondial* (Fayard, 1980).—Eds.]

4. [Senghor is referring to the "Pacte colonial," also called the Metropolitan Commercial Exclusive, which was a system of commercial regulations imposed by France on its colonies, essentially establishing a trade monopoly.—Eds.]

5. [The passage in question occurs in Book 2, Section 104, of *The Histories*. The original Greek reads: "μελάγχροες εἰσὶ καὶ οὐλότριχες" (They are dark-skinned and woolly-

haired); Herodotus, *The Histories*, trans. A. D. Godley (Harvard University Press, 1920), 392.—Eds.]

6. [Paul Rivet, *Sumérien et Océanien* (E. Champion, 1929).—Eds.]

7. [Alexandre Moret, *Histoire de l'Orient* (Presses universitaires de France, 1929).—Eds.]

8. [Roger Garaudy, "Les Occasions perdues," in *Pour un dialogue des civilisations: l'Occident est un accident* (Denoël, 1977), 79–105.—Eds.]

9. [The exhibition *L'Orient des Provençaux* consisted of a series of seventeen exhibits at the Musée d'histoire in Marseille (November 1982–February 1983).—Eds.]

10. [The citation in question is to Book 6, part 2. Senghor is misquoting; the three factors are "sensation, *intellect*, and desire" (our emphasis). Elsewhere—for instance, in chapter 6 of this volume—Senghor translates this triad as "sensation, reason, and desire." The Greek word is *νοῦς*, which has the sense of "intellect" or the rational part of the soul. See Aristotle, *Éthique à Nicomaque*, trans. Jules Tricot (Librairie philosophique J. Vrin, 1959), 276–77.—Eds.]

11. [*Méditations* first appeared in Latin in 1641, followed by a French translation in 1647. Senghor seems to be alluding to Mediation 6, in which Descartes writes of "les facultés de vouloir, de sentir, de *concevoir*" (the faculties of desiring, feeling, and *conceiving*) (our emphasis). *Œuvres de Descartes*, tome IX, vol. 2, edited by Charles Adam and Paul Tannery (Cerf, 1904), 68. In *Les principes de la philosophie* (1647), Descartes writes that "Vouloir, [. . .] mais aussi sentir, est la même chose ici que penser" (To desire, but also to feel, is the same here as to think). *Œuvres*, 28.—Eds.]

12. [This appears to be a paraphrase of some of Garaudy's early thought. Garaudy elaborates a similar claim in "De l'empirisme logique à la sémantique: Essai d'un bilan du néo-positivisme," *Revue philosophique* 146 (1956): 217–35, see esp. 223. We are grateful to Julian Roche for guidance in locating possible sources for this citation.—Eds.]

13. [This lecture was published as Léopold Sédar Senghor, "La Révolution de 1889 et Leo Frobenius," in *Éthiopiques: Revue socialiste de culture négro-africaine* 30 (1982): 301–12.—Eds.]

14. [Friedrich Nietzsche, *Also sprach Zarathustra: Ein Buch für Alle und Keinen* (Chemnitz: Ernst Schmeitzner, 1883–85); Friedrich Nietzsche, *Ainsi parlait Zarathoustra: Un livre pour tout le monde et personne*, trans. Henri Albert (Paris: Société du Mercure de France, 1898).—Eds.]

15. [Henri Bergson, *Essai sur les données immédiates de la conscience* (Paris: Félix Alcan, 1889). Paul Claudel's play was composed in 1889 and published the following year. Paul Claudel, *Tête d'or* (Paris: Librairie de l'art indépendant, 1890). Senghor had access to the 1889 play in the Pléiade edition. Paul Claudel, *Théâtre I*, ed. Jacques Madaule and Jacques Petit (Gallimard, Bibliothèque de la Pléiade, 1967).—Eds.]

16. [Arthur Rimbaud, *Une saison en enfer* (Brussels: Alliance Typographique, 1873).—Eds.]

17. [Senghor is juxtaposing two well-known passages that are quite far apart in the original. The first part of the passage, up to ". . . Cham" (Rimbaud, *Une saison en enfer*, 9–10), occurs in the "Mauvais sang" section, and the second, beginning with "I invented . . ." (30), occurs in "Délires II: Alchimie du verbe" (our translation).—Eds.]

Index